SPIKE ISLAND'S REPUBLICAN PRISONERS, 1921

TOM O'NEILL, MA

The History Press

This book is dedicated to my wife Ann and our
sons Finbarr and Philip.
Thanks again for your support and patience.
This book is also dedicated to the memory of
the men who were imprisoned or interned on
Spike Island during 1921.

First published 2021
Reprinted with revisions 2021, 2023

The History Press
The Mill, Brimscombe Port
Stroud, Gloucestershire, GL5 2QG
www.thehistorypress.co.uk

British Library Cataloguing in Publication Data.
A catalogue record for this book is available from the British Library.

ISBN 978 0 7509 9627 3

Typesetting and origination by Typo•glyphix, Burton-on-Trent
Printed in Great Britain by TJ International Ltd, Padstow, Cornwall

CONTENTS

ACKNOWLEDGEMENTS

My primary reason for writing this book is to record the details of the men who were imprisoned or interned on Spike Island during 1921 and to ensure that their names and sacrifices will never be forgotten.

In the course of researching this book, I was very fortunate to have access to comprehensive original documents from the Irish and British perspectives. My principal source of Irish-related documents was from the Bureau of Military History witness statements. I wish to thank the Officer in Charge, Irish Military Archives, Comdt Daniel Ayiotis and his staff in Cathal Brugha Barracks, Dublin, for their work in digitalising the original copies and making them available online. Seventy-eight witness statements contain information about Spike Island during 1921 and one for 1916. All seventy-eight statements are listed in the Primary Source section.

The completion of this book would not have been possible without the availability of so much of the original British Army paperwork relating to the Spike Island Military Prison in the Field, 1921, which is available in the United Kingdom National Archives, Kew, London. The material was easily located on their website and on my many visits to Kew, the files were promptly made available to me for my research. The British material greatly assisted me in my goal of producing, as far as possible, a complete and balanced account of the men and events on Spike Island during 1921. My very sincere thanks to the staff at Kew.

Other original documents that I availed of include the Spike Island diary written by internee John Hennessy, late of Ballynoe, and the Spike Island notebook written by internee Richard Brett, late of

Kilmacthomas and Australia. Also, the Spike Island autographs books, once belonging to former prisoners and internees. These were very kindly donated to Spike Island by their families. The known Spike Island autograph books from 1921 are listed in Appendix 15.

Many thanks to our son Finbarr for providing the IT support for this project. Your patience was appreciated. Thanks also to my long-standing friend Eugene Power for proof-reading the various early drafts. Similarly, I want to acknowledge the advice, assistance and support of a number of other individuals.

My sincere thanks to Mai Kerins for her invaluable work in proof-reading the final drafts of this book. Her experience and attention to detail has resulted in a polished publication.

A special thanks also to the relatives of the almost 1,200 Republican prisoners and internees that were held on Spike Island during 1921. The photographs and information they provided was very much appreciated. It is impossible to thank each of you personally, and any attempt to do so would result in some being omitted. So, I hope you will accept my collective words of sincere appreciation to you all. I am confident that between us we have ensured that the sacrifices made by your fathers, uncles, grandfathers, etc. during the struggle for Irish independence will continue to be remembered with pride.

I wish to thank Eileen Horgan for the advice required to compile the details of the prisoners and internees. Thanks to Mr Dan Breen, acting curator of the Cork City Public Museum, Fitzgerald Park, for locating some original autograph books and photographs relating to Spike Island, and to Mr Brian McGee, chief archivist and his staff at the Cork City and County Archives, for their assistance.

Local historians have provided me with information and photographs used in this book. These include: Sheila O'Sullivan from Newmarket, Christy and Tim O'Sullivan from Clonmult, Donie O'Sullivan from Lombardstown, Gerry White from Cork City and John Mulcahy from Whitechurch. Thanks to Conor Kenny from Grenagh, for providing photographs of the Cork Male Gaol hunger strikers imprisoned on Spike Island. Thanks to Tom Toomey from Limerick, Pat Kirby from Ennis, and John Connors from Borrisoleigh, Co. Tipperary, for information about their respective counties. Thanks also to Fr Pat Kelleher for his assistance.

I want to acknowledge Spike Island staff member Arek Maciak for his outstanding work in producing the five drawings in this book. Also, for his work in preparing the photographs of the prisoners and internees for display in the Independence Museum on Spike Island and for publication in this book.

Thanks to Carmel McDonnell, Martin Lynch, Ross McBride, Anita O'Riordan and Noel McCarthy, for their work during the early years of this project.

Thanks to the directors of the Spike Island Steering Committee and the Spike Island Development Company, Denis Deasy, Brendan Tuohy, David Keane, Sean O'Callaghan, John Forde, the Cobh Municipal District Officer, Paraig Lynch and the General Manager, John Crotty, for supporting my research visits to the UK National Archives, Kew, London.

Many thanks to my wife Ann, for her patience, again.

All of these individuals have helped me in the course of researching and writing this book. Any errors or omissions are entirely mine.

LIST OF ABBREVIATIONS

ASU	Active Service Unit
CA	Competent Authority
CO	Commanding Officer
Comdt	Commandant, Irish equivalent to British Army major
Cork M G	Cork Male Gaol, Western Road, also called HMP Cork
Cork M H	Cork Military Hospital, Victoria Barracks, Cork
DCM	District Court Martial
DI	District Inspector, RIC
Div	Division, army formation
DORA	Defence of the Realm Act
FGCC	Field General Court Martial
GHQ	General Headquarters
HMP	His or Her Majesty's Prison
HMS	His or Her Majesty's Ship
HQ	Headquarters
I	Imprisonment
Interned	Arrested and imprisoned without trial
IRA	Irish Republican Army
KB	Kerry Brigade (British Army) arrest prefix
Lt	Lieutenant
M Court	Military Court
MPIF	Military Prison in the Field
OAML	Offence against Martial Law
OC	Officer Commanding
PQ	Parliamentary Question from Westminster
Prisoner	Captured or arrested, charged, tried, convicted and sentenced
PS	Penal Servitude
RC	Roman Catholic
RIC	Royal Irish Constabulary
RN	Royal Navy
ROIR	Restoration of Order in Ireland Regulations
S Court	Summary Court
Vol	Volunteer, IRA rank
16 I.B.	16th Infantry Brigade of the British Army, arrest prefix
17 I.B.	17th Infantry Brigade of the British Army, arrest prefix
18 I.B.	18th Infantry Brigade of the British Army, arrest prefix
WD	War Department, (British)
WS	Witness Statement

1

THE BREAKDOWN OF CIVIL LAW

The prisoners and internees that were incarcerated on Spike Island during 1921 were almost exclusively from the six counties of Munster: Cork, Clare, Kerry, Limerick, Tipperary and Waterford. The remainder were from counties Wexford and Kilkenny. These were the counties that were placed under Martial Law by the British government at the end of 1920 and early 1921 because they were the most violent counties in Ireland at the time.

The urgent requirement by the British authorities and specifically the British Army for the opening of a prison on Spike Island was due to the high number of attacks on the RIC and the British Army by the IRA, resulting in a large increase in the numbers of Republicans captured and imprisoned for participating in these attacks and for their support for independence. Prior to and during the War of Independence, the British government in London carried out the administration of Ireland through their representatives and civil servants in Dublin Castle and throughout the country. The path that led to the breakdown of the British civil administration and the introduction of Martial Law, or Military Law, began shortly after the 1916 Rising.

In the aftermath of the 1916 Rising, the surviving senior Irish Volunteer officers studied the principal actions and strategies of that momentous week and analysed their mistakes. They concluded that when the next attempt at independence by force of arms would begin there would be major changes in their strategy and tactics.

It was decided that never again would they take on the might of the Crown Forces using conventional warfare.[1] The next war would be one of guerrilla warfare, hit and run. No more taking over buildings and waiting to be attacked and overwhelmed by Crown Forces.

It was recognised that the priority for the Irish Volunteers, better known as the Irish Republican Army (IRA), must be to neutralise the Royal Irish Constabulary (RIC), a force that was seen as the eyes and ears of Dublin Castle in every part of Ireland. Throughout Ireland, with the exception of Dublin City, law and order was the responsibility of the RIC. Dublin was under the responsibility of the Dublin Metropolitan Police (DMP). The British Army was used in a support role for the police. Prior to 1920, the RIC was one of the most efficient police forces in the world. During the War of Independence, the members of the RIC were the most dangerous adversaries of the IRA because of their local knowledge and their ability to identify members of the organisation. To have any chance of succeeding in their goal of achieving independence, the IRA had to neutralise the RIC's ability to operate as an efficient force.

Initially, the effectiveness of the RIC was due to the vast numbers of RIC barracks that were located throughout the country. Almost every village had a permanent RIC presence. What had been their strength prior to 1920 was now their weakness. There were simply too many barracks to reinforce and defend against IRA attack. Throughout Ireland, approximately 60 per cent of the RIC barracks were evacuated and in effect, abandoned.

Beginning in 1919, the Irish Republican Army (IRA) certainly focussed on their priority of neutralising the RIC. The first two members of the RIC killed by the IRA were killed at Soloheadbeg, near Tipperary Town, on 21 January 1919. This was the same day that the members of the First Dáil held their inaugural meeting in the Mansion House in Dublin. Fifteen members of the RIC were killed by the IRA during 1919.[2] During 1920, the IRA killed 176 members of the police, including regular RIC, Black and Tans and Auxiliary Police.[3] During 1921, the IRA killed a total of 235 police officers, with the worst single

---

1   Michael Hopkinson, *The War of Independence*, p.13.
2   Richard Abbott, *Police Casualties in Ireland, 1919–1922*, p.48.
3   Ibid., p.169.

month of the War of Independence for police casualties being May 1921, when fifty-six policemen were killed.[4]

The highest percentage of attacks on the RIC and on the British Army occurred in Munster; this was also the area of operations of the 6th Division of the British Army and the first part of Ireland to come under Martial Law. Its area of operations covered one-third of the island of Ireland. A staggering 60 per cent of the deaths of combatants, IRA and Crown Forces, during the War of Independence occurred within that area. Between 1919 and 1921, Cork was the most violent county in Ireland, followed in order by Tipperary, Clare, Kerry and Limerick.[5] An affidavit sworn by Gen. Sir Nevil Macready, the Commander-in-Chief of the British Forces in Ireland, highlighted the Crown Forces casualties in the Martial Law area. In it he stated that between 1 June 1920 and 10 February 1921, six military officers, twenty-four soldiers and sixty-two members of the police had been murdered. In a later affidavit he updated the figures to include fatalities among Crown Forces up to 10 April 1921. They had increased to fourteen military officers, fifty-four soldiers and 101 police.[6] Civil law had indeed collapsed and the police became almost totally reliant on the close support of the British Army. From 1 January to the Truce on 11 July 1921, 119 members of the RIC were killed in the Martial Law area and two more were killed after the Treaty was signed, one in Co. Kerry, the other in Co. Limerick.

The IRA campaign against the RIC was so successful that by the beginning of 1920, the strength of the force fell dramatically and recruitment fell to a trickle. The British government's reaction was to recruit former British soldiers as temporary constables for the RIC. All of the former soldiers had extensive service during the First World War. After completing the briefest of RIC recruit training, they were transferred to RIC barracks all over Ireland in small numbers and placed under the command of the local RIC sergeant. Because of the numbers involved, there were insufficient stocks of RIC uniforms available for them. The shortage of RIC uniforms was made up by issuing British Army uniforms. This resulted in the new RIC recruits appearing in the

4   Ibid., p.272.
5   *The Irish Rebellion in the 6th Division Area*, Imperial War Museum London, EPS/2/2 also Patrick McCarthy, *The Irish Sword, Spring 2010, No. 107.*
6   *The Irish Reports, 1921, Vol. 2, The King's Bench Division*, pp.328–329.

streets from around March 1920 wearing a mix of police dark green and army khaki. They quickly received the nickname the 'Black and Tans'. By the middle of 1920, sufficient RIC uniform material was produced and the original Black and Tan uniforms disappeared. However, far worse persecution of the Irish by elements of the Crown Forces was to follow.

The next force recruited by the British government to reinforce the police was the Auxiliary Division RIC (ADRIC) and was also referred to as the 'Black and Tans', or more accurately as the Auxiliaries or 'Auxies'. This force was made up of former commissioned officers with wartime service from all three British armed forces: Royal Navy, Army and the Royal Air Force. The role of the Auxiliaries was to terrorise the country and to bring the war to the IRA. Beginning in August 1920, the Auxiliaries were deployed throughout Ireland in Company strength of approximately 120 men.[7] They had their own transport and roamed the country freely, where they created fear among the population and caused widespread destruction. One location that the Auxiliaries were based in was Woodstock House, Inistioge, Co. Kilkenny, a place that several of the Kilkenny internees and prisoners were taken to on their journey to imprisonment on Spike Island. Other locations in Cork were Moore's Hotel and Victoria Barracks, the former workhouse in Dunmanway, Macroom Castle and the Lakeside Hotel in Killaloe, Co. Clare.[8]

Meanwhile, the IRA attacks and ambushes against the RIC continued. One of the first major ambushes, in what would later become the Martial Law area, took place at Rineen, between Ennistymon and Miltown Malbay, Co. Clare, on 22 September 1920. In a well-planned and executed ambush against a mobile patrol, the local IRA killed six members of the force, including one Black and Tan.[9]

Because of the fear generated by the activities of the Auxiliaries and their impression of invincibility, the IRA had to do battle with them. The opportunity to do so was taken on 28 November 1921, when a two-vehicle mobile patrol of Auxiliary Police from Macroom Castle was ambushed by an IRA Flying Column at Kilmichael, in west Cork.

7   Ernest McCall, *The Auxies, 1920–1922*.

8   Ernest McCall, *The First Anti-Terrorist Unit, The Auxiliary Division RIC*, pp.312–313.

9   P. Ó Ruairc, *Blood on the Banner*, pp.165–171. Also Richard Abbott, *Police Casualties in Ireland 1919–1922*, pp.123–126.

Seventeen of the eighteen members of the patrol were killed as a result of the ambush. One of the Auxiliaries, Cadet Guthrie, the driver of the second Crossley Tender, escaped from the ambush location and made the mistake of going into a public house in uniform, looking for directions to get back to Macroom Castle. He was duly abducted by two IRA men and shot dead with his own revolver. Kilmichael was the greatest loss of life suffered by the RIC during the War of Independence.[10]

The next major incident was in Cork City on the night of 10/11 December 1920. The evening of the 10th began with an attack on a mobile patrol of Auxiliaries at Dillon's Cross, near Victoria Barracks. A grenade was thrown into one of the Crossley Tenders and some of the Auxiliaries were seriously wounded, one dying later from his wounds. Reinforcements arrived quickly from Victoria Barracks and they used bloodhounds to follow a trail that led to the Delaney home, on Dublin Hill, on the outskirts of the city. Two of the Delaney brothers were found inside and dragged out. The two brothers, Jeremiah and Con, both Volunteers, were killed out of hand by the Crown Forces. That was only the beginning of a terrible night.[11]

Later, Auxiliary Police from 'K' Company set out to have their revenge on the people of Cork City. Bringing petrol and explosives with them from Victoria Barracks, the Auxiliaries set fire to the centre of the city. By morning, the city centre and the City Hall were smouldering ruins. After their night of burning and destruction in Cork, members of 'K' Company that were involved wore burned 'cork bottle tops' behind the cap badges of their Balmoral headdress. As a consequence of their night of destruction, the entire 'K' Company of Auxiliaries was transferred from the city to the old workhouse in Dunmanway. A few days later, Cadet Harte of 'K' Company murdered the elderly Canon Magner and a civilian, Tadhg Crowley, outside Dunmanway, Co. Cork.[12]

Such was the level of violence at the end of 1920 in the 6th Division area, and in particular as a result of the Kilmichael ambush, the British authorities declared Martial Law on 10 December 1920. The Lord Lieutenant proclaimed the following areas to be under and subject to Martial Law: 'The County of Cork, (East Riding), the County of

10 Tom Barry, *Guerrilla Days in Ireland*.
11 Gerry White and Brendan O'Shea, *The Burning of Cork*.
12 Fr Donal O'Donovan, *The Murder of Canon Magner and Tadhg Crowley*.

Cork (West Riding), the County of the City of Cork, the County of Tipperary (North Riding), the County of Tipperary (South Riding), the County of Kerry, the County of Limerick and the County of the City of Limerick'.[13]

It was also decreed that within the Martial Law area:

Any unauthorised person found in possession of arms, ammunition or explosives would, on conviction by a Military Court, suffer death.

Any person taking part in or aiding and abetting those taking part in insurrection would be considered guilty of waging war against the King and would, on conviction by a Military Court, be liable to suffer death.

This decree was used to the full on several occasions. There were fourteen Republican prisoners executed by military firing squads in the Martial Law area during 1921.[14] Thirteen were executed in Cork Military Detention Barracks and one in New Barracks, Limerick. The introduction of Martial Law by the British authorities was a reluctant acceptance that civil law had collapsed and now the British military were governing the area.

The British government also introduced official reprisals, to be carried out by the Crown Forces as a consequence of attacks by the IRA. The first were carried out in Midleton, Co. Cork, on New Year's Day 1921. The reprisals followed an IRA ambush on a joint RIC–Black and Tan foot patrol in the Main Street on 29 December 1920.[15] In the course of the ambush, an RIC constable and two Black and Tans were killed. As a result, seven houses were officially burned down in Midleton.

On 4 January 1921, Gen. Macready issued Proclamation No. 2, which extended Martial Law to Co. Clare, Co. Waterford, City of Waterford, Co. Wexford and Co. Kilkenny. This came into force one week later, on 11 January 1921.[16]

---

13 UKNA, Kew, London, WO 71/380.
14 See Appendix 2 for the full list.
15 *Rebel Cork's Fighting Story*, Anvil edition, pp.189–190.
16 UKNA, Kew, London, WO 71/380.

The Crown Forces, combined RIC and British Army, were having some successes in their war against the IRA, and several hundred members of the organisation and their support network were arrested. In order to hasten the detention of those suspected of Republican activities, the British authorities re-introduced internment throughout Ireland in August 1920 and not confined to the Martial Law area.[17] In the early months of 1921, the vast majority of Republicans held in custody were internees. On 17 January 1921, throughout Ireland, there were 1,478 internees in custody and that number had reached 4,454 by 11 July 1921, the day the Truce came into effect.[18] Internees continued to be held in custody until after the Treaty was signed in December 1921. The convicted Republican prisoners were released immediately after the Treaty was ratified by the three governments in London, Belfast and Dublin in January 1922.

The Truce, resulting in a temporary cessation of hostilities in the War of Independence, came into effect at noon, on Monday, 11 July 1921. It was the first major step in an attempt to bring the two warring sides to the negotiating table and reach an agreement to end the war.

At the time, the IRA was very much in need of the truce. The year 1921 had been a difficult time for the IRA, in particular in the Martial Law area. Approximately 2,000 of their men were imprisoned or interned, a significant percentage of their fighting force. Also, within the Martial Law area, the IRA had suffered a number of reversals during the early months of 1921. The temporary cessation of hostilities gave both sides breathing space after the intensity of the war. It was now time for the negotiations to begin in an attempt to find a permanent peaceful solution after centuries of conflict.

17 William Murphy, *Political Imprisonment and the Irish, 1912–1921*, p.193.
18 Ibid., p.269.

2

THE IRA IN THE MARTIAL LAW AREA

Martial Law was declared in the eight previously mentioned counties because of the ferocity and frequency of the armed attacks on the Crown Forces by members of the IRA, and in particular, by the flying columns during the last months of 1920 and 1921. The largest formation of the IRA at regional level for most of the War of Independence was the brigade. The IRA brigades in the Martial Law area were as follows:[1]

Mid Clare Brigade and West Clare Brigade.

North Kerry No. 1 Brigade, Mid Kerry No. 2 Brigade, South Kerry No. 3 Brigade.

East Limerick Brigade, Mid Limerick Brigade and West Limerick Brigade.

No. 1 (North Tipperary) Brigade, No. 2 (Mid Tipperary) Brigade and No. 3 (South Tipperary) Brigade.

First (East, Mid, South and City) Cork Brigade, Second (North) Cork Brigade and Third (West) Cork Brigade. In July 1921, the Second Cork Brigade was divided in half. After that, the Second Brigade covered the north-east of the county and the newly formed Fourth

---

1 *With the IRA in the Fight for Freedom, 1919 to the Truce, The Red Path to Glory*, pp.13–25.

Cork Brigade covered the north-west of the county.

West Waterford Brigade and East Waterford Brigade.

Kilkenny Brigade.

Wexford Brigade.

All of the brigades were subdivided into battalions and some of the larger brigades had as many as ten battalions, numbered one to ten. In practice, battalion areas were made up of a number of the larger towns and these individual towns and villages within the battalion areas were designated as companies. Again, some of the larger battalions had as many as eighteen companies and these were designated by letters, 'A' Company, 'B' Company, etc. To give an example, Midleton, Co. Cork, was designated 'B' Company, Fourth Battalion, First Cork Brigade.

All of the individual IRA brigades throughout the country were directly under the command of IRA General Headquarters (GHQ) in Dublin. The Crown Forces in Dublin were constantly raiding houses in search of GHQ officers. This meant that an efficient chain of command and effective lines of communications between GHQ and the brigades were virtually impossible. During March 1921, IRA GHQ took steps to address these difficulties. In the Martial Law area, Gen. Liam Lynch was appointed Officer Commanding, the First Southern Division of the IRA. The West Limerick, Kerry, Cork and Waterford Brigades were placed under his command and control.[2] Gen. Lynch was now the local commander of the brigades and their link in the chain of command to GHQ in Dublin. Comdt Gen. Ernie O'Malley was appointed Officer Commanding, the Second Southern Division, which included South and Mid Tipperary Brigades, East and Mid Limerick Brigades and the Kilkenny Brigade.[3] This resulted in a more efficient IRA force and enabled local brigade commanders to receive quicker permission or refusal for their proposed operations against the Crown Forces. The creation of the IRA divisions resulted in much

2   Jim Maher, *The Flying Column, West Kilkenny, 1916–1922*, p.191.
3   Dorothy Macardle, *The Irish Republic*, p.439.

larger flying columns being armed, equipped and prepared for military engagements.

As previously mentioned, the Kilmichael ambush was the specific incident that drove the British authorities to declare Martial Law. This ambush was carried out by the brigade flying column of the 3rd West Cork Brigade under the command of Tom Barry. Barry received his military training in the British Army during the First World War.

The other IRA brigades were also very active. The following are some of the engagements and incidents between the IRA and Crown Forces in the Martial Law area during 1921 until the Truce on 11 July. Not all engagements had successful outcomes for the IRA. The prisoners incarcerated on Spike Island would have been involved in quite a number of these attacks and ambushes.

On 20 January 1921, RIC DI Tobias O'Sullivan was walking from the RIC barracks in Listowel, Co. Kerry, to his home, with his 7-year-old son when he was shot dead by an IRA squad. He was frequently reported as having been killed to prevent him identifying prisoners on Spike Island. This is incorrect, as Spike Island was opened as a prison and internment camp on 19 February 1921, almost a month after he was killed. The specific prisoner that the British Army and RIC wanted DI O'Sullivan to identify was Tom Malone, alias Sean Forde. At the time, Malone was a prisoner in either Cork Male Gaol or on Bere Island. On 15 April he was moved from Bere Island to Spike, from where he escaped on 30 April.

At about 4 p.m., on 20 January, an RIC mobile patrol was ambushed at Glenwood, near Sixmilebridge, Co. Clare. The patrol commander was DI Clarke, who had been an Auxiliary before being commissioned into the RIC. An RIC sergeant, two constables and two Black and Tans were killed in that ambush.[4]

On 24 January 1921, the flying column of the Second Tipperary Brigade, under the command of Jerry Ryan, ambushed a combined British Army and RIC mobile patrol at Poynstown, between Killenaule and Gortnahoe. Two British soldiers were killed. Two days later, the column commander Jerry Ryan was arrested. He was subsequently convicted and imprisoned on Spike Island.[5]

---

4   Richard Abbot, *Police Casualties in Ireland 1919–1922*, pp.186–187.
5   Seán Hogan, *The Black and Tans in North Tipperary*, pp.317–319.

On the morning of 28 January 1921, the members of the Flying Column of the 6th Battalion, First Cork Brigade, set up an ambush for Crown Forces near Dripsey Bridge. Unfortunately, the location of the ambush was revealed in conversation to a local Loyalist lady, Mrs Lindsey. In an unusual move, she sent a message to the IRA officers in charge of the ambush that she was reporting the ambush to the troops in Ballincollig Barracks. The IRA officers refused to believe the message. By chance, the IRA sentry who was guarding the avenue of approach used by British soldiers advancing on the ambush position had left his post to go to a local house for food. Those in the ambush position were taken by surprise, and in their withdrawal under fire from the advancing soldiers, two IRA men were killed and ten captured by the military. Five of the prisoners were subsequently executed. Denis Murphy, one of the prisoners, was sentenced to death but this was commuted. He was transferred to Spike as a prisoner.[6]

On the afternoon of 3 February 1921, a combined force of IRA from the Mid Limerick and East Limerick Brigade flying columns ambushed a two-vehicle mobile patrol of RIC at Dromkeen, near Pallasgreen, Co. Limerick. Eleven policemen were killed, this included three RIC constables and eight Black and Tans.[7]

On the morning of 8 February 1921, soldiers from Victoria Barracks surrounded Rahanisky House, on the northern side of Cork City. When the soldiers searched the house, they found a considerable quantity of small arms and they captured thirteen men and one woman, the owner of the house. She was the source of the information to Victoria Barracks. Eleven of the male prisoners were convicted and sentenced to long terms of imprisonment. All were transferred as prisoners to Spike.

On 15 February, the British Army received information as to the location of an IRA ambush on the main Cork to Mallow road, at Mourne Abbey. British troops from Ballincollig and Buttevant, assisted by the RIC from Mallow, attempted to surround the IRA's ambush position. In the engagement, four IRA men were killed and

---

6 Dripsey Ambush Committee, *Glory O, Glory O, Ye Bold Fenian Men.*

7 Thomas Toomey, *The War of Independence in Limerick, 1912–1921.* Also, *Limerick's Fighting Story,* 1916–21, pp. 107–110.

the two men captured were subsequently executed together on 28 April 1921 in Cork Military Detention Barracks.

On the afternoon of Sunday, 20 February, at Clonmult, near Midleton, Co. Cork, almost the entire East Cork flying column was wiped out, having been surprised by a British Army patrol, later reinforced by Auxiliary Police. Only one IRA man escaped. Twelve IRA men were killed, seven after they had surrendered. Two of the eight men captured were executed on the same day as the two men captured at Mourne Abbey. Clonmult was the worst defeat ever suffered by the IRA. Five of the men captured at Clonmult – Garde, Harty, O'Leary, Terry and Walsh – were transferred to Spike as prisoners.[8]

On 21 February, the IRA in Kilkenny City ambushed British soldiers in Friary Street. The soldiers were transporting rations between the military barracks and Kilkenny Gaol. A terrified woman screamed when she saw the soldiers being attacked. This alerted other soldiers, who immediately opened fire. Two of the attacking IRA men were killed and a corporation worker was accidentally killed by the soldiers.[9]

On 5 March, in a very successful operation, a combined force of IRA drawn from the Second Cork Brigade and the Second Kerry Brigade ambushed a British Army mobile patrol at Clonbanin Cross, on the Mallow to Killarney road. The commanding officer of the British Army's Kerry Brigade, Col Comdt Cumming, Lt Maligny and two soldiers were killed. There were no IRA men killed.[10] Col Comdt Cumming was the most senior British Army officer killed during the War of Independence.

On 19 March, a joint RIC and British Army mobile patrol was ambushed near Dungarvan, Co. Waterford, an RIC sergeant and a Black and Tan were killed.

Also on that day, a major battle took place at Crossbarry, West Cork, when superior forces of the British Army attempted to surround the flying column of the Third (West) Cork Brigade in a pincer movement. One of the British Army units failed to close the encirclement and this gap was exploited by the column and enabled the IRA men to withdraw and escape. The Third Brigade commander, Charlie

8 Tom O'Neill, *The Battle of Clonmult*.
9 Jim Maher, *The Flying Column West Kilkenny, 1916–1922*, pp.139–152.
10 *Rebel Cork's Fighting Story*, Anvil edition, pp.147–155.

Hurley, was killed early that morning by troops involved in the sweep. Crown Forces stated that seven soldiers and an RIC constable were killed at Crossbarry.

On 27 April 1921, the flying column of the Third Tipperary Brigade ambushed a British Army mobile patrol near Clogheen and two soldiers were killed. A car being driven by RIC, DI Potter drove into the ambush position. The DI was captured and taken away by the IRA men. The IRA informed the British authorities that DI Potter would released if Thomas Traynor, a prisoner under sentence of death in Mountjoy, would be reprieved. When Traynor was hanged, Potter was executed.[11]

On 4 May 1921, eight members of the RIC were killed near Rathmore, Co. Kerry, in an IRA ambush carried out by a combined force drawn from the Second Kerry and Second Cork Brigades. An RIC sergeant, a regular RIC constable and six Black and Tans were killed. One RIC constable survived.

On 8 May, an RIC cycle patrol was ambushed at Inch, near Gorey, Co. Wexford. An RIC sergeant was seriously wounded and a Black and Tan killed.[12]

In the middle of May, troops from the Gloucestershire Regiment carried out a series of searches in north-west Cork. While searching Riordan's farm at Knockavoureen, Kiskeam, on Monday, 16 May, they captured their primary target, the flying column commander Sean Moylan. He was found in possession of a loaded revolver and two Mills bombs (grenades). During a follow-up search of Riordan's farm, the soldiers found one of the two Hotchkiss machine guns taken by the IRA in the raid on Mallow Military Barracks. This machine gun had been used effectively by the IRA during the Clonbanin ambush. Moylan and others captured that day became prisoners on Spike Island.

On the morning of 31 May, the IRA detonated a 6in artillery shell that had been primed by Capt. Paddy Whelan at Clonmult, beside the band of the Hampshire Regiment, in the outskirts of Youghal, Co. Cork.[13] The band was leading a company of the regiment from the army barracks in Youghal to the shooting range on the western side

11 Richard Abbott, *Police Casualties in Ireland 1919–1921*, pp. 225–226.
12 Ibid., p.232.
13 Patrick Whelan, WS No. 1449, p.56.

of the town for Lewis Gun practice. Seven members of the band were killed or died of their injuries.

On 1 June, a combined RIC and Black and Tan bicycle patrol was ambushed near Castlemaine, Co. Kerry. An RIC district inspector, three RIC constables and a Black and Tan were killed.[14]

On 2 June, members of the North Tipperary flying column, reinforced by men from the Cloughjordan Company, ambushed an RIC bicycle patrol at Kallebeg Cross, Co. Tipperary. One Black and Tan and three RIC constables were killed.

On the morning of 2 June 1921, the flying column of the First Tipperary Brigade ambushed a twelve-man RIC cycle patrol at Modreeney (Kylebeg). A well-decorated Black and Tan was killed and three RIC constables died of their wounds the following day.[15]

Near Castlecomer, Co. Kilkenny, on 18 June, a local informer had reported an IRA ambush position to the military. The IRA group in the ambush position were surprised by British soldiers. During the firefight, two IRA men were killed in action and two were wounded and captured. One of the prisoners later died of his wounds.

On 2 July, a ten-man RIC patrol was ambushed near Tallow, Co.Waterford, by IRA men using a machine gun. One RIC constable was killed.

On 10 July, a Black and Tan was speaking to a girl in O'Connell Street, Ennis, Co. Clare, when they were attacked. Both were seriously wounded and removed to hospital, where the Black and Tan died of his injuries. It is believed that the girl was his wife and that they had been married earlier that morning.

At around 8.30 p.m. on the night of 10 July, four British soldiers were captured in Cork City by a patrol of seven IRA men. They were searched and no arms were found on them. Their bodies were found the following day. They were the last British soldiers to be killed in Cork during the War of Independence.[16]

At 8.30 a.m. on 11 July, just hours before the Truce came into effect, an RIC constable from Tipperary was attacked and killed by four

---

14 *Kerry's Fighting Story,* The Kerryman edition, pp.153–154.

15 Richard Abbot, *Police Casualties in Ireland 1919–1921,* pp.49 and 250. Also Seán Hogan, *The Black and Tans in North Tipperary,* pp.371–381.

16 Barry Keane, *Cork's Revolutionary Dead 1916–1923,* pp.276–277.

armed men in Townsend Street, Skibbereen, Co. Cork. He was the last member of the RIC and, indeed, the last member of the Crown Forces, to be killed before the Truce.[17]

At noon, on Monday, 11 July 1921, the Truce came into effect and the guns fell silent. The Truce was expected to be just a temporary cessation of hostilities. However, it held and a negotiated settlement was agreed that led to the British and Irish representatives signing the Anglo–Irish Treaty on 6 December 1921. One month later, the Treaty was ratified by the three governments in Dublin, London and in Northern Ireland. The War of Independence was over.

---

17 Richard Abbot, *Police Casualties in Ireland 1919–1922*, p.266.

3

THE BRITISH ARMY IN THE MARTIAL LAW AREA

Militarily, the entire Martial Law area was the area of operations of the British Army's 6th Division. The Division was commanded by Lt Gen. Sir E.P. Strickland, with headquarters in Victoria Barracks, now Collins Barracks, Cork City. Geographically, it consisted of the six counties of Munster and counties Wexford and Kilkenny, in Leinster.

The 6th Division area was subdivided into Brigade areas, see Map 1. The 17th Infantry Brigade, with headquarters in Victoria Barracks, was responsible for Cork City and south, east and west Cork. The 16th Brigade, with headquarters in Fermoy Military Barracks, was responsible for north Cork and counties Tipperary, Waterford, Wexford and Kilkenny. The 18th Infantry Brigade had its headquarters in Limerick City and was responsible for counties Limerick, Clare and part of Tipperary. The British Army's Kerry Brigade had its headquarters in Buttevant Military Barracks, Co. Cork, and was responsible for north-west Cork and all of Co. Kerry.[1]

---

1   Charles Townshend, *The British Campaign in Ireland 1912–1921*, p.86.

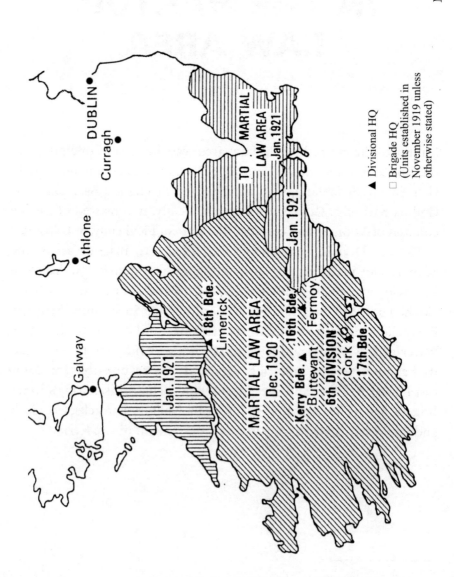

Map 1: Martial Law Area.

4

THE MILITARY TRIALS AND IMPRISONMENT OF CIVILIANS

In the Martial Law area, the military authorities had a number of options available to them for trying civilian prisoners for charges against the Restoration of Order in Ireland Act 1920. Because members of the IRA's flying columns and Active Service Units (ASU) engaged in armed attacks against the Crown Forces were not wearing an identifiable uniform and meeting other criteria, they were not entitled to the protection of the Geneva Convention. Therefore, they were tried and referred to as civilians.

At the lower end of the scale was the Summary Court (S Court). This could impose up to six months' imprisonment, with or without Hard Labour (HL), impose a fine up to £100, or recommend an accused for internment or refer the case for trial by Military Court.[1] A District Court Martial (DCM) could not award any punishment higher than two years imprisonment, with or without Hard Labour (HL).[2]

A Field General Court Martial (FGCM) of civilians in the Martial Law area was cumbersome and slow. The Military Court was swifter and less cumbersome. The military High Command also believed, incorrectly as it later transpired, that the Military Court was not subject to interference by the High Court. Where charges were punishable

---

1   Sean Enright, *The Trial of Civilians by Military Courts 1921*, p.34.
2   *British Army Manual of Military Law, War Office 1914*, p.35.

by death, the FGCM was required to include a person with legal knowledge and experience, the Military Court was not. The FGCM could only pass a sentence available under common law; the Military Court could impose their own sentence. Where a FGCM imposed the death penalty, clemency was the preserve of the Lord Lieutenant. With the Military Court, the Army reserved the question of clemency to the Commander in Chief.[3] Most of the IRA men executed in the Martial Law area during 1921 were convicted and sentenced to death following trials by Military Court and as a result of losing their appeals.

During June and July 1921, two men, Patrick Clifford and Michael O'Sullivan, who had been sentenced to death by Military Courts and who had lost their first appeals to have their death sentences overturned, took their appeals to the House of Lords in London. One of their grounds for appeal was the illegality of the Military Courts. The Master of the Rolls found in favour of the men and ruled the Military Courts were indeed illegal and that the men should have been tried by Field General Court Martial. Their death sentences were overturned and the men were released. Capt. Patrick Higgins, captured at Clonmult and also awaiting the outcome of his appeal against his death sentence, benefitted from the ruling and he too was released. Unfortunately, the ruling came too late to save the men who had already been executed in Cork and Limerick during 1921.[4]

Another option was the drumhead court martial, used on a maximum of three occasions during 1921. All of the individuals officiating at a drumhead court martial were British Army officers. The IRA prisoner was defended by a British officer, the jurors were British Army officers and the judge advocate was a senior army officer. The first occasion that a captured IRA prisoner was tried by drumhead court martial in the Martial Law area was on Monday, 2 May 1921. The day before, a Crown Forces mobile patrol was ambushed near Kildorrery, north Cork, at approximately 5.30 p.m. The patrol overwhelmed the ambush party, and in the ensuing battle two IRA men were killed. Volunteer Patrick Casey was spotted by two soldiers firing his rifle. After firing a round at the same two soldiers, the IRA man dropped

3   *British Army Manual of Military Law, War Office* 1914, p.35.
4   See Appendix 2.

his rifle and surrendered. He was taken to Victoria Barracks, where he was tried by drumhead court martial the following day. He was found guilty, sentenced to death and executed at 6 p.m. that evening. The entire process, from capture to execution, took twenty-five hours.

From August 1920, internment was also available to the authorities throughout the island of Ireland and not confined to the Martial Law area. By the early part of 1921, the vast majority of Republicans held in custody were internees.

Internees were the second category detained on Spike Island. They were suspected Republicans who were arrested, charged, tried and found not guilty in a military court but were, however, detained as internees. When the Crown Forces wanted to intern an individual, an application was made to the General Officer Commanding 6th Division and Military Governor of the Martial Law area, Gen. Strickland, along with the evidence to support the application. If satisfied, which he usually was, Strickland signed the application approving the internment. The individuals were transferred to an internment camp, where they received and signed their Internment Order, stating that they were to be interned on either Spike Island or Bere Island. Unlike convicted prisoners, there was no time limit stated on their internment order.

A third subcategory of internee involved convicted prisoners. When convicted Republicans received short custodial sentences from military courts they were also informed of their earliest and latest release dates. On occasions where the release date was prior to the signing of the Anglo–Irish Treaty in December 1921, and if the individual was still considered a threat to the Crown, an application to intern was sent to Gen. Strickland. When it was accepted and signed, the document was delivered to the prison. The prisoner was released on or before his release date and immediately served with his internment order. What that specifically meant on Spike Island was that the individual was released from the prison compound in the casemates, served with his internment order and taken to the internment compound, and thus remained in custody.

The British Army Brigade arrest details that are given in this book, for either the internees or the prisoners, specify the British Army Brigade area where the individual was captured or arrested, and are followed by the individual's unique arrest number. All those arrested by Crown

Forces in the 17th Brigade area were given the prefix 17 I.B. before their unique arrest reference number. Likewise for the Republicans arrested in the other brigade areas, with 16 I.B., 18 I.B. and K.B. preceding the arrest numbers.

The Brigade arrest numbers are essential when carrying out research. It is the only definite means of identifying an individual, particularly where there are men with the same name and from the same area. For example, there are four men named Jim or James Barry in the internee list, three of them from Cork City and two of them had addresses in Evergreen Road. In addition, arrested Republicans and internees were sometimes given a 6th Division arrest number.

Internees continued to be detained until after the Anglo–Irish Treaty was signed in London in December 1921. The convicted Republican prisoners were not released until after the Treaty was ratified by the three governments in London, Belfast and Dublin in January 1922.

5

THE PRISONS AND INTERNMENT CAMPS IN THE MARTIAL LAW AREA

For imprisoning and interning Republicans in the Martial Law area during the War of Independence, existing permanent prisons were used initially. Following the introduction of Martial Law there was a very large increase in the numbers being imprisoned, and in particular in the numbers being interned. There were five types of places of detention in use: civilian prisons, Military Prisons in the Field (MPIF), internment camps, the Military Detention Barracks Cork, which was part of the Victoria Barracks complex, and also the Brigade Cage in Victoria Barracks. The civil gaols were administered by the Prison Board in Dublin. The military authorities were responsible for seeing that all gaols in the Martial Law area did not become overcrowded and for their defence.[5]

The Cork Military Detention Barracks, Military Prisons in the Field, the Brigade Cage and the internment camps were entirely the responsibility of the 6th Division for discipline, interior economy and defence. At the height of the conflict during 1921, the following locations were used for the incarceration of political prisoners and internees in the 6th Division area of operations, which was the Martial Law area.[6]

---

5   UKNA, Kew, London, WO 35/141.
6   Ibid.

Cork Male Gaol, located on the western side of UCC.
Limerick Civilian Gaol.
Waterford Civilian Gaol.
Kilkenny Civilian Gaol.
Spike Island Military Prison in the Field (MPIF), referred to as the prison compound, in effect the north-east casemates.
Spike Island Internment Camp, referred to as the internment compound and initially the north-east casemates, later the 'A' and 'B' Blocks.
Bere Island Military Prison in the Field and internment camp.
Kilworth Army Camp.
Cork Military Detention Barracks.
The Brigade Cage in Victoria Barracks.

The 6th Division policy as regards prisoners was as follows:

Prisoners sentenced to less than six months imprisonment served their sentences in the following prisons:[7]

16th Brigade area, Waterford and Kilkenny Gaols. Except for Mitchelstown and Fermoy areas; these were sent to Cork Male Gaol.
17th Infantry Brigade, Cork Male Gaol.
18th Brigade area, Limerick Gaol.
Kerry Brigade area, Cork Male Gaol.
The Military Detention Barracks was used for men awaiting trial under the 6th Division's Law Branch in Victoria Barracks.

Republican prisoners sentenced by a Military Court to a period of six months or more could not be sent outside the Martial Law area and were initially sent to Bere Island. On 15 April 1921, all eighty-five Republican prisoners were removed from Bere Island and transferred to Spike Island, and from that date forward all Republican prisoners were sent to the MPIF on Spike Island or to Cork Male Gaol, also referred to as HMP (for men), Cork. From 15 April until its closure in December 1921, only internees were sent to Bere Island. Following

---

7   UKNA, Kew, London, WO 35/141.

the transfer of all Republican prisoners from Bere Island, Republican prisoners sentenced by a Court Martial could be sent to the MPIF on Spike or to England.

Commencing on 18 June 1921, 18th Brigade, OC Troops Waterford, OC Troops Kilkenny, the Governor Cork Male Gaol and the commandant of the Detention Barracks rendered a report every Saturday, by telegram, to 6th Division HQ, showing the numbers of prisoners in their custody under the following subheadings:[8]

a) Ameliorative Penal Servitude.
b) Ameliorative Imprisoned Hard Labour.
c) Ameliorative not Hard Labour.
d) Non-Ameliorative Penal Servitude.
e) Non-Ameliorative Imprisoned Hard Labour over six months.
f) Non-Ameliorative not Hard Labour over six months.
g) Non-Ameliorative Imprisoned Hard Labour under six months.
h) Untried.
i) Internees.
to (h) above referred only to persons apprehended for crimes in connection with Republican activities.

Men awaiting trial in Cork were confined in the Military Detention Barracks until after the conclusion of their trail, when their sentences were confirmed. Twelve cells were retained in the Detention Barracks for staging prisoners to Spike Island.

Men sentenced by Summary Court (S Court) in Cork and Kerry Brigades to terms of imprisonment of six months and under were sent to Cork Male Gaol.

Men sentenced to terms of imprisonment of over six months were detained in the Brigade area where they were arrested. They remained there until their sentences were confirmed and until orders for their transfers were received from Divisional Headquarters.

All Republican prisoners sentenced to death appealed their conviction and sentence. When the appeals failed and their death sentence was confirmed by the Gen. Macready, the men were executed by firing

---

8 Ibid.

squad in the yard of Cork Military Detention Barracks. Their bodies were removed by military ambulance for burying in the grounds of Cork Male Gaol. Comdt Thomas Kent, of Castlelyons, was the only man executed and buried in the grounds of the Detention Barracks. He was executed on 9 May 1916 and buried close to where he was shot. Because the subsoil was rock, his grave was very shallow, and this was just one reason why there were no other burials in the grounds of the Detention Barracks. Another practical reason was the lack of space for graves; there was far more space within the grounds of Cork Male Gaol and no shortage of trustee prisoners to dig them. All executions in the Martial Law area were by firing squad. In the remainder of the country, because it was under civil law, all executions were carried out by hanging.

Female Republican prisoners detained in the 16th and 17th Brigade areas were sent to Waterford Gaol. Those in the 18th and Kerry Brigade areas were sent to the female wing of Limerick Gaol. These were the only two prisons in the Martial Law area where female Republican activists were incarcerated. The decision was taken by the British authorities not to intern female Republican activists.

Female civilian, non-Republican prisoners were imprisoned in the Female Gaol in Sunday's Well, Cork City.

There were three 'Staging Camps' in the 6th Division area where Crown Forces foot patrols and mobile patrols handed over men they had detained. They were located in Victoria Barracks, Kilworth Army Camp and in Buttevant Military Barracks. While in the Staging Camps, the detainees were processed, during which the decision was taken by the military authorities, sometimes liaising with members of the Royal Irish Constabulary (RIC), as regards releasing them or transferring them to Cork Military Detention Barracks for trial or recommending the men for internment.[9]

The Staging Camp in Victoria Barracks was called the Brigade Cage. It consisted of wooden huts surrounded with barbed wire and was located on a corner of the parade ground. For a short while a notice stating, 'This is a cage for rebels and murderers', was placed above the gate into the Cage.[10] When internee Professor Alfred O'Rahilly saw it,

---

9   UKNA, Kew, London, WO 35/141.
10 See Denis Collins, WS No. 827, p.22.

he created such consternation that the sign was removed. Quite a lot of the men imprisoned or interned on Spike Island passed through the Brigade Cage.

Kilworth Army Camp, located in north Cork between Fermoy and Mitchelstown, was the staging area for internees arrested in the 16th Infantry Brigade area. The most dangerous time for prisoners and internees was the days and even weeks after their arrest. They usually found the regime much easier in Kilworth, and as a result, Kilworth was often referred to as a 'rest camp' by the internees. Almost all of the internees held in Kilworth were transferred to Spike Island and Bere Island. During mid-September 1921 it was decided by 16th Brigade Headquarters to remove all internees from Kilworth and transfer them to Spike Island in three rotations.

All of the aforementioned prisons, places of detention and proce-dures remained in use and in force until independence was achieved in early 1922. An unusual situation occurred after the Truce was declared on 11 July 1921. Republican prisoners or internees who had escaped prior to the Truce and those who escaped during the Truce could not be rearrested by Crown Forces. As a result of the Truce, Crown Forces were not permitted to arrest members of the IRA. This was most impor-tant for the seven internees who escaped from Spike in November 1921 as they could not be rearrested for escaping.

6

THE MILITARY PRISON IN THE FIELD (MPIF), SPIKE ISLAND, 1921

Because of the very large increase in the numbers of convicted Republican prisoners and internees in the British Army's 6th Division area, the decision was taken to open the fort on Spike Island as a prison. This chapter is a chronological account of the main events that occurred on Spike Island during 1921, from the opening in February to the closing of the prison in November, a total of nine months.

On 15 February 1921, the Officer Commanding Spike Island received orders from 6th Division Headquarters that it had been decided to utilise Spike Island for the accommodation of internees and prisoners. From 19 February 1921, Spike Island became a Military Prison in the Field (MPIF), consisting of an internment compound and a prison compound. This new role as an MPIF was in addition to the garrison's primary role of coastal defence.

Col Gregory, Royal Garrison Artillery (RGA), was appointed the prison commandant. He arrived on Thursday, 16 February, accompanied by another officer. He was responsible for the safe custody of the prisoners and the internees, the organisation and interior economy of the prison, and the general administration of the prison and the staff.

It was also decreed that the Officer Commanding the Cameron Highlanders would detail approximately sixty men for guard duty in the prison. Armed soldiers patrolled the perimeter of the compounds on a twenty-four-hour rota. The families of the military living on Spike Island, approximately 200 women and children, were issued with a special military pass. A notice stating that no civilians were permitted to land on the island, unless in possession of a pass, was published in local newspapers.

There were three locations within the fort on Spike Island where the men were held during 1921. *(See Map 2.)* The north-east casemates were used from the very beginning and were initially used for internees. This changed on 1 April, when all the internees were moved across the parade ground to the 'A' Block.[1] The first prisoners were accommodated in the casemates on Friday, 15 April, after they were transferred from Bere Island. After this, the casemates were only used for prisoners. These casemates consisted of fifteen bomb-proof arched buildings, running in parallel. Fourteen were used to accommodate the internees and later the prisoners. The casemates were referred to as 'huts' by the Republican prisoners and were numbered 15 to 28. *(See detailed Map 3.)*

The casemates or 'huts' extend from the inner wall of the fort, under the ramparts and as far as the dry moat. The back wall of each case-mate is the inner wall of the moat. The only door to each casemate is on the fort side, with a window on either side. There is one other window in each casemate, looking out into the moat. The casemates are approximately 13.5m long, are approximately 4m wide and have a brick arched ceiling/roof, 2.9m at its apex. The roof is approximately 1m thick and covered with clay. Each casemate housed fourteen men.[2] The fifteenth casemate was originally designed as a pedestrian access to the fort and was not used for incarceration. A secure exercise yard was created in front of the casemates by erecting barbed wire on top of an existing wall. A gap in the western end of the wall was fenced off using high wooden poles and several strands of barbed wire. Communal ablutions, wash rooms and toilets were within the exercise yard.

The second location was the 'A' Block, on the south-west of the fort, and it was used only for internees. This block was previously used as accommodation for the British Army enlisted ranks. It is a two-storey building of cut limestone and has a bomb-proof roof. There were and

---

1   Spike Island diary of internee John Hennessy, Ballynoe.
2   ibid..

still are eleven rooms on the ground floor and eleven more on the first floor. The rooms were generally referred to as huts by the internees. The hut numbers are shown on the diagram of the 'A' Block.

The third location was 'B' Block and this consisted of twenty-five army wooden huts used only for internees. The huts would have been erected during the First World War to provide temporary accommodation for troops on short-term assignment to Spike Island. The huts were located in the lawn in front of 'A' Block. There are no known surviving photographs or drawings showing these huts. The gable of some of the 'B' Block huts can be seen in the background of the photograph of the internee staff officers. There are no known details of the numbering sequence of the huts.

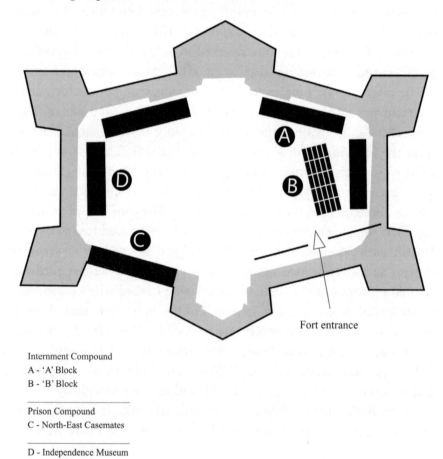

Fort entrance

Internment Compound
A - 'A' Block
B - 'B' Block

Prison Compound
C - North-East Casemates

D - Independence Museum
    Opened in 2019

Map 2: Military Prison in the Field.

The huts, in the three locations, were the sleeping quarters. Simply by removing and stowing the bed boards and mattresses every morning, they converted the sleeping quarters into their day room. They were given tables consisting of a wooden top that fitted on top of two high trestles, which could be quickly cleared to make room for the beds. Wooden and steel benches were used for seating.

It was decided that bed cots would not to be given to the inmates in the huts. Instead, to make up their beds, they were given two trestles, three bed boards, a horse hair mattress and four army blankets.[3] The two trestles were approximately 6in (150mm) high and 2ft (600mm) wide and were placed at right angles to the three bed boards. The three bed boards, approximately 6ft (1.8m) long, were placed on top of the two trestles and provided support for the mattress and kept the bed about 6in (150mm) off the ground. Instructions were given to the Spike Island logistics officer that he was to retain sufficient material to provide a least 900 beds.

On Saturday, 19 February 1921, the first eighty four internees were transferred to Spike Island. Fifty came from the Cork Male Gaol, four from Cork Military Detention Barracks and thirty from the Brigade Cage in Victoria Barracks. A large percentage of the internees were from the Bandon, Clonakilty and Timoleague areas of west Cork. Most of the remainder were from Cork City, Clare and Kerry. A second batch of sixty-one internees arrived on Spike on Thursday, 24 February. Forty-four were sent from the Cork Male Gaol, three from the Detention Barracks and fourteen from the Brigade Cage. All of the internees were accommodated in the north-east casemates. Investigating their Brigade arrest numbers, the majority were arrested in groups in west Cork.

On 28 February, Lt Victor Bickersteth Murray fatally shot himself on Spike Island.[4] He was a platoon commander with the company from the Second Battalion, Cameron Highlanders, carrying out security duties on Spike Island.

On 1 April all the internees were moved from the north-east casemates to 'A' and 'B' Blocks in preparation for the arrival of the first Republican prisoners from Bere Island.

---

3   Spike Island diary of internee John Hennessy, Ballynoe.
4   O'Halpin, E., & Ó Corráin, D., *The Dead of the Irish Revolution*, p.318.

On 10 April, the camp commandants on Spike Island and Bere Island received orders from 6th Division Headquarters changing the policy that had existed in both camps. The orders stated that with effect from Wednesday, 13 April, all eighty-five prisoners sentenced to Penal Servitude (PS) and those to Hard Labour (HL) were to be removed from Bere Island and transferred to the MPIF on Spike Island.[5] However, the prisoners were transferred from Bere Island on 15 April. This meant that with effect from 15 April, Bere Island was only used as an internment camp. 'Bere Island was used as an internment camp for dangerous internees who were not likely to be released and who it was desired to separate from the remainder.'[6]

During 14/15 April, a total of sixty internees from Spike Island, Cork Male Gaol and Kilworth were transported to Bere Island on a Royal Navy destroyer.[7] On arrival in Berehaven, and following the disembarking of the internees, the destroyer conveyed all of the prisoners from Bere Island to Spike Island.[8] The camp commandant on Spike Island provided all transferred internees and prisoners with twenty-four hours' rations and a blanket.[9] The 17th Brigade had detailed an escort of one officer and six other ranks to accompany the internees and prisoners. The military were provided with forty-eight hours' rations and one blanket each. There were two other transfers of prisoners and internees from Cork Male Gaol to Spike during the remainder of April 1921.

---

5   UKNA, Kew, London, WO 35/141.
6   Ibid.
7   Ibid.
8   UKNA, Kew, London, WO 35/138.
9   UKNA, Kew, London, WO 35/141.

7

THE PRISON ROUTINE ON SPIKE ISLAND

While camp security was the responsibility of the British Army camp commandant, the prisoners and internees ran their individual compounds. Within the compounds, a senior IRA officer was in command and the British Army camp commandant Maj. Kennedy liaised closely with him on matters that arose.

The prisoners and internees were held in different types of accommodation on Spike Island. Some were in stone and brick, single-storey casemates. Those in the 'A' Block were in the two-storey, dormitory-type accommodation previously used by the British soldiers. The 'B' Block consisted of twenty-five wooden huts. Regardless of which one they were held in, the men generally referred to their room as their 'hut'.[1]

The men in every hut elected their own hut leader. The block leader was elected from the hut leaders and that was the chain of command within every compound. For administration within the compound, staff officers were elected for various appointments. These appointments included a postal officer, catering officer, medical officer, recreation officer and a canteen officer. The running of the prisons and internment camps was very much in the style of a prisoner-of-war camp.

Reveille, wake-up time, was at 7.30 a.m. Between then and 9 a.m., the internees had the opportunity for stowing their beds, erecting tables, washing and having breakfast and cleaning their casemate. At 9 a.m.,

---

1 See, William Desmond, WS No. 832.

the first check parade of the day occurred, to count the internees to ensure all were present and that none had escaped during the night. The second parade consisted of a roll call at 2 p.m. Later, another check parade was added at 4.30 p.m. Weather permitting, the check parades were held in the exercise yard. During inclement weather, the men were counted standing by their beds. At approximately 8 p.m. every night all able-bodied men were formed up in formation in front of their huts. On the order of their commanding officer, they were brought to the position of attention, ordered to fall out and march into their huts. This was a message to the British that the men were finishing their day on the orders of their own officers.

While the principal difficulty for the men was the loss of their freedom, this was followed closely by boredom. Their staff officers were constantly planning and arranging events and activities to address the boredom.

Examples of some of these activities were football and hurling matches that were organised by the internees. These included inter-county, ground floor 'A' Block versus first floor, inter-Block, etc. Concerts were another very successful way of passing time and included rehearsals, making costumes, organising the concerts and the performances. Irish language classes were also very popular, with both elementary and advanced classes available. The advanced classes were taught by Pádraig Ó Siochfhradha, Patrick Sugrue, better known by his pen name An Seabhac (The Hawk), and by Tom Ryan from Thomastown. The opportunity was also availed of for one of the senior IRA men to give lectures of a military nature. Another successful pastime was making silver jewellery from coins that were smuggled into Spike in cakes and bread. In keeping with their Nationalistic ideals, the jewellery often took the form of Celtic design, including Tara brooches, and was often engraved with 'Spike 1921'. Many items of jewellery made on Spike during 1921 still survive as treasured family heirlooms and are worn with pride. Examples are on display in the 'Independence' museum on Spike and illustrated in the photograph section of this book.

Autograph books were very popular with prisoners and internees. Surviving autograph books are full of poetry, reflecting the men's love of their country and their families. Others record the arrest of individuals, their trials and transfers, including their arrival on Spike. Nineteen autograph books, some original and some copies, are on display in the 'Independence' museum on Spike. All are listed in Appendix 15.

Despite some conflicts between the clergy and the IRA in the community and the threat of excommunication for active IRA men, several surviving written accounts mention the importance of religion to the men while in prison. In addition to the members of clergy that were incarcerated with the prisoners, every prison and internment camp had a clergyman from the local diocese appointed as a prison chaplain. Fr John Callanan was the prison chaplain for Spike Island. Mass was celebrated daily for the internees, while prisoners were only permitted to attend Mass on Sundays and holy days. In addition, Rosaries, Novenas to the Blessed Sacrament, Benediction, confession and confraternity were organised regularly and were very well attended.

There is no record of a clergyman being incarcerated on Spike during 1921. They were held elsewhere, including Bere Island and in Kilkenny Gaol. What is interesting is that during the tunnel escape from Kilkenny Gaol in November 1921, Fr Delahunty, the Catholic Curate from Callan, Co. Kilkenny, was among the escapees. Some members of the clergy certainly did play their part in the struggle for independence.

The men who were imprisoned or interned on Spike Island during 1921 represent a full cross section of Irish society at the time. In the British Army ledgers used to record their details, prisoner and internee records differed. The recorded details of the prisoners included their religion, age and occupation, while these three details were not recorded for the internees.

Studying these three categories reveals that all of the prisoners on Spike were Roman Catholic. The youngest Republicans held on Spike Island were 16 years old, of which four were internees and two were prisoners. The oldest man on Spike was John O'Keeffe, 66, an engineer, from Clogheen Cottage, Clonakilty, Co. Cork, who was held as both an internee and a prisoner.

The variety of occupations reveals the breadth of support for the fight for independence. Every occupation and profession in the wider community was represented on Spike, including labourer, driver, shopkeeper, saddler, tradesman, dentist, and there were politicians at local and national level and clergymen. Interestingly, the records show William Maurice Swanton, an internee from Castletownbere, Co. Cork, was a pharmaceutical chemist.

The majority of the incarcerated men were the breadwinners or principal providers for their families. Thus, incarceration placed a double strain on the families of the men. Firstly, the income from the breadwinner was lost, and secondly, the breadwinner was now a dependent. Very few internees or prisoners were as fortunate as internee Joe Cosgrove, from Whitegate, Co. Cork. Prior to his arrest, he was employed by Capt. Clarke of Trabolgan House, who paid his salary for the duration of his internment.[2] The financial and material support for the men, from their families, was essential for their well-being during their incarceration. These included sending basic foodstuffs to the men to supplement the meagre military rations. The surviving letters and diaries are full of accounts of the welcome parcels of foodstuffs, clothing, cash, cigarettes, etc. There is no doubt that the families endured difficult times to support their imprisoned menfolk.

Everyday rations for the prisoners and internees were meagre. The internees on Spike were not all fortunate enough to share their hut with men such as John Hennessy, from Ballynoe, Co. Cork. John was a baker and his surviving diary contains full accounts of him and his comrades in their hut receiving eggs, meat, cakes, bread, etc. from their families. John would then gather all the foodstuffs and using his culinary skills make a substantial meal for his colleagues in their hut.

To help alleviate these difficulties, the Irish Volunteers at national level established the Irish Volunteer Dependants' Fund. Two of the leading ladies in this organisation were its President, Mrs Kathleen Clarke, and Vice-President, Mrs Éamon Ceannt, the widows of two of the executed 1916 leaders. Eventually the various Volunteer funds amalgamated to form the Irish National Aid and Volunteer Dependents Fund with branches throughout the country. This charitable organisation organised events and collected funds from the wider community

---

2 Information received from J. Cosgrove's daughter. Joe Cosgrove's brother, Cpl William Cosgrove, won the Victoria Cross with the First Battalion Royal Munster Fusiliers at Gallipoli during the First World War.

to assist those in prison and their families. Members of the Irish Volunteers also contributed to the fund.

Overall, the men imprisoned or interned on Spike Island managed their incarceration very well. This was primarily due to the team spirit, the shared hardships and dangers they experienced in their common goal for Irish Independence. From the numbers and diversity of internees and prisoners it is clear that the support for freedom was indeed widespread and had the support of their families.

8

THE ESCAPE OF THREE PRISONERS

The first escape from Spike Island during 1921 took place in broad daylight on Saturday, 30 April. Three prisoners were involved: Sean MacSwiney and Cornelius Twomey, both from Cork City, and Tom Malone alias Sean Forde, from Tyrrellspass, Co. Westmeath, and active with the IRA in Co. Limerick.

The two Cork men had been arrested by British soldiers at Rahanisky House, near Whitechurch, Co. Cork, and both were serving fifteen-year prison sentences. Of the three prisoners, it was most important to free Tom Malone because the British authorities were not aware that he was actually the much-wanted IRA man Sean Forde.[1] Following his escape from the exercise yard in Mountjoy Prison, Dublin, with twenty-two other prisoners on 20 March 1919, Malone went on the run in Co. Limerick.[2] He made a reputation for himself in East Limerick for attacking RIC barracks. He quickly rose in importance on the Crown Forces' most wanted list under his alias Sean Forde.

Unknown to the British authorities, Malone/Forde had been arrested by Auxiliary Police in Cork City on Christmas morning 1920, when he gave his real name, Tom Malone. He was tried, convicted and sentenced to death for the attempted murder of an Auxiliary Policeman while resisting arrest in King Street, now Mc Curtain Street in Cork. His death sentence was commuted to fifteen years Penal Servitude, and was he transferred to

1 Tomas Malone, WS Nos. 218 and 845.
2 Tom Malone, *Alias Sean Forde*, pp.38–41.

Bere Island Military Prison in the Field, later to Spike Island on 15 April.

While attending Mass on Spike, Malone was recognised by one of the internees, who knew him under his alias. Mass time was the only occasion when prisoners and internees were in the same location, but still separated. The internee attempted to give Malone/Forde cigarettes and when he failed, he asked a British officer to give the cigarettes to Malone/Forde. Recognising the name, the British officer set the wheels in motion to have Malone/Forde correctly identified. The net was closing in and Malone was due to be transferred back to Cork Male Gaol on the evening of 30 April, possibly to be identified. The internee told his CO what had happened and Malone/Forde was alerted to the possible threat of him being identified.

In the days following the incident with the cigarettes, a plan was made to rescue Malone from Spike. The prison chaplain, Fr Callanan, conveyed the escape details between the IRA in Cobh and the prisoners. The date set for the rescue was between 10 and 11 a.m. on Saturday, 30 April. The three prisoners, Sean MacSwiney, Cornelius Twomey and Tom Malone, volunteered to assist in the maintenance of the army golf course on the island, ensuring they were outside the security of the fort.

Comdt Michael Burke, Officer Commanding the Cobh Company of the IRA, assembled a rescue party and secured a boat for the mission. On the morning of the planned rescue the boat, flying the Union Jack, put out from Cobh for the ten-minute trip to Spike. On board were the Cobh IRA men Michael Burke, George O'Reilly, Frank Barry and Andrew Butterly.[3]

When the boat reached Spike, the prisoners were in position and working on the golf course. There was a sentry armed with a rifle with fixed bayonet, a sergeant and a corporal, both unarmed, guarding the prisoners. The launch moved into position and the occupants pretended to be fishing.[4] The lawnmower being used by the prisoners had broken down and they were pretending to repair it. This gave Malone the opportunity to steal a hammer. Suddenly, the prisoners sprang into action as Malone attacked the armed sentry.[5] He grabbed his rifle and hit him twice in the head with the hammer and the sentry collapsed.

---

3   *Rebel Cork's Fighting Story*, Anvil edition, pp.167–168. Also, *Sworn to be Free, The Complete book of IRA Jailbreaks, 1918–1921*, pp.179–182.

4   *Rebel Cork's Fighting Story*, Anvil edition, pp.167–168.

5   Tom Malone, *Alias Sean Forde*, pp.78–84.

The other two prisoners overpowered the two soldiers, forced them into a hollow in the ground and tied them up. The boat was brought in near the shore and the three prisoners jumped aboard.

The plan was to take the boat to Paddy's Block, the nearest point on the mainland near Ringaskiddy. However, seaweed had been ingested into the water intake pipe of the engine and the boat barely moved. When the boat was about 200m from Spike, the occupants were horrified to see the two soldiers emerge from the bushes and run towards the fort. While still a considerable distance from the mainland, a party of armed soldiers appeared from the fort and began searching the bushes for the escaped prisoners.

Eventually, the boat was beached near Paddy's Block and the IRA men and the three prisoners quickly made their way to the village of Ringaskiddy, where they found Jerome Crowley, captain of the Ballinhassig Company, and Sean Hyde waiting for them with transport. The transport only consisted of a horse and trap, incapable of transporting nine men. It was quickly decided that the two local volunteers and the three prisoners would use the trap to escape. They drove it to Ballinhassig village, where Capt. Jerome Crowley and Capt. Michael Walsh of the local IRA Company assisted the three fugitives. The Cobh men returned home using a combination of ferry, rowing boat and train.[6] The three escaped prisoners spent that night in a dugout near Ballinhassig before going their separate ways. Within a few days, Malone was safely back in East Limerick and on the way swapped the captured rifle for a parabellum hand gun.[7] The escape plan had worked to perfection. The soldier that Forde had struck twice on the head with the hammer died of his injuries approximately three weeks later.

On 11 May, thirteen Penal Servitude prisoners and twenty internees were transferred from Cork Male Gaol to Spike Island. The thirty-three men were transported from the gaol to Customs House Quay in the city and placed on a War Department (WD) vessel at 5.45 a.m.

During the remainder of May, more transfers of prisoners and internees took place to Spike from the 17th Brigade Cage in Victoria Barracks, Cork Male Gaol and Kilworth Army Camp.

---

6   *Rebel Cork's Fighting Story*, Anvil edition, pp.167–168.
7   Tom Malone, *Alias Sean Forde*, pp.78–84.

9

THE FATAL
SHOOTING OF
CAPT. PATRICK WHITE

On the evening of 31 May, the most dramatic and tragic event of the year took place on Spike Island: the shooting dead of internee Capt. Patrick White. White had been an active member of the Irish Volunteers since 1914. He was one of a group of Clare Volunteers that mobilised during Easter 1916 in an unsuccessful attempt to receive arms from the gun-running ship *Aud*. He was also very active during the War of Independence. On 13 January 1921, White participated in a success-ful ambush against Crown Forces at Cratloe, Co. Clare, during which two RIC sergeants were killed. In follow-up raids by Crown Forces on 21 January, White was arrested. His friend and colleague, Thomas Ringrose, was also arrested later that night.[1]

Following their arrests, both men were regularly taken on board British military vehicles as human shields in an attempt to prevent IRA ambushes on these mobile patrols. On 12 April, both men were trans-ferred from Cork Male Gaol to Spike Island as internees. On reaching the fort on Spike Island, White turned to Ringrose and said, 'We are safe now.' Both men were held in the 'A' Block.

The internees were held in the internment compound, which con-sisted of the 'A' Block and in wooden huts that made up 'B' Block. A 5m-high barbed-wire fence separated the internment compound from

---

1   Capt P. White Commemorative Booklet.

the adjoining parade ground. Internees were permitted to play hurling and football on the parade ground every evening. To enable them to participate, the British Army sentries would allow them out of their compound through a gate in the fence leading on to the parade ground.

At approximately 5.45 p.m., on 31 May, White was playing hurling with fellow internees on the parade ground, when the ball rolled under the barbed-wire fence that separated the parade ground from the internment compound. White rushed over to the wire to retrieve the ball and was almost immediately shot by a British Army sentry, Pte Whitehead, who occupied No. 2 sentry post.[2] Pte Whitehead was from the Second Battalion, King's Own Scottish Borderers.

The camp commandant quickly arrived on the scene and instructed the sentry to unload his rifle. The military doctor arrived and rendered first aid to the mortally wounded internee. The prison chaplain, Fr Callanan, was also quickly on the scene and administered the last rites of the Catholic Church on the dying volunteer. White was removed by stretcher from the scene of the shooting to the prison hospital, where he died at approximately 7.20 p.m. that evening of shock and haemorrhage as a result of a bullet wound.

White's body remained overnight in 'A' Block, Hut 1, surrounded by a guard of honour of his fellow internees.[3] At 8.30 a.m. the following day his body was removed to the prison chapel, where Mass was said for the repose of his soul. After Mass, his body was brought back to Hut 1, where it remained guarded by volunteers.

On 3 June, a Military Court of Inquiry in lieu of an inquest was held on Spike Island to investigate the circumstances of the death.[4]

The first witness was the sentry Pte Whitehead, who stated: 'That his orders were to fire at any internee tampering with the wire. The deceased was stretching out his hand through the wire to get a ball. In accordance with my orders I fired at him and hit him.'

The military case was that the sentries were given written orders to fire on any internee, without warning, when they saw them interfering with the wire.

2   Barry Keane, *Cork's Revolutionary Dead, 1916–1923*, p.251.

3   The Prison Diary of Tom Ryan from Thomastown, Co. Kilkenny, and a Spike Island internee.

4   UKNA, Kew, London, WO 35/159B/35, *The Military Court of Enquiry in Lieu of an inquest into the shooting of internee Patrick White on Spike Island.*

The two principal findings of the Military Court of Inquiry were:

> That the deceased was himself to blame, in as much as he tampered with the wire surrounding the compound in defiance of orders.
>
> That no blame attaches in the matter to Pte Whitehead, who fired at the deceased in the execution of his duty, or to the military authorities.

It was also decided that when internees were playing football or hurling on the parade ground, that an internee would be designated to retrieve the ball from the wire and that internee would wear a white coat to identify him to the sentries.[5]

The commanding officer of the 17th Brigade in Victoria Barracks, Col Comdt Higginson, concluded however:

> That while Pte Whitehead had followed orders, he displayed gross stupidity in the interpretation of the order. That the sentry was aware that the deceased was attempting to get a ball and was not evidently tampering with the wire with any intention of escaping and that it was therefore, quite unnecessary for him to have fired.

IRA internee Richard O'Connell was one of those hurling with White. He stated:

> We were out this day hurling and the ball went into the wire. Paddy White rushed over to pull the ball out with the hurley. If he got through that wire, it would have been into his own hut, which was nothing to do with escaping from the place. The next thing was the soldier on sentry duty put up his rifle and shot White dead. We did not know at the time that there had been an ambush in Cork and that five or six of this Regiment had been killed. This was their revenge.[6]

5   Seamus Healy's audio recording of former internee Timothy Herlihy.
6   Richard O'Connell, WS No. 656, pp.27–28.

Early on the morning of 31 May, the day White was killed, the IRA detonated a roadside bomb beside the band of the Hampshire Regiment on the outskirts of Youghal, in east Cork. The band playing was leading a company from the regiment from the army barracks in Youghal towards the shooting range west of the town for Lewis Gun practice. 'When the clouds of dust settled, some twenty men and boys were seen lying on the ground and pitiful groans and cries for help were heard. Seven members of the band were killed or died of their wounds.'[7]

On Friday, 3 June, White's body was taken from 'A' Block, Hut 1, to the prison chapel for requiem Mass. After Mass, his coffin was carried by fellow internees from the chapel to the pier, escorted by armed British soldiers. All the prisoners and internees stood on the parade ground until the cortège had passed.[8] His coffin was taken to Cobh railway station and from there to his home town, Meelick, Co. Clare, for burial.

With the obvious exception of planned executions, the shooting dead of IRA men in prison by British Army sentries was very rare. The suggestion by IRA internee Richard O'Connell that the killing of Patrick White was an act of revenge for the killings in Youghal that morning was a very real possibility.

A plaque commemorating the death of Capt. Patrick White was unveiled on Spike Island in 1957 by Minister for Agriculture Sean Moylan, TD. The Minister had been a Republican prisoner on Spike Island during 1921.

---

7 *Regimental History of the Royal Hampshire Regiment, Vol.* 3, p.11.
8 The Prison Diary of Tom Ryan from Thomastown, Co. Kilkenny.

10

HUNGER STRIKES AND RIOTS

During June, more transfers of prisoners and internees took place to Spike from the Brigade Cage in Victoria Barracks, Cork Male Gaol and Kilworth Army Camp. A major transfer of approximately 110 internees from Spike to Bere Island took place on Monday, 11 July 1921, the day the Truce between the IRA and Crown Forces came into effect.

The majority of the internees transferred to Bere Island on 11 July were from Cork, including Dick Barrett of Upton, Joseph Kenny of Grenagh, who was one of the Cork Male Gaol hunger strikers during 1920, the three Lehane brothers and Jim (Tough) Barry. Barry later managed the Cork senior hurling team between 1926 and 1966. While most of the internees remained on Bere Island until they were released in December, others were later transferred back to Spike.

On 18 August, eighteen internees were transferred from Waterford Gaol to Spike by Royal Navy destroyer.

In late August, the prisoners in the north-east casemates held a meeting in the large building in their compound and demanded political treatment. They demanded the following conditions:[1]

That they be allowed to write three letters weekly in place of the one allowed on Sundays by the prison rule.
That they get full prisoner of war treatment.
That they be allowed tobacco and cigarettes for smoking purposes.

1 Jim Maher, *The Flying Column – West Kilkenny, 1916–1921*, 2015 edition, pp. 268–269.

Soon afterwards, the military authorities informed the prisoners that these concessions would not be allowed.

Because of this refusal, a hunger strike began in the prison compound at 6 p.m. on 30 August. Sean Twomey, the CO of the prisoners, believed that the hunger strike was not sanctioned by IRA GHQ and he resigned as he was not in favour. His place as CO of the prisoners was taken by Jerry Ryan, from Thurles. The strike lasted four days and was then abandoned.

Also in late August, the senior Spike Island internee officers handed the following written demand to the camp commandant:[2]

To the Governor of the Military Prison in Field, Spike Island,

Sir, Take notice that we, on behalf of the internees here, demand immediate and unconditional release on the grounds that the English Government has neither legal nor moral right to hold us by force. If the internees here are not released by Tuesday 30th inst at 6 pm, we will refuse to partake of any food until or just demand is complied with and thus bring the opinion of the civilized world to bear on the inhuman manner in which the British people and their hired government are treating one of the small nations for which the late war is alleged to have been fought.

Henry Mahony, 1st officer in Charge
William Quirke, 2nd officer in Charge

Their demand for unconditional release was refused and the hunger strike began at 6 p.m. on 30 August. All 293 medically fit internees participated in the hunger strike.[3] The men who were medically unfit and not in hospital supported the hunger strikers by taking over the duties of hut orderlies. The hunger strike was called off three days later, on 2 September at 4.30 p.m., without achieving their release.

On 13 September 1921, the OC Troops Kilworth received orders from his Brigade commander in Fermoy Barracks that all internees in Kilworth, fifty-six in number, were to be transferred to Spike Island.

---

2   See Michael O'Sullivan's autograph book on Spike Island, AB 5, p.92.
3   See Appendix 5.

The transfer was to be carried out by road 'to Queenstown and thence by WD boat to Spike Island'.[4] It was ordered that the internees were to be divided into three parties and were to be sent to Queenstown (Cobh) on consecutive nights as follows:[5]

19 internees on Tuesday night 13/14 Sept.
19 internees on Wednesday night 14/15 Sept.
18 internees on Thursday night 15/16 Sept.
All cash belonging to the internees was to be sent with the last batch.

Transport from Fermoy was in Kilworth at 8 p.m. on each of the three nights. The internees departed Kilworth at 1 a.m. and arrived at the Yacht Club, Queenstown, at 5 a.m. The internees were put on the WD boat and taken to Spike Island.

The exact route of the convoy was specified as Kilworth–Fermoy–Rathcormac–Lisgoold–Carrigtwohill–Queenstown. When the internees were handed over to the escort for Spike Island, the Fermoy escort proceeded to Belmont huts on the eastern side of Queenstown, where 2nd Battalion Cameron Highlanders provided them with breakfast. Afterwards, transport conveyed the escort to Kilworth and the transport returned to Fermoy.

The internees in Kilworth for Spike were held in three separate huts. The transfer arrangement worked perfectly for the first two nights. However, when the soldiers entered the third hut at around 11 p.m. for the last convoy, it was empty. The internees in that hut had been digging an escape tunnel for a number of weeks and when the first transfers began on the Tuesday night, they knew they had forty-eight hours to finish the tunnel and escape. Luckily for the last batch of internees, their hut was the last to be vacated. The escaping internees were actually in the tunnel when the soldiers were above their heads. All eighteen internees made a successful escape from Kilworth that night.

On the night of Saturday/Sunday, 24/25 September, eighty-five prisoners, other than those serving sentences of Penal Servitude, were transferred from Spike to Cork Male Gaol. The transfers took place

4   UKNA, Kew, London, WO 35/140.
5   Ibid.

in two phases, the first consisting of forty prisoners and the second the remaining forty-five. The transfers were by WD vessels directly to Custom House Quay in the city. The first group arrived at the city quay at 2 a.m. and the second group one hour later. An Army searchlight lorry was used during the disembarking of the prisoners and armoured cars were provided to reinforce the escort from the quay to the gaol. A prison officer was detailed to proceed with the first group with all property and documentation for the governor of Cork Male Gaol. This was the beginning of the closure of the prison compound in Spike.

On 23 September, orders were issued by 17th Brigade Headquarters for the rotation of the security company on Spike Island. A Company from the 2nd Battalion Cameron Highlanders was to relieve the Company from the 2nd Battalion the King's Own Scottish Borderers (KOSB) that were providing security duties. The rotation took place on 27/28 September. The KOSB's embarked from Spike at 9.30 a.m. on 28 September on HMS *Salmon* and re-joined their battalion on Bere Island. The orders were issued by Maj. B.L. Montgomery, Brigade Major of the 17th Brigade.[6]

Having failed to obtain unconditional release by hunger strike, the internees decided to wreck their accommodation. Their belief was that if their accommodation was destroyed, the authorities would be forced to release them. On Sunday, 16 October, the internees on Spike began breaking up their huts. The two senior internee commanders, William Quirke and Henry O'Mahony, were removed by the military and placed in the cells. The following day, 17 October, the internees declared that a hunger strike would begin at 3 p.m. unless their two colleagues were released. The next morning the two men were released, the hunger strike continued, and at 9 a.m. the destruction of their huts recommenced.

The British soldiers began to take back control of the internment compound by weight of numbers. Later that day the soldiers forced all of the internees, except those in hospital, out into the dry moat.

While in the moat, the hunger strike continued and the internees were put on bread and water. The internees endured three cold and very wet October nights in the moat. Internee Daniel Clancy, from Kanturk, had his big toe shot off by indiscriminate firing from British soldiers around 2 a.m. on 19 October. He was removed to the

---

6   Later Field Marshal Montgomery (Monty) of El Alamein during the Second World War.

The Night
on the Moat.

prison hospital and from there he was transferred to Cork Military Hospital in Victoria Barracks on 20 October. He died in hospital on 11 November.[7] Internee Tom Ryan stated in his diary that, 'at approximately 6 a.m. on the same morning, Patrick Mulhall from Castlecomer, was also shot in the foot by a British soldier, while in the moat and had one of his toes blown off. He too was transferred to Cork Military Hospital later that day.'

Hot tea was brought to the moat gate at 8 a.m. and it was refused until the soldiers provided them with full rations. An hour later, the full rations arrived. After spending three miserable days and nights in the moat without a roof over their heads, the internees were permitted to return to their partially destroyed huts at 6 p.m. on Wednesday evening.[8] They had a slightly less uncomfortable time, with a roof over their heads but without glass in the windows and sleeping on the floor without blankets, until Friday night.

7 Barry Keane, *Cork's Revolutionary Dead 1916–1923*, pp.280–281.
8 Jim Maher, *The Flying Column – West Kilkenny, 1916–1921*, 2015 edition, p.269.

The Col Comdt and Superintendent of the Internee Camps and Prisons in Ireland visited Spike Island on 25 October. He was accompanied on his inspection by Mr Staines, the Sinn Féin representative on the visiting commission, and by the camp commandant, Maj. Kennedy. The purpose of their visit and inspection was to inquire into the circumstances and conditions regarding the recent riot. They inspected the living quarters (huts), cook houses, latrines and hospital rooms, both of the internees and the prisoners. The prisoners' compound was found to be normal, i.e. the same as during their previous inspection.

The conditions in the internment compound were as follows:

> The rooms (huts), windows, doors, fire-places and floors were destroyed. The wash houses were partially destroyed, the electric lights and the fittings were also found to be destroyed. The remainder of the articles of furniture in the Huts had been removed by the troops. These included shelves spiked into the walls, cupboards, bed-boards, tables and forms (seat benches). The swill from the cook-house, ashes, debris of all kinds, including bread and vegetables, were lying in heaps in the area of the cook-house and entrance gate to the living blocks. The ground was also littered with torn-up clothing and paper and sanitation was found to be almost nonexistent. As living quarters, the blocks containing the internees have been completely destroyed, practically nothing escaped except the roof.

The unnamed internee supervisor stated that 'one thing led to another and in the end we destroyed everything'. He also stated that the internees had no grudge or ill feeling towards the commandant, Maj. Kennedy, who carried out his duties with fairness and consideration. The riot was entirely aimed at highlighting the plight of the internees and their demand to be released.

The inspecting team concluded that 'the conditions under which the internees at Spike are now living – conditions in which they, themselves, have made – are, of course, unsatisfactory and bad'.

11

THE ESCAPE OF SEVEN INTERNEES

As a result of the escape of the three prisoners from Spike in April, neither prisoners nor internees were taken outside the fort on work parties. Being prisoners, and particularly being members of a fighting force, escape was uppermost in their minds. The men possessed the required organisational skills and team effort to succeed. Therefore, another plan to escape was devised.

However, escape from Spike presented many challenges. During 1921, tunnels had been used successfully in Kilworth, the Curragh, Bere Island, Kilkenny and elsewhere but this was definitely not an option from Spike. Most of the fort, including the prison compound, is built on limestone, which is impossible to tunnel through, and the remainder on sandstone shale, which is unstable. The prisoners or internees had to get out of their compounds without being seen by the sentries on the ground. They then had to scale a 7m-high wall to get up to the ramparts, which is the high ground between the fort and the dry moat. The rampart at the rear of 'A' Block had rolls of barbed wire with sentries posted there, and searchlights illuminated the area at night. It they managed to get through all these obstacles and security, they then had to drop down the same height to get into the dry moat surrounding the fort and scale another high wall to escape the moat. They also had to avoid being seen on the outer island because all the families were British Army, unlike Bere Island where the vast majority of the families were Irish. The last hurdle was getting off the island, and unless the escape had been liaised with the local IRA Company, either in Cobh or Ringaskiddy, this part would be very difficult because all boats on the island were required to be chained and padlocked with the oars removed. In addition, a motor launch with an armed crew made a continuous tour of the island.[1] Within the two blocks, all the internees were counted by a British Army officer at 4 p.m. every evening. A plan had to be devised to disguise the possibility that seven men would be missing from one of those inspections.

In the immediate aftermath of the internee riots in September, the internees were taken out into the dry moat as punishment. They had to endure three miserable, cold, wet nights without shelter there. In order to get the internees into the moat from 'A' and 'B' Blocks, the soldiers opened up the sally port at the rear of 'A' Block. The sally port was a type of tunnel under the ramparts leading directly into the moat and in design and size was quite similar to the casemates. On the fort side, the sally port entrance was screened with barbed wire and was bricked up, the inside was obstacle free and a cast-iron gate secured access from the moat. While in the moat, the internee staff officers studied the layout of the sally port and recognised its potential for future escape plans.

In early November, when the preparations for the escape attempt were complete, the first phase of their plan using the sally port was put into action. The internees complained to the British Army that the sally port at the rear of 'A' Block was full of rubbish and infested with rats. The internees even offered to clean it out. Having received permission from the Army to do so, the internees set to work, removing bricks in order to gain access to the tunnel. This was part of the bigger plan because, by removing the bricks, it would enable the escaping internees access to the sally port and it also enabled work to be carried out to get through the gate into the moat. A cat ladder to scale the wall out of the moat had been made from light planks, chair rungs and electric light flex.

Finally, it was agreed that the escape attempt would be made on the night of 10/11 November 1921 and seven internees were selected. They were Bill Quirke, Moss Twomey, Tom Crofts, Dick Barrett, Henry O'Mahony, Paddy Buckley and Jack Eddy. Six of the men were in 'A' Block and, as an added complication, Bill Quirke was in 'B' Block.[2]

---

1 *Sworn to be Free, The Complete book of IRA Jailbreaks, 1918–1921*, p.180.
2 Ibid., pp.179–182.

A little after 5 p.m. on 10 November, the seven escapees went through the hole in the wall at the rear of 'A' Block and into the sally port. The stones in the 'A' Block and the bricks and barbed wire were quickly put back in place.[3] They then had to get across the moat at intervals, scale the wall with the cat ladder without being seen by the sentries on the ramparts. Eventually, all seven were outside the outer wall of the moat.

They made their way cautiously to the shoreline, where they had been told a boat had been beached. However, when they found the boat, it was far too heavy to lift or drag to the water. They were determined to find a means of getting off the island. They made their way to the main pier to see if any of the boats were unlocked. All the boats near the pier were locked but in the darkness they could barely see a boat further out from the pier. Jack Eddy swam to it, only to find it was tied to an anchor with a rope. Silently, he swam out again and with a pocket knife and began to cut the rope. The knife slipped from his frozen hands and he had to sever the remaining strands with his teeth. He pushed the boat ashore and a search revealed a pair of oars, while bits of furze branches served as oar locks. All seven men now piled into the boat and pulled away from the island as quickly and quietly as possible to avoid the searchlights and the motor launch.[4]

Helped by Henry O'Mahony's local knowledge, they came ashore near the Belmont Army huts, on the east side of Cobh, at about 10 p.m. Their planning and efforts had paid off. They were now safe, and because of the Truce they could not be rearrested by Crown Forces for escaping from custody.

---

3   Ibid., p.181.
4   Ibid. pp. 179-182.

12

THE CLOSING OF THE MILITARY PRISON IN THE FIELD

Just before midnight on 14 November, the last transfer of internees to Spike from Cork Male Gaol took place. Ten internees were transferred by WD vessel from Custom House Quay directly to Spike. This was a very unusual transfer because of the ten internees transferred, seven of them had previously been held as prisoners on Spike. The seven had been given short custodial sentences by summary courts and were shortly due for release. They were transferred from Spike back to Cork Male Gaol on 24 September. The authorities obviously still considered the men a threat to the Crown because, while in Cork Male Gaol, instead of being allowed to finish their sentences, the authorities had remitted the unexpired portion of their sentence and served them with internment orders and reclassified the men as internees. On arrival at Spike, the vessel disembarked the ten internees and transported twenty prisoners to Cork Male Gaol. The ten internees were only on Spike for four days before being moved again, this time to Maryborough (Portlaoise) Prison.

On the night of 16/17 November, the last seventy-one Republican prisoners were moved from Spike to Kilkenny Gaol. They travelled by sea from Spike to Waterford City. On arrival at the city docks they were escorted to a special train to take them to Kilkenny. One week later, on Tuesday, 22 November, forty-four prisoners escaped from Kilkenny Gaol through a tunnel.[1] The successful completion of the tunnel was made possible only with the cooperation of a friendly prison warder named Power. When the prisoners were prioritising the names of the men being selected for escape, they gave priority to those with the longest sentences. Therefore, those sentenced to death, penal servitude for life and sentences of more than fifteen years imprisonment were top of the list. The first man through the tunnel was Larry Condon, of Fermoy. Unfortunately for the escaping prisoners, the tunnel began to collapse as Maurice Walsh of Limerick was making his way through, otherwise a greater number would have escaped. By examining the list of names of the men that escaped that night, published in the *Kilkenny People* newspaper, I have concluded that at least thirteen escapees were former Spike prisoners. The thirteen men are listed in Appendix 10.

As a result of the destruction caused by the internees during the riot, and in particular the smashing of the windows, coupled with the onset of winter, the internment compound was deemed uninhabitable by a joint committee of British and Irish representatives. On 16 November, just a few days after the successful escape, a Movement Order was received by the British Army commander on Spike to transfer all of the remaining internees to Maryborough Prison. The precise date for the transfer had not been decided. The main points of the Movement Order dated 15 November stated that:[2]

The following will proceed from Spike Island to Maryborough (Portlaoise) Prison at a time and on a date to be notified later:

532 Internees
Prison Staff (less advance and rear parties)
One Medical Officer (Major Wilson), and
R.A.M.C. Orderlies as requires by the Commandant,
Spike Island.
The move will be carried out by rail, entraining station, Queenstown.

---

1 Jim Maher, *The Flying Column West Kilkenny, 1916–1922*, pp. 257–263.
2 UKNA, Kew, London, WO 35/140.

An escort of two Companies (of not less than 134 privates) from the detachment, 2nd Bn, Queen's Own Cameron Highlanders at Spike Island, reinforced from Battalion Headquarters.

The Commandant, Spike Island will arrange with OC, Royal Army Service Corps, Queenstown, for War Department ships to transfer the internees from Spike Island to the Deep Water Quay in Queenstown.

Internees will be handcuffed, four together for the duration of the train journey.

Guides will meet the party on arrival at Maryborough. The officer in charge of the escort will be responsible for the detrainment and safe custody of the internees until they are handed over in Maryborough Prison.

It is realised that it is impossible to keep secret the fact that the internees are shortly to be moving from Spike to Maryborough (Portlaoise) Prison. What can and must be kept secret however is the actual date of the transfer. It should be easy to put people off the scent by mentioning false dates.

The very detailed Movement Order was put into operation on the night of 18 November. The internees were paraded beside their beds for the nightly head count by the army officer. At 7.30 p.m., when the head count was completed, all the internees, including those in hospital, were ordered outside with all their belongings packed in their luggage. They then assembled in the narrow muddy enclosures in front of the huts. All the internees, including those in hospital, were handcuffed together in pairs and ordered to make their way to Spike pier. The journey from the fort to the pier, a distance of approximately 650m, took five hours and all were on the boats by half past midnight. After the short boat journey, the internees disembarked at the Deep Water Quay in Cobh, beside the railway station, and boarded the special train waiting for them for the night journey to Maryborough (Portlaoise) Prison.

There were British troops on picket duty at every railway station on the route, with strict orders that they were not permitted to return to their barracks until after the special train had passed through their station. The internees and their escort arrived at Maryborough (Portlaoise) Prison at 8 p.m. on Saturday, 19 November 1921. This transfer to a prison outside the Martial Law area was only made possible with the introduction of the Truce. While Martial Law was in force, it was not legally permitted to transfer prisoners or internees in or out of the Martial Law area. When the Truce came into effect, Martial Law was suspended, therefore transfers were permitted. This may have been the only occasion when this happened.

The Spike internment compound was now empty. All the internees transferred from Spike Island were released from Maryborough (Portlaoise) Prison on Thursday, 8 December 1921.[1]

---

1   Jim Maher, *The Flying Column – West Kilkenny, 1916–1921,* 2015 edition, pp.269–270.

CONCLUSION

Examining the diverse representation of occupations, the representation of prisoners and internees from almost every town and village in the Martial Law area and the large numbers imprisoned on Spike, it is easy to conclude that almost the entire population was either involved in or supportive of the struggle for independence. In addition, considering the fact that the men involved in the flying columns had local knowledge, mutual support and were fighting for the liberation of their country against the Crown Forces, it is accurate to say that, certainly by 1921, victory was achievable.

Meanwhile, the Crown Forces had inexhaustible military resources, but they were weakened due to a lack of support from their politicians. The British politicians were primarily focussed on their own and their party's reputation. The achievements and success of the Sinn Féin/IRA propaganda machine, particularly in America, were a major factor in persuading the British politicians to seek a political solution to the Irish question. There is no doubt that the indiscipline of the Auxiliary Police, such as during the burning of Cork, greatly helped the Republican propaganda machine.

At the same time, it should be noted that the Truce was certainly a welcome respite for the IRA. The British military pressure was certainly being felt at IRA company and battalion level. The population was becoming war weary and, most importantly, resupply of weapons and small arms ammunition were becoming problematic. While the Truce on 11 July 1921 was a welcome relief to the IRA, there was still plenty of enthusiasm for the cause should the Truce fail.

Following the declaration and implementation of the Truce, the Republican prisoners and internees nationally were adamant that they should be released. This was never going to happen because the men incarcerated were a major reason for the Republican commitment to the Truce, in particular the approximately thirty-five convicted Republicans under sentence of death. As long as the Truce held, these men could not be executed. Prior to the Truce, there were fourteen Republicans executed by military firing squads in the Martial Law area during 1921, thirteen executed in Cork Military Detention Barracks and one in Limerick Army Barracks.

Five months after the Truce, and as a result of sustained political negations, the Treaty was signed in London on 6 December 1921 and all internees nationwide were released. The Republican prisoners remained in prison over Christmas and were released immediately after the Treaty was ratified by the three governments in London, Belfast and Dublin on 7 January 1922.

The War of Independence was over and peace restored to Ireland. However, the IRA was divided because of a failure to achieve a republic and the country was partitioned. Within six short months, peace was shattered and war returned in a dreadful and devastating Civil War, brother against brother.

The legacy of the internees and prisoners incarcerated on Spike Island during the nine months of 1921 was the securing of Irish independence. It is the goal of this book and of those working in the Spike Island Heritage Centre to ensure that their names and sacrifices will never be forgotten.

Ar Dheis Dé go raibh a n-Anam Dhilís.

LIST OF REPUBLICAN PRISONERS ON SPIKE ISLAND

The alphabetical list and details of the Republican prisoners held on Spike Island between April and November 1921 follows.

When searching for an individual where the status is unknown, i.e. prisoner or internee, check the internee list first. There are three times more internees listed: 900 internees and 300 prisoners approximately. The names are in chronological sequence. The surname may or may not have an 'O' or have Mc or Mac included. The vast majority of the records were handwritten and in many cases the British soldiers on clerical duties wrote the names as they sounded and some were misspelt. I have corrected errors where possible.

There were also several occasions where prisoners intentionally furnished incorrect details to their captives. For example, the men from Ballylongford, Co. Kerry, gave Co. Cork as their home address. Where incorrect names were given, I have provided the alias and correct name(s) where known.

In many of the records, the details of the hut an individual prisoner was held in while on Spike was included. The detailed map of the north-east casemates on the next page will enable the reader to identify the hut location.

Not all records survived, therefore it is possible that names have been inadvertently omitted, or that details are incorrect. Some of the town lands listed in the records were particularly difficult to locate, and indeed some have been impossible to identify.

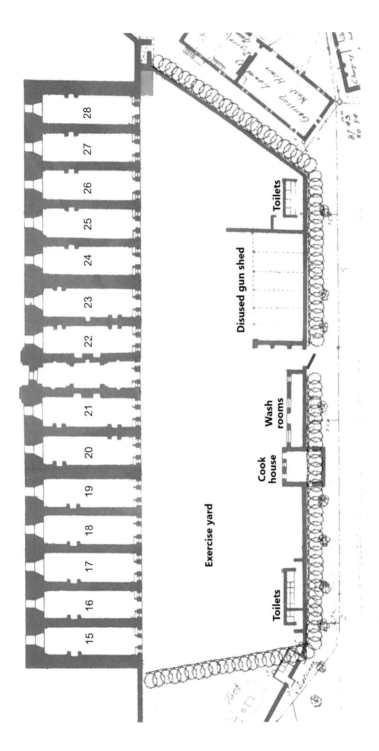

Map 3: Map of the north-east casemates.

Please make contact with the Spike Island manager with original records to have a name added or details amended. Any new information, photographs, etc. are always most welcome. Please send any correspondence to: The Manager, Spike Island, Cobh, Co. Cork, email admin@spikeislandcork.ie, www.spikeislandcork.ie.

Prisoners

Bailey, John
Lough Gur, Herbertstown, Co. Limerick.
He was transferred from Bere Island Military Prison in the Field to Spike prison compound on 15 Apr 1921.

Barry, Florence
Oldcourt, Ballinspittle, Co. Cork.
Age: 22. Occupation: Labourer.
Religion: R.C.
6th Division arrest No. 520.
Offence under Martial Law.
He was tried by Summary Court on 20 June 1921 and sentenced to 6 months imprisonment.
Earliest release date, 20 Nov 1921.
His sentence expired on 19 Dec 1921.
He was transferred from Cork Male Gaol to Spike prison compound on 25 June 1921.
He was transferred from Spike, back to Cork Male Gaol on 24 Sept 1921.

Barry, Thomas
String, Glanworth, Co. Cork.
Age: 23. Occupation: Farmer.

Religion: R.C.
6th Division arrest No. 347.
Offence under Martial Law.
He was tried by Summary Court on 3 May 1921 and sentenced to 6 months imprisonment.
Earliest release date, 4 Oct 1921.
His sentence expired on 2 Nov 1921.
He was transferred from Cork Male Gaol to Spike prison compound on 22 June 1921.

Baylor, Michael
His alias was Michael Fitzgerald.
Cassidy's Avenue, off Old Youghal Road, Cork City.
Occupation: Shirt cutter.
Religion: R.C.
He was arrested by British soldiers at Rahanisky House, Whitechurch, Co. Cork, on 8 Feb 1921 and taken to Victoria Barracks, Cork.[1]
6th Division arrest No. 197.
Offences against Martial Law, conspiring to levy war against the King and possession of arms.

---

1   Seán Enright, *The Trial of Civilians by Military Courts in Ireland 1921*, pp.128–133.

He was tried by Military Court in Victoria Barracks on 26 Feb 1921 and sentenced to 15 years imprisonment. His sentence expired on 25 Feb 1936. He was transferred from Bere Island Military Prison in the Field to Spike prison compound on 15 Apr 1921. He was transferred to Kilkenny Gaol on 17 Nov 1921 and released from there in Jan 1922.

See also: Bowles, Michael; Conroy, Cornelius; Dennehy, Jerh; MacSwiney, John; Murphy, Timothy; O'Driscoll, Laurence; O'Keeffe, John; Thompson, James; Twomey, Cornelius; and Twomey. John.

Bland, William J.

Also listed as Bliand.
Killeagh & Church St, Youghal, Co. Cork.
Age: 25.
Occupation: Coach painter.
Religion: R.C.
He was arrested on 24 June 1921 in Killeagh, Co. Cork, and taken to Victoria Barracks, Cork.
6th Division arrest No. 581.
Brigade arrest No. 17 I.B. 1011.
Offence against Martial Law, he was found in possession of arms.
He was tried by Military Court in Victoria Barracks on 25 June 1921 and sentenced to 5 years Penal Servitude (PS). He was transferred from Cork Male Gaol to Spike prison compound on 6 July 1921.

Bohane, Edward (Ned)

Kinsale, Co. Cork.
Age: 20. Occupation: Farmer.
Religion: R.C.
6th Division arrest No. 71.
Brigade arrest No. 17 I.B. 1032.
Offence against Martial Law, illegal assembly.
He was tried by Summary Court on 19 Jan 1921 and sentenced to 6 months imprisonment.
Earliest release date, 19 June 1921.
His sentence expired on 18 July 1921.
He was transferred from Bere Island Military Prison in the Field to Spike prison compound on 15 Apr 1921. While on Spike, his sentence was reserved. He was served with an Internment Order and immediately transferred to Spike internment compound.

See also: Bohane, Ned, in the Spike internee list.

Bourke, George

93 Bandon Road, Cork City.
Age: 26. Occupation: Pipe Fitter.
Religion: R.C.
6th Division arrest No. 497.
Offence under Martial Law.
He was tried by Summary Court on 17 June 1921 and sentenced to 6 months imprisonment.
His sentence expired on 16 Dec 1921.
He was transferred from Cork Male Gaol to Spike prison compound on 22 June 1921.

He was transferred from Spike back to Cork Male Gaol on 24 Sept 1921.

Bowles, Michael

Clogheen, Co. Cork.
Age: 23. Occupation: Blacksmith.
Religion: R.C.
He was arrested by British soldiers at Rahanisky House, Whitechurch, on 8 Feb 1921 and taken to Victoria Barracks, Cork.
6th Division arrest No. 195.[2]
Offences against Martial Law, levying war against the King and carrying arms.
He was tried by Military Court in Victoria Barracks on 26 Feb 1921 and sentenced to 10 years Penal Servitude.
His sentence expired on 25 Feb 1931.
He was transferred from Bere Island Military Prison in the Field to Spike prison compound on 15 Apr 1921.
He was transferred from Spike to Cork Military Hospital on 20 Sept 1921 and returned to Spike on 7 Nov from Cork Male Gaol.
He was transferred to Kilkenny Gaol on Thursday, 17 Nov 1921, and released from there in Jan 1922.
See also: Conroy, Cornelius; Dennehy, Jerh; Fitzgerald, Michael; MacSwiney, John; Murphy, Timothy; O'Driscoll, Laurence; O'Keeffe, John; Thompson, James; Twomey, Cornelius; and Twomey, John.

Michael Bowles, Clogheen, Co. Cork.

Brennan, Thomas

Lough Gur, Herbertstown, Co. Limerick.
He was transferred from Bere Island Military Prison in the Field to Spike prison compound on 15 Apr 1921.

Brown, Dominic

Blennerbinne, Tralee, Co. Kerry.
Age: 27. Occupation: Engineer.
Religion: R.C.
6th Division arrest No. 453.
Offence under the ROIR.
He was tried by Summary Court on 28 May 1921 and sentenced to 6 months imprisonment.
Earliest release date, 29 Oct 1921.
His sentence expired on 27 Nov 1921.
He was transferred from Cork Male Gaol to Spike prison compound on 13 June 1921.
He was transferred from Spike back to Cork Male Gaol on 24 Sept 1921.

Brown, Edward

Church Street, Listowel, Co. Kerry.

---

2   Seán Enright, *The Trial of Civilians by Military Courts in Ireland 1921*, pp.128–133.

Age: 31. Occupation: Cattle dealer.
Religion: R.C.
6th Division arrest No. 575.
Brigade arrest No. K.B. 266.
Offence under Martial Law,
organising Sinn Féin police.
He was tried by Summary Court
on 22 June 1921 and sentenced to
3 months imprisonment.
His sentence expired on 21 Sept 1921.
He was transferred from Cork Male
Gaol to Spike prison compound on
6 July 1921.
He was released from Spike on 7 Sept
1921, authority received from CA 693,
dated 5 Sept 1921.

Brown, Matthew

Castletownroche, Co. Cork.
Age: 27. Occupation: Labourer.
Religion: R.C.
6th Division arrest No. 420.
Offence under the ROIR.
He was tried by Summary Court
on 21 May 1921 and sentenced to
6 months imprisonment.
Earliest release date, 21 Oct 1921.
His sentence expired on 20 Nov 1921.
He was transferred from Cork Male
Gaol to Spike prison compound on
13 June 1921.
He was transferred from Spike back
to Cork Male Gaol on 24 Sept 1921.

Brown, Richard

New Street, Macroom, Co. Cork.
Age: 19. Occupation: Van Driver.

Religion: R.C.
He was arrested by Crown Forces on
30 June 1921 for giving a false name.
6th Division arrest No. 590.
Brigade arrest No. 17 I.B. 1038.
Offence under Martial Law, giving a
false name.
He was tried by Summary Court
on 30 June 1921 and sentenced to
6 months imprisonment.
Earliest release date, 30 Nov 1921.
His sentence expired on 29 Dec 1921.
He was transferred from Cork Male
Gaol to Spike prison compound on
15 July 1921.
He was transferred from Spike back
to Cork Male Gaol on 24 Sept 1921.

Buckley, Daniel

Telephone Terrace, Blarney,
Co. Cork.
Age: 23. Occupation: Clerk.
Religion: R.C.
Offence under the ROIR.
He was tried by FGCM on 10 June
1921 and sentenced to 15 years
Penal Servitude.
His sentence expired on 9 June 1936.
He was transferred from Cork to Spike
prison compound on 18 June 1921.
He was transferred from Spike to
Kilkenny Gaol on 17 Nov 1921 and
released from there in Jan 1922.

Burke, Edmund

Bruff, Co. Limerick.
He was transferred from Bere Island

Military Prison in the Field to Spike prison compound on 15 Apr 1921.

Burke, Michael

Folkstown, Ballinure, Thurles, Co. Tipperary.
Age: 23. Occupation: Mechanic.
Religion: R.C.
On 1 Aug 1920 the military were searching the village of Moyglass in Co. Tipperary. When searched, Michael Burke was found with a grenade, a Colt semi-automatic pistol and eight rounds of ammunition in his pockets.[3]
He was taken to Cork Male Gaol, where he survived 94 days on hunger strike, from 11 Aug to 12 Nov 1920. When he had recovered from his hunger strike, he was tried by FGCM in Victoria Barracks, Cork, on 16 May 1921, for an offence against Martial Law, the possession of bombs and ammunition.
He was found guilty and sentenced to

Michael Burke, Thurles, Co. Tipperary.

10 years Penal Servitude.
His sentence expired on 15 May 1931.
He was transferred from Cork Male Gaol to Spike prison compound on 28 May 1921.
He was transferred from Spike to Kilkenny Gaol on 17 Nov 1921. On Tuesday, 22 Nov, he escaped through a tunnel from Kilkenny Gaol with 43 others.

Burke, William

Windmill, Limerick City.
Age: 16. Occupation: Labourer.
Religion: R.C.
Offence under the ROIR.
He was tried by FGCM on 26 May 1921 and sentenced to 3 years Penal Servitude.
His sentence expired on 25 May 1924.
He was transferred from Limerick to Spike prison compound on 1 June 1921.
He was transferred from Spike to Kilkenny Gaol on 17 Nov 1921 and released from there in Jan 1922.

Butler, John J.

Thomona, Limerick City.
Age: 22. Occupation: Well borer.
Religion: R.C.
6th Division arrest No. 289.
Offence under the ROIR.
He was tried by FGCM on 5 Apr 1921 and sentenced to 5 years

---

3   UKNA, Kew, London, WO 35/136, p.80.

imprisonment, which was reduced to 1 year imprisonment.

His sentence expired on 4 Apr 1922. He was transferred from Limerick to Spike prison compound on 2 June 1921. He was transferred from Spike to Cork Male Gaol on 24 Sept 1921.

Byrns, Pat
Tullig, Beaufort and Killflynn, Abbeydorney, Co. Kerry.
Age: 24. Occupation: Labourer.
Religion: R.C.
6th Division arrest No. 567.
Brigade arrest No. K.B. 270.
Offence under Martial Law, being a suspected person and refusing to enter into recognisance.
He was tried by Summary Court in Ballymullen Barracks, Tralee, on 16 June 1921 and sentenced to 3 months imprisonment.
His sentence expired on 15 Sept 1921. He was transferred from Cork Male Gaol to Spike prison compound on 6 July 1921.
He was released from Spike on 1 Sept 1921, authority received from CA 693, dated 30 Aug 1921.

Casey, Pat
Friar Street, Cashel, Co. Tipperary.
Age: 25.
Occupation: Creamery Manager.
Religion: R.C.
6th Division arrest No. 483.
Offence under Martial Law.

He was tried by Summary Court on 8 June 1921 and sentenced to 9 months imprisonment.
Earliest release date, 22 Jan 1922.
His sentence expired on 7 Mar 1922. He was transferred from Cork Male Gaol to Spike prison compound on 22 June 1921.
He was transferred from Spike back to Cork Male Gaol on 24 Sept 1921.

Clancy, John
31 Cross Road, Thomond Gate, Limerick City.
Age: 22. Occupation: Sawyer.
Religion: R.C.
6th Division arrest No. 164.
Offence against the ROIR.
He was tried by FGCM on 13 Apr 1921 and sentenced to 1 year imprisonment.
Earliest release date, 12 Feb 1922.
His sentence expired on 12 Apr 1922. He was transferred from Cork Male Gaol to Spike prison compound on 25 June 1921.
He was transferred from Spike back to Cork Male Gaol on 24 Sept 1921.

Clancy, Maurice
Farrangeel, Kanturk, Co. Cork.
Age: 26. Occupation: Farmer.
Religion: R.C.
Offence under the ROIR.
He was tried by Summary Court on 31 May 1921 and sentenced to 6 months imprisonment.

Earliest release date, 31 Oct 1921.
His sentence expired on 30 Nov 1921.
He was transferred from Cork to Spike
prison compound on 18 June 1921.
He was transferred from Spike to
Cork Male Gaol on 24 Sept 1921.

Cleary, Michael
Herbertstown, County Limerick.
He was transferred from Bere Island
Military Prison in the Field to Spike
prison compound on 15 Apr 1921.

Clifford, John
Russincartin.
Age: 26. Occupation: Farmer.
6th Division arrest No. 95.
Offence against the ROIR.
He was tried by District Court
Martial (DCM) on 5 Jan 1921 and
sentenced to 2 years imprisonment.
He had 6 months remitted, 18 months
to serve.
Earliest release date, 5 Apr 1922.
His sentence expired on 4 July 1922.
He was transferred from Cork to Spike
prison compound on 2 June 1921.
He was transferred from Spike to
Cork Male Gaol on 24 Sept 1921 and
released from there on 12 Jan 1922.

Cogan, Charles
33 Cove Street, Cork City.
Age: 33. Occupation: Joiner.
Religion: R.C.
6th Division arrest No. 495.
Offence under the ROIR.

He was tried by Summary Court
on 11 June 1921 and sentenced to
6 months imprisonment.
Earliest release date, 17 Nov 1921.
His sentence expired on 16 Dec 1921.
He was transferred from Cork Male
Gaol to Spike prison compound on
22 June 1921. He was transferred back
to Cork Male Gaol on 24 Sept 1921.

Cohalan, Thomas
Charles Fort, Kinsale, Co. Cork.
Age: 36. Occupation: Carpenter.
Religion: R.C.
6th Division arrest No. 65.
Offence against the ROIR, illegal
assembly.
He was tried by Summary Court
on 20 Jan 1921 and sentenced to
6 months imprisonment.
Earliest release date, 19 June 1921.
His sentence expired on 18 July 1921.
He was transferred from Bere Island
Military Prison in the Field to Spike
prison compound on 15 Apr 1921.
While on Spike, his sentence was
vacated. He was served with an
Internment Order and immediately
transferred to Spike internment
compound, no date given.
See also: Cohalan, Thomas, in the
Spike internee list.

Connors, John
Pilltown, Co. Waterford.
Age: 19. Occupation: Labourer.
Religion: R.C.

On 1 July 1921, he was arrested
by Crown Forces for possession of
information and for not reporting rebels.
6th Division arrest No. 600.
Brigade arrest No. 17 I.B. 1113.
Offences against Martial Law, for
possession of information and for not
reporting rebels.
He was tried by Summary Court
on 1 July 1921 and sentenced to
6 months imprisonment.
Earliest release date, 2 Dec 1921.
His sentence expired on 31 Dec 1921.
He was transferred from Cork to
Spike prison compound on 15 July
1921. He was transferred to Cork
Male Gaol on 24 Sept 1921.

Conroy, Cornelius

3 South Terrace, Cork City.
Age: 26. Occupation: He was
employed by the British Army as
a confidential clerk in Victoria
Barracks, Cork.

Cornelius Conroy, South Terrace,
Cork City.

Religion: R.C.
He was arrested by British soldiers
at Rahanisky House, Whitechurch,
Co. Cork on 8 Feb 1921 and taken to
Victoria Barracks, Cork.[4]
6th Division arrest No. 204.
Offences against Martial Law,
conspiring to levy war against the
King and possession of arms.
He was tried by Military Court in
Victoria Barracks on 26 Feb 1921 and
sentenced to 15 years Penal Servitude.
His sentence expired on 25 Feb 1936.
He was transferred from Bere Island
Military Prison in the Field to Spike
prison compound on 15 Apr 1921.
He was transferred from Spike to
Kilkenny Gaol on 17 Nov 1921. On
Tuesday, 22 Nov, he escaped through
a tunnel from Kilkenny Gaol with
43 others.
See also: Bowles, Michael; Dennehy,
Jerh; Fitzgerald, Michael; MacSwiney,
John; Murphy, Timothy; O'Driscoll,
Laurence; O'Keeffe, John; Thompson,
James; Twomey, Cornelius; and
Twomey, John.

Conway, Thomas

Carnane, Fedamore, Kilmallock,
Co. Limerick.
Age: 20. Occupation: Farmer.
Religion: R.C.
He was captured while on sentry duty
at Caherguillamore House, Bruff,

---

4   Seán Enright, *The Trial of Civilians by Military Courts in Ireland 1921*, pp.128–133.

Thomas Conway, Kilmallock,
Co. Limerick.

Co. Limerick, on 27 Dec 1920.[5]
6th Division arrest No. 526.
Offence against the ROIR.
He was tried by FGCM on 23 Feb
1921 and sentenced to 5 years
Penal Servitude.
Earliest release date, 28 Nov 1924.
His sentence expired on 22 Feb 1926.
He was transferred from Limerick
via Cork Male Gaol to Spike prison
compound on 11 May 1921, to Hut 24.
He was transferred from Spike to
Kilkenny Gaol on 17 Nov 1921 and
released from there in Jan 1922.

Cooney, Francis

O'Connell Avenue, Limerick City.
O/C 'B' Company, Na Fianna, Limerick.
Age: 18. Occupation: Shop assistant.
Religion: R.C.
He was arrested by RIC at Rosbrien,
Limerick, on 22 May 1921 and taken
to William Street RIC Barracks in
Limerick City.

6th Division arrest No. 244.
Offence against the ROIR.
He was tried by FGCM in Limerick
on 26 May 1921 and sentenced to
3 years Penal Servitude (PS).
Earliest release date, 25 Aug 1923.
His sentence expired on 25 May 1924.
He was transferred from Limerick to
Spike prison compound on 1 June 1921.
He was transferred from Spike to
Kilkenny Gaol on 17 Nov 1921 and
released from there in Jan 1922.

Corr, Gerard

9 Mount Vincent Cottages, Rosbrien,
Limerick City.
Age: 19. Occupation: Printer.
Religion: R.C.
6th Division arrest No. 239.
Offence against the ROIR.
He was tried by FGCM in Limerick,
on 26 May 1921 and sentenced to
3 years Penal Servitude (PS).
Earliest release date, 25 Aug 1923.
His sentence expired on 25 May 1924.
He was transferred from Limerick to
Spike prison compound on 1 June 1921.
He was transferred from Spike to
Kilkenny Gaol on 17 Nov 1921 and
released from there in Jan 1922.

Crampton, Patrick J.

Rathpeacon, Co. Cork.
Age: 27.
Occupation: Machine Operator.

---

5   Thomas Toomey, *The War of Independence in Limerick, 1912–1921*, pp. 485–496.

Religion: R.C.

Offence against the ROIR.

He was tried by FGCM in Victoria Barracks, Cork, on 10 June 1921 and sentenced to 15 years Penal Servitude. His sentence expired on 9 June 1936. He was transferred from Cork to Spike prison compound on 18 June 1921. He was transferred from Spike to Kilkenny Gaol on 17 Nov 1921 and released from there in Jan 1922.

Creedon, William

Sleeveen West, Macroom, Co. Cork.

Age: 26.

Occupation: Labourer.

Religion: R.C.

6th Division arrest No. 475.

Offence against the ROIR.

He was tried by Summary Court on 7 June 1921 and sentenced to 6 months imprisonment. Earliest release date, 7 Nov 1921. His sentence expired on 6 Dec 1921. He was transferred from Cork Male Gaol to Spike prison compound on 22 June 1921.

He was transferred from Spike to Cork Military Hospital in Victoria Barracks.

Cregan, Patrick

Collooney Street, Limerick City.

Age: 20. Occupation: Mechanic.

Religion: R.C.

6th Division arrest No. 211.

Offence against Martial Law.

He was tried by Military Court

on 27 May 1921 and sentenced to 12 years Penal Servitude. Earliest release date, 27 May 1930. His sentence expired on 26 May 1933. He was transferred from Limerick to Spike prison compound on 1 June. He was transferred from Spike to Kilkenny Gaol on 17 Nov 1921 and released from there in Jan 1922.

Cremin, John

3 Friars Walk, Cork City.

Age: 23. Occupation: Labourer.

Religion: R.C.

6th Division arrest No. 493.

Offence against the ROIR.

He was tried by Summary Court on 17 June 1921 and sentenced to 6 months imprisonment. Earliest release date, 17 Nov 1921. His sentence expired on 16 Dec 1921. He was transferred from Cork Male Gaol to Spike prison compound on 22 June 1921. He was transferred back to Cork Male Gaol on 24 Sept 1921.

Croke, Denis

Laffans Bridge, Killenaule, Co. Tipperary.

Age: 22. Occupation: Labourer.

Religion: R.C.

6th Division arrest No. 642.

Offence against the ROIR.

He was tried by FGCM on 22 July 1921 and sentenced to 10 years Penal Servitude (PS).

He was transferred from Cork Male

Gaol to Spike prison compound on
11 Aug 1921.

He was transferred from Spike to
Kilkenny Gaol on 17 Nov 1921 and
released from there in Jan 1922.

Cronin, John J.

John Joe Cronin, Charleville, Co. Cork.

Charleville, Co. Cork.
Age: 17.
Occupation: Student.
Religion: R.C.
6th Division arrest No. 115.
Offences against the ROIR, he was
found in possession of IRA documents
and in breach of Martial Law.
He was tried by Summary Court
on 28 Jan 1921 and sentenced to
6 months imprisonment.
Earliest release date, 18 June 1921.
His sentence expired on 27 July 1921.
He was transferred from Bere Island
Military Prison in the Field to Spike
prison compound on 15 Apr 1921.
He was released from Spike on
28 June 1921, authority received from
CA 693, dated 21 June 1921.

Cronin, Pat

Gurrinebann.
Age: 21. Occupation: Farmer.
Religion: R.C.
6th Division arrest No. 448.
Offence against Martial Law.
He was tried by Summary Court
on 23 May 1921 and sentenced to
6 months imprisonment.
Earliest release date, 24 Oct 1921.
His sentence expired on 22 Nov 1921.
He was transferred from Cork to Spike
prison compound on 13 June 1921.
He was given parole from Spike from
2 to 11 July. He was transferred to
Cork Male Gaol on 24 Sept 1921.

Cronin, Patrick

Finuge, Lixnaw, Co. Kerry.
Age: 22. Occupation: Farmer.
Religion: R.C.
6th Division arrest No. L. 726.
Offences against Martial Law, he was
found carrying arms and ammunition.
He was tried by Military Court on
8 June 1921 and sentenced to Penal
Servitude for Life.
He was transferred from Cork Male
Gaol to Spike prison compound on
13 June 1921.
He was transferred from Spike, to
Kilkenny Gaol on 17 Nov 1921 and
released from there in Jan 1922.

Cronin, William

Ballinphellic, Ballygarvan, Co. Cork.
Age: 21. Occupation: Farmer.

Religion: R.C.

6th Division arrest No. 544.

Brigade arrest No. 17 I.B. 643.

Offence under the ROIR.

He was tried by Summary Court on 20 June 1921 and sentenced to 3 months imprisonment.

Earliest release date, 5 Sept 1921.

His sentence expired on 19 Sept 1921.

He was transferred from Cork Male Gaol to Spike prison compound on 30 June 1921.

He was released from Spike on 6 Sept 1921 with authority from CA 693, dated 3 Sept 1921.

Crowley, John

Templeglantine, Co. Limerick.

Age: 22.

Occupation: Draper.

Religion: R.C.

Offence against the ROIR.

He was tried by FGCM on 23 Mar 1921 and sentenced to 10 years Penal Servitude.

Earliest release date, 19 Sept 1928.

His sentence expired on 22 Mar 1931.

He was transferred from Limerick, via Cork Male Gaol to Spike prison compound on 11 May 1921.

He was transferred from Spike to Kilkenny Gaol on 17 Nov 1921 and released from there in Jan 1922.

Crowley, John

Ballylanders, Co. Limerick.

Age: 28. Occupation: Shop assistant.

Religion: R.C.

He was arrested on 16 July 1920.

A party of police arrived in Ballylanders, Co. Limerick, at 1.15 a.m. on 16 July 1920 and were fired upon from Crowley's public house. The police returned fire and after half an hour rushed the house. Michael O'Reilly, John and Peter Crowley were found in a top room. Revolvers and ammunition were found in a trap in the ceiling. Christopher Upton was found in the same house, hiding under the stairs. All four were arrested by the RIC.

6th Division arrest No. L. 465.

Offences against the ROIR, found carrying firearms.

Michael O'Reilly, John and Peter Crowley were found not guilty of attacking the police with firearms. They were found guilty of being present and abetting certain persons unknown in the attack.[6] See Upton, Christopher, in the Spike internee list. Both brothers, John and Peter below, survived 94 days on hunger strike in Cork Male Gaol from 11 Aug to 12 Nov 1920.

After recovering from the effects of his hunger strike, John was tried by FGCM in Victoria Barracks, Cork, on

---

6   UKNA, Kew, London, WO 35/135, p.150.

John (Jack) Crowley, Ballylanders,
Co. Limerick.

Peter Crowley, Ballylanders,
Co. Limerick.

2 June 1921 and sentenced to 2 years
imprisonment.
His sentence expired on 1 June 1923.
He was transferred from Cork
Military Detention Barracks to Spike
prison compound on 9 June 1921.
He was transferred from Spike to Cork
Male Gaol on 24 Sept 1921. He was
released from there on 12 Jan 1922.

Military Detention Barracks to Spike
prison compound on 9 June 1921.
He was transferred from Spike to Cork
Male Gaol on 24 Sept 1921. He was
released from there on 12 Jan 1922.
Both brothers, Peter and John (above)
survived 94 days on hunger strike
in Cork Male Gaol from 11 Aug to
12 Nov 1920.

Crowley, Peter

Ballylanders, Co. Limerick.
Age: 19. Occupation: Drapers assistant.
Religion: R.C.
Arrested on 16 July 1920, details as
for his brother John above.
6th Division arrest No. L. 466.
Offences against the R.O.I.R, found
carrying firearms.
After recovering from the effects of
his hunger strike, he was tried by
FGCM in Victoria Barracks, Cork, on
2 June 1921 and sentenced to 2 years
imprisonment.
His sentence expired on 1 June 1923.
He was transferred from Cork

Daly, Tim

Ballymacus, Kinsale, Co. Cork.
Age: 23. Occupation: Labourer.
Religion: R.C.
6th Division arrest No. 554.
Brigade arrest No. 17 I.B. 1042.
Offence against Martial Law, refusing
to obey a military order.
He was tried by Summary Court in
Victoria Barracks on 20 June 1921 and
sentenced to 3 months imprisonment.
Earliest release date, 5 Sept 1921.
His sentence expired on 19 Sept 1921.
He was transferred from Cork Male
Gaol to Spike prison compound on
6 July 1921.

He was released from Spike on 6 Sept 1921, authority from CA 693, dated 3 Sept 1921.

Dargan, Thomas[7]

Thomas Dargan, Rutland Street, Limerick City.

15 Rutland Street, Limerick City.
Age: 17. Occupation: Printer.
Religion: R.C.
He was arrested by RIC at Rosbrien, on 22 May 1921 and taken to William St RIC Barracks, Limerick.
6th Division arrest No. 240.
Offence against the ROIR.
He was tried by FGCM on 26 May 1921 and sentenced to 3 years Penal Servitude.
Earliest release date, 25 Aug 1923.
His sentence expired on 25 May 1924.
He was transferred from Limerick to Spike prison compound on 1 June 1921.
He was transferred from Spike to Kilkenny Gaol on 17 Nov 1921.
After the mass escape from Kilkenny Gaol on 22 Nov, he was transferred to Limerick Gaol. He was released from there in Jan 1922.

Dee, John

Ballylongford, Co. Kerry.
Age: 27. Occupation: Farmer.
Religion: R.C.
6th Division arrest No. 577.
Brigade arrest No. K.B. 250.
Offences against Martial Law, he was found drilling, being a member of the IRA and for refusing to enter into recognisance.
He was tried by Summary Court in Ballymullen Barracks, Tralee, on 22 June 1921 and sentenced to 3 months imprisonment.
Earliest release date, 7 Sept 1921.
His sentence expired on 21 Sept 1921.
He was transferred from Cork Male Gaol to Spike prison compound on 6 July 1921. He was released from Spike on 7 Sept 1921, authority from CA 693.

Dee, Patrick

Ballylongford, Co. Kerry.
Age: 24. Occupation: Farmer.
Religion: R.C.
6th Division arrest No. 576.
Brigade arrest No. K.B. 251.
Offences against Martial Law, drilling, being a member of the IRA and for refusing to enter into recognisance.
He was tried by Summary Court

---

7   See his WS, No. 1404.

in Ballymullen Barracks, Tralee,
on 22 June 1921 and sentenced to
3 months imprisonment.
Earliest release date, 7 Sept 1921.
His sentence expired on 21 Sept 1921.
He was transferred from Cork Male
Gaol to Spike prison compound on
6 July 1921. He was released from
Spike on 7 Sept 1921, authority from
CA 693.

Deegan, Michael
John's Bridge, Kanturk, Co. Cork.
Age: 27.
Occupation: Cheese Maker.
Religion: R.C.
6th Division arrest No. 449.
Offence against Martial Law, failing
to report damage to a bridge.
He was tried by Summary Court
on 22 June 1921 and sentenced to
6 months imprisonment.
Earliest release date, 11 Aug 1921.
His sentence expired on 26 Aug 1921.
He was transferred from Cork Male
Gaol to Spike prison compound on
13 June 1921. He was released from
Spike on 11 Aug 1921.

Dennehy, Henry
Charleville, Co. Cork.
Age: 24.
Occupation: Engine Driver.
Religion: R.C.
6th Division arrest No. 113.

Offence against Martial Law.
He was tried by Summary Court
on 28 Jan 1921 and sentenced to
6 months imprisonment.
Earliest release date, 28 June 1921.
His sentence expired on 27 July 1921.
He was transferred from Bere Island
Military Prison in the Field to Spike
prison compound on 15 Apr 1921.
He was released from Spike on
28 June 1921, authority of CA 693,
dated 21 June 1921.

Dennehy, Jeremiah
232 Blarney Street, Cork City.
Age: 23. Occupation: Clerk.
Religion: R.C.
He was arrested by British soldiers
at Rahanisky House, Whitechurch,
Co. Cork, on 8 Feb 1921 and taken to
Victoria Barracks, Cork.[8]
6th Division arrest No. 198.
Offences against Martial Law,
conspiring to levy war against the
King and possession of arms.
He was tried by Military Court in
Victoria Barracks on 26 Feb 1921 and
sentenced to 15 years Penal Servitude.
His sentence expired on 25 Feb 1936.
He was transferred from Bere Island
Military Prison in the Field to Spike
prison compound on 15 Apr 1921.
He was transferred from Spike to
Cork Military Hospital in Victoria
Barracks on 27 Aug 1921 and

8   Seán Enright, *The Trial of Civilians by Military Courts in Ireland 1921*, pp.128–133.

released in Jan 1922.
See also: Bowles, Michael; Conroy,
Cornelius; Fitzgerald, Michael;
MacSwiney, John; Murphy, Timothy;
O'Driscoll, Laurence; O'Keeffe,
John; Thompson, James; Twomey,
Cornelius; and Twomey, John.

Desmond, Dan

Desmond, Ben, in all British documents.
10 Mangerton Terrace, Blarney,
Co. Cork.
Age: 21.
Occupation: Factory Hand.
Religion: R.C.
6th Division arrest No. 380.
Offence against the ROIR, causing
harm to a bridge.
He was tried by FGCM in Victoria
Barracks on 13 May 1921 and
sentenced to 2 years imprisonment.
Earliest release date, 12 Jan 1923.
His sentence expired on 12 May 1923.
He was transferred from Cork to Spike
prison compound on 2 June 1921.
He was transferred from Spike to Cork
Male Gaol on 24 Sept 1921. He was
released from there on 12 Jan 1922.
Brother of Michael below.

Desmond, Michael

10 Mangerton Terrace, Blarney,
Co. Cork.
Age: 18.
Occupation: Factory Hand.
Religion: R.C.

Offence under the ROIR.
He was tried by FGCM in Victoria
Barracks on 10 June 1921 and
sentenced to 15 years Penal Servitude.
His sentence expired on 19 June 1936.
He was transferred from Cork to Spike
prison compound on 18 June 1921.
He was transferred from Spike to
Kilkenny Gaol on 17 Nov 1921. He
was released from there in Jan 1922.
Brother of Dan above.

Desmond, William

Ballythomas, Kinsale, Co. Cork.
Age: 25. Occupation: Farmer.
Religion: R.C.
6th Division arrest No. 553.
Brigade arrest No. 17 1.B. 1043.
Offence against Martial Law, refusing
to obey a military order.
He was tried by Summary Court
on 20 June 1921 and sentenced to
3 months imprisonment.
Earliest release date, 5 Sept 1921.
His sentence expired on 19 Sept 1921.
He was transferred from Cork Male
Gaol to Spike prison compound on
6 July 1921.
He was released from Spike on 6 Sept
1921, authority from CA 693, dated
3 Sept 1921.

Dineen, Edward

Knockderk, Kilmallock, Co. Limerick.
He was transferred from Bere Island
Military Prison in the Field to Spike
prison compound on 15 Apr 1921.

Divan, Michael
Pike St., Thurles, Co. Tipperary.
Age: 24.
Occupation: Coach Builder.
6th Division arrest No. 119.
Offences against Martial Law.
He was tried by FGCM on 23 Mar
1921 and sentenced to 10 years
Penal Servitude.
He was transferred from Limerick
via Cork Male Gaol to Spike prison
compound on 11 May 1921.
He was transferred from Spike to
Kilkenny Gaol on 17 Nov 1921. He
was released from there in Jan 1922.

Donoghue, Dan
Coomacullen, Glenflesk, Co. Kerry.
Age: 22. Occupation: Labourer.
Religion: R.C.
6th Division arrest No. 571.
Brigade arrest No. K.B. 275.
Offences against Martial Law, for
being a member of the IRA and
being found in possession of illegal
documents, relating to the IRA.
He was tried by Summary Court
in Ballymullen Barracks, Tralee,
on 27 June 1921 and sentenced to
6 months imprisonment.
Earliest release date, 27 Nov 1921.
His sentence expired on 26 Dec 1921.
He was transferred from Cork Male
Gaol to Spike prison compound on
6 July 1921. He was transferred back
to Cork Male Gaol on 24 Sept 1921.

Donoghue, Michael
Annemore, Glenflesk, Co. Kerry.
Age: 28. Occupation: Labourer.
Religion: R.C.
6th Division arrest No. 573.
Brigade arrest No. K.B. 277.
Offences against Martial Law, aiding
the destruction of public roads, being
a member of the IRA and being
in possession of illegal documents,
relating to the IRA.
He was tried by Summary Court
in Ballymullen Barracks, Tralee,
on 27 June 1921 and sentenced to
6 months imprisonment.
Earliest release date, 27 Nov 1921.
His sentence expired on 26 Dec 1921.
He was transferred from Cork Male
Gaol to Spike prison compound on
6 July 1921. He was transferred back
to Cork Male Gaol on 24 Sept 1921.

Donovan, James
Cross House, Clonakilty, Co. Cork.
Age: 20.
Occupation: Labourer.
Religion: R.C.
6th Division arrest No. 397.
Offences against the ROIR, acting as
a policeman.
He was tried by Summary Court
on 17 May 1921 and sentenced to
6 months imprisonment.
Earliest release date, 18 Oct 1921.
His sentence expired on 16 Nov 1921.
He was transferred from Cork Male
Gaol to Spike prison compound on

13 June. He was transferred back to Cork Male Gaol on 24 Sept 1921.

Donovan, Michael

Michael Donovan, Clonakilty, Co. Cork.

15 Patrick Street, Clonakilty, Co. Cork. Age: 22. Occupation: Labourer. Religion: R.C. 6th Division arrest No. 398. Offence against the ROIR, acting as a policeman. He was tried by Summary Court on 17 May 1921 and sentenced to 6 months imprisonment. Earliest release date, 18 Oct 1921. His sentence expired on 16 Nov 1921. He was transferred from Cork Male Gaol to Spike prison compound on 13 June. He was transferred back to Cork Male Gaol on 24 Sept 1921.

Dooley, Daniel
Castlelyons, Fermoy, Co. Cork. Age: 28. Occupation: Farmer. Religion: R.C. 6th Division arrest No. 233. Offence against the ROIR. He was tried by FGCM on 12 Mar

1921 and sentenced to 12 months imprisonment. Earliest release date, 11 Jan 1922. His sentence expired on 11 Mar 1922. He was transferred from Cork to Spike prison compound on 2 June 1921, to Hut 24, in the north-east casemates. He was transferred from Spike to Cork Male Gaol on 24 Sept 1921.

Doran, James
Mullinahone, Co. Tipperary. Age: 22. Occupation: Chauffeur. Religion: R.C. 6th Division arrest No. 516. Offence under the ROIR. He was tried by Summary Court on 20 June 1921 and sentenced to 3 years imprisonment. Earliest release date, 7 Sept 1921. His sentence expired on 21 Sept 1921. He was transferred from Cork Male Gaol to Spike prison compound on 25 June. He was released from Spike on 7 Sept 1921, authority received from CA 693, dated 5 Sept 1921.

Dower, William
Villierstown, Co. Waterford. Age: 22. Occupation: Mechanic. Religion: R.C. 6th Division arrest No. 482. Offence under the ROIR. He was tried by Summary Court on 11 June 1921 and sentenced to 6 months imprisonment. Earliest release date, 10 Nov 1921.

William Dower, Villierstown,
Co. Waterford.

His sentence expired on 10 Dec 1921.
He was transferred from Cork Male
Gaol to Spike prison compound on
22 June 1921. He was transferred back
to Cork Male Gaol on 24 Sept 1921.

Dowling, Michael

Moyderwell, Tralee, Co. Kerry.
Age: 21. Occupation: Carpenter.
Religion: R.C.
6th Division arrest No. L. 462.
He was charged with four offences
under the ROIR:
1. Attempted murder.
2. Wounding with intent to murder.
3. Wounding with intent.
4. False imprisonment.
The charge stated that, near Tralee
on the night of 5/6 February 1921, he
assaulted an ex-soldier, imprisoned
him for approximately eighteen hours
and shot him with intent to murder.[9]
The arrested men were convinced that
the ex-soldier was an informer.

He was tried by FGCM in Victoria
Barracks, Cork, on 19 May 1921 and
found guilty of the 4th charge only.
He was sentenced to 2 years
imprisonment with Hard Labour.
Earliest release date, 19 Jan 1923.
His sentence expired on 18 May 1923.
He was transferred from Cork Male
Gaol to Spike prison compound on
18 June 1921.
He was transferred from Spike back to
Cork Male Gaol on 24 Sept 1921. He
was released from there on 12 Jan 1922.
See also: Duggan, Michael; Hanafin,
Michael; and McMahon, Bryan in
this list.

Dowling, William

Ballydwyer, Tralee, Co. Kerry.
Age: 24.
Occupation: Farmer.
Religion: R.C.
6th Division arrest No. 318.
Offence against the ROIR.
He was tried by FGCM on 16 Apr
1921 and sentenced to 1 year
imprisonment.
Earliest release date, 15 Feb 1922.
His sentence expired on 15 Apr 1922.
He was transferred from Cork to
Spike prison compound on 2 June
1921. He was transferred back to
Cork Military Hospital in Victoria
Barracks on 12 Sept 1921.

---

9   UKNA, Kew, London, WO 35/124 and WO 35/136, p.166.

Doyle, Jeremiah

Killeen, Gould's Cross, Co. Tipperary.
6th Division arrest No. 480.
Offence against Martial Law.
He was tried by Summary Court
on 11 June 1921 and sentenced to
6 months imprisonment.
Earliest release date, 11 Nov 1921.
His sentence expired on 10 Dec 1921.
He was transferred from Cork Male
Gaol to Spike prison compound on
22 June. He was transferred back to
Cork Male Gaol on 24 Sept 1921.

Doyle, Thomas

Ballytrehy, Clogheen, Co. Tipperary.
Age: 19. Occupation: Farmer.
Religion: R.C.
6th Division arrest No. 229.
Offence against the ROIR.
He was tried by FGCM on 12 Mar
1921 and sentenced to 12 months
imprisonment with Hard Labour.
Earliest release date, 11 Jan 1922.
His sentence expired on 11 Mar 1922.
He was transferred from Cork to
Spike prison compound on 2 June. He
was transferred back to Cork Male
Gaol on 24 Sept 1921.

Duggan, Daniel

Shinagh, Bandon, Co. Cork.
Age: 20. Occupation: Collier.
Religion: R.C.
6th Division arrest No. 364.

Offence against the ROIR.
He was tried by Summary Court
on 12 May 1921 and sentenced to
6 months imprisonment.
Earliest release date, 13 Oct 1921.
His sentence expired on 11 Nov 1921.
He was transferred from Cork Male
Gaol to Spike prison compound on
13 June. He was transferred back to
Cork Male Gaol on 24 Sept 1921.

Duggan, Michael (Mocy)

Farmers Bridge, Tralee, Co. Kerry.
Age: 21.
Occupation: Motor driver.
Religion: R.C.
Charged with four offences under
the ROIR:
1. Attempted murder.
2. Wounding with intent to murder.
3. Wounding with intent.
4. False imprisonment.
His charge stated that, near Tralee on
the night of 5/6 February 1921, he
assaulted an ex-soldier, imprisoned
him for approximately eighteen hours
and shot him with intent to murder.[10]
The arrested men were convinced that
the ex-soldier was an informer.
He was tried by FGCM in Victoria
Barracks, Cork, on 19 May 1921 and
found guilty of 1st and 4th charges only.
He was sentenced to Penal Servitude
for Life.
He was transferred from Cork to Spike

---

10 UKNA, Kew, London, WO 35/124 and WO 35/136, p.166.

prison compound on 18 June 1921.
He was transferred from Spike to
Kilkenny Gaol on 17 Nov 1921 and
released from there in Jan 1922.
See also: Dowling, Michael; Hanafin,
Michael; and McMahon, Bryan, in
this list.

Driscoll, Laurence

Kilmore, Bandon, Co. Cork.
Age: 22. Occupation: Labourer.
Religion: R.C.
6th Division arrest No. 194.
Offence against Martial Law,
carrying arms.
He was tried by Military Court
on 26 Feb 1921 and sentenced to
10 years Penal Servitude.
He was transferred from Bere Island
Military Prison in the Field to Spike
prison compound on 15 Apr 1921.
He was transferred from Spike to
Kilkenny Gaol on 17 Nov 1921. He
was released from there in Jan 1922.

Dwyer, Daniel

Tubbercurry, Killorglin, Co. Kerry.
Age: 24.
Occupation: Shop Assistant.
Religion: R.C.
6th Division arrest No. 562.
Brigade arrest No. K.B. 274.
Offence against Martial Law, being a
member of an unlawful association,
the Irish Volunteers.
He was tried by Summary Court
in Ballymullen Barracks, Tralee,

on 22 June 1921 and sentenced to
3 months imprisonment.
Earliest release date, 7 Sept 1921.
His sentence expired on 21 Sept 1921.
He was transferred from Cork Male
Gaol to Spike prison compound on
6 July 1921. He was released from
Spike on 7 Sept 1921, authority
received from CA 693.

Dwyer, Frank

Toomevara, Co. Tipperary.
Age: 30. Occupation: Labourer.
Religion: R.C.
6th Division arrest No. 288.
Offences against the ROIR.
He was tried by FGCM on 5 Apr
1921 and sentenced to 5 years Penal
Servitude, commuted to 2 years
Imprisonment.
Earliest release date, 5 Dec 1922.
His sentence expired on 4 Apr 1923.
He was transferred from Limerick to
Spike prison compound on 2 June 1921.
He was transferred from Spike to Cork
Male Gaol on 24 Sept 1921. He was
released from there on 12 Jan 1922.

Dwyer, John

Castletownbere, Co. Cork.
Occupation: Farmer.
Religion: R.C.
Brigade arrest No. 17 I.B. 476.
Offence against Martial Law.
He was tried by Summary Court
on 8 Mar 1921 and sentenced to
6 months imprisonment.

Earliest release date, 8 Aug 1921.
His sentence expired on 7 Sept 1921.
He was transferred from Bere Island
Military Prison in the Field to Spike
prison compound on 15 Apr 1921,
to Hut 24 in the north-east casemates.
On 8 Aug 1921, while on Spike,
his sentence was vacated. He was
served with an Internment Order
and immediately transferred to Spike
internment compound and remained
in custody.
See also: Dwyer, John, in the Spike
internee list.

Dwyer, Michael
Seafield Spa, County Kerry
Age: 20. Occupation: Clerk.
Religion: R.C.
6th Division arrest No. 580.
Offence against the ROIR, he was
found by Crown Forces carrying time
fuses for explosives.
He was tried by FGCM in Ballymullen
Barracks, Tralee, on 27 June 1921 and
sentenced to 2 years imprisonment.
Earliest release date, 25 Feb 1923.
His sentence expired on 26 June 1923.
He was transferred from Cork Male
Gaol to Spike prison compound on
6 July.
He was transferred back to Cork
Male Gaol on 24 Sept 1921. He was
released from there on 12 Jan 1922.

Dwyer, Patrick
Killeen, Gould's Cross, Co. Tipperary.

Age: 20. Occupation: Farmer.
Religion: R.C.
6th Division arrest No. 515.
Brigade arrest No. 16 I.B. 487.
Offence under the ROIR.
He was tried by Summary Court
on 18 June 1921 and sentenced to
6 months imprisonment.
Earliest release date, 7 Sept 1921.
His sentence expired on 17 Dec 1921.
He was transferred from Cork Male
Gaol to Spike prison compound on
25 June 1921. He was transferred back
to Cork Male Gaol on 24 Sept 1921.
He was transferred from Cork Male
Gaol back to Spike on 14 Nov as
an internee and held in the
internment compound.
See also: Dwyer, Patrick, in the Spike
internee list.

Fenton, Michael
Roula, Ballina, Killaloe, Co. Clare.
Age: 22.
Occupation: Post office assistant.
Religion: R.C.
He was arrested on the night of
22/23 May 1921. As a Post Office
official, he was charged with making
copies of Crown Forces telegrams
and communicating same to persons
unknown. In a follow-up search, John
Kent of Killaloe was arrested, having
been found in possession of Crown
Forces telegrams. See also: Spike
prisoner Kent, John.
6th Division arrest No. 246.

Offence under the ROIR.
He was tried by FGCM in Limerick
on 17 June 1921 and sentenced to
12 years Penal Servitude (PS), 5 years
were remitted, and he had 7 years PS
to serve.
Earliest release date, 16 Sept 1926.
His sentence expired on 16 June 1928.
He was transferred from Cork Male
Gaol to Spike prison compound on
25 June 1921.
He was transferred to Kilkenny Gaol
on 17 Nov 1921 and released from
there in Jan 1922.

Finn, John
Ballinphelic, Ballygarvan, Co. Cork.
Age: 21. Occupation: Farmer.
Religion: R.C.
6th Division arrest No. 545.
Brigade arrest No. 17 I.B. 644.
Offence under the ROIR.
He was tried by Summary Court
on 20 June 1921 and sentenced to
3 months imprisonment.
Earliest release date, 5 Sept 1921.
His sentence expired on 19 Sept 1921.
He was transferred from Cork Male
Gaol to Spike prison compound on
30 June. He was released from Spike
on 6 Sept, authority received from
CA 693, dated 3 Sept 1921.

Finn, John
Dooneen, Old Head, Kinsale, Co. Cork.
Age: 23. Occupation: Labourer.

Religion: R.C.
Brigade arrest No. 17 I.B. 344.
6th Division arrest No. 518.
Offence under the ROIR.
He was tried by FGCM on 20 June
1921 and sentenced to 6 months
imprisonment.
Earliest release date, 25 Nov 1921.
His sentence expired on 19 Dec 1921.
He was transferred from Cork Male
Gaol to Spike prison compound on
25 June. He was transferred back to
Cork Male Gaol on 24 Sept.
He was transferred from Cork Male
Gaol back to Spike on 14 Nov as
an internee and held in the
internment compound.
See also: Finn, John, in the Spike
internee list.

Fitzgerald, Denis
Caherleaheen, Tralee, Co. Kerry.
Listed as Caheralaheen.
Age: 23. Occupation: Labourer.
Religion: R.C.
Brigade arrest No. K.B. 253.
6th Division arrest No. 579.
Offence under Martial Law, he was
found in possession of and wearing
Royal Irish Constabulary
uniform trousers.
He was tried by Summary Court
on 22 June 1921 and sentenced to
6 months imprisonment.
Earliest release date, 12 Nov 1921.
His sentence expired on 23 Dec 1921.
He was transferred from Cork Male

Gaol to Spike prison compound on 6 July. He was transferred back to Cork Male Gaol on 24 Sept 1921.

Fitzgerald, James
Cork City.
Age: 23. Occupation: Traveller.
Religion: R.C.
Brigade arrest No. 17 1.B. 890.
6th Division arrest No. 539.
Offence against Martial Law, avoiding arrest.
He was tried by Summary Court on 24 June 1921 and sentenced to 6 months imprisonment.
Earliest release date, 24 Nov 1921.
His sentence expired on 23 Dec 1921.
He was transferred from Cork to Spike prison compound on 15 July 1921. He was transferred back to Cork Male Gaol on 24 Sept 1921.

Fitzgerald, John
Bruff, Co. Limerick.
He was transferred from Bere Island Military Prison in the Field to Spike prison compound on 15 Apr 1921.

Fitzgerald, Michael
His real name was Michael Baylor, see Baylor in this list.
Cassidy's Avenue off Old Youghal Road, Cork City.
Occupation: Shirt Cutter.
Religion: R.C.

He was arrested by British soldiers at Rahanisky House, Whitechurch, Co. Cork, on 8 Feb 1921 and taken to Victoria Barracks, Cork.[11]
6th Division arrest No. 197.
Offences against Martial Law, conspiring to levy war against the King and possession of arms.
He was tried by Military Court in Victoria Barracks on 26 Feb 1921 and sentenced to 15 years imprisonment.
His sentence expired on 25 Feb 1936.
He was transferred from Bere Island Military Prison in the Field to Spike prison compound on 15 Apr 1921.
He was transferred to Kilkenny Gaol on 17 Nov 1921. He was released from there in Jan 1922.
See also: Bowles, Michael; Conroy, Cornelius; Dennehy, Jerh; MacSwiney, John; Murphy, Timothy; O'Driscoll, Laurence; O'Keeffe, John; Thompson, James; Twomey, Cornelius; and Twomey, John.

Fitzgerald, Phillip
Lough Gur, Herbertstown, Co. Limerick.
He was transferred from Bere Island Military Prison in the Field to Spike prison compound on 15 Apr 1921.

Fitzgerald, William
Killballowen, Co. Clare.
He was transferred from Bere Island

---

11 Seán Enright, *The Trial of Civilians by Military Courts in Ireland 1921*, pp.128–133.

Military Prison in the Field to Spike prison compound on 15 Apr 1921.

Fox, Patrick

Princess St, Fermoy, Co. Cork.
Age: 26. Occupation: Labourer.
Religion: R.C.
Arrested on 22 June 1921.
Two offences under the ROIR.[12]
He attempted to persuade a soldier to join the Irish Volunteers.
He attempted to seduce a soldier from his duty.
He was tried by FGCM in Fermoy on 22 July 1921.
He was found guilty of first charge, not guilty of second and sentenced to 3 years Penal Servitude (PS).
His sentence expired on 21 July 1924.
According to the ledger of prisoners, he was transferred from Waterford Barracks to Spike prison compound on 18 Aug 1921. He was released from Spike on 28 Sept, authority received from CA 693, dated 26 Sept 1921.

Fraher, James[13]

Ballyguiry, Dungarvan, Co. Waterford.
Age: 23.
Occupation: Shop Assistant.
Religion: R.C.
He was arrested by Auxiliary Police near Thurles, Co. Tipperary, on 30 Mar 1921 for participating in the

seizure and destruction of Littleton RIC Barracks on 31 Oct 1920.[14]
6th Division arrest No. 65.
Offence against the ROIR.
He was tried by FGCM in Limerick, on 11 Apr 1921 and sentenced to 5 years Penal Servitude.
Earliest release date, 9 Jan 1925.
His sentence expired on 10 Apr 1926.
He was transferred from Limerick via Cork Male Gaol to Spike prison compound on 11 May 1921.
He was transferred from Spike to Kilkenny Gaol on 17 Nov 1921 and released from there in Jan 1922.
See also: his co-accused Spike prisoners Leamy, Michael and McCarthy, John of Thurles.

Gabbett, Gus

81 High Road, Limerick City.
Age: 17. Occupation: Labourer.
Religion: R.C.
6th Division arrest No. 238.
Offences against the ROIR.
He was tried by FGCM on 26 May 1921 and sentenced to 3 years Penal Servitude.
Earliest release date, 25 Aug 1923.
His sentence expired on 25 May 1924.
He was transferred from Limerick to Spike prison compound on 1 June 1921.
He was transferred from Spike

---

12 UKNA, Kew, London, WO 35/136, p.159.
13 See his WS, No. 1232.
14 UKNA, Kew, London, WO 35/135, p.278.

to Kilkenny Gaol on 17 Nov and released from there in Jan 1922.

Gallaghan, Richard

Herbertstown, Co. Limerick.
He was transferred from Bere Island Military Prison in the Field to Spike prison compound on 15 Apr 1921.

Galvin, Dan

Newcestown, Enniskean, Co. Cork.
Age: 23. Occupation: Farmer.
Religion: R.C.
6th Division arrest No. 349.
Offence under Martial Law.
He was tried by Summary Court on 4 May 1921 and sentenced to 6 months imprisonment.
Earliest release date, 5 Oct. 1921.
His sentence expired on 3 Nov 1921.
He was transferred from Cork Male Gaol to Spike prison compound on 22 June. He was transferred back to Cork Male Gaol on 24 Sept 1921.

Garde, William

Ballinamona, Ballycotton, Co. Cork.
Age: 18.
Occupation: Farmer.
Religion: R.C.
He was captured by British soldiers and Auxiliary Police with seven others, after the battle of Clonmult, near Midleton, in Co. Cork, on 20 Feb 1921. Twelve of his colleagues

William Garde, Ballycotton, Co. Cork.

were killed during the battle and two later executed.[15]
6th Division arrest No. L. 402.
Offence, Levying War against the King.
He was tried by Military Court in Victoria Barracks, from 8 to 19 Mar 1921. He was sentenced to Penal Servitude for Life.
He was transferred from Cork Military Detention Barracks to Spike prison compound on 30 Apr 1921.
He was transferred to Kilkenny Gaol on 17 Nov 1921 and later to Waterford Gaol. He was released from there in Jan 1922.
See also: Harty, J.; O'Leary, J.; Terry, E.; and Walsh, R. in this list.

Grace, Daniel

Boyle Street, Bandon, Co. Cork.
Age: 19. Occupation: Carpenter.
Religion: R.C.
Brigade arrest No. 17 I.B. 995.
6th Division arrest No. 546.
Offence under Martial Law.

---

15 UKNA, Kew, London, WO 71/380 and Tom O'Neill, *The Battle of Clonmult, the IRA's Worst Defeat.*

He was tried by Summary Court
on 20 June 1921 and sentenced to
6 months imprisonment.
Earliest release date, 20 Nov 1921.
His sentence expired on 19 Dec 1921.
He was transferred from Cork Male
Gaol to Spike prison compound on
30 June. He was transferred back to
Cork Male Gaol on 24 Sept 1921.

Griffin, Patrick
Ballinspittle, Kinsale, Co. Cork.
Age: 25. Occupation: Labourer.
Religion: R.C.
6th Division arrest No. 68.
Brigade arrest No. 1034.
Offence against Martial Law,
illegal assembly.
He was tried by Summary Court
on 19 Jan 1921 and sentenced to
6 months imprisonment.
Earliest release date, 19 June 1921.
His sentence expired on 18 July 1921.
He was transferred from Bere Island
Military Prison in the Field to Spike
prison compound on 15 Apr 1921.
On 20 June, while on Spike, his sentence
was vacated. He was served with an
Internment Order and immediately
transferred to Spike internment
compound and remained in custody.
See also: Griffin, Patrick, in the Spike
internee list.

Halloran, Michael
Old Chapel, Bandon, Co. Cork.
Age: 21. Occupation: Carpenter.

Religion: R.C.
Brigade arrest No. 17 I.B. 996.
6th Division arrest No. 547.
Offence under the ROIR.
He was tried by Summary Court
on 20 June 1921 and sentenced to
6 months imprisonment.
Earliest release date, 20 Nov 1921.
His sentence expired on 19 Dec 1921.
He was transferred from Cork Male
Gaol to Spike prison compound on
30 June. He was transferred back to
Cork Male Gaol on 24 Sept 1921.

Hanafin, Michael
Clonlour, Boherla, Tralee, Co. Kerry.
Age: 25. Occupation: Labourer.
Religion: R.C.
6th Division arrest No. L. 460.
He was charged with four offences
under the ROIR:
1. Attempted murder.
2. Wounding with intent to murder.
3. Wounding with intent.
4. False imprisonment.
His charge stated that, near Tralee on
the night of 5/6 February 1921, he

Michael Hannafin, Tralee, Co. Kerry.

assaulted an ex-soldier, imprisoned him for approximately eighteen hours and shot him with intent to murder.[16] The arrested men were convinced that the ex-soldier was an informer.

He was tried by FGCM in Victoria Barracks, Cork, on 19 May 1921 and found guilty of the 1st and 4th charges only. He was sentenced to Penal Servitude for Life.

He was transferred from Cork to Spike prison compound on 18 June 1921. He was transferred from Spike to Kilkenny Gaol on 17 Nov 1921. He was released from there in Jan 1922. See also: Duggan, Michael; Dowling, Michael; and McMahon, Bryan.

Hanafin, Jeremiah

17 Nelson St, Tralee, Co. Kerry.
Age: 21. Occupation: Clerk.
Religion: R.C.
6th Division arrest No. 455.
Offence against Martial Law.
He was tried by Summary Court on 28 May 1921 and sentenced to 6 months imprisonment.

His sentence expired on 27 Nov 1921. He was transferred from Cork Male Gaol to Spike prison compound on 13 June. He was transferred back to Cork Male Gaol on 24 Sept 1921.

Hannon, Jeremiah

Ballinspittle, Kinsale, Co. Cork.
Age: 29. Occupation: Labourer.
Religion: R.C.
Brigade arrest No. 17 I.B. 1035.
6th Division arrest No. 66.
Offence against Martial Law,
Illegal assembly.
He was tried by Summary Court on 19 Jan 1921 and sentenced to 6 months imprisonment.

Earliest release date, 19 June 1921.
His sentence expired on 18 July 1921.
He was transferred from Bere Island Military Prison in the Field to Spike prison compound on 15 Apr 1921.
On 22 June 1921, while on Spike, his sentence was vacated. He was served with an Internment Order and immediately transferred to Spike internment compound and remained in custody. See also: Hannon, Jeremiah, in the Spike internee list.

Harty, John

Ballyroe, Cloyne, Co. Cork.
Age: 19. Occupation: Farmer
Religion: R.C.
He was captured by British soldiers and Auxiliary Police with seven others, after the battle of Clonmult, near Midleton, in Co. Cork, on 20 Feb 1921. Twelve of his colleagues were killed during the battle and two later executed.[17]

16 UKNA, Kew, London, WO 35/124 and WO 35/136, p.166.
17 UKNA, Kew, London, WO 71/380 and Tom O'Neill, *The Battle of Clonmult, the IRA's Worst Defeat.*

John Harty, Cloyne, Co. Cork.

6th Division arrest No. L. 403.
Offence, Levying War against the King.
He was tried by Military Court in
Victoria Barracks, from 8 to
19 Mar 1921.
He was sentenced to Penal Servitude
for Life.
He was transferred from Cork
Military Detention Barracks to Spike
prison compound on 30 Apr 1921.
He was transferred from Spike to
Kilkenny Gaol on 17 Nov 1921 and
later to Waterford Gaol.
He was released from there in Jan 1922.
See also: Garde, W.; O'Leary, J.; Terry,
E.; and Walsh, R. in this list.

Hassett, John[18]
Moyriesk, Quinn, Co. Clare.
Age: 34. Occupation: Farmer.
Religion: R.C.
6th Division arrest No. 99.
Offence, participating in an
armed attack.
He was tried by Military Court, from

Jack Hassett, Quin, Co. Limerick.

28 Mar to 1 Apr 1921, and sentenced
to 10 years Penal Servitude (PS).
Earliest release date, 29 Sept 1928.
His sentence expired on 31 Mar 1931.
He was transferred from Limerick
via Cork Male Gaol to Spike prison
compound on 11 May 1921.
He was transferred from Spike to
Kilkenny Gaol on 17 Nov 1921. He
was released from there in Jan 1922.

Hayes, John TD
10 Sullivan's Quay, Cork City.
Age: 37.
Occupation: Insurance Agent.
Religion: R.C.
6th Division arrest No. 281.
Offence under Martial Law.
He was tried by Summary Court
on 19 Apr 1921 and sentenced to
6 months imprisonment.
Earliest release date, 19 Sept 1921.
His sentence expired on 18 Oct 1921.
He was transferred from Cork Male
Gaol to Spike prison compound on

---

18 See William McNamara, WS No. 1135.

22 June. He was released from there on 11 Aug, authority received from CA 805, dated 11 Aug 1921.

Healy, Daniel

Gurrane, Donoughmore, Co. Cork.
Age: 21. Occupation: Farmer.
Religion: R.C.
6th Division arrest No. 386.
Offences against Martial Law.
He was tried by Summary Court on 17 May 1921 and sentenced to 6 months imprisonment.
Earliest release date, 18 Oct 1921.
His sentence expired on 16 Nov 1921.
He was transferred from Cork Male Gaol to Spike prison compound on 13 June. He was transferred back to Cork Male Gaol on 24 Sept 1921.

Healy, Denis

Ballinore, Blackrock, Co. Cork.
Age: 21.
Occupation: Porter.
Religion: R.C.
6th Division arrest No. 276.
Offences under Martial Law, membership of the IRA and possession of illegal documents relating to the IRA.
He was tried by Summary Court on 16 Apr 1921 and sentenced to 6 months imprisonment.
Earliest release date, 16 Sept 1921.
His sentence expired on 15 Oct 1921.
He was transferred from Cork Male Gaol to Spike prison compound on

22 June 1921. He was released from Spike on 16 Sept, authority received from CA 693, dated 14 Sept 1921.

Heaphy, Patrick

Cahircorney, Herbertstown, Co. Limerick.
He was transferred from Bere Island Military Prison in the Field to Spike prison compound on 15 Apr 1921.

Hedderman, William

Lough Gur, Herbertstown, Co. Limerick.
He was transferred from Bere Island Military Prison in the Field to Spike prison compound on 15 Apr 1921.

Hennessey, John

114 Carey's Road, Limerick City.
Age: 20.
Occupation: Irish Teacher.
Religion: R.C.
6th Division arrest No. 319.
Offences against the Defence of the Realm Act (DORA).
He was tried by FGCM on 27 Apr 1921 and sentenced to 2 years imprisonment.
Earliest release date, 27 Dec 1922.
His sentence expired on 26 Apr 1923.
He was transferred from Cork Military Detention Barracks to Spike prison compound on 2 June 1921. He was transferred back to Cork Male Gaol on 24 Sept 1921 and released from there on 12 Jan 1922.

Hickey, Denis

Glenville, Co. Cork.
Age: 38. Occupation: Farmer.
Religion: R.C.
6th Division arrest No. 585.
Brigade arrest No. 16 I.B. 457
& S.C/206.
Offence against Martial Law, using a
false name.
He was tried by Summary Court
on 27 June 1921 and sentenced to
3 months imprisonment.
Earliest release date, 12 Sept 1921.
His sentence expired on 26 Sept 1921.
He was transferred from Cork Male
Gaol to Spike prison compound on
6 July 1921.
On 12 Sept 1921, while on Spike,
his sentence was vacated. He was
served with an Internment Order
and immediately transferred to Spike
internment compound, authority from
GS 348/306/D dated 3 Sept 1921.
See also: Hickey, Denis, in the Spike
internee list.

Hickey, John

Lough Gur, Herbertstown,
Co. Limerick.
He was transferred from Bere Island
Military Prison in the Field to Spike
prison compound on 15 Apr 1921.

Hickey, Phillip

Curraheen, Tallow, Co. Waterford.

Age: 19. Occupation: Farmer.
Religion: R.C.
6th Division arrest No. 378.
Offences against Martial Law.
He was tried by Summary Court
on 13 May 1921 and sentenced to
6 months imprisonment.
Earliest release date, 14 Oct 1921.
His sentence expired on 12 Nov 1921.
He was transferred from Cork Male
Gaol to Spike prison compound on
13 June. He was transferred back to
Cork Male Gaol on 24 Sept 1921.

Hogan, John

Meanus, Co. Limerick.
He was transferred from Bere Island
Military Prison in the Field to Spike
prison compound on 15 Apr 1921.

Holland, Dan[19]

Timoleague, Courtmacsherry, Co. Cork.
Age: 37. Occupation: Farmer.
Religion: R.C.
6th Division arrest No. 550.
Brigade arrest No. 17 I.B. 993.
Offence under the ROIR, giving a
false name and address.
He was tried by Summary Court
on 19 June 1921 and sentenced to
6 months imprisonment.
Earliest release date, 19 Nov 1921.
His sentence expired on 18 Dec 1921.
He was transferred from Cork Male
Gaol to Spike prison compound on

---

19 See his WS, No. 1341.

30 June. He was transferred back to Cork Male Gaol on 24 Sept 1921. He was transferred back to Spike again from Cork Male Gaol on 14 Nov, as an internee and held in the internment compound.
See also: Holland, Dan, in the Spike internee list.

Horan, William
Ballywalter, Golden, Co. Tipperary.
Age: 20.
Occupation: Labourer.
Religion: R.C.
6th Division arrest No. 606.
Brigade arrest No. 18 I.B S.C/63.
Offence against Martial Law, acting contrary to the ROIR, part 79.
He was tried by Summary Court on 22 June 1921 and sentenced to 6 months imprisonment.
Earliest release date, 22 Nov 1921.
His sentence expired on 21 Dec 1921.
He was transferred from Cork to Spike prison compound on 15 July.
He was transferred back to Cork Male Gaol on 24 Sept 1921. He was released from there in Jan 1922.

Horan, William
Hollyford, Co. Tipperary.
Age: 24. Occupation: Farmer.
Religion: R.C.
6th Division arrest No. 468.
Brigade arrest No. 16 I.B. 488.
Offences against the ROIR.
He was tried by FGCM on 1 June

1921 and sentenced to 6 months imprisonment.
Earliest release date, 1 Nov 1921.
His sentence expired on 30 Nov 1921.
He was transferred from Cork Male Gaol to Spike prison compound on 13 June 1921. He was transferred back to Cork Male Gaol on 24 Sept 1921.
He was transferred back from Cork Male Gaol again on 14 Nov as an internee and held in the internment compound.
See also: Horan, William, in the Spike internee list.

Horgan, John
Ballycarthy, Tralee, Co. Kerry.
Age: 20. Occupation: Porter.
Religion: R.C.
6th Division arrest No. 60.
Offences against the ROIR.
He was tried by FGCM on 17 Jan 1921 and sentenced to 2 years imprisonment.
Earliest release date, 16 Sept 1922.
His sentence expired on 16 Jan 1923.
He was transferred from Cork to Spike prison compound on 2 June 1921. He was transferred back to Cork Male Gaol on 24 Sept 1921. He was released from there on 12 Jan 1922.

Hourigan, John
Holy Cross, Co. Tipperary.
He was transferred from Bere Island Military Prison in the Field to Spike prison compound on 15 Apr 1921.

Hourigan, Thomas

Holy Cross, Co. Tipperary.

He was transferred from Bere Island Military Prison in the Field to Spike prison compound on 15 Apr 1921.

Hurley, John

Patrickswell, Co. Limerick.

He was transferred from Bere Island Military Prison in the Field to Spike prison compound on 15 Apr 1921.

Hurley, John

Barrack St, Clonakilty, Co. Cork.
Age: 17. Occupation: Mechanic.
Religion: R.C.
6th Division arrest No. 469.
Offences against the ROIR.
He was tried by Summary Court on 2 June 1921 and sentenced to 6 months imprisonment.
Earliest release date, 2 Nov 1921.
His sentence expired on 1 Dec 1921.
He was transferred from Cork Male Gaol to Spike prison compound on 13 June 1921. He was transferred back to Cork Male Gaol on 24 Sept 1921. He was released from there on 12 Jan 1922.

Hurley, John

Convent Street, Listowel, Co. Kerry.
Age: 22.
Occupation: Labourer.
Religion: R.C.
6th Division arrest No. 303.
Offence under Martial Law.
He was tried by Summary Court

on 21 Apr 1921 and sentenced to 6 months imprisonment.
Earliest release date, 21 Sept 1921.
His sentence expired on 20 Oct 1921.
He was transferred from Cork Male Gaol to Spike prison compound on 22 June 1921. He was transferred back to Cork Male Gaol on 28 June 1921.

Ivers, John

136 Lower Glanmire Road, Cork City.
Age: 24.
Occupation: Railway Man.
Religion: R.C.
His house was searched by Crown Forces on 19 Jan 1921. Letters addressed to Sean Ivers and envelopes addressed to O/C Cork 1 and O/C Cork 3 Bandon were found in a pocket of a coat. He was immediately arrested.
6th Division arrest No. 168.
Offences against the ROIR.
He was tried by FGCM in Victoria Barracks, Cork, on 8 and 10 Feb 1921. He was found guilty and sentenced to 18 months imprisonment with Hard Labour.
Earliest release date, 11 May 1922.
His sentence expired on 9 Aug 1922.
He was transferred from Cork to Spike prison compound on 2 June 1921. He was transferred back to Cork Male Gaol on 24 Sept 1921. He was released from there on 12 Jan 1922.

Kane, John J.

Duggan's Court, Davis St,
Limerick City.
Age: 19. Occupation: Labourer.
Religion: R.C.
6th Division arrest No. 234.
Offence against the ROIR.
He was tried by FGCM on 27 May
1921 and sentenced to 10 years
Penal Servitude.
His sentence expired on 26 June 1931.
He was transferred from Limerick to
Spike prison compound on 1 June
1921. He was transferred to Kilkenny
Gaol on 17 Nov and released from
there in Jan 1922.

Keane, John J.

Cahircorney, Herbertstown,
Co. Limerick.
He was sentenced to 10 years
imprisonment.
He was transferred from Bere Island
Military Prison in the Field to Spike
prison compound on 15 Apr 1921.

Keane, William

Lisduffbally.
Age: 28. Occupation: Farmer.
Religion: R.C.
He was arrested by Crown Forces on
2 July 1921 for false imprisonment.
6th Division arrest No. 609.
Offence against Martial Law, for false
imprisonment.

He was tried by FGCM on 2 July
1921 and sentenced to 2 years
imprisonment.
Earliest release date, 3 Mar 1923.
His sentence expired on 1 July 1923.
He was transferred from Cork Male
Gaol to Spike prison compound on
15 July 1921. He was transferred back
to Cork Male Gaol on 24 Sept 1921. He
was released from there on 12 Jan 1922.

Kearney, John[20]

Durra, Innis, Co. Clare.
Age: 65. Occupation: Farmer.
Religion: R.C.
6th Division arrest No. 292.
Offence, levying war against the King.
He was tried by Military Court,
from 28 Mar to 1 Apr 1921. He was
sentenced to 1 year imprisonment.
Earliest release date, 31 Jan 1922.
His sentence expired on 31 Mar 1922.
He was transferred from Limerick
via Cork Male Gaol to Spike prison
compound on 9 June 1921.
He was transferred from Spike to Cork
Military Hospital in Victoria Barracks
on 28 Oct 1921.

Kearney, Michael

Shannon St, Bandon, Co. Cork.
Age: 20. Occupation: Labourer.
Religion: R.C.
6th Division arrest No. 325.
Offence under Martial Law.

20 See William McNamara, WS No. 1135.

He was tried by Summary Court
on 29 Apr 1921 and sentenced to
6 months imprisonment.
Earliest release date, 29 Sept 1921.
His sentence expired on 28 Oct 1921.
He was transferred from Cork Male
Gaol to Spike prison compound on
22 June 1921. He was transferred back
to Cork Male Gaol on 24 Sept 1921.

Kearns, Thomas
33 Bowman Street, Limerick City.
Age: 17. Occupation: Tailor.
Religion: R.C.
6th Division arrest No. 236.
Offences against the ROIR.
He was tried by FGCM on 26 May
1921 and sentenced to 3 years
Penal Servitude.
Earliest release date, 25 Aug 1923.
His sentence expired on 25 May 1924.
He was transferred from Limerick
to Spike prison compound on
1 June 1921 and transferred. He was
transferred from Spike to Kilkenny
Gaol on 17 Nov.
 On Tuesday, 22 Nov, he escaped
through a tunnel from Kilkenny Gaol
with 43 others.

Kelleher, Michael
3 North Main St, Youghal, Co. Cork.
Age: 27. Occupation: Potter.
Religion: R.C.
6th Division arrest No. 236.
Offence, possession of arms.
He was tried by Military Court on

6 Mar 1921 and sentenced to 10 years
Penal Servitude (PS).
His sentence expired on 6 Mar 1931.
He was transferred from Bere Island
Military Prison in the Field to Spike
prison compound on 15 Apr 1921.
He was transferred from Spike to
Kilkenny Gaol on 17 Nov 1921 and
released from there in Jan 1922.

Kelly, Bryan
Pear St, Mallow, Co. Cork.
Age: 35. Occupation: Shoemaker.
Religion: R.C.
6th Division arrest No. P19.
Offence under Martial Law.
He was tried by Summary Court
on 14 June 1921 and sentenced to
18 months imprisonment.
Earliest release date, 14 Sept 1921.
His sentence expired on 13 Dec 1922.
He was transferred from Cork Male
Gaol to Spike prison compound on
22 June 1921.
He was transferred from Spike to
Cork Male Gaol on 24 Sept and
released from there on 12 Jan 1922.

Kelly, John
Ballylongford, County Kerry, listed as
Co. Cork.
Age: 22. Occupation: Labourer.
Religion: R.C.
Brigade arrest No. K.B. 245.
6th Division arrest No. 569.
Offence under Martial Law, obstruct-
ing and assaulting members of the RIC.

He was tried by Summary Court in Ballymullen Barracks, Tralee, on 20 June 1921 and sentenced to 6 months imprisonment with Hard Labour. Earliest release date, 20 Nov 1921. His sentence expired on 19 Dec 1921. He was transferred from Cork Male Gaol to Spike prison compound on 6 July. He was transferred back to Cork Male Gaol on 24 Sept 1921.

Kenny, John
Killarney, Co. Kerry.
Age: 44. Occupation: Miner.
Religion: R.C.
6th Division arrest No. 451.
Offence under Martial Law.
He was tried by Summary Court on 18 May 1921 and sentenced to 6 months imprisonment.
Earliest release date, 19 Oct 1921.
His sentence expired on 17 Nov 1921.
He was transferred from Cork Male Gaol to Spike prison compound on 22 June and transferred back to Cork Male Gaol on 28 June 1921.

John Kenny, Killarney, Co. Kerry.

Kent, John
Ballymalone, Killaloe, Co. Clare.
Age: 30. Occupation: Farmer.
Religion: R.C.
He was arrested by Crown Forces near Ballina on 23 May 1921. He was found in possession of an undated Crown Forces telegram purporting to be sent from OC 'G' Coy, (Auxiliary Police). Also two telegrams dated 23 May '21, purporting to be sent from Auxiliaries, Killaloe. Michael Fenton of Ballina was arrested for copying and passing on the telegrams. See Spike prisoner Fenton, Michael.
6th Division arrest No. 247.
Offence under Martial Law.
He was tried by FGCM on 17 June 1921 and sentenced to 1 year imprisonment.
Earliest release date, 18 Apr 1921.
His sentence expired on 16 June 1922.
He was transferred from Cork Male Gaol to Spike prison compound on 25 June 1921. He was transferred back to Cork Male Gaol on 24 Sept 1921. He was released from there on 12 Jan 1922.

Keogh, James
Grattan St, Youghal, Co. Cork.
Age: 27.
Occupation: Carpenter.
Religion: R.C.
6th Division arrest No. 235.
Offence, possession of arms.
He was tried by Military Court on

6 Mar 1921 and sentenced to 10 years Penal Servitude (PS).

His sentence expired on 6 Mar 1931. He was transferred from Bere Island Military Prison in the Field to Spike prison compound on 15 Apr 1921. He was transferred from Spike to Kilkenny Gaol on 17 Nov 1921 and released from there in Jan 1922.

Keohane, John
Lislevane, Timoleague, Co. Cork.
Age: 27. Occupation: Farmer.
Religion: R.C.
Brigade arrest No. 17 I.B 994.
6th Division arrest No. 543.
Offence under the ROIR.
He was tried by Summary Court on 19 June 1921 and sentenced to 6 months imprisonment.
Earliest release date, 19 Nov 1921.
His sentence expired on 18 Dec 1921.
He was transferred from Cork Male Gaol to Spike prison compound on 30 June. He was transferred back to Cork Male Gaol on 24 Sept 1921.

Keohane, Tim
Ballinroher, Timoleague, Co. Cork.
Age: 22. Occupation: Labourer.
Religion: R.C.
6th Division arrest No. 542.
Brigade arrest No. 17 I.B. 991.
Offence under the ROIR, giving a false name and address.
He was tried by Summary Court on 19 June 1921 and sentenced to

6 months imprisonment.
Earliest release date, 19 Nov 1921.
His sentence expired on 18 Dec 1921. He was transferred from Cork Male Gaol to Spike prison compound on 30 June. He was transferred back to Cork Male Gaol on 24 Sept 1921. On 14 Nov, he was transferred back to Spike again from Cork Male Gaol as an internee and held in the internment compound.
See also: Keohane, Tim in the Spike internee list.

King, Denis
Fethard, Co. Tipperary.
Age: 24. Occupation: Labourer.
Religion: R.C.
6th Division arrest No. 275.
Offence against Martial Law.
He was tried by FGCM on 4 Mar 1921 and sentenced to 9 months imprisonment.
Earliest release date, 20 Oct 1921.
His sentence expired on 3 Dec 1921.
He was transferred from Cork Male Gaol to Spike prison compound on 9 June. He was transferred back to Cork Male Gaol on 24 Sept 1921.

Langford, Aeneas
Milltown, Co. Kerry.
Age: 22.
Occupation: Drapers assistant.
Religion: R.C.
6th Division arrest No. 564.
Brigade arrest No. K.B. 272.

Aeneas Langford, Milltown, Co. Kerry.

Offence against Martial Law, being a member of an unlawful association, the Irish Volunteers.
He was tried by Summary Court in Ballymullen Barracks, Tralee, on 22 June 1921 and sentenced to 6 months imprisonment.
Earliest release date, 20 Nov 1921.
His sentence expired on 21 Dec 1921.
He was transferred from Ballymullen Barracks to Cork Male Gaol via Buttevant Military Barracks.
He was transferred from Cork Male Gaol to Spike prison compound on 6 July 1921, to Hut 27 in the northeast casemates.
He was transferred from Spike to Cork Male Gaol on 24 Sept 1921.
First cousin of John Langford below.

Langford, John
Killorglin, Co. Kerry.
Age: 28. Occupation: Farmer.
Religion: R.C.
6th Division arrest No. 563.
Brigade arrest No. K.B. 273.
Offence against Martial Law, being a member of an unlawful association, the Irish Volunteers.
He was tried by Summary Court in Ballymullen Barracks, Tralee, on 22 June 1921 and sentenced to 3 months imprisonment.
Earliest release date, 7 Sept 1921.
His sentence expired on 21 Sept 1921.
He was transferred from Ballymullen Barracks to Cork Male Gaol via Buttevant Military Barracks.
He was transferred from Cork Male Gaol to Spike prison compound on 6 July 1921. He was released from Spike on 7 Sept, authority received from CA 693, dated 5 Sept 1921. First cousin of Aeneas Langford above.

Langton, Lawrence
Cumber, Kinnitty, Birr, Co. Offaly.
Age: 25.
Occupation: Farmer.
Religion: R.C.
6th Division arrest No. 206.
Offence under the ROIR.
He was tried by FGCM on 21 June 1921 and sentenced to 7 years Penal Servitude.
Earliest release date, 20 Sept 1926.
His sentence expired on 20 June 1928.
He was transferred from Cork Male Gaol to Spike prison compound on 25 June 1921.
He was transferred from Spike to Kilkenny Gaol on 17 Nov 1921 and released from there in Jan 1922.

Leamy, Michael

Michael Leamy, Thurles, Co. Tipperary.

Horse and Jockey, Thurles,
Co. Tipperary.
Age: 21. Occupation: Labourer.
Religion: R.C.
He was arrested by Crown Forces
for participating in the seizure and
destruction of Littleton RIC Barracks
on 31 Oct 1920.[21]
6th Division arrest No. 146.
Offence against the ROIR.
He was tried by FGCM on 11 Apr
1921 in Limerick and sentenced to
5 years Penal Servitude (PS).
Earliest release date, 9 Jan 1925.
His sentence expired on 10 Apr 1926.
He was transferred from Limerick
via Cork Male Gaol to Spike prison
compound on 11 May 1921.
He was transferred from Spike to
Kilkenny Gaol on 17 Nov 1921 and
released from there in Jan 1922.
See also: his co-accused Spike
prisoners Fraher, James, of Dungarvan,
and McCarthy, John of Thurles.

He was the Commanding Officer
of Collins Barracks, Cork, formerly
Victoria Barracks, from Feb 1947 to
Jan 1953.

Leary, James

Killard, Blarney, Co. Cork.
Age: 21. Occupation: Labourer.
Religion: R.C.
Offence under the ROIR.
He was tried by FGCM on 10 June
1921 and sentenced to 15 years Penal
Servitude (PS).
His sentence expired on 9 June 1936.
He was transferred from Cork to Spike
prison compound on 18 June 1921.
He was transferred from Spike to
Kilkenny Gaol on 17 Nov 1921 and
released from there in Jan 1922.

Leary, Pat

Lisanslea, Upton, Co. Cork.
Age: 28. Occupation: Farmer.
Religion: R.C.
Brigade arrest No. 17 I.B. 1030.
6th Division arrest No. 587.
Offence against Martial Law, giving a
false name.
He was tried by Summary Court
on 30 June 1921 and sentenced to
6 months imprisonment.
Earliest release date, 30 Nov 1921.
His sentence expired on 29 Dec 1921.
He was transferred from Cork Male
Gaol to Spike prison compound on

---

21 UKNA. Kew, London, WO 35/135, p.278.

6 July 1921. He was transferred back to Cork Male Gaol on 24 Sept. On 14 Nov he was transferred back again from Cork Male Gaol as an internee and held in the internment compound.
See Leary, Pat, in the Spike internee list.

Lehane, Daniel

Scart, Bantry, Co. Cork.
Age: 19. Occupation: Farmer.
Religion: R.C.
6th Division arrest No. 537.
Brigade arrest No. 17 I.B. 999.
Offence under the ROIR.
He was tried by Summary Court on 22 June 1921 and sentenced to 3 months imprisonment.
Earliest release date, 7 Sept 1921.
His sentence expired on 21 Sept 1921.
He was transferred from Cork Male Gaol to Spike prison compound on 30 June 1921.
On 7 Sept 1921 while on Spike, his sentence was vacated. He was served with an Internment Order and immediately transferred to Spike internment compound, authority from CA 671 dated 5 Sept 1921 and remained in custody.
See also: Lehane, Daniel, in the Spike internee list.

Lynch, Dan

118 Masseytown, Mallow, Co. Cork.
Age: 31. Occupation: Butcher.
Religion: R.C.

He was arrested by Crown Forces on 30 June 1921 for being out after curfew and trying to avoid arrest.
6th Division arrest No. 591.
Brigade arrest No. 17 I.B. 1037.
Offences against Martial Law, out after curfew and trying to avoid arrest.
He was tried by Summary Court on 30 June 1921 and sentenced to 3 months imprisonment.
Earliest release date, 15 Sept 1921.
His sentence expired on 29 Sept 1921.
He was transferred from Cork Male Gaol to Spike prison compound on 15 July. He was released from Spike on 15 Sept, authority CA 693, dated 13 Sept 1921.

Lynch, Michael

Brewsterfield, Glenflesk, Killarney, Co. Kerry.
Age: 22.
Occupation: Labourer.
Religion: R.C.
6th Division arrest No. 572.
Brigade arrest No. K.B. 276.
Offences against Martial Law, being a member of the IRA and found in possession of documents relating to the IRA.
He was tried by Summary Court on 27 June 1921 and sentenced to 6 months imprisonment.
Earliest release date, 27 Nov 1921.
His sentence expired on 26 Dec 1921.
He was transferred from Cork Male Gaol to Spike prison compound on

6 July. He was transferred back to
Cork Male Gaol on 24 Sept 1921.

Lyons, Cornelius

Rathcool, Banteer, Co. Cork.
Age: 21. Occupation: Labourer.
Religion: R.C.
Offence against the ROIR.
He was tried by Summary Court
on 15 June 1921 and sentenced to
3 months imprisonment.
Earliest release date, 31 Aug 1921.
His sentence expired on 14 Sept 1921.
He was transferred from Cork to
Spike prison compound on 18 June
1921. He was released from Spike on
31 Aug, authority from CA 693, dated
29 Aug 1921.

Lyons, Martin

Kiltankin, Ballyporeen, Co. Tipperary.
Age 20.
Occupation: Farmer.
Religion: R.C.
6th Division arrest No. 586.
Brigade arrest No. C.M.C. 80.
Offence against Martial Law, found in
possession of illegal documents.
He was tried by Summary Court
on 17 June 1921 and sentenced to
3 months imprisonment.
Earliest release date, 2 Sept 1921.
His sentence expired on 16 Sept 1921.
He was transferred from Cork Male
Gaol to Spike prison compound on

6 July 192. He was released from
Spike on 3 Sept, authority CA 693,
31 Aug 1921.

MacSwiney, John (Sean)

4 Belgrave Place, Cork City.
Religion: R.C.
He was arrested by British soldiers at
Rahanisky House, Whitechurch, Co.
Cork, on 8 Feb 1921 and taken to
Victoria Barracks, Cork.[22]
He was charged with offences
against Martial Law. Conspiring
to levy war against the King and
possession of arms.
He was tried by Military Court
on 26 Feb 1921 and sentenced to
15 years Penal Servitude.
His sentence expired on 25 Feb 1936.
He was transferred from Bere Island
Military Prison in the Field to Spike
prison compound on 15 Apr 1921.
He escaped from Spike on 30 Apr 1921,
with Tom Malone and Con Twomey.

Sean MacSwiney, Belgrave Street,
Cork City.

---

22 Seán Enright, *The Trial of Civilians by Military Courts in Ireland 1921*, pp.128–133.

He was a brother of Terence MacSwiney, former Lord Mayor of Cork. See also: Bowles, Michael; Conroy, Cornelius; Dennehy, Jerh; Fitzgerald, Michael; Murphy, Timothy; O'Driscoll, Laurence; O'Keeffe, John; Thompson, James; Twomey, Cornelius; and Twomey, John.

Madden, Michael
Grange, Co. Limerick.
He was transferred from Bere Island Military Prison in the Field to Spike prison compound on 15 Apr 1921.

Maher, Peter
Gould's Cross, Co. Tipperary.
Age: 18. Occupation: Labourer.
Religion: R.C.
He was arrested by Crown Forces on 28 Apr 1921.
6th Division arrest No. 639.
Offences against the ROIR, shooting with intent to murder on 28 Apr 1921.
He was tried by FGCM in Cork on 26 July 1921 and sentenced to 3 years Penal Servitude.
His sentence expired on 26 July 1923.
He was transferred from Cork Male Gaol to Spike prison compound on 11 Aug 1921.
He was transferred from Spike to Cork Military Hospital on 31 Oct 1921 and released on 9 Dec 1921.[23]

Mahony, Thomas
Newtown Sands, Co. Kerry.
Age: 18.
Occupation: Shop Assistant.
Religion: R.C.
6th Division arrest No. 390.
Offence under Martial Law.
He was tried by Summary Court on 30 Apr 1921 and sentenced to 6 months imprisonment.
Earliest release date, 30 Sept 1921.
His sentence expired on 29 Oct 1921.
He was transferred from Cork Male Gaol to Spike prison compound on 22 June 1921. He was transferred back to Cork Male Gaol on 24 Sept 1921.

Malone, Thomas
Alias Sean Forde
Tyrrellspass, Co. Westmeath.
Age: 24. Occupation: Teacher.
Religion: R.C.
He was arrested by Auxiliary Police on Christmas Day 1920, in King Street,

Tom Malone, Tyrell's Pass, Co. Westmeath.

---

23 UKNA, Kew, London, WO 35/136, p.87.

now McCurtain Street, Cork City.
Offence, the attempted murder of an
Auxiliary and improper possession
of ammunition.
He was tried by Military Court in
Victoria Barracks, Cork, convicted
and sentenced to death, commuted to
15 years Penal Servitude.
He was transferred from Bere Island
Military Prison in the Field to Spike
prison compound on 15 Apr 1921.
He escaped from Spike on 30 Apr
1921 with Sean MacSwiney and Con
Twomey. During the escape Malone
mortally wounded a British soldier
with a hammer.[24]

McAuliffe, John

5 Mangerton Terrace, Blarney, Co. Cork.
Age: 27.
Occupation: Labourer.
Religion: R.C.
Offence against the ROIR.
He was tried by FGCM on 10 June
1921 and sentenced to 15 years Penal
Servitude (PS).
His sentence expired on 9 June 1936.
He was transferred from Cork to
Spike prison compound on 18 June
1921. He was transferred back to
Cork Male Gaol on 17 Nov 1921.

McAuliffe, John

Charleville, Co. Cork.
He was transferred from Bere Island
Military Prison in the Field to Spike
prison compound on 15 Apr 1921.

McAuliffe, William

Baggotstown, Co. Limerick.
He was transferred from Bere Island
Military Prison in the Field to Spike
prison compound on 15 Apr 1921.

McCarthy, Cal (Callaghan)

Kilnamartyra, Macroom, Co. Cork.
Age: 25. Occupation: Farmer.
Religion: R.C.
Offence against Martial Law.
He was tried by Summary Court,
on 26 Jan 1921 and sentenced to
6 months imprisonment.
Earliest release date, 26 May 1921.
His sentence expired on 25 July 1921.
He was transferred from Bere Island
Military Prison in the Field to Spike
prison compound on 15 Apr 1921.
While on Spike, his sentence was
vacated on 26 June 1921. He was
served with an Internment Order
and immediately transferred to Spike
internment compound and remained
in custody.
See also: McCarthy, Cal, in the Spike
internee list.

McCarthy, Con

Lissane, Drimoleague, Co. Cork.
Age: 28. Occupation: Labourer.
Religion: R.C.

---

24 See his WS, No. 845.

He was arrested by Crown Forces with his brothers Timothy and James on 4 July 1921 for consorting with rebels. 6th Division arrest No. 598. Brigade arrest No. 17 I.B. 923. Offence against Martial Law, consorting with rebels.

He was tried by Summary Court on 1 July 1921 and sentenced to 6 months imprisonment with Hard Labour. Earliest release date, 2 Dec 1921. His sentence expired on 31 Dec 1921. He was transferred from Cork to Spike prison compound on 15 July 1921. He was transferred back to Cork Male Gaol on 24 Sept 1921.

McCarthy, Daniel[25]

Daniel McCarthy, Lombardstown, Co. Cork.

Creggane, Lombardstown, Co. Cork.
Age: 26.
Occupation: Farmer.
Religion: R.C.
He was one of the founding members of the Lombardstown Company of the Irish Volunteers. He became a first lieutenant in the Company. After Gen. Lucas was captured by the IRA near Fermoy he was moved to O'Connell's of Lackendarra and later to McCarthy's house. Daniel McCarthy was detailed to guard him in both houses.

Because his brigade and battalion HQ were frequently in the Lombardstown area, he was regularly detailed for guard duty.

He was arrested at home by British soldiers and Auxiliary Police on 17 Jan 1921. He was taken to Buttevant Military Barracks and to Cork Military Detention Barracks. 6th Division arrest No. 161.

Offence against the ROIR, he was found in possession of seditious documents relating to Sinn Féin. He was tried by FGCM on 9 Feb 1921 and sentenced to 1 year imprisonment.

Earliest release date, 11 Dec 1921. His sentence expired on 8 Feb 1922. He was transferred from Cork Male Gaol to Spike prison compound on 2 June 1921.

He was transferred back to Cork Male Gaol on 24 Sept and released from there on 10 Dec 1921. Brother of internee McCarthy, Michael.

25 See his WS, No. 1239.

McCarthy, Florence

Skibbereen, Co. Cork.

He was transferred from Bere Island
Military Prison in the Field to Spike
prison compound on 15 Apr 1921.

McCarthy, Frank

Quaker Road, Cork City.
Age: 26. Occupation: Stone Cutter.
Religion: R.C.
6th Division arrest No. 472.
Offence against Martial Law.
He was tried by Summary Court, on
7 July 1921 and sentenced to 6 months
imprisonment with Hard Labour.
Earliest release date, 7 Nov 1921.
His sentence expired on 6 Dec 1921.
He was transferred from Cork Male
Gaol to Spike prison compound on
13 June. He was transferred back to
Cork Male Gaol on 24 Sept 1921.

McCarthy, James[26]

Eyeries, Castletownbere, Co. Cork.
Age: 20. Occupation: Farmer.
Religion: R.C.
He was arrested by British soldiers on
4 Mar 1921, near Eyeries, and taken
to Furious Pier, near Castletownbere.
Offence against Martial Law.
He was tried by Summary Court,
on 8 Mar 1921 at Furious Pier and
sentenced to 6 months imprisonment
with Hard Labour.
Earliest release date, 8 Aug 1921.

His sentence expired 7 Sept 1921.
Following his trial he was sent to Bere
Island Military Prison in the Field.
He was transferred from Bere Island
to Spike prison compound on
15 Apr 1921.
On 8 Aug 1921, while on Spike
his sentence was vacated. He was
served with an Internment Order
and immediately transferred to Spike
internment compound and remained
in custody.
See also: McCarthy, James, in the
Spike internee list.

McCarthy, James

Lissane, Drimoleague, Co. Cork.
Age: 32. Occupation: Farmer.
Religion: R.C.
He was arrested with his brothers
Con and Timothy on 4 July 1921 for
consorting with rebels.
6th Division arrest No. 599.
Brigade arrest No. 17 I.B. 922.
Offence against Martial Law,
consorting with rebels.
He was tried by Summary Court on
1 July 1921 and sentenced to 6 months
imprisonment with Hard Labour.
Earliest release date, 2 Dec 1921.
His sentence expired on 31 Dec 1921.
He was transferred from Cork to
Spike prison compound on 15 July
1921. He was transferred back to
Cork Male Gaol on 24 Sept 1921.

---

26 See his WS, No. 1567.

McCarthy, John

Thurles, Co. Tipperary
Age: 20. Occupation: Mechanic.
Religion: R.C.
He was arrested by Auxiliary Police
near Thurles, Co. Tipperary, on
30 Mar 1921 for participating in the
seizure and destruction of Littleton
RIC Barracks on 31 Oct 1920.[27]
6th Division arrest No. 166.
Offence against the ROIR.
Tried by FGCM on 11 Apr 1921 and
sentenced to 10 years Penal Servitude.
His sentence expired on 10 Apr 1931.
He was transferred from Limerick
via Cork Male Gaol to Spike prison
compound on 11 May 1921
He was transferred from Spike to
Kilkenny Gaol on 17 Nov 1921 and
released from there in Jan 1922.
See also: his co-accused Spike
prisoners, Leamy, Michael, of Thurles
and Fraher, James, of Dungarvan.

McCarthy, John

Sackville, Ardfert, Co. Kerry.
Age: 23. Occupation: Farmer.
Religion: R.C.
6th Division arrest No. 79.
Offence against the ROIR.
He was tried by FGCM on 18 January
1921 and sentenced to 2 years
imprisonment.
Earliest release date, 19 Sept 1922.
His sentence expired on 17 Jan 1923.

He was transferred from Cork Male
Gaol to Spike prison compound on
2 June 1921. He was transferred back
to Cork Male Gaol on 24 Sept 1921.
He was released from there on
12 Jan 1922.

McCarthy, Mortimer

Castletownbere, Co. Cork.
Age: 25. Occupation: Farmer.
Religion: R.C.
Offences against Martial Law.
He was tried by Summary Court on
8 Mar 1921 and sentenced to 6 months
imprisonment with Hard Labour.
Earliest release date, 8 Aug 1921.
His sentence expired on 7 Sept 1921.
He was transferred from Bere Island
Military Prison in the Field to Spike
prison compound on 15 Apr 1921, to
Hut 24 in the north-east casemates.
On 8 Aug 1921 while on Spike, his
sentence was vacated. He was served
with an Internment Order and
immediately transferred to Spike
internment compound and remained
in custody.
See also: McCarthy, Mortimer, in the
Spike internee list.

McCarthy, Patrick

Meanus, Co. Limerick.
He was transferred from Bere Island
Military Prison in the Field to Spike
prison compound on 15 Apr 1921.

---

27 UKNA, Kew, London, WO 35/135, p.278.

McCarthy, Richard

Chapel Street, Bantry, Co. Cork.
Age: 23.
Occupation: Coach painter.
Religion: R.C.
He was arrested with William
McCarthy, Thomas Tobin and John
Turner, on 27 Feb 1921, at Loughtagalla,
Thurles. They were arrested for being
assembled together with others
unknown and for attempting to oppose
the Forces of H.M.[28]
6th Division arrest No. 176.
Offences under the ROIR.
He was tried by FGCM on 10 May
1921 and sentenced to 18 months
imprisonment with Hard Labour.
Earliest release date, 11 Aug 1922.
His sentence expired on 9 Nov 1922.
He was transferred from Cork Male
Gaol to Spike prison compound on
25 June 1921. He was transferred back
to Cork Male Gaol on 24 Sept 1921.
He was released from there on
12 Jan 1922.

McCarthy, Timothy

Lissane, Drimoleague, Co. Cork.
Age: 24. Occupation: Farmer
Religion: R.C.
He was arrested with his brothers
James and Con on 4 July 1921 for
consorting with rebels.
6th Division arrest No. 597.

Brigade arrest No. 17 I.B. 924.
Offence against Martial Law,
consorting with rebels.
He was tried by Summary Court on
1 July 1921 and sentenced to 6 months
imprisonment with Hard Labour.
Earliest release date, 2 Dec 1921.
His sentence expired 31 Dec 1921.
He was transferred from Cork to
Spike prison compound on 15 July
1921. He was transferred back to
Cork Male Gaol on 24 Sept 1921.

McCarthy, William

Thurles, Co. Tipperary.
Age: 23. Occupation: Chauffer.
Religion: R.C.
He was arrested with Richard
McCarthy, Thomas Tobin and John
Turner on 27 Feb 1921 at Loughtagalla,
Thurles. They were arrested for being
assembled together with others
unknown and for attempting to
oppose the Forces of H.M.[29]
6th Division arrest No. 117.
Offence under the ROIR.
He was tried by FGCM on 10 May
1921 and sentenced to 18 months
imprisonment with Hard Labour.
Earliest release date, 11 Aug 1922.
His sentence expired on 9 Nov 1922.
He was transferred from Cork Male
Gaol to Spike prison compound on
25 June 1921.

---

28 UKNA, Kew, London, WO 35/136, p.103.
29 Ibid.

He was transferred back to Cork Male Gaol on 24 Sept and released from there on 12 Jan 1922.

McDonnell, James

Pallas, Co. Tipperary.

Age: 25. Occupation: Farmer.

Religion: R.C.

6th Division arrest No. 203.

Offence under the ROIR.

He was tried by FGCM on 4 June 1921 and sentenced to 3 years Penal Servitude.

Earliest release date, 8 Sept 1923.

His sentence expired on 3 June 1924.

He was transferred from Cork Male Gaol to Spike prison compound on 25 June 1921.

He was transferred from Spike to the Military Hospital in Victoria Barracks on 1 Sept and released from Cork Male Gaol on 12 Jan 1922.

McEllistrim, Tom

Ballymacelligott, Co. Kerry.

Age: 35. Occupation: Farmer.

Religion: R.C.

6th Division arrest No. 566.

Brigade arrest No. K.B. 267.

Offence against Martial Law, being a suspected person and refusing to enter into recognisance.

He was tried by Summary Court in Ballymullen Barracks, Tralee, on 20 June 1921 and sentenced to 3 months

imprisonment with Hard Labour.

Earliest release date, 5 Sept 1921.

His sentence expired on 19 Sept 1921.

He was transferred from Cork Male Gaol to Spike prison compound on 6 July 1921. He was released from Spike in Sept, authority received from CA 693, dated 3 Sept 1921.

McMahon, Bryan

Lismore, Abbeydorney, Co. Kerry.

Age: 17. Occupation: Farmer.

Religion: R.C.

6th Division arrest No. 472.

He was charged with four offences under the ROIR:

1. Attempted murder.

2. Wounding with intent to murder.

3. Wounding with intent.

4. False imprisonment.

His charge stated that near Tralee on the night of 5/6 February 1921, he assaulted an ex-soldier, imprisoned him for approximately eighteen hours and shot him with intent to murder. The arrested men were convinced that the ex-soldier was an informer.

He was tried by FGCM in Victoria Barracks, Cork, on 19 May 1921 and found guilty of the 4th charge only and sentenced to 18 months imprisonment with Hard Labour.[30]

Earliest release date, 19 Aug 1922.

His sentence expired on 18 Nov 1922.

He was transferred from Cork to

---

30 UKNA, Kew, London, WO 35/124 and WO 35/136, p.166.

Spike prison compound on 18 June 1921. He was transferred back to Cork Male Gaol on 24 Sept 1921. He was released from there on 12 Jan 1922.

See also: Dowling, Michael; Duggan, Michael; and Hanafin, Michael.

McNamara, William[31]

Ennis, Co. Clare.

Age: 28. Occupation: Grocer.

Religion: R.C.

6th Division arrest No. 100.

Offences, Levying War against the King and possession of firearms.

He was tried by Military Court on 28 Mar to 1 Apr 1921 and sentenced to 15 years Penal Servitude (PS).

Earliest release date, 1 July 1932.

His sentence expired on 31 Mar 1936.

He was transferred from Limerick via Cork Male Gaol to Spike prison compound on 11 May 1921.

He was transferred from Spike to Kilkenny Gaol on 17 Nov 1921. On Tuesday, 22 Nov, he escaped through a tunnel from Kilkenny Gaol with 43 others.

McSweeney, John

Also listed as Sweeney.

7 Muskerry Terrace, Blarney, Co. Cork.

Age: 29.

Occupation: Factory Hand.

Religion: R.C.

6th Division arrest No. 384.

Offence against the ROIR.

He was tried by FGCM on 13 May 1921 in Victoria Barracks and sentenced to 2 years imprisonment with Hard Labour.

Earliest release date, 12 Jan 1923.

His sentence expired on 12 May 1923.

He was transferred from Cork to Spike prison compound on 2 June 1921. He was transferred back to Cork Male Gaol on 14 Nov 1921. He was released from there on 12 Jan 1922.

Meehan, Richard

Rushmount, Kilworth, Co. Cork.

Age: 40. Occupation: Labourer.

Religion: R.C.

6th Division arrest No. 552.

Brigade arrest No. 16 I.B. S.C/22.

Offence under the ROIR.

He was tried by Summary Court on 27 May 1921 and sentenced to 3 months imprisonment with Hard Labour.

Earliest release date, 12 Aug 1921.

His sentence expired on 26 Aug 1921.

He was transferred from Cork Male Gaol to Spike prison compound on 6 July 1921. He was released from Spike on 12 Aug, authority received from CA 693, dated 12 Aug 1921.

Mescil, Thomas

Kilmacdurine, Co. Clare.

Age: 28. Occupation: Labourer.

---

31 See his WS, No. 1135.

Religion: R.C.

6th Division arrest No. 290.

Offence against the ROIR.

He was tried by FGCM on 8 Apr 1921 and sentenced to 18 months imprisonment with Hard Labour.

Earliest release date, 9 Jan 1922.

His sentence expired on 7 Oct 1922.

He was transferred from Cork to Spike prison compound on 2 June 1921. He was transferred back to Cork Male Gaol on 24 Sept 1921. He was released from there on 12 Jan 1922.

Morris, James

Ballineen, Co. Cork.

Age: 21.

Occupation: Creamery Worker.

Religion: R.C.

6th Division arrest No. 376.

Offence against the ROIR.

He was tried by Summary Court on 29 Apr 1921 and sentenced to 6 months imprisonment.

Earliest release date, 18 Oct 1921.

His sentence expired on 16 Nov 1921.

He was transferred from Cork Male Gaol to Spike prison compound on 13 June. He was transferred back to Cork Male Gaol on 24 Sept 1921.

Morrissey, John

Clashmore, Co. Waterford.

Age: 19. Occupation: Labourer.

Religion: R.C.

He was arrested by Crown Forces on 1 July 1921, for consorting with rebels.

6th Division arrest No. 601.

Brigade arrest No. 17.I.B 114.

Offence against Martial Law, consorting with rebels.

He was tried by Summary Court on 1 July 1921 and sentenced to 3 months imprisonment with Hard Labour.

Earliest release date, 16 Sept 1921.

His sentence expired on 30 Sept 1921.

He was transferred from Cork to Spike prison compound on 15 July 1921. He was released from Spike on 16 Sept, authority received from CA 693, dated 14 Sept 1921.

Moylan, John R. TD[32]

Kiskeam, Newmarket, Co. Cork.

Age: 31. Occupation: Carpenter.

Religion: R.C.

He was arrested by British troops from the Gloucestershire Regiment, at Riordan's farm at Knockavoureen, Kiskeam, Co. Cork, on Monday, 16 May 1921. He was found in possession of a loaded revolver and two Mills bombs (grenades).

After being interrogated, Moylan and the other prisoners were marched several miles to military trucks. They were then taken to Kanturk Military Barracks. During their search of Riordan's farm, the British soldiers found one of the two Hotchkiss

---

32 See his WS, Nos. 505 & 838.

Sean Moylan, Kiskeam, Co. Cork.

machine guns taken by the IRA in the raid on Mallow Military Barracks. From Kanturk, he was taken to Buttevant Military Barracks and later to Victoria Barracks, Cork. He was tried by Military Court in Victoria Barracks on 30 May 1921 for the illegal possession of arms and sentenced to 15 years Penal Servitude. He was transferred from Cork to Spike prison compound on 13 June 1921. As an elected TD, he received early release from Spike prison compound on 8 Aug 1921. This was to enable him to participate in the Dáil debate on the proposed Treaty negotiations. The authority for his release came from the General Officer Commanding (GOC) 6th Division, Gen. Strickland.

Mulcahy, John

Ballyloundash, Herbertstown, Co. Limerick.
Age: 25. Occupation: Farmer.

Religion: R.C.
He was captured by Crown Forces while on sentry duty at Caherguillamore House, Bruff, Co. Limerick, on 27 Dec 1920.[33]
6th Division arrest No. 522.
Offence against the ROIR.
He was tried by FGCM on 23 Feb 1921 and sentenced to 5 years Penal Servitude (PS).
Earliest release date, 23 Jan 1924.
His sentence expired on 22 Feb 1926.
He was transferred from Limerick via Cork Male Gaol to Spike prison compound on 11 May 1921, to Hut 24 in the north-east casemates.
He was transferred to Kilkenny Gaol on 17 Nov 1921 and released from there in Jan 1922.

Mulcahy, Patrick

Meanus, Co. Limerick.
He was transferred from Bere Island Military Prison in the Field to Spike prison compound on 15 Apr 1921.

Mulcahy, Richard

Dyrick, Lower Cappoquin, Co. Waterford.
Age: 19. Occupation: Farmer.
Religion: R.C.
6th Division arrest No. 394.
Offence against the ROIR.
He was tried by Summary Court on 17 May 1921 and sentenced to

---

33 Thomas Toomey, *The War of Independence in Limerick, 1912–1921*, pp.485–496.

6 months imprisonment with
Hard Labour.
Earliest release date on 18 Oct 1921.
His sentence expired on 16 Nov 1921.
He was transferred from Cork Male
Gaol to Spike prison compound on
13 June. He was transferred back to
Cork Male Gaol on 24 Sept 1921.

Mulcahy, Timothy

Meanus, Co. Limerick.
He was transferred from Bere Island
Military Prison in the Field to Spike
prison compound on 15 Apr 1921.

Mulcahy, William

Cork.
He was transferred from Bere Island
Military Prison in the Field to Spike
prison compound on 15 Apr 1921.

Mulchinock, Denis

Banteer, Co. Cork.
Age: 25. Occupation: Signalman.
Religion: R.C.
6th Division arrest No. 446.
Offence against Martial Law.
He was tried by Summary Court on
23 May 1921 and sentenced to 6 months
imprisonment with Hard Labour.
Earliest release date, 24 Oct 1921.
His sentence expired on 22 Nov 1921.
He was transferred from Cork Male
Gaol to Spike prison compound on
13 June. He was transferred back to
Cork Male Gaol on 24 Sept 1921.

Mullins, James

Droum, Castletownbere, Co. Cork.
Age: 25. Occupation: Farmer.
Religion: R.C.
6th Division arrest No. 644.
Offence under the ROIR.
He was tried by FGCM on 7 Mar
1921 and sentenced to 12 years Penal
Servitude (PS).
His sentence expired on 6 Mar 1933.
He was transferred from Cork Male
Gaol to Spike prison compound on
11 Aug 1921. He was transferred
from Spike to Kilkenny Gaol on
17 Nov 1921 and released from there
in Jan 1922.

Mulvihill, Brian

Rathpeacon, Co. Cork.
Age: 21. Occupation: Painter.
Religion: R.C.
Offence against the ROIR.
He was tried by FGCM on 10 June
1921 and sentenced to 15 years Penal
Servitude (PS).
His sentence expired on 9 June 1936.
He was transferred from Cork to
Spike prison compound on 18 June.
He was transferred back to Cork
Male Gaol on 24 Sept 1921.

Mulvihill, Daniel

Ballylongford, County Kerry, listed as
Co. Cork.
Age: 33. Occupation: Labourer.
Religion: R.C.
Brigade arrest No. K.B. 248.

6th Division arrest No. 565.
Offence against Martial Law,
assaulting and obstructing members
of the RIC.
He was tried by Summary Court in
Ballymullen Barracks, Tralee, on 20 June
1921 and sentenced to 6 months
imprisonment with Hard Labour.
Earliest release date, 20 Nov 1921.
His sentence expired on 19 Dec 1921.
He was transferred from Cork Male
Gaol to Spike prison compound on
6 1921. He was transferred back to
Cork Male Gaol on 24 Sept 1921.

Murnane, David
Lough Gur, Herbertstown, Co. Limerick.
He was transferred from Bere Island
Military Prison in the Field to Spike
prison compound on 15 Apr 1921.

Murnane, James
Lough Gur, Herbertstown, Co. Limerick.
He was transferred from Bere Island
Military Prison in the Field to Spike
prison compound on 15 Apr 1921.

Murphy, Daniel
Castletownbere, Co. Cork.
He was transferred from Bere Island
Military Prison in the Field to Spike
prison compound on 15 Apr 1921.

Murphy, Daniel
Convent Street, Listowel, Co. Kerry.
Age: 20. Occupation: Labourer.
Religion: R.C.

6th Division arrest No. 302.
Offence under Martial Law.
He was tried by Summary Court on
21 Apr 1921 and sentenced to 6 months
imprisonment with Hard Labour.
Earliest release date, 21 Sept 1921.
His sentence expired on 20 Oct 1921.
He was transferred from Cork Male
Gaol to Spike prison compound on
22 June 1921. He was transferred back
to Cork Male Gaol on 28 June, authority
from 6th Division HQ by telephone.

Murphy, Denis
Dripsey, Co. Cork.
Age: 22. Occupation: Labourer.
Religion: R.C.
He was captured by British soldiers
after the failed ambush at Dripsey, Co.
Cork, on 28 Jan 1921.
6th Division arrest No. 237.
Offence levying war against the King.
He was tried by Military Court in
Victoria Barracks on 9 Mar 1921.
He was sentenced to death and his
sentence was commuted to Penal
Servitude for Life.

Denis Murphy, Dripsey, Co. Cork.

He was transferred from Bere Island Military Prison in the Field to Spike prison compound on 15 Apr 1921, to Hut 24 in the north-east casemates. He was transferred from Spike to Kilkenny Gaol on 17 Nov 1921 and released from there in Jan 1922.

Five of his colleagues captured with him at Dripsey – Timothy McCarthy, Thomas O'Brien, Daniel O'Callaghan, John Lyons and Patrick O'Mahoney – were also sentenced to death and executed in the exercise yard of Cork Military Detention Barracks, on 28 Feb 1921.

Murphy, James

Stanton's Lane, Bandon, Co. Cork.
Age: 25.
Occupation: Insurance Agent.
Religion: R.C.
Brigade arrest ref No. 17 I.B. 998.
6th Division arrest No. 548.
Offence under the ROIR.
He was tried by Summary Court on 20 June 1921 and sentenced to 6 months imprisonment with Hard Labour.
Earliest release date, 20 Nov 1921.
His sentence expired on 19 Dec 1921.
He was transferred from Cork Male Gaol to Spike prison compound on 30 June. He was transferred back to Cork Male Gaol on 24 Sept 1921.
He was transferred back from Cork Male Gaol again on 14 Nov as an internee and confined in the Spike internment compound.

See also: Murphy, James, Bandon, in list of Spike internees.

Murphy, John

6 King's Terrace, Cork City.
Age: 46. Occupation: Clerk.
Religion: R.C.
6th Division arrest No. 484.
Offence under Martial Law.
He was tried by Summary Court on 13 June 1921 and sentenced to 6 months imprisonment with Hard Labour.
Earliest release date, 13 Nov 1921.
His sentence expired on 12 Dec 1921.
He was transferred from Cork Male Gaol to Spike prison compound on 22 June 1921. He was released from Spike on 13 Nov, authority received from CA 692, dated 11 Nov 1921.

Murphy, Michael

Sovereign St, Clonakilty, Co. Cork.
Age: 19.
Occupation: Harness Maker.
Religion: R.C.
6th Division arrest No. 401.
Offence against Martial Law.
He was tried by Summary Court on 17 May 1921 and sentenced to 6 months imprisonment with Hard Labour.
Earliest release date, 18 Oct 1921.
His sentence expired on 16 Nov 1921.
He was transferred from Cork Male Gaol to Spike prison compound on 13 June. He was transferred back to Cork Male Gaol on 24 Sept 1921.

Murphy, Patrick

Sovereign St, Clonakilty, Co. Cork.
Age: 18.
Occupation: Boat assistant.
Religion: R.C.
6th Division arrest No. 400.
Offence against Martial Law.
He was tried by Summary Court on
17 May 1921 and sentenced to 6 months
imprisonment with Hard Labour.
Earliest release date, 18 Oct 1921.
His sentence expired on 16 Nov 1921.
He was transferred from Cork Male
Gaol to Spike prison compound on
13 June. He was transferred back to
Cork Male Gaol on 24 Sept 1921.

Murphy, Thomas

Convent Street, Listowel, Co. Kerry.
Age: 21.
Occupation: Boot Maker.
Religion: R.C.
6th Division arrest No. 301.
Offence under Martial Law.
He was tried by Summary Court on
21 Apr 1921 and sentenced to 6 months
imprisonment with Hard Labour.
Earliest release date, 21 Sept 1921.
His sentence expired on 20 Oct 1921.
He was transferred from Cork Male
Gaol to Spike prison compound on
22 June. He was transferred back to
Cork Male Gaol on 28 June 1921,
authority from 6th Division HQ
by telephone.

Murphy, Timothy

Killeendaniel, Rathpeacon, Co. Cork.
Age: 20. Occupation: Labourer.
Religion: R.C.
He was arrested by British soldiers
at Rahanisky House, Whitechurch,
Co. Cork on 8 Feb 1921 and taken to
Victoria Barracks, Cork.[34]
6th Division arrest No. 202.
Offences against Martial Law,
conspiring to levy war against the
King and possession of arms.
He was tried by Military Court
in Victoria Barracks on 26 Feb
1921 and sentenced to 15 years Penal
Servitude (PS).
His sentence expired on 25 Feb 1936.
He was transferred from Bere Island
Military Prison in the Field to Spike
prison compound on 15 Apr 1921.
He was transferred from Spike to
Kilkenny Gaol on 17 Nov. On Tuesday,
22 Nov, he escaped through a tunnel
from Kilkenny Gaol with 43 others.
See also: Bowles, Michael; Conroy,
Cornelius; Dennehy, Jerh; Fitzgerald,
Michael; MacSwiney, John; O'Driscoll,
Laurence; O'Keeffe, John; Thompson,
James; Twomey, Cornelius; and
Twomey, John.

Murphy, Timothy

Carey's Road, Limerick City.
Age: 21. Occupation: Mill Hand.
Religion: R.C.

---

34 Seán Enright, *The Trial of Civilians by Military Courts in Ireland 1921*, pp.128–133.

He participated in the Dromkeen
Ambush against the RIC and the
attack on the Black and Tans at
Carey's Road, Limerick City, shortly
before his capture.[35]
6th Division arrest No. 204.
Offence under Martial Law.
He was tried by Military Court
in Limerick from 17 to 19 May
1921, and sentenced to death. His
sentence was commuted to Penal
Servitude for Life.
He was transferred from Cork Male
Gaol to Spike prison compound on
25 June 1921.
He was transferred from Spike
to Kilkenny Gaol on 17 Nov. On
Tuesday, 22 Nov, he escaped through
a tunnel from Kilkenny Gaol with
43 others.
See also: Spike prisoner Edward
Punch of Limerick.

Murray, John
Kinsale, Co. Cork.
Age: 25.
Occupation: Farmer.
Religion: R.C.
6th Division arrest No. 70.
Offence against Martial Law.
He was tried by Summary Court on
19 Jan 1921 and sentenced to 6 months
imprisonment with Hard Labour.
Earliest release date, 19 June 1921.
His sentence expired on 18 July 1921.

He was transferred from Bere Island
Military Prison in the Field to Spike
prison compound on 15 Apr 1921.
On 8 Aug 1921, while on Spike,
his sentence was vacated. He was
served with an Internment Order
and immediately transferred to Spike
internment compound and remained
in custody.
See also: Murray John, in list of
Spike internees.

Nagle, Michael
The Hill, Blarney, Co. Cork.
Age: 21. Occupation: Labourer.
Religion: R.C.
Offence against the ROIR.
He was tried by FGCM in Victoria
Barracks on 10 June 1921 and
sentenced to 15 years imprisonment
with Hard Labour.
His sentence expired on 9 June 1936.
He was transferred from Cork to Spike
prison compound on 18 June 1921.
He was transferred from Spike to
Kilkenny Gaol on 17 Nov 1921 and
released from there in Jan 1922.

Nelligan, Pat
Ballymacphilip, Ballyhooly, Co. Cork.
Age: 29. Occupation: Farmer.
Religion: R.C.
6th Division arrest No. 486.
Offence under Martial Law.
He was tried by Summary Court on

---

35 Thomas Toomey, *The War of Independence in Limerick 1912–1921*, pp.616–617.

13 June 1921 and sentenced to 6 months
imprisonment with Hard Labour.
Earliest release date, 13 Nov 1921.
His sentence expired on 12 Dec 1921.
He was transferred from Cork Male
Gaol to Spike prison compound on
22 June. He was transferred back to
Cork Male Gaol on 24 Sept 1921.

Neville, Pat

Ballinlough Road, Cork City.
Age: 20. Occupation: Caretaker.
Religion: R.C.
He was arrested in late May 1921 at
Old Court, Riverstown, Co. Cork.
6th Division arrest No. 359.
Offence against Martial Law.
Tried by Summary Court in Victoria
Barracks on 10 May 1921 and
sentenced to 6 months imprisonment
with Hard Labour.
Earliest release date, 11 Oct 1921.
His sentence expired on 9 Nov 1921.
He was transferred from Cork to
Spike prison compound on 13 June.
He was transferred back to Cork
Male Gaol on 24 Sept 1921.[36]

Neylon, John J.

Emlagh, Kilfenora, Co. Clare.
Age: 26.
Occupation: Shop assistant.
Religion: R.C.
He was arrested by RIC & Black
and Tans near Kilfenora on 7 Feb

John Joe Neylon, Kilfenora, Co. Clare.

1921 and taken to Ennistymon and
later to Ennis.
6th Division arrest No. 95.
Offence against Martial Law, suspected
robbery of rate money & books.
He was tried by FGCM on 4 Mar
1921 and sentenced to 7 years
Penal Servitude.
Earliest release date, 5 June 1926.
His sentence expired on 3 Mar 1928.
He was transferred from Limerick,
via Cork Male Gaol to Spike prison
compound on 11 May 1921.
He was transferred from Spike to
Kilkenny Gaol on 17 Nov 1921 and
released from there in Jan 1922.

Nolan, James

Cork.
Age: 30. Occupation: Engineer.
Religion: R.C.
6th Division arrest No. 59.
Offence against Martial Law, he was
found in possession of arms.
He was tried by Military Court in

---

36 See Laurence Neville, (brother), WS No. 1639, p.17.

Victoria Barracks on 14 Jan 1921 and sentenced to 10 years Penal Servitude. His sentence expired on 13 Jan 1931. He was transferred from Bere Island Military Prison in the Field to Spike prison compound on 15 Apr 1921. He was transferred from Spike to Kilkenny Gaol on 17 Nov 1921 and released from there in Jan 1922.

O'Brien, Bernard

East Main Street, Lismore,
Co. Waterford.
Age: 19. Occupation: Labourer.
Religion: R.C.
6th Division arrest No. 393.
Offence against Martial Law.
He was tried by Summary Court on 17 May 1921 and sentenced to 6 months imprisonment with Hard Labour. Earliest release date, 18 Oct 1921. His sentence expired on 16 Nov 1921. He was transferred from Cork Male Gaol to Spike prison compound on 13 June. He was released from Spike on 18 Oct, authority received from CA 693, dated 16 Oct 1921.

O'Brien, Charles

Clashduff, Drimoleague, Co. Cork.
Age: 27. Occupation: Farmer.
Religion: R.C.
He was arrested by Crown Forces on 4 July 1921, for consorting with rebels.
Brigade arrest No. 17 I.B. 921.
6th Division arrest No. 596.
Offence against Martial Law,

consorting with rebels.
He was tried by Summary Court on 1 July 1921 and sentenced to 6 months imprisonment with Hard Labour. Earliest release date, 30 Nov 1921. His sentence expired on 31 Dec 1921. He was transferred from Cork Male Gaol to Spike prison compound on 15 July 1921. He was transferred back to Cork Male Gaol on 14 Nov, authority from CA 1083, dated 12 Nov 1921.

O'Brien, John

97 Barrack Street, Cork City.
Age: 28. Occupation: Carpenter.
Religion: R.C.
6th Division arrest No. 521.
Brigade arrest No. 17 I.B. 886.
Offence against Martial Law, attempting to evade arrest.
He was tried by Summary Court on 20 June 1921 and sentenced to 6 months imprisonment with Hard Labour. Earliest release date, 20 Nov 1921. His sentence expired on 19 Dec 1921. He was transferred from Cork Male Gaol to Spike prison compound on 6 July 1921. He was transferred back to Cork Male Gaol on 14 Nov, authority from CA 1083, dated 12 Nov 1921.

O'Brien, Michael

Lough Gur, Herbertstown, Co. Limerick.
He was transferred from Bere Island Military Prison in the Field to Spike prison compound on 15 Apr 1921.

O'Brien, Thomas

Rawlingstown.

He was transferred from Bere Island Military Prison in the Field to Spike prison compound on 15 Apr 1921.

O'Brien, Richard

Ballingoue.

He was transferred from Bere Island Military Prison in the Field to Spike prison compound on 15 Apr 1921.

O'Connell, Michael

Carrigmartin, Ballyneety, Co. Limerick.

He was transferred from Bere Island Military Prison in the Field to Spike prison compound on 15 Apr 1921.

O'Connell, Michael

12 Caledonia Place, Edward Street, Limerick City.

Age: 19. Occupation: Sawyer.

Religion: R.C.

6th Division arrest No. 210.

Offence under Martial Law.

He was tried by Military Court on 27 May 1921 and sentenced to 12 years Penal Servitude.

Earliest release date, 27 May 1930.

His sentence expired on 26 May 1933.

He was transferred from Limerick to Spike prison compound on 1 June 1921.

He was transferred from Spike to Kilkenny Gaol on 17 Nov 1921 and released from there in Jan 1922.

O'Connor, Patrick

Castle Park, Kinsale, Co. Cork.

Age: 25.

Occupation: Labourer.

Religion: R.C.

6th Division arrest No. 402.

Offences against Martial Law.

He was tried by Summary Court on 17 May 1921 and sentenced to 6 months imprisonment with Hard Labour.

Earliest release date, 18 Oct 1921.

His sentence expired on 16 Nov 1921.

He was transferred from Cork Male Gaol to Spike prison compound on 13 June 1921. He was released from Spike on 18 Oct, authority from CA 693, dated 16 Oct 1921.

O'Connor, Thomas

Scart, Gortatlea, Co. Kerry.

Age: 39. Occupation: Farmer.

Religion: R.C.

6th Division arrest No. 320.

Offence under the ROIR.

He was tried by FGCM on 16 Apr 1921 and sentenced to 18 months imprisonment with Hard Labour.

Earliest release date, 17 July 1922.

His sentence expired on 15 Oct 1922.

He was transferred from Cork to Spike prison compound on 2 June 1921. He was transferred back to Cork Male Gaol on 14 Nov, authority from CA 1083, 12 Nov 1921. He was released from there on 12 Jan 1922.

O'Dea, Andrew

Lough Gur, Herbertstown, Co. Limerick. He was transferred from Bere Island Military Prison in the Field to Spike prison compound on 15 Apr 1921.

O'Donnell, Cornelius

Ballinacaloe near Bruff, Co. Limerick. He was transferred from Bere Island Military Prison in the Field to Spike prison compound on 15 Apr 1921.

O'Donnell, Jim

Castletownbere, Co. Cork.
Age: 22. Occupation: Clerk.
Religion: R.C.
Brigade arrest No. 17 I.B. 704.
Offence against Martial Law.
He was tried by Summary Court on 8 Mar 1921 and sentenced to 6 months imprisonment.
Earliest release date, 9 Aug 1921.
His sentence expired on 8 Sept 1921.
He was transferred from Bere Island Military Prison in the Field to Spike prison compound on 15 Apr 1921.
On 9 Aug 1921, while on Spike, his sentence was vacated. He was served with an Internment Order and immediately transferred to Spike internment compound and remained in custody.
See O'Donnell, Jim, in the list of Spike internees.

O'Donnell, Michael

Grange, Co. Limerick.
He was transferred from Bere Island Military Prison in the Field to Spike prison compound on 15 Apr 1921.

O'Donnell, Patrick

Dooradoyle, Mungret, Limerick City.
Age: 17. Occupation: Porter.
Religion: R.C.
6th Division arrest No. 237.
Offences under the ROIR.
He was tried by FGCM on 26 May 1921 and sentenced to 3 years Penal Servitude.
Earliest release date, 25 Mar 1923.
His sentence expired on 15 May 1924.
He was transferred from Limerick to Spike prison compound on 1 June 1921.
He was transferred from Spike to Kilkenny Gaol on 17 Nov 1921 and released from there in Jan 1922.

O'Donnell, Timothy

Fedamore, Co. Limerick.
He was transferred from Bere Island Military Prison in the Field to Spike prison compound on 15 Apr 1921.

O'Donoghue, Florence

24 Victoria Avenue, Cork City.
Age: 24. Occupation: Machinist.
Religion: R.C.
6th Division arrest No. 498.
Offence under Martial Law.
He was tried by Summary Court on 17 June 1921 and sentenced to 6 months imprisonment with Hard Labour.
Earliest release date, 17 Nov 1921.
His sentence expired on 16 Dec 1921.

He was transferred from Cork Male Gaol to Spike prison compound on 22 June 1921.

He was transferred back to Cork Male Gaol on 14 Nov, authority from CA 1083 dated 12 Nov 1921. He was released from there on 17 Nov, authority received from CA 693, dated 15 Nov 1921.

O'Donovan, Dan
The Quay, Bantry, Co. Cork.
Age: 18.
Occupation: Fishmonger.
Religion: R.C.
6th Division arrest No. 481.
Offence under the ROIR.
He was tried by Summary Court on 10 June 1921 and sentenced to 6 months imprisonment with Hard Labour.
Earliest release date, 10 Nov 1921.
His sentence expired on 9 Dec 1921.
He was transferred from Cork Male Gaol to Spike prison compound on 22 June 1921. He was released from

Daniel O'Donovan, Bantry, Co. Cork.

Spike on 10 Nov, authority from CA 963, dated 8 Nov 1921.
He was the last-known surviving Spike prisoner or internee from 1921, and died in 2006, aged 104.

O'Donovan, Peter J.
10 Maymount, Friars Walk, Cork City.
Age: 24.
Occupation: Blacksmith.
Religion: R.C.
6th Division arrest No. 395.
Offences against Martial Law.
He was tried by Summary Court in Victoria Barracks on 19 May 1921 and sentenced to 6 months imprisonment with Hard Labour.
Earliest release date, 20 Oct 1921.
His sentence expired on 18 Nov 1921.
He was transferred from Cork Male Gaol to Spike prison compound on 13 June 1921.
He was released from Spike on 20 Oct, authority from CA 693, dated 18 Oct 1921.

O'Driscoll, Dan[37]
Also listed as Driscoll.
Rockmount, Drimoleague, Co. Cork.
Age: 21. Occupation: Farmer.
Religion: R.C.
He was arrested by Auxiliary Police on 2 June 1921. He was taken to Dunmanway and later to Cork Male Gaol.

---

37 See his WS, No. 1352.

6th Division arrest No. 645.
Offence, shooting with intent to
murder on 13 May 1921.[38]
He was tried by FGCM in Victoria
Barracks, Cork, from 18 to 21 July
1921 and sentenced to 10 years
Penal Servitude.
He was transferred from Cork Male
Gaol to Spike prison compound
on 11 Aug. He was transferred to
Kilkenny Gaol on 17 Nov. Following
the mass escape from Kilkenny
on 22 Nov, he was transferred to
Waterford Gaol and released from
there on 12 Jan 1922.

O'Driscoll, John

Mill Street, Timoleague, Co. Cork.
Age: 25. Occupation: Farmer.
Religion: R.C.
6th Division arrest No. 551.
Brigade arrest No. 17 I.B. 992.
Offence under the ROIR.
He was tried by Summary Court on
19 June 1921 and sentenced to 6 months
imprisonment with Hard Labour.
Earliest release date, 19 Nov 1921.
His sentence expired on 18 Dec 1931.
He was transferred from Cork Male
Gaol to Spike prison compound on
30 June 1921.
On 14 Nov 1921, while he was on
Spike, his sentence was vacated. He
was served with an Internment Order

and immediately transferred to Spike
internment compound, authority
from CA 1083, dated 11 Nov 1921.
See O'Driscoll, John, in the Spike
internee list.

O'Driscoll, Laurence

Dublin Pike, Cork City.
Age: 22. Occupation: Labourer.
Religion: R.C.
He was arrested by British soldiers at
Rahanisky House, Whitechurch, Co.
Cork, on 8 Feb 1921 and taken to
Victoria Barracks, Cork.[39]
6th Division arrest No. 194.
Offences against Martial Law,
conspiring to levy war against the
King and possession of arms.
He was tried by Military Court in
Victoria Barracks on 26 Feb 1921 and
sentenced to 10 years Penal Servitude.
His sentence expired on 25 Feb 1931.
He was transferred from Bere Island
Military Prison in the Field to Spike
prison compound on 15 Apr 1921.
He was transferred from Spike to
Kilkenny Gaol on 17 Nov 1921and
released from there in Jan 1922.
See also: Bowles, Michael; Conroy,
Cornelius; Dennehy, Jerh; Fitzgerald,
Michael; MacSwiney, John; Murphy,
Timothy; O'Keeffe, John; Thompson,
James; Twomey, Cornelius; and
Twomey, John.

---

38 UKNA, Kew, London, WO 35/136, p.91.
39 Seán Enright, *The Trial of Civilians by Military Courts in Ireland 1921*, pp.128–133.

O'Dwyer, Edward

27 Denmark Street, Limerick City.
Age: 19. Occupation: Carpenter.
Religion: R.C.
6th Division arrest No. 157.
Offences against the ROIR.
He was tried by FGCM on 13 Apr
1921 and sentenced to 5 years
Penal Servitude.
Earliest release date, 11 Jan 1925.
His sentence expired on 12 Apr 1926.
He was transferred from Limerick
via Cork Male Gaol to Spike prison
compound on 11 May 1921.
He was transferred from Spike
to Kilkenny Gaol on 17 Nov. On
Tuesday, 22 Nov, he escaped through
a tunnel from Kilkenny Gaol with
43 others.

O'Dwyer, William

Tarrants Cross, Freemount,
Charleville, Co. Cork.
Age: 24.
Occupation: Creamery manager.
Religion: R.C.
Offence against the ROIR.
He was tried by FGCM on 11 June
1921 and sentenced to 5 years
Penal Servitude.
Earliest release date, 11 Aug 1921.
His sentence expired on 10 June 1926.
He was transferred from Cork to Spike
prison compound on 18 June 1921.
He was transferred from Spike to
Kilkenny Gaol on 17 Nov 1921 and
released from there in Jan 1922.

O'Halloran, Patrick

Scallagheen, Tipperary Town.
Age: 24. Occupation: Farmer.
Religion: R.C.
He was arrested by British soldiers
in Tipperary Town on the night of
26 Nov 1920. That night an Army
patrol was proceeding down Main
Street and the British soldiers saw
two men ahead of them, the accused
and John Withero of Spittle Street,
Tipperary Town. The officer called
on them to halt. Both men ran off
and were pursued by the officer. One
of the men turned around and fired
on the officer, who returned fire. In a
follow-up search, John Withero was
found at home with a bullet wound in
his leg. Patrick O'Halloran was found
in a doctor's surgery with a chest
wound. He was also identified as the
man who fired on the officer.[40]

Patrick O'Halloran, Tipperary Town.

40 UKNA, Kew, London, WO 35/136, p.79.

Offence, shooting with intent to commit murder on 26 Nov 1920. He was tried by FGCM on 16 May 1921 and sentenced to 15 years Penal Servitude. His sentence expired on 16 May 1936. He was transferred from Cork to Spike prison compound on 28 May 1921. He was transferred from Spike to Kilkenny Gaol on 17 Nov 1921. On Tuesday, 22 Nov, he escaped through a tunnel from Kilkenny Gaol with 43 others. See also: Withero, John, in the internee list.

O'Halloran, Pat
8 Springview Terrace, Commons Rd, Cork City.
Age: 23. Occupation: Clerk.
Religion: R.C.
Brigade arrest No. 17 I.B. 898.
6th Division arrest No. 589.
Offence against Martial Law, failing to report rebels.
He was tried by Summary Court on 30 June 1921 and sentenced to 6 months imprisonment with Hard Labour. Earliest release date, 30 Nov 1921. His sentence expired on 29 Dec 1921. He was transferred from Cork Male Gaol to Spike prison compound on 6 July 1921. He was transferred back to Cork Male Gaol on 14 Nov, authority from CA 1083, dated 12 Nov 1921.

O'Hehir, Michael
Also listed as Hahir.
Mount Prospect, South Circular Road, Limerick City.
Age: 16. Occupation: Carpenter.
Religion: R.C.
6th Division arrest No. 242.
Offences against the ROIR.
He was tried by FGCM on 26 May 1921 and sentenced to 3 years Penal Servitude (PS).
Earliest release date, 25 Aug 1923. His sentence expired on 25 May 1924. He was transferred from Limerick to Spike prison compound on 1 June 1921. He was transferred from Spike to Kilkenny Gaol on 17 Nov 1921 and released from there in Jan 1922.

O'Keeffe, John
Rahanisky, Dublin Pike, Cork City.
Age 21.
Occupation: Student.
Religion: R.C.
He was arrested by British soldiers at Rahanisky House, Whitechurch, Co. Cork, on 8 Feb 1921 and taken to Victoria Barracks, Cork.[41]
6th Division arrest No. 196.
Offences against Martial Law, conspiring to levy war against the King and possession of arms.
He was tried by Military Court on 26 Feb 1921 and sentenced to 10 years Penal Servitude.

41 Seán Enright, *The Trial of Civilians by Military Courts in Ireland 1921*, pp.128–133.

His sentence expired on 25 Feb 1931.
He was transferred from Bere Island
Military Prison in the Field to Spike
prison compound on 15 Apr 1921.
He was transferred from Spike to
Kilkenny Gaol on 17 Nov 1921 and
released from there in Jan 1922.
See also: Bowles, Michael; Conroy,
Cornelius; Dennehy, Jerh; Fitzgerald,
Michael; MacSwiney, John; Murphy,
Timothy; O'Driscoll, Laurence;
Thompson, James; Twomey,
Cornelius; and Twomey, John.

O'Keeffe, John

Clogheen Cottage, Clonakilty,
Co. Cork.
Age: 66. Occupation: Engineer.
Religion: R.C.
6th Division arrest No. 470.
Offence against Martial Law.
He was tried by Summary Court on
2 June 1921 and sentenced to 6 months
imprisonment with Hard Labour.
Earliest release date, 2 Nov 1921.
His sentence expired on 1 Dec 1921.
He was transferred from Cork Male
Gaol to Spike prison compound on
13 June 1921. He was transferred back
to Cork Male Gaol on 24 Sept 1921.
At age 66 he was both the oldest
prisoner and internee on Spike Island
during 1921.
See also: O'Keeffe, John, internee list.

O'Leary, Cornelius

Market Street, Bandon, Co. Cork.
Age: 28. Occupation: Saddler.
Religion: R.C.
6th Division arrest No. 549.
Brigade arrest No. 17 I.B. 997.
Offence under the ROIR.
He was tried by Summary Court on
20 June 1921 and sentenced to 6 months
imprisonment with Hard Labour.
Earliest release date, 20 Nov 1921.
His sentence expired on 19 Dec 1921.
He was transferred from Cork Male
Gaol to Spike prison compound on
30 June 1921.
On 14 Nov 1921, while he was on
Spike, his sentence was vacated. He
was served with an Internment Order
and immediately transferred to Spike
internment compound, authority from
CA 1083, dated 11 Nov 1921.
See also: O'Leary, Cornelius, in the
Spike internee list.

O'Leary, Jeremiah (Diarmuid)

Cork Road, Killeagh, Co. Cork.
Age: 19. Occupation: Labourer.
Religion: R.C.
He was captured by British soldiers
and Auxiliary Police with seven
others after the battle of Clonmult
near Midleton, in Co. Cork, on
20 Feb 1921. Twelve of his colleagues
were killed during the battle and two
later executed.[42]

---

42 UKNA, Kew, London, WO 71/380 and Tom O'Neill, *The Battle of Clonmult, the IRA's Worst Defeat*. Also Diarmuid O'Leary, WS No. 1589.

Diarmuid O'Leary, Killeagh, Co. Cork.

6th Division arrest No. L. 410.
Offence, levying war against the King.
He was tried by Military Court in
Victoria Barracks, from 8 to
19 Mar 1921.
He was sentenced to death and his
sentence was later commuted to
Penal Servitude for Life. Two of his
colleagues, Patrick O'Sullivan and
Maurice Moore, were executed.
He was transferred from Cork
Military Detention Barracks to Spike
prison compound on 30 Apr 1921.
He was transferred to Kilkenny Gaol
on 17 Nov 1921 After the mass escape
from Kilkenny Gaol on 22 Nov he was
transferred to Waterford Gaol. He was
released from there in Jan 1922.
See also: Harty, J.; Garde, W.; Terry,
E.; and Walsh, R.

O'Mahony, Francis
29 South Terrace, Cork City.
Age: 23. Occupation: Insurance Agent.
Religion: R.C.
6th Division arrest No. 494.
Offence under Martial Law.

He was tried by Summary Court on
11 June 1921 and sentenced to 6 months
imprisonment with Hard Labour.
Earliest release date, 17 Nov 1921.
His sentence expired on 16 Dec 1921.
He was transferred from Cork Male
Gaol to Spike prison compound on
22 June 1921.
He was transferred from Spike and
admitted to Cork Military Hospital
in Victoria Barracks on 25 June,
authority from CA 632, dated 24 June.
He escaped from Cork Military
Hospital on 15 Oct 1921.

O'Mahony, Patrick
65 Catherine Street, Limerick City.
Age: 17. Occupation: Clerk.
Religion: R.C.
6th Division arrest No. 291.
Offences under the ROIR.
He was tried by FGCM on 5 Mar
1921 and sentenced to 2 years
imprisonment with Hard Labour.
Earliest release date, 4 Nov 1922.
His sentence expired on 4 Mar 1923.
He was transferred from Limerick to
Spike prison compound on 2 June 1921.
He was transferred from Spike to
Cork Male Gaol on 14 Nov, authority
from CA 1083, dated 12 Nov 1921.
He was released from there on
12 Jan 1922.

O'Neill, Patrick J.
Annascaul, Co. Kerry.
Age: 37. Occupation: Dentist.

Religion: R.C.
6th Division arrest No. 169.
Offences against the ROIR.
He was tried by FGCM on 9 February
1921 and sentenced to 5 years
Penal Servitude.
His sentence expired on 8 Feb 1926.
He was transferred from Cork Male
Gaol to Spike prison compound on
25 Apr 1921.
He was transferred from Spike to
Kilkenny Gaol on 17 Nov 1921 and
released from there in Jan 1922.

O'Neill, Patrick

Thomas Street, Limerick City.
Age: 25. Occupation: Hair Dresser.
Religion: R.C.
6th Division arrest No. 140.
Offences against the ROIR.
He was tried by FGCM on 5 Apr
1921 and sentenced to 7 years
Penal Servitude.
Earliest release date, 5 July 1926.
His sentence expired on 4 Apr 1928.
He was transferred from Limerick,
via Cork Male Gaol to Spike prison
compound on 11 May 1921.
He was transferred from Spike to
Kilkenny Gaol on 17 Nov 1921 and
escaped from there on 22 Nov 1921.

O'Regan, Dan

18 Evergreen Street, Cork City.
Age: 22. Occupation: Fitter's Mate.
Religion: R.C.
6th Division arrest No. 496.

Offence under Martial Law.
He was tried by Summary Court on
11 June 1921 and sentenced to 6 months
imprisonment with Hard Labour.
Earliest release date, 17 Nov 1921.
His sentence expired on 16 Dec 1921.
He was transferred from Cork Male
Gaol to Spike prison compound on
22 June 1921.
He was transferred from Spike to
Cork Male Gaol on 14 Nov, authority
from CA 1083, dated 12 Nov 1921.
He was released from Cork Male
Gaol on 17 Nov, authority from
CA 693, dated 15 Nov 1921.

O'Reilly, Michael

Ballysaskin, Ballylanders,
Co. Limerick.
Age: 22.
Occupation: Labourer.
Religion: R.C.
He was arrested on 16 July 1920.
A party of police arrived in
Ballylanders, Co. Limerick, at
1.15 a.m. on 16 July 1920 and were
fired upon from Crowley's public
house. The police returned fire
and after half an hour rushed the
house. Michael O'Reilly, John and
Peter Crowley were found in a top
room. Revolvers and ammunition
were found in a trap in the ceiling.
Christopher Upton was found in the
same house, hiding under the stairs.
All four were arrested by the RIC.
6th Division arrest No. L. 468.

Offences against the ROIR, found carrying firearms.

He was taken to Cork Male Gaol and survived 94 days on hunger strike there from 11 Aug to 12 Nov 1920. After he recovered from the effects of his hunger strike he was tried by FGCM on 2 June 1921. He was found not guilty of attacking the police with firearms. He was found guilty of being present and abetting certain persons unknown.[43] He was sentenced to 2 years imprisonment with Hard Labour.

His sentence expired on 1 June 1923. He was transferred from Cork Military Detention Barracks to Spike prison compound on 9 June 1921.

He was transferred from Spike to Cork Male Gaol on 14 Nov 1921, authority from CA 1083 of 12 Nov 1921. He was released from there on 12 Jan 1922.

See Upton, Christopher, in the Spike internee list.

See Crowley, Peter and John, in this list.

O'Shea, Daniel

Fossa, Killarney, Co. Kerry.
Age: 22. Occupation: Labourer.
Religion: R.C.
6th Division arrest No. 96.
Offences under the ROIR.
He was tried by District Court Martial on 5 Jan 1921 and sentenced to 2 years imprisonment with Hard Labour. He had 6 months remitted, resulting in 18 months to serve.
Earliest release date, 5 Apr 1922.
His sentence expired on 4 July 1922.
He was transferred from Cork to Spike prison compound on 2 June 1921.
He was transferred from Spike to Cork Military Hospital on 20 July. He was released from Cork Male Gaol on 12 Jan 1922.

O'Shea, Denis

Gortacootler, Co. Kerry.
Age: 23.
Occupation: Farmer.
Religion: R.C.
6th Division arrest No. 92.
Offences under the ROIR.
He was tried by District Court Martial on 5 Jan 1921 and sentenced to 2 years imprisonment with Hard Labour.
Earliest release date, 6 Sept 1922.
His sentence expired on 4 Jan 1923.
He was transferred from Cork to Spike prison compound on 2 June 1921.
He was transferred from Spike to Cork Military Hospital on 20 July and returned on 16 Aug.
He was transferred to Cork Male Gaol on 14 Nov 1921 and released from there on 12 Jan 1922.

O'Shea, Florence

Curragh, Skibbereen, Co. Cork.
Age: 24.

43 UKNA, Kew, London, WO 35/135, p.150.

Occupation: Trade Union Secretary.
Religion: R.C.
6th Division arrest No. 588.
Brigade arrest No. 17 I.B. 1090.
Offence against Martial Law,
possession of illegal documents.
He was tried by Summary Court on
30 June 1921 and sentenced to 6 months
imprisonment with Hard Labour.
Earliest release date, 30 Nov 1921.
His sentence expired on 29 Dec 1921.
He was transferred from Cork Male
Gaol to Spike prison compound on
6 July 1921.
On 14 Nov 1921, while he was on
Spike, his sentence was vacated. He
was served with an Internment Order
and immediately transferred to Spike
internment compound, authority from
CA 1083, dated 11 Nov 1921.
See also: O'Shea, Florence, in the
Spike internee list.

O'Shea, John
Gortacootler, Co. Kerry.
Age: 18.
Occupation: Labourer.
Religion: R.C.
6th Division arrest No. 91.
Offences under the ROIR.
He was tried by District Court Martial
on 5 Jan 1921 and sentenced to 2 years
imprisonment with Hard Labour.
Earliest release date, 6 Sept 1922.
His sentence expired on 4 Jan 1923.
He was transferred from Cork Male
Gaol to Spike prison compound on

2 June 1921, to Hut 24 in the north-
east casemates.
He was transferred from Spike to
Cork Male Gaol on 24 Sept 1921. He
was released from there on
12 Jan 1922.

O'Sullivan, Christopher
Castleconnell, Co. Limerick.
He was transferred from Bere Island
Military Prison in the Field to Spike
prison compound on 15 Apr 1921.

O'Sullivan, Jeremiah
Beaufort, Co. Kerry.
Age: 18.
Occupation: Farmer.
Religion: R.C.
6th Division arrest No. 98.
Offence against the ROIR
He was tried by District Court
Martial on 5 Jan 1921. He was
sentenced to 2 years imprisonment
with Hard Labour, 6 months remitted,
resulting in 18 months imprisonment,
with HL to serve.
His sentence expired on 4 July 1922.
He was transferred from Cork to Spike
prison compound on 2 June 1921.
He was transferred back to Cork
Male Gaol on 14 Nov, authority from
CA 1083, dated 12 Nov 1921. He was
released from there on 12 Jan 1922.

O'Sullivan, John
30 Winters Hill, Sunday's Well, Cork City.
Age: 24. Occupation: Gas Fitter.

Religion: R.C.

6th Division arrest No. 499.

Offence under Martial Law.

He was tried by Summary Court on 17 June 1921 and sentenced to 6 months imprisonment with Hard Labour. Earliest release date, 17 Nov 1921. His sentence expired on 16 Dec 1921. He was transferred from Cork Male Gaol to Spike prison compound on 22 June 1921. He was transferred back to Cork Male Gaol on 14 Nov, authority from CA 1083, dated 12 Nov 1921.

He was released from Cork Male Gaol on 17 Nov, authority from CA 693, dated 15 Nov 1921.

He was Pipe Major of the Irish Volunteer Pipe Band, Cork City.

O'Sullivan, Michael

Grillough, Lismire, Co. Cork.

He was transferred from Bere Island Military Prison in the Field to Spike prison compound on 15 Apr 1921.

O'Sullivan, Timothy

Skibbereen, Co. Cork.

He was transferred from Bere Island Military Prison in the Field to Spike prison compound on 15 Apr 1921.

Page, Charles

6 Albert Place, Fermoy, Co. Cork.

Age: 34. Occupation: Painter.

Religion: R.C.

6th Division arrest No. 485.

Offence under Martial Law.

He was tried by Summary Court on 13 June 1921 and sentenced to 6 months imprisonment with Hard Labour. Earliest release date, 19 Nov 1921. His sentence expired on 12 Dec 1921. He was transferred from Cork Male Gaol to Spike prison compound on 22 June 1921. He was released from Spike on 13 Nov, authority from CA 692, dated 11 Nov 1921.

Pollock, James

34 Mary Street, Cork City.

Age: 21. Occupation: Printer.

Religion: R.C.

He was arrested by Crown Forces at Farmer's Cross on the outskirts of Cork City on 24 Apr 1921. He was seen to throw something away. One live round and some empty cartridges were found where he had thrown them.[44]

6th Division arrest No. L. 647.

Offence under the ROIR.

He was tried by FGCM in Victoria Barracks on 18 May 1921 and sentenced to 5 years Penal Servitude. His sentence expired on 17 May 1925. He was transferred from Cork Male Gaol to Spike prison compound on 13 June 1921.

He was transferred from Spike to Kilkenny Gaol on 17 Nov. On

---

44 UKNA, Kew, London, WO 35/135, p.196.

Jim Pollock, Mary Street, Cork City.

Tuesday, 22 Nov, he escaped through a tunnel from Kilkenny Gaol with 43 others.

Power, James

Kilmacthomas, Co. Waterford.
Age: 18.
Occupation: Shop assistant.
Religion: R.C.
6th Division arrest No. 676.
Offence under the ROIR.
He was tried by FGCM and sentenced to 5 years Penal Servitude.
He was admitted to Cork Military Hospital in Victoria Barracks on 20 July 1921.
He was transferred from Cork Male Gaol to Spike prison compound on 19 Sept 1921.
He was transferred from Spike to Kilkenny Gaol on 17 Nov 1921. On Tuesday, 22 Nov, he escaped through a tunnel from Kilkenny Gaol with 43 others.

Power, Patrick J.

86 Main Street, Youghal, Co. Cork.
Age: 22. Occupation: Draper.
Religion: R.C.
6th Division arrest No. 358.
Offence under Martial Law.
He was tried by Summary Court on 7 May 1921 and sentenced to 6 months imprisonment with Hard Labour.
Earliest release date, 8 Oct 1921.
His sentence expired on 6 Nov 1921.
He was transferred from Cork Male Gaol to Spike prison compound on 22 June. He was released from Spike on 8 Oct, authority from CA 693, dated 6 Oct 1921.

Punch, Edward

31 Frederick Place, Limerick City.
Age: 28.
Occupation: Sawyer.
Religion: R.C.
He participated in the Dromkeen Ambush against the RIC and the attack on the Black and Tans at Carey's Road, Limerick City shortly before his capture.[45]
6th Division arrest No. 208.
Offence under Martial Law.
He was tried by Military Court on 19 May 1921.
He was sentenced to death and his sentence was later commuted to Penal Servitude for Life.
He was transferred from Cork Male

---

45 Thomas Toomey, *The War of Independence in Limerick 1912–1921*, pp.616–617.

Gaol to Spike prison compound on 25 June 1921.

He was transferred from Spike to Kilkenny Gaol on 17 Nov 1921. On Tuesday, 22 Nov, he escaped through a tunnel from Kilkenny Gaol with 43 others.

See also: Spike prisoner Timothy Murphy of Limerick.

Pyne, Frank

Ballyporeen, Co. Tipperary.
Age: 30. Occupation: Labourer.
Religion: R.C.
6th Division arrest No. 415.
Offence under Martial Law.
He was tried by FGCM on 23 May 1921 and sentenced to 10 years Penal Servitude.
His sentence expired on 22 May 1931.
He was transferred from Cork to Spike prison compound on 28 May 1921.
He was transferred from Spike to Kilkenny Gaol on 17 Nov. On Tuesday, 22 Nov, he escaped through a tunnel from Kilkenny Gaol with 43 others.

Quinlan, James

Ballysheida, Annacarthy, Co. Tipperary.
Age: 30. Occupation: Farmer.
Religion: R.C.
6th Division arrest No. 375.
Offence against Martial Law.
He was tried by Summary Court on 11 May 1921 and sentenced to 6 months imprisonment with Hard Labour.

Earliest release date, 12 Oct 1921.
His sentence expired on 10 Nov 1921.
He was transferred from Cork Male Gaol to Spike prison compound on 13 June. He was released from Spike on 12 Oct, authority from CA 693, dated 10 Oct 1921.

Quinlan, William

Annacarty, Co. Tipperary.
Age: 22.
Occupation: Book keeper.
Religion: R.C.
He was arrested by Crown Forces for acting contrary to the ROIR, part 79.
6th Division arrest No. 607.
Brigade arrest No. 18 I.B. S.C/ 62.
Brigade arrest No. 16 I.B. 489 & S.C/62.
Offence against Martial Law, acting contrary to the ROIR, part 79.
He was tried by Summary Court on 22 June 1921 and sentenced to 6 months imprisonment with Hard Labour.
Earliest release date, 22 Nov 1921.
His sentence expired on 21 Dec 1921.
He was transferred from Cork to Spike prison compound on 15 July 1921.
On 14 Nov 1921, while still on Spike, his sentence was reserved. He was served with an Internment Order and immediately transferred to Spike internment compound, authority from CA 1083, dated 11 Nov 1921.
See also: Quinlan, William, in the Spike internee list.

Quirke, James

Ballyduff, Co. Waterford.
Age: 28.
Occupation: Farmer.
Religion: R.C.
6th Division arrest No. 560.
Brigade arrest No. 16 I.B. 490
& S.C/215.
Offence under the ROIR, possession
of illegal documents.

He was tried by Summary Court on
27 June 1921 for possession of illegal
documents and sentenced to 6 months
imprisonment with Hard Labour.
Earliest release date, 27 Nov 1921.
His sentence expired on 26 Dec 1921.
He was transferred from Cork Male
Gaol to Spike prison compound on
6 July 1921.

On 14 Nov 1921, while on Spike,
his sentence was reserved. He was
served with an Internment Order
and immediately transferred to Spike
internment compound, authority from
CA 1083, dated 11 Nov 1921.
See also: Quirke, James, in the Spike
internee list.

Rahilly, Jack

Knockatoon, Rockchapel, Co. Cork.
Age: 20.
Occupation: Farmer.
Religion: R.C.
Offence against Martial Law.
He was tried by Summary Court on
10 June 1921 and sentenced to 6 months

Jack Rahilly, Rockchapel, Co. Cork.

imprisonment with Hard Labour.
Earliest release date, 10 Nov 1921.
His sentence expired on 9 Dec 1921.
He was transferred from Cork to
Spike prison compound on 18 June
1921. He was released from Spike on
10 Nov, authority from CA 693, dated
8 Nov 1921.

Regan, Patrick

2 Patrick Street, Clonakilty, Co. Cork.
Age: 22. Occupation: Labourer.
Religion: R.C.
6th Division arrest No. 399.
Offence against Martial Law.
He was tried by Summary Court
on 17 May 1921 and sentenced to
6 months imprisonment with
Hard Labour.
Earliest release date, 18 Oct 1921.
His sentence expired on 16 Nov 1921.
He was transferred from Cork Male
Gaol to Spike prison compound on
13 June. He was released from Spike
on 18 Oct, authority from CA 693,
dated 16 Oct 1921.

Ryan, Jeremiah (Jerry)[46]

Jerry Ryan, Thurles, Co. Tipperary.

Horse and Jockey, Thurles ,
Co. Tipperary.
Age: 28. Occupation: Farmer.
Religion: R.C.
He was arrested by members of the
RIC near Thurles on 26 Jan 1921.[47]
6th Division arrest No. 57.
Offence against the ROIR, levying
war against the King in the attack on
Littleton RIC Barracks.
He was tried by FGCM in Limerick
Military Barracks on 23 Feb 1921 and
sentenced to 15 years Penal Servitude.
His sentence expired on 22 Feb 1936.
He was transferred from Limerick
via Cork Male Gaol to Spike prison
compound on 11 May 1921.
He was transferred from Spike to
Kilkenny Gaol on 17 Nov 1921. On
Tuesday, 22 Nov, he escaped through
a tunnel from Kilkenny Gaol with
43 others.

Ryan, Peter

Peter Ryan, Drombane Cross,
Co. Tipperary.

Drombane Cross, Thurles,
Co. Tipperary.
Age: 22. Occupation: Grocer.
Religion: R.C.
6th Division arrest No. 193.
Offence under the ROIR.
He was tried by FGCM on 4 May
1921 and sentenced to 1 year
imprisonment with Hard Labour.
Earliest release date, 5 Mar 1922.
His sentence expired on 3 May 1922.
He was transferred from Cork Male
Gaol to Spike prison compound on
25 June 1921. He was transferred
back to Cork Male Gaol on 14 Nov,
authority from CA 1083, dated
12 Nov 1921.
Brother of John Ryan, Spike internee.

Scanlon, Martin

Cahircorney, Co. Limerick.
He was transferred from Bere Island

---

46 See his WS, No. 1487.
47 Seán Hogan, *The Black and Tans in North Tipperary*, pp.317–319.

Military Prison in the Field to Spike prison compound on 15 Apr 1921.

Sexton, Timothy
Kinsale, Co. Cork.
Age: 17. Occupation: Labourer.
Religion: R.C.
6th Division arrest No. 67.
Offence against Martial Law.
He was tried by Summary Court on 19 Jan 1921 and sentenced to 6 months imprisonment with Hard Labour.
Earliest release date, 19 June 1921.
His sentence expired on 18 July 1921.
He was transferred from Bere Island Military Prison in the Field to Spike prison compound on 15 Apr 1921.
On 4 July 1921, while on Spike, his sentence was reserved. He was served with an Internment Order and immediately transferred to Spike internment compound.
See also: Sexton, Timothy, in the Spike internee list.

Shea, John
Castletownbere, Co. Cork.
Age: 20. Occupation: Farmer.
Religion: R.C.
Offence against Martial Law.
He was tried by Summary Court on 8 Mar 1921 and sentenced to 6 months imprisonment with Hard Labour.
Earliest release date 8 Aug 1921.
His sentence expired on 7 Sept 1921.
He was transferred from Bere Island Military Prison in the Field to Spike

prison compound on 15 Apr 1921.
On 8 Aug 1921, while on Spike, his sentence was reserved. He was served with an Internment Order and immediately transferred to Spike internment compound.
See also: Shea, John, in the Spike internee list.

Sheehan, Thomas
Lough Gur, Herbertstown, Co. Limerick.
He was transferred from Bere Island Military Prison in the Field to Spike prison compound on 15 Apr 1921.

Sisk, John
6 Dunlock, Blackrock, Co. Cork.
Age: 21. Occupation: Fireman.
Religion: R.C.
6th Division arrest No. 277.
Offence against Martial Law.
He was tried by Summary Court on 16 Apr 1921 and sentenced to 6 months imprisonment with Hard Labour.
Earliest release date, 16 Sept 1921.
His sentence expired 15 Oct 1921.
He was transferred from Cork Male Gaol to Spike prison compound on 22 June. He was released from Spike on 16 Sept, authority from CA 693, dated 14 Sept 1921.

Slattery, William
Herbertstown, Co. Limerick.
He was transferred from Bere Island Military Prison in the Field to Spike prison compound on 15 Apr 1921.

Smith, Richard

Charleville, Co. Cork.

Age: 23.

Occupation: Coach Builder.

Religion: R.C.

6th Division arrest No. 114.

Offence against Martial Law.

He was tried by Summary Court on
28 Jan 1921 and sentenced to 6 months
imprisonment with Hard Labour.
Earliest release date, 28 June 1921.
His sentence expired on 27 July 1921.
He was transferred from Bere Island
Military Prison in the Field to
Spike prison compound on 15 Apr
1921. He was released from Spike
on 27 June, authority from CA
693 dated 27 Apr 1921.

Stack, Humphrey

Ballyconra, Lisselton Cross, Co. Kerry.

Age: 22.

Occupation: Farmer.

Religion: R.C.

6th Division arrest No. 342.

Offence against Martial Law.

He was tried by Summary Court on
22 Apr 1921 and sentenced to 6 months
imprisonment with Hard Labour.
Earliest release date, 22 Sept 1921.
His sentence expired on 21 Oct 1921.
He was transferred from Cork Male
Gaol to Spike prison compound on
22 June. He was released from Spike
on 22 Sept, authority from CA 693,
dated 20 Sept 1921.

Stack, James

Ballyconra, Lisselton Cross, Co. Kerry.

Age: 30. Occupation: Farmer.

Religion: R.C.

6th Division arrest No. 341.

Offence against Martial Law.

He was tried by Summary Court on
22 Apr 1921 and sentenced to 6 months
imprisonment with Hard Labour.
Earliest release date, 22 Sept 1921.
His sentence expired on 21 Oct 1921.
He was transferred from Cork Male
Gaol to Spike prison compound on
22 June. He was released from Spike
on 22 Sept, authority from CA 693,
dated 20 Sept 1921.

Sugrue, Timothy

Lahard, Killarney, Co. Kerry.

Age: 22. Occupation: Farmer.

Religion: R.C.

6th Division arrest No. 97.

Offence against the ROIR.

He was tried by District Court Martial
on 5 Jan 1921 and sentenced to 2 years
imprisonment with Hard Labour. He
had 6 months remitted, resulting in
18 months with HL to serve.
Earliest release date, 5 Apr 1922.
His sentence expired on 4 July 1922.
He was transferred from Cork Male
Gaol to Spike prison compound on
2 June 1921.
He was transferred back to Cork
Male Gaol on 14 Nov, authority from
CA 1083, dated 12 Nov 1921. He was
released from there on 12 Jan 1922.

Sullivan, Denis
Cladanure, Kenmare, Co. Kerry.
Age: 23. Occupation: Farmer.
Religion: R.C.
Brigade arrest No. K.B. 268.
6th Division arrest No. 574.
Offence under Martial Law, he
was found in possession of illegal
documents relating to the IRA.
He was tried by Summary Court on
22 June 1921 and sentenced to 6 months
imprisonment with Hard Labour.
Earliest release date, 22 Nov 1921.
His sentence expired on 31 Dec 1921.
He was transferred from Cork Male
Gaol to Spike prison compound on
6 July 1921.
He was transferred back to Cork
Male Gaol on 14 Nov, authority
from CA 1083, dated 12 Nov 1921.

Sullivan, James
Killballyowen, Co. Clare.
He was transferred from Bere Island
Military Prison in the Field to Spike
prison compound on 15 Apr 1921.

Sullivan, Michael
Castletownbere, Co. Cork.
Age: 22.
Occupation: Labourer.
Religion: R.C.
Brigade arrest No. 17 I.B. 613.
Offence against Martial Law.
He was tried by Summary Court on
8 Mar 1921 and sentenced to 6 months
imprisonment with Hard Labour.

Earliest release date, 8 Aug 1921.
His sentence expired 7 Sept 1921.
He was transferred from Bere Island
Military Prison in the Field to Spike
prison compound on 15 Apr 1921.
On 8 Aug 1921, while on Spike,
his sentence was reserved. He was
served with an Internment Order
and immediately transferred to Spike
internment compound.
See also: Sullivan, Michael, in the
Spike internee list.

Sullivan, Michael
Limerick.
He was transferred from Bere Island
Military Prison in the Field to Spike
prison compound on 15 Apr 1921.

Swanton, John
Castletownbere, Co. Cork.
He was transferred from Bere Island
Military Prison in the Field to Spike
prison compound on 15 Apr 1921.

Sweeney, Daniel
Cork Street, Macroom, Co. Cork.
Age 28. Occupation: Labourer.
Religion: R.C.
6th Division arrest No. 535.
Offence under Martial Law.
He was tried by FGCM on 20 June
1921 and sentenced to 6 months
imprisonment with Hard Labour.
Earliest release date, 20 Nov 1921.
His sentence expired on 19 Dec 1921.
He was transferred from Cork Male

Gaol to Spike prison compound on 25 June 1921.
He was transferred back to Cork Male Gaol on 14 Nov, authority from CA 1083, dated 12 Nov 1921.

Terry, Edmund
Churchtown South, Co. Cork.
Age: 17.
Occupation: Apprentice carpenter.
Religion R.C.
He was captured by British soldiers and Auxiliary Police with seven others after the battle of Clonmult, near Midleton, Co. Cork, on 20 Feb 1921. Twelve of his colleagues were killed during the battle and two later executed.[48]
6th Division arrest No. L. 404.
Offence, levying war against the King. He was tried by Military Court in Victoria Barracks from 8 to 19 Mar 1921 and sentenced to Penal Servitude for Life.

Edmond Terry, Churchtown South, Co. Cork.

He was transferred from Cork Military Detention Barracks to Spike prison compound on 30 Apr 1921.
He was transferred from Spike to Kilkenny Gaol on 17 Nov 1921. After the mass escape from Kilkenny Gaol on 22 Nov he was transferred to Waterford Gaol and released from there in Jan 1922.
See also: Harty, J., Garde, W., O'Leary, J., and Walsh, R.

Thompson, James
77 Thomas Davis Street, Cork City.
Age: 25. Occupation: Labourer.
Religion: R.C.
He was arrested by British soldiers at Rahanisky House, Whitechurch, Co. Cork, on 8 Feb 1921 and taken to Victoria Barracks, Cork.[49]
6th Division arrest No. 201.
Offences against Martial Law, conspiring to levy war against the King and possession of arms.
He was tried by Military Court in Victoria Barracks on 26 Feb 1921 and sentenced to 15 years Penal Servitude. His sentence expired on 25 Feb 1936.
He was transferred from Bere Island Military Prison in the Field to Spike prison compound on 15 Apr 1921.
He was transferred from Spike to Kilkenny Gaol on 17 Nov 1921. After the mass escape from Kilkenny

---

48 UKNA, Kew, London, WO 71/380 and Tom O'Neill *The Battle of Clonmult, the IRA's Worst Defeat,* also Diarmuid O'Leary, WS No. 1589.
49 Seán Enright, *The Trial of Civilians by Military Courts in Ireland 1921,* pp.128–133.

Gaol on 22 Nov he was transferred to Waterford Gaol and released from there in Jan 1922.

See also: Bowles, Michael; Conroy, Cornelius; Dennehy, Jerh; Fitzgerald, Michael; MacSwiney, John; Murphy, Timothy; O'Driscoll, Laurence; O'Keeffe, John; Twomey, Cornelius; and Twomey, John.

Tobin, Daniel

Cloughleafin, Mitchelstown, Co. Cork.
Age: 24. Occupation: Labourer.
Religion: R.C.
6th Division arrest No. 538.
Brigade arrest No. 16 I.B. 78.
Offence under the ROIR.
He was tried by FGCM on 21 June 1921 and sentenced to 2 years imprisonment with Hard Labour.
Earliest release date, 20 Feb 1923.
His sentence expired on 20 June 1923.
He was transferred from Cork Male Gaol to Spike prison compound on 30 June 1921.
He was transferred back to Cork Male Gaol on 14 Nov and released from there on 12 Jan 1922.

Tobin, John

Ballynoe, Carrigtwohill, Co. Cork.
Age: 25. Occupation: Labourer.
Religion: R.C.
He was arrested by Crown Forces on 6 July 1921, for shooting with intent

to murder, on 23 June 1921.[50]
6th Division arrest No. 643.
Offence under the ROIR, shooting with intent to murder, on 23 June 1921.
He was tried by FGCM in Victoria Barracks, Cork, on 22 July 1921 and sentenced to 15 years Penal Servitude (PS).
His sentence expired on 21 July 1931.
He was transferred from Cork Male Gaol to Spike prison compound on 11 Aug 1921.
He was transferred from Spike to Kilkenny Gaol on 17 Nov and released from there in Jan 1922.

Tobin, Maurice

Kilmaloo, Co. Waterford.
Age: 26. Occupation: Farmer.
Religion: R.C.
He was arrested by Crown Forces on 1 July 1921 while riding a bicycle during curfew.
Brigade arrest No. 17 I.B. 1111.
6th Division arrest No. 602.
Offence against Martial Law, riding a bicycle during curfew.
He was tried by Summary Court on 1 July 1921 and sentenced to 2 months imprisonment.
Earliest release date, 22 Aug 1921.
His sentence expired on 31 Aug 1921.
He was transferred from Cork to Spike prison compound on 15 July 1921. He was released from Spike on

50 UKNA, Kew, London, WO 35/136, p.92.

22 Aug, authority received from CA 693, dated 19 Aug 1921.

Tobin, Thomas

3 Harr Street, Thurles, Co. Tipperary.
Age: 22.
Occupation: Coach Builder.
Religion: R.C.
He was arrested by Crown Forces, with William McCarthy, Richard McCarthy and John Turner, on 27 Feb 1921 at Loughtagalla, Thurles, for being assembled together with others unknown and for attempting to oppose the Forces of H.M.[51]
6th Division arrest No. 116.
Offence under the ROIR, see above.
He was tried by FGCM on 10 May 1921 and sentenced to 18 months imprisonment with Hard Labour.
Earliest release date, 11 Aug 1922.
His sentence expired on 9 Nov 1922.
He was transferred from Cork Male Gaol to Spike prison compound on 25 June 1921.
He was transferred back to Cork Male Gaol on 14 Nov 1921 and released from there on 12 Jan 1922.

Turner, John

West Gate, Thurles, Co. Tipperary.
Age: 19. Occupation: Shop assistant.
Religion: R.C.
He was arrested with William

McCarthy, Richard McCarthy and Thomas Tobin on 27 Feb 1921 at Loughtagalla, Thurles, for being assembled together with others unknown and for attempting to oppose the Forces of H.M.[52]
6th Division arrest No. 118.
Offence under the ROIR, see above.
He was tried by FGCM on 10 May 1921 and sentenced to 18 months imprisonment with Hard Labour.
Earliest release date, 11 Aug 1922.
His sentence expired on 9 Nov 1922.
He was transferred from Cork Male Gaol to Spike prison compound on 25 June 1921.
He was transferred back to Cork Male Gaol on 14 Nov 1921 and released from there on 12 Jan 1922.

Tuthill, Patrick

Little Wesley Place, Limerick City.
Age: 18. Occupation: Labourer.
Religion: R.C.
6th Division arrest No. 241.
Offences against the ROIR.
He was tried by FGCM on 26 May 1921 and sentenced to 3 years Penal Servitude.
Earliest release date, 25 Aug 1923.
His sentence expired on 25 May 1924.
He was transferred from Limerick to Spike prison compound on 1 June 1921.
He was transferred from Spike to

---

51 UKNA, Kew, London, WO 35/136, p.103.
52 Ibid.

Kilkenny Gaol on 17 Nov 1921 and released from there in Jan 1922.

Twomey, Cornelius
Dublin Hill, Kilbarry, Cork City.

Con Twomey, Dublin Hill, Co. Cork.

Religion: R.C.
He was arrested by British soldiers at Rahanisky House, Whitechurch, Co. Cork on 8 Feb 1921 and taken to Victoria Barracks, Cork.[53]
Offences against Martial Law, conspiring to levy war against the King and possession of arms.
He was tried by Military Court in Victoria Barracks on 26 Feb 1921 and sentenced to 15 Years Penal Servitude.
His sentence expired on 25 Feb 1936.
He was transferred from Bere Island Military Prison in the Field to Spike prison compound on 15 Apr 1921.
He escaped from Spike on 30 Apr 1921.
See also: MacSwiney, J., and Malone ,T.
See also: Bowles, Michael; Conroy, Cornelius; Dennehy, Jerh; Fitzgerald, Michael; MacSwiney, John; Murphy, Timothy; O'Driscoll, Laurence; O'Keeffe, John; Thompson, James; and Twomey, John.

Twomey, Daniel
Killowney, Old Head, Kinsale, Co. Cork.
Age: 28.
Occupation: Farmer.
Religion: R.C.
6th Division arrest No. 517.
Offence under the ROIR.
He was tried by Summary Court on 20 June 1921 and sentenced to 6 months imprisonment with Hard Labour.
Earliest release date, 20 Nov 1921.
His sentence expired on 19 Dec 1921.
He was transferred from Cork Male Gaol to Spike prison compound on 25 June 1921.
On 14 Nov 1921, while on Spike, his sentence was reserved. He was served with an Internment Order and immediately transferred to Spike internment compound.
See also: Twomey, Daniel, in the Spike internee list.

Twomey, Daniel
32 North Main Street and 34 Princes Street, Cork City.
Age: 23. Occupation: Hardware Assistant.
Religion: R.C.
6th Division arrest No. 559.
Brigade arrest No. 17.I.B. 1024.
Offence against Martial Law, not having the names of all occupants of his house listed inside his front door.
He was tried by Summary Court on

---

53 Seán Enright, *The Trial of Civilians by Military Courts in Ireland 1921*, pp.128–133.

29 June 1921 and sentenced to 4 months imprisonment with Hard Labour. Earliest release date, 9 Oct 1921. His sentence expired on 28 Oct 1921. He was transferred from Cork Male Gaol to Spike prison compound on 6 July 1921.

On 8 Aug he had two months remitted from his sentence. He was released from Spike on 18 Aug 1921. Brother of internees James and Michael.

Twomey, James

32 North Main Street and 34 Princes Street, Cork City. Age: 29. Occupation: Shop assistant. Religion R.C. 6th Division arrest No. 561. Brigade arrest No. 17 I.B. 1026. Offence against Martial Law, not having the names of all occupants of his house listed inside his front door. He was tried by Summary Court in Victoria Barracks, Cork, on 29 June 1921 and sentenced to 4 months imprisonment with Hard Labour. Earliest release date, 9 Oct 1921. His sentence expired on 28 Oct 1921. He was transferred from Cork Male Gaol to Spike prison compound on 6 July 1921.

On 8 Aug he had two months remitted from his sentence. He was released from Spike on 18 Aug 1921. Brother of internees Daniel and Michael.

Twomey, John

Kilbarry, Dublin Pike, Cork City. Age: 38. Occupation: Worked in Fords. Religion: R.C. He was arrested by British soldiers at Rahanisky House, Whitechurch, Co. Cork, on 8 Feb 1921 and taken to Victoria Barracks, Cork.[54] 6th Division arrest No. 200. Offences against Martial Law, conspiring to levy war against the King and possession of arms. He was tried by Military Court, on 26 Feb 1921 and sentenced to 15 years Penal Servitude. His sentence expired on 25 Feb 1936. He was transferred from Bere Island Military Prison in the Field to Spike prison compound on 15 Apr 1921. He was transferred to Kilkenny Gaol on 17 Nov 1921 and released from there in Jan 1922. See also: Bowles, Michael; Conroy, Cornelius; Dennehy, Jerh; Fitzgerald, Michael; MacSwiney, John; Murphy, Timothy; O'Driscoll, Laurence; O'Keeffe, John; Thompson, James; and Twomey, Cornelius.

Twomey, Michael

32 North Main Street and 34 Princes Street, Cork City. Age: 25. Occupation: Accountant. Religion: R.C.

---

54 Ibid.

6th Division arrest No. 558.
Brigade arrest No. 17 I.B. 1025.
Offence against Martial Law, not
having the names of all occupants of
his house listed inside his front door.
He was tried by Summary Court on
29 June 1921 and he was sentenced to
4 months imprisonment with
Hard Labour.
His sentence expired on 28 Oct 1921.
He was transferred from Cork Male
Gaol to Spike prison compound on
6 July 1921.
On 8 Aug 1921 he had two months
remitted from his sentence. He was
released from Spike on 18 Aug 1921.
Brother of internees Daniel and James.

Twomey, Patrick

Killowney, Old Head, Kinsale, Co. Cork.
Age: 21. Occupation: Farmer.
Religion: R.C.
6th Division arrest No. 519.
Offence under the ROIR.
He was tried by Summary Court on
20 June 1921 and sentenced to 6 months
imprisonment with Hard Labour.
Earliest release date, 20 Nov 1921.
His sentence expired on 19 Dec 1921.
He was transferred from Cork Male
Gaol to Spike prison compound on
25 June. He was transferred back to
Cork Male Gaol on 14 Nov 1921.

Veale, Patrick

Moord, Waterford.
Occupation: Farmer.

Religion: R.C.
He was arrested by Crown Forces
on 1 July 1921, while riding a bicycle
during curfew.
6th Division arrest No. 603.
Brigade arrest No. 17 I.B. 1112.
Offence against Martial Law, riding a
bicycle during curfew.
He was tried by Summary Court
on 1 July 1921 and sentenced to
2 months imprisonment.
Earliest release date, 22 Aug 1921.
His sentence expired on 31 Aug 1921.
He was transferred from Cork Male
Gaol to Spike prison compound on
15 July. He was released from Spike
on 24 Aug 1921.

Wall, Thomas P.

6 George's Quay, Cork City.
Age: 23. Occupation: Clerk.
Religion: R.C.
He was arrested by Crown Forces
when found in possession of a uniform.
6th Division arrest No. 608.
Brigade arrest No. 17 I.B. 1059.
Offence under Martial Law, found in
possession of a uniform.
He was tried by Summary Court on
7 July 1921 and sentenced to 6 months
imprisonment with Hard Labour.
Earliest release date, 8 Dec 1921.
His sentence expired on 6 Jan 1922.
He was transferred from Cork Male
Gaol to Spike prison compound on
15 July. He was transferred back to
Cork Male Gaol on 14 Nov 1921.

Wallace, Thomas

Ballylongford, Co. Kerry, listed as
Co. Cork.
Age: 47. Occupation: Farmer.
Religion: R.C.
6th Division arrest No. 568.
Brigade arrest No. K.B. 249.
Offence under Martial Law, acting as
a Sinn Féin magistrate.
He was tried by Summary Court on
4 June 1921 and sentenced to 3 months
imprisonment with Hard Labour.
Earliest release date, 20 Aug 1921.
His sentence expired on 3 Sept 1921.
He was transferred from Cork Male
Gaol to Spike prison compound on
6 July 1921.
He was released from Spike on 20 Aug
1921, authority received from CA 693,
dated 19 Aug 1921.

Walsh, Christopher

Blarney Road, Blarney, Co. Cork.
Age: 24.
Occupation: Factory Hand.
Religion: R.C.
Offence under the ROIR.
He was tried by FGCM on 10 June
1921 and sentenced to 15 years
Penal Servitude.
His sentence expired on 9 June 1936.
He was transferred from Cork to Spike
prison compound on 18 June 1921.
He was transferred from Spike to
Kilkenny Gaol on 17 Nov 1921 and
released from there in Jan 1922.

Walsh, James

Knockea, Clonakilty, Co. Cork.
Age: 47. Occupation: Farmer.
Religion: R.C.
6th Division arrest No. L. 624.
Brigade arrest No. 17 I.B. 657.
Offence under DORA.
He was tried by FGCM on 13 June
1921 and sentenced to 84 days
imprisonment with Hard Labour.
Earliest release date, 24 Aug 1921.
His sentence expired on 5 Sept 1921.
He was transferred from Cork Male
Gaol to Spike prison compound on
18 June 1921.
On 25 Aug 1921, while on Spike,
his sentence was vacated. He was
served with an Internment Order
and immediately transferred to Spike
internment compound.
See also: Walsh, James, in the Spike
internee list.

Walsh, Joseph

Tipperary Town.
Age: 25. Occupation: Book Keeper.
Religion R.C.
He was arrested by Crown Forces,
when he was found in possession of a
message regarding Crown Forces.
6th Division arrest No. 605.
Brigade arrest No. 16 I.B. S/C 654
Offence under Martial Law, found
in possession of a message regarding
Crown Forces.
He was tried by Summary Court on
27 June 1921 and sentenced to 6 months

imprisonment with Hard Labour.
Earliest release date, 27 Nov 1921.
His sentence expired on 26 Dec 1921.
He was transferred from Cork Male
Gaol to Spike prison compound on
15 July. He was transferred back to
Cork Male Gaol on 24 Sept 1921.

Walsh, Maurice

Carraghtarna, Fethard, Co. Tipperary.
Age: 17.
Occupation: Farmer.
Religion: R.C.
6th Division arrest No. 641.
Offence under the ROIR.
He was tried by FGCM on 22 July
1921 and sentenced to 5 years
Penal Servitude.
His sentence expired on 21 July 1926.
He was transferred from Cork Male
Gaol to Spike prison compound on
11 August 1921.
He was transferred from Spike to
Kilkenny Gaol on 17 Nov 1921 and
released from there in Jan 1922.

Walsh, Robert

Ballybraher, Ballycotton, Co. Cork.
Age 20.
Occupation: Farmer.
Religion: R.C.
He was captured by British soldiers
and Auxiliary Police with seven
others after the battle of Clonmult,
near Midleton, in Co. Cork, on

Robert Walsh,
Ballycotton,
Co. Cork.

20 Feb 1921. Twelve of his colleagues
were killed during the battle and two
later executed.[55]
6th Division arrest No. L. 406.
Offence, levying war against the King.
He was tried by Military Court in
Victoria Barracks on 8 to 19 Mar
1921 and sentenced to Penal Servitude
for life.
He was transferred from Cork
Military Detention Barracks to Spike
prison compound on 30 Apr 1921, to
Hut 24 in the north-east casemates.
He was transferred from Spike to
Kilkenny Gaol on 17 Nov 1921.
After the mass escape from Kilkenny
Gaol on 22 Nov he was transferred
to Waterford Gaol and released from
there in Jan 1922.
See also: Harty, J.; Garde, W.; O'Leary,
J.; and Terry, E.

Walsh, William

Ivy Cottage, Killard, Blarney, Co. Cork.
Age: 19. Occupation: Factory Hand.
Religion: R.C.
6th Division arrest No. 377.
Offence against the ROIR.

55 UKNA, Kew, London, WO 71/380 and Tom O'Neill, *The Battle of Clonmult, the IRA's Worst Defeat.*

He was tried by FGCM in Victoria
Barracks on 13 May 1921 and
sentenced to 2 years imprisonment
with Hard Labour.
Earliest release date, 12 Apr 1923.
His sentence expired on 12 May 1923.
He was transferred from Cork Male
Gaol to Spike prison compound on
2 June 1921, to Hut 24 in the north-
east casemates.
He was transferred from Spike
back to Cork Male Gaol on 24 Sept
1921 and released from there on
12 Jan 1922.

Ware, Michael

Kilelton, Ballylongford, Co. Kerry
listed as Co. Cork.
Age: 23. Occupation: Farmer.
Religion: R.C.
Brigade arrest No. K.B. 246.
6th Division arrest No. 570.
Offence under Martial Law,
obstructing and assaulting members
of the RIC.
He was tried by Summary Court
on 20 June 1921 and sentenced to
6 months imprisonment with
Hard Labour.
Earliest release date, 20 Nov 1921.
His sentence expired on 19 Dec 1921.
He was transferred from Cork Male
Gaol to Spike prison compound on
6 July 1921. He was transferred back
to Cork Male Gaol on 14 Nov 1921.

White, Jack

Main Street, Charleville, Co. Cork,
Age: 21. Occupation: Butcher.
Religion: R.C.
Offence under Martial Law.
He was tried by Summary Court
on 10 June 1921 and sentenced to
6 months imprisonment with
Hard Labour.
Earliest release date, 10 Nov 1921.
His sentence expired on 9 Dec 1921.
He was transferred from Cork Male
Gaol to Spike prison compound on
18 June 1921. He was transferred back
to Cork Male Gaol on 24 Sept 1921.

Woulfe, Thomas

Lahinch Road, Ennis, Co. Clare.
Age: 25. Occupation: Farmer.
Religion: R.C.
6th Division arrest No. 264.
Offence under the ROIR.
He was tried by FGCM on 17 June
1921 and sentenced to 2 years
imprisonment with Hard Labour.
Earliest release date, 16 Feb 1921.
His sentence expired on 16 June 1921.
He was transferred from Cork Male
Gaol to Spike prison compound on
25 June 1921.
He was transferred back to Cork
Male Gaol on 24 Sept 1921 and
released from there on 12 Jan 1922.

LIST OF INTERNEES ON SPIKE ISLAND

The alphabetical list and details of suspected Republican internees held on Spike Island between April and November 1921 follows. The original British Army records do not contain the same volume of information for the internees as is the case with the prisoners. Also, because the internees were not processed through the military courts, the reason for their arrest is generally not available.

When searching for an individual where the status is unknown, i.e. prisoner or internee, check the internee list first. There are three times more internees listed, 900 internees as against 300 prisoners. The names are in chronological sequence. The surname may or may not have an 'O' or have Mc or Mac included. The vast majority of the records were handwritten and in many cases the British soldiers on clerical duties wrote the names as they sounded and quite a few were misspelt. I have corrected errors where possible. There were also several occasions where prisoners intentionally furnished incorrect details to their captives. Where incorrect names were given, I have provided the alias and correct name(s) where known. It has not been possible to locate a list of the internees that were transferred from Spike Island to Maryborough (Portlaoise) Prison on 18/19 November 1921.

Not all records survived. Therefore, it is possible that names have been omitted inadvertently. Some of the town lands listed in the records were particularly difficult to locate and indeed some have been impossible to identify.

In many of the records, the details of the hut an internee was held in while on Spike were included. The detailed map of the 'A' Block on the next page will enable the reader to identify the location of that hut. There is a drawing on the second next page of what the 'B' Block may have looked like. It has not been possible to determine hut numbers in 'B' Block.

Please make contact with the Spike Island manager, with original records, to have names added or details amended. Any new information, photographs, etc., are always most welcome. Please send any correspondence to: The Manager, Spike Island, Cobh, Co. Cork, admin@spikeislandcork.ie, www.spikeislandcork.ie.

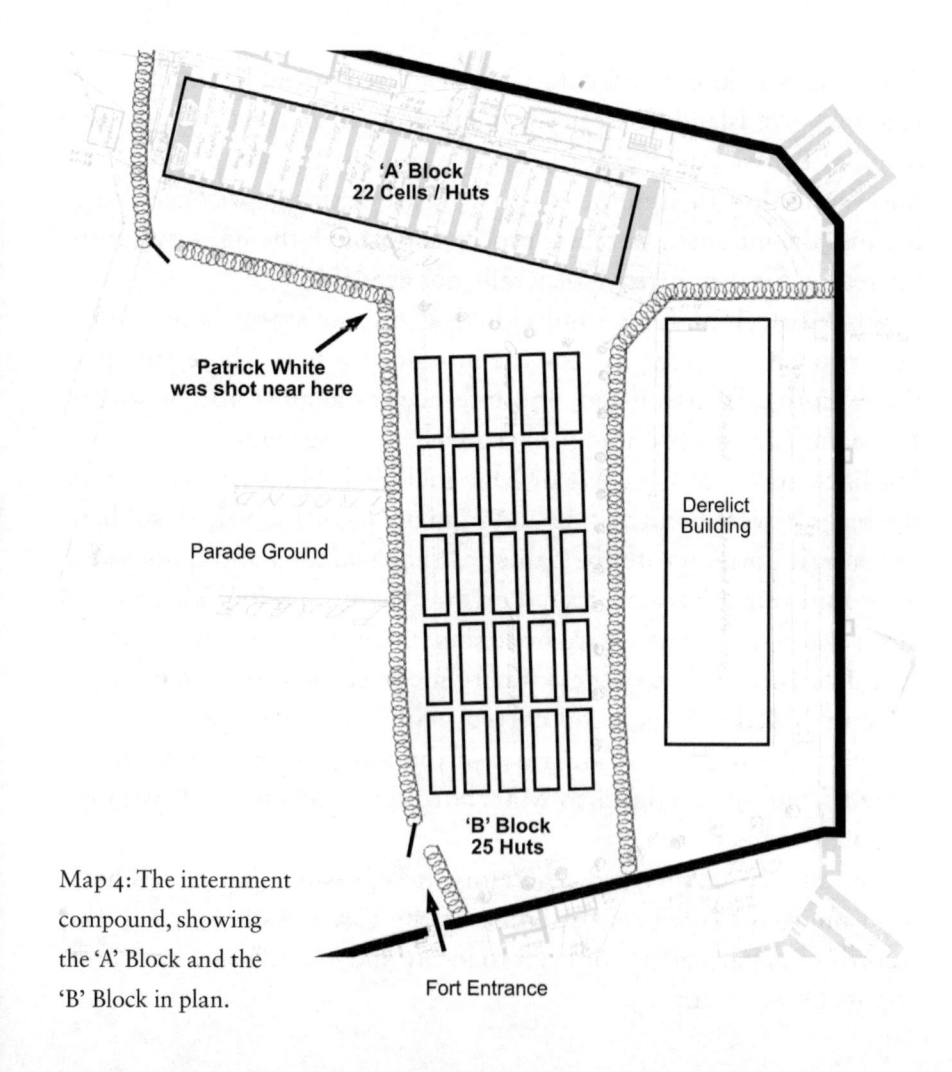

'A' Block
22 Cells / Huts

Patrick White
was shot near here

Parade Ground

Derelict
Building

'B' Block
25 Huts

Map 4: The internment compound, showing the 'A' Block and the 'B' Block in plan.

Fort Entrance

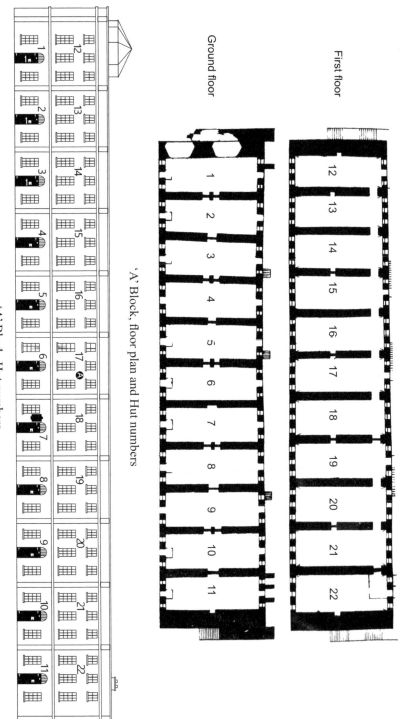

First floor

Ground floor

'A' Block, floor plan and Hut numbers

'A' Block, Hut numbers

Map 5: Detailed plan and elevation of the 'A' Block.

Internees

Aherne, Michael

Burrane, Timoleague, Co. Cork.
6th Division arrest No. 343.
Brigade arrest No. 17 I.B. 274.
He was transferred from Cork Male
Gaol to Spike Island internment
compound on 19 Feb 1921.

Aherne, Pat

Monard, College Road, Cork City.
6th Division arrest No. 610.
Brigade arrest No. 17 I.B. 582.
He was transferred from Cork Male
Gaol to Spike Island internment
compound on 25 Apr 1921.
He was transferred from Spike to Bere
Island internment camp on 11 July
1921 on HMS *Vidette*.

Arnold, Ned

Knockboola, Rathcormac, Co. Cork.
Age: 19.
6th Division arrest No. 759.
Brigade arrest No. 16 I.B. 480.
He was arrested on 26 Aug
1920 and interned after a period of
imprisonment.
He was transferred from Cork Male
Gaol to Spike Island internment
compound on 20 Sept 1921.
He was transferred from Spike to
Maryborough (Portlaoise) Prison on
18/19 Nov and released from there in
Dec 1921.

Barrett, Daniel

Ivy Hook & 18 Watercourse Rd,
Cork City and Monkstown, Co. Cork.
6th Division arrest No. 492.
Brigade arrest No. 17 I.B. 410.
He was transferred from Cork Male
Gaol to Spike Island internment
compound on 12 Apr 1921.
He was transferred from Spike to Bere
Island internment camp on 11 July
1921 on HMS *Vidette*.

Barrett, Edward

Kilmoylorane, Ballinascarthy, Co. Cork.
6th Division arrest No. 447.
Brigade arrest No. 17 I.B. 383.
He was transferred to Spike Island
internment compound, to 'B' Block,
Hut 23, to be moved to Bere Island.
He was transferred from Spike to Bere
Island internment camp on 11 July
1921 on HMS *Vidette*.

Barrett, James

Anaharlick, Coppeen, Co. Cork.
6th Division arrest No. 407.
Brigade arrest No. 17 I.B. 337.
He was transferred to Spike Island
internment compound, to be moved
to Bere Island.
He was transferred from Spike to Bere
Island internment camp on 11 July
1921 on HMS *Vidette*.

Barrett, John

Waterloo, Blarney, Co. Cork. Age: 21.
Brigade arrest No. 17 I.B. 1125.
He was transferred from Cork Male
Gaol to Spike Island internment
compound on 25 July 1921, to 'A'
Block, Hut 19.
He was transferred to Maryborough
(Portlaoise) Prison on the night of
18/19 Nov and released from there in
Dec 1921.

Barrett, Richard

Tullyglass, Bandon, Co. Cork.
Brigade arrest No. 17 I.B. 204.
He was arrested at the end Apr 1921.
He was transferred from the Brigade
Cage in Victoria Barracks, Cork, to
Spike Island internment compound on
19 Feb 1921.

Barrett, Richard (Dick)

Upton, Bandon, Co. Cork.
Age: 29.
Occupation: National school teacher.
6th Division arrest No. 604.
Brigade arrest No. 17 I.B. 571.
He was transferred from Cork Male
Gaol to Spike Island internment
compound on 30 Apr 1921, to 'A'
Block, Hut 16.
He was appointed a Staff Officer for
the internees.
He was transferred from Spike to Bere
Island internment camp on 11 July

Dick Barrett, Upton, Co. Cork.

1921 on HMS *Vidette*.
He was transferred back to Spike
from Bere Island and escaped from
Spike with six other internees on the
night of 10/11 Nov 1921.
See detailed account of their escape in
this book.
Prior to being interned he was the
brigade quartermaster for the Third
(West) Cork Brigade.
He took the anti-Treaty side during
the Irish Civil War and he was
captured when the Four Courts
garrison in Dublin surrendered on
Friday, 30 June 1922.
He was imprisoned in Mountjoy Jail
in Dublin. Following the assassination
of the pro-Treaty TD, Sean Hales,
by the IRA in Dublin on 7 Dec
1922, Barrett and three of his fellow
prominent anti-Treaty prisoners were
executed by firing squad in Mountjoy
Gaol the following morning as an
Irish government reprisal.[1]

---

1   *Dick Barrett (1889–1922) his Life and Death*, published by the Ballineen and Enniskeane Area
    Heritage Group. See also Frank Neville, WS No. 443, p.15.

Barrett, William

Coppeen, Co. Cork.
Brigade arrest No. 17 I.B. 199.
He was transferred from Cork Male
Gaol to Spike Island internment
compound on 24 Feb 1921.

Barrett, William (Bill)

William Barrett, Killenaule,
Co. Tipperary.

Crohane, Killenaule, Co. Tipperary.
Age: 22.
Brigade arrest No. 16 I.B. 100.
He was transferred to Spike Island
internment compound, for transfer to
Bere Island.
He was transferred from Spike to Bere
Island internment camp on 14/15 Apr
1921 by RN destroyer.
He was transferred back from Bere
Island to Spike on 20 Sept on HMS
Stormcloud, D 89.
He was transferred from Spike to
Maryborough (Portlaoise) Prison on
the night of 18/19 Nov and released
from there in Dec 1921.

Barron, Jack (John)

Ballyheeny, Clashmore, Co. Waterford.
Age: 20.
Brigade arrest No. 17 I.B. 1116.
He was transferred from Cork Male
Gaol to Spike Island internment
compound on 25 July 1921, to 'A'
Block, Hut 15.
He was transferred to Maryborough
(Portlaoise) Prison on the night of
18/19 Nov and released from there in
Dec 1921.

Barron, Thomas

Hugginstown, Dunnamaggan,
Co. Kilkenny.
Age: 30.
He was arrested by Crown Forces in
Kilkenny during 1920. He was taken
to Kilkenny Goal and to Belfast Gaol.
He was transferred to Wormwood
Scrubs prison in London and went on
hunger strike there for 18 days.
He was arrested by Auxiliary
Police in 1921 and was taken to
their Company Headquarters in
Woodstock House, near Inistioge,
Co. Kilkenny. From there he was
taken to Waterford Gaol, Kilworth
Army Camp and Cork Male Gaol.
Brigade arrest No. 16 I.B. 420.
He was transferred from Cork Male
Gaol to Spike Island internment
compound on 30 June 1921, to 'B'
Block, Hut 20. He was later moved to
'A' Block, Hut 2.
He was transferred to Maryborough

(Portlaoise) Prison on the night of 18/19 Nov and released from there in Dec 1921.

Barry, Edmond

Cork City.
Brigade arrest No. 17 I.B. 229.
He was transferred from Cork Male Gaol to Spike Island internment compound on 19 Feb 1921.

Barry, Edmond

5 Windsor Cottages, Cork City.
6th Division arrest No. 561.
Brigade arrest No. 17 I.B. 481.
He was transferred from Cork Male Gaol to Spike Island internment compound on 25 Apr 1921.
He was transferred from Spike to Bere Island internment camp on 11 July 1921 on HMS *Vidette*.
Brother of internees James and John.

Barry, Jack

Victoria Cross, Cork City.
6th Division arrest No. 534.
Brigade arrest No. 17 I.B. 436.
He was transferred from Spike to Bere Island internment camp on 11 July 1921 on HMS *Vidette*.

Barry, James

Fermoy, Co. Cork.
Age: 27.
On the night of 4/5 June 1920, a British Army mobile patrol, under the command of Lt G.T. Milnes, drove into The Square in Fermoy. The lead vehicle was an armoured car. Lt Milnes spotted two men on top of a telegraph pole outside the Munster and Leinster Bank. He ordered the two men to climb down and they were taken to the local RIC barracks. They gave their names as James Barry and Michael Casey, both of Fermoy. Casey was searched and a pair of pliers was found in his pocket. When questioned, they stated that they were putting a flag on the pole. The soldiers and police believed that they were about to cut the telephone lines to the local barracks. They were duly arrested.[2]
Brigade arrest No. 16 I.B. 158.
He was transferred from Kilworth Army Camp to Spike Island internment compound on 17 May 1921.
He was transferred to Maryborough (Portlaoise) Prison on the night of 18/19 Nov and released from there in Dec 1921.
See also: Casey, Michael, Fermoy.

Barry, James

5 Windsor Cottages, Cork City.
6th Division arrest No. 559.
Brigade arrest No. 17 I.B. 480.
He was transferred from Cork Male Gaol to Spike Island internment compound on 25 Apr 1921.

---

2   UKNA, Kew, London, CO 904/196/48.

He was transferred from Spike to Bere Island internment camp on 11 July 1921 on HMS *Vidette*.
Brother of internees Edmond and John.

Barry, James (Jim, Tough)

James (Tough) Barry, Morrough Terrace, Cork City.

49 Morrough Terrace, Evergreen Road, Cork City.
Age: 27. Brigade arrest No. 17 I.B. 468.
He was transferred from Cork Male Gaol to Spike Island internment compound on 12 Apr 1921.
He was transferred from Spike to Bere Island internment camp on 14/15 Apr 1921 by RN destroyer.
He was transferred from Bere Island back to Spike on 20 Sept on HMS *Stormcloud*, D 89.
He was transferred from Spike to Maryborough (Portlaoise) Prison on the night of 18/19 Nov and released from there in Dec 1921.

Barry, James Patrick

15 Marville Terrace, Evergreen Road, Cork City.

James Barry, Maiville Terrace, Evergreen Road, Cork City.

Age: 33.
Brigade arrest No. 17 I.B. 850.
He was transferred from Cork Male Gaol to Spike Island internment compound on 6 July 1921.
He was transferred to Maryborough (Portlaoise) Prison on the night of 18/19 Nov and released from there in Dec 1921.

Barry, John

13 Barrack Street, Cork City.
Brigade arrest No. 17 I.B. 507.
He was transferred from Cork Male Gaol to Spike Island internment compound on 12 Apr 1921.
He was transferred from Spike to Bere Island internment camp on 14/15 Apr 1921 by RN destroyer.

Barry, John

5 Windsor Cottages, Cork City.
6th Division arrest No. 560.
Brigade arrest No. 17 I.B. 482.
He was transferred from Cork Male Gaol to Spike Island internment

compound on 25 Apr 1921.
He was transferred from Spike to Bere
Island internment camp on 11 July
1921 on HMS *Vidette*.
Brother of internees Edmond and James.

Barry, Patrick

396 Blarney Lane, Cork City.
Age: 19.
6th Division arrest No. 789.
Brigade arrest No. 17 I.B. 606.
He was transferred from Cork Male
Gaol to Spike Island internment
compound on 15 July 1921, to 'A'
Block, Hut 16.
He was transferred to Maryborough
(Portlaoise) Prison on the night of
18/19 Nov and released from there in
Dec 1921.

Barry, Tadhg

Cork City.
He was transferred from Cork Male
Gaol to Spike Island internment
compound on 19 Feb 1921.

Beausang, Daniel

Kilmagner, Youghal, Co. Cork.
Age: 23.
6th Division arrest No. 829.
Brigade arrest No. 17 I.B. 919.
He was transferred from Cork Male
Gaol to Spike Island internment
compound on 15 July 1921, to 'A'
Block, Hut 15.
He was transferred to Maryborough
(Portlaoise) Prison on the night of

18/19 Nov and released from there in
Dec 1921.

Beckett, Thomas A.

Cromane House, Kilgarvan, Co. Kerry.
Age: 23.
Brigade arrest No. 17 I.B. 876.
He was transferred from the Brigade
Cage in Victoria Barracks, Cork, to
Spike Island internment compound on
30 June 1921.
He was transferred to Maryborough
(Portlaoise) Prison on the night of
18/19 Nov and released from there in
Dec 1921.

Beechinor, Thomas

Thomas Beechinor, Courtmacsherry,
Co. Cork.

Courtmacsherry, Co. Cork.
6th Division arrest No. 391.
Brigade arrest No. 17 I.B. 353.
He was transferred from Spike to Bere
Island internment camp on 11 July
1921 on HMS *Vidette*.

Begley, Eugene

Ballymurphy, Crossbarry, Bandon,

Maj. C.F. Kennedy, King's
Own Scottish Borderers, Camp
Commandant, Spike Island.

Fr Callanan, Prison Chaplain.

Spike Island internee Staff Officers, rear L to R: Michael Shelley, Richard
Barrett, Henry O'Mahony, Bill Quirke, John J. Dunne. Front, L to R:
Timothy Lehane, Thomas Griffin, Philip O'Donnell, J. McCarthy.

Capt. Michael Burke,
Cobh Company, IRA.

Vice-Comdt Michael Walsh,
Ballinhassig Company, IRA.

L to R: Sean Hyde, Ballinhassig; Capt. Jerome Crowley, Ballinhassig
Company IRA; Frank Barry, Cobh.

All five men assisted in the escape of the three prisoners from Spike Island
on 30 April 1921.

Spike Island prisoners, L to R: Lar Conroy, Cork City, Timmy Carey, Limerick City and Jerry Ryan, Upperchurch, Co. Tipperary.

Spike Island prisoners, L to R: James Keogh, William Bland, Michael Kelleher and Patrick Power, all from Youghal, Co. Cork.

Spike Island prisoners: 1. Michael Leamy, Thurles, 2. Thomas Dargan, Limerick City, 3.Diarmuid O'Leary, Killeagh, Co. Cork, 4. Father Callanan, Prison Chaplain and 5. Michael Hannafin, Tralee, Co. Kerry.

Type of hut used for 'B' Block, internment compound.

The plaque on
'A' Block
commemorating
the killing of
Capt. Patrick White.

ORDER UNDER MARTIAL LAW.

WHEREAS it appears to me that for securing the restoration and maintenance of Order in the Martial Law Area in Ireland, it is expedient that **John**

HENNESSY of **Ballynoe**

in the County of **Waterford**

should, in view of the fact that he is a person suspected of acting, having acted, and being about to act in a manner prejudicial to the restoration and maintenance of Order in the Martial Law Area in Ireland, be subjected to such obligations and restrictions as are hereinafter mentioned :

Now I HEREBY ORDER that the said **John HENNESSY**

shall be interned in **the Military Internment Camp at Spike or Bere Island** and shall be subject to all the rules and conditions applicable to persons there interned and shall remain there until further orders.

If within seven days from the date on which this Order is served on the said

John HENNESSY

he shall submit to me any representations against the provisions of this Order, such representation will have due consideration. If I am satisfied that this Order may be revoked or varied without injury to the restoration and maintenance of Order in the Martial Law Area in Ireland I will revoke or vary this Order by a further Order in writing under my hand. Failing such revocation or variation this Order shall remain in force.

Dated at CORK this 30 day of June 1921

Lieut Col
A.A.G

MAJOR-GENERAL,
Commanding 6th Division,
MILITARY GOVERNOR.

[OVER.

John Hennessy's Internment Order.

A tea cosy embroidered from an old rope by internee John Kelleher, Midleton, while on Spike Island.

Celtic-style jewellery made from coins by the internees and prisoners on Spike Island.

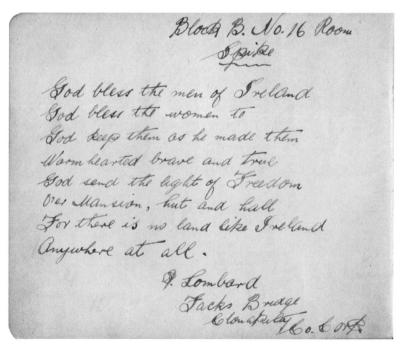

Block B. No. 16 Room
Spike

God bless the men of Ireland
God bless the women to
God keep them as he made them
Warm hearted brave and true
God send the light of Freedom
Over Mansion, hut and hall
For there is no land like Ireland
Anywhere at all.

P. Lombard
Jacks Bridge
Clonakilty Co. Cork

Patrick Lombard, Clonakilty, Co. Cork.

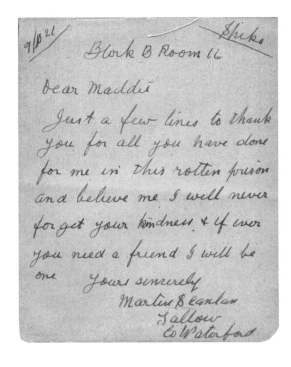

9/10/21   Spike

Block B Room 16

Dear Maddie

Just a few lines to thank
you for all you have done
for me in this rotten prison
and believe me I will never
forget your kindness. & if ever
you need a friend I will be
one   Yours sincerely
      Martin Scanlon.
       Tallow
        Co Waterford

Martin Scanlon, Tallow,
Co. Waterford.

Left: Florence O'Leary, Cork City.   Right: Pat Brady, Crosshaven, Co. Cork.

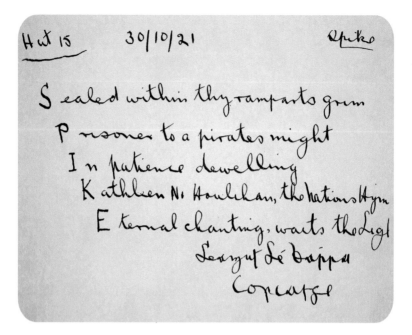

James Barry, Cork City.

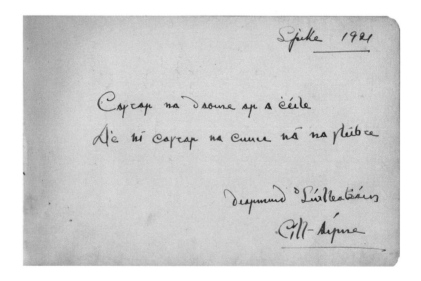

Jeremiah O'Sullivan, Killarney, Co. Kerry. Translation:

The people meet one another.

But the hills never meet, nor the mountains.

Co. Cork.

Age: 31.

6th Division arrest No. 605.

Brigade arrest No. 17 I.B. 572.

He was arrested at the end Apr 1921.

He was transferred from Cork Male
Gaol to Spike Island internment
compound on 30 Apr 1921, to 'A'
Block, Hut 16.[3]

He was transferred from Spike to Bere
Island internment camp on 11 July
1921 on HMS *Vidette*.

He was transferred back to
Spike Island and transferred to
Maryborough (Portlaoise) Prison on
the night of 18/19 Nov and released
from there in Dec 1921.

Behan, Michael

Lixnaw, Co. Kerry.

Age: 22.

Brigade arrest No. K.B. 296.

He was transferred from Cork
Military Detention Barracks to Spike
Island internment compound on
6 July 1921.

He was transferred from Spike to
Cork Military Hospital in Victoria
Barracks, Cork, on 21 July. He
returned to Spike from there on
11 Aug 1921.

He was transferred to Maryborough
(Portlaoise) Prison on the night of
18/19 Nov and released from there in
Dec 1921.

Bent, Nicholas

Ballycow, Banntown, Gorey,
Co. Wexford.

Age: 24.

Brigade arrest No. 16 I.B. 469.

He was transferred from Waterford
Gaol by RN destroyer to Spike Island
internment compound on 18 Aug 1921.

He was transferred to Maryborough
(Portlaoise) Prison on the night of
18/19 Nov and released from there in
Dec 1921.

Bohane, Edward (Ned)

Ballinspittle, Kinsale, Co. Cork.

Age: 20. Occupation: Farmer.

Brigade arrest No. 17 I.B. 103?

6th Division arrest No. 71.

While he was in the Spike prison
compound, he was served with an
Internment Order before his release
date. Instead of being released, he was
further detained as an internee.

He was transferred to Spike
internment compound on 20 Sept
1921, to 'A' Block, Hut 3.

He was transferred from Spike to
Maryborough (Portlaoise) Prison
on the night of 18/19 Nov. He was
released from there on 8 Dec 1921.

See Bohane, Ned, in the list of
Spike prisoners.

---

3   See Frank Neville, WS No. 443, p.15.

Boland, William

Lower Cork St, Mitchelstown and
Kilworth, Co. Cork.
Age: 34. Brigade arrest No. 16 I.B. 444.
He was transferred from Kilworth
Army Camp to Spike Island internment
compound on 15 Sept 1921.
He was transferred to Maryborough
(Portlaoise) Prison on the night of
18/19 Nov and released from there in
Dec 1921.

Bowen, Frank

Knockgorm, Ballinspittle, Kinsale,
Co. Cork.
Age: 21.
Brigade arrest No. 17 I.B. 1083.
He was arrested by Crown Forces on
4 Aug 1921.
He was transferred from Cork Male
Gaol to Spike Island internment
compound on 22 Aug 1921.
He was transferred to Maryborough
(Portlaoise) Prison on the night of
18/19 Nov and released from there in
Dec 1921.

Bowen, Michael

Knockgorm, Ballinspittle, Kinsale,
Co. Cork.
Brigade arrest No. 17 I.B. 470.
He was transferred from Cork Male
Gaol to Spike Island internment
compound on 12 Apr 1921.
He was transferred from Spike to Bere
Island internment camp on 14/15 Apr
1921 by RN destroyer.

Bowler, Michael

Fermoy, Co. Cork.
6th Division arrest No. 210.
He was transferred from Kilworth
Army Camp to Spike Island internment
compound on 13 Apr 1921.
He was transferred from Spike to Bere
Island internment camp on 14/15 Apr
1921 by RN destroyer.

Boyle, Patrick

John's Gate St, Wexford Town.
Age: 20.
Brigade arrest No. 16 I.B. 468.
He was transferred from Waterford
Gaol by RN destroyer to Spike Island
internment compound on 18 Aug
1921, to 'A' Block, Hut 11.
He was transferred to Maryborough
(Portlaoise) Prison on the night of
18/19 Nov and released from there in
Dec 1921.

Boyle, Thomas

Dungarvan, Co. Waterford.
6th Division arrest No. 129.
Brigade arrest No. 16 I.B. 129.
He was transferred from Kilworth
Army Camp to Spike Island internment
compound on 13 Apr 1921.
He was transferred from Spike to Bere
Island internment camp on 14/15 Apr
1921 by RN destroyer.

Brady, Michael

Bluepool, Kanturk, Co. Cork.
Age: 22.

6th Division arrest No. 777.
Brigade arrest No. K.B. 261.
He was transferred from Cork Male
Gaol to Spike Island internment
compound on 22 June 1921.

Brady, Pat

Crosshaven, Co. Cork and
13 North Main Street, Cork City.
Age: 43.
Brigade arrest No. 17 I.B. 931.
He was arrested by Crown Forces on
22 June 1921.
He was transferred from Cork Male
Gaol to Spike Island internment
compound on 30 June 1921.
He was transferred to Maryborough
(Portlaoise) Prison on the night of
18/19 Nov and released from there in
Dec 1921.

Breen, Jeremiah J.

Ballyconry, Lisselton, Ballybunnion,
Co. Kerry.
Age: 23.
6th Division arrest No. 866.
Brigade arrest No. K.B. 303.
He was transferred from Cork Male
Gaol to Spike Island internment
compound on 15 July 1921, to
'A' Block, Hut 5.
He was transferred to Maryborough
(Portlaoise) Prison on the night of
18/19 Nov and released from there in
Dec 1921.

Brennan, Edward

Rosslare Strand, Rosslare,
Co. Wexford.
Age: 25.
Brigade arrest No. 16 I.B. 185.
He was transferred from Kilworth
Army Camp to Spike Island
internment compound on 17 May
1921, to 'A' Block, Hut 18.
He was transferred to Maryborough
(Portlaoise) Prison on the night of
18/19 Nov and released from there in
Dec 1921.
Brother of internee George Brennan.

Brennan, Francis

Ballinadee, Co. Cork.
He was transferred from the Brigade
Cage in Victoria Barracks, Cork, to
Spike Island internment compound on
19 Feb 1921.

Brennan, George

Rosslare Strand, Rosslare, Co.
Wexford.
Brigade arrest No. 16 I.B. 184.
He was transferred from Kilworth
Army Camp to Spike Island internment
compound on 13 Apr 1921.
He was transferred from Spike to Bere
Island internment camp on 14/15 Apr
1921 by RN destroyer.
Brother of internee Edward Brennan.

Brennan, Matthew

Camolin, Co. Wexford.
Age: 25. Brigade arrest No. 16 I.B.

366. He was transferred from Cork to Spike Island internment compound on 6 July 1921, to 'A' Block, Hut 20. He was transferred to Maryborough (Portlaoise) Prison on the night of 18/19 Nov and released from there in Dec 1921.

Brett, John (Jack)

Knockinkit, Killenaule, Co. Tipperary.
Age: 22.
Brigade arrest No. 16 I.B. 114.
He was arrested on 15 Jan 1921 and taken to Tipperary Military Barracks. On 24 Jan he was moved to Kilworth Army Camp.
He was transferred from Kilworth Army Camp to Spike Island internment compound on 13 Apr 1921, to 'B' Block, Hut 10.
He was transferred from Spike to Bere Island internment camp on 14/15 Apr 1921 by RN destroyer.
He was transferred back to Spike from Bere Island on 20 Sept on HMS *Stormcloud*, D 89.
He was transferred to Maryborough (Portlaoise) Prison on the night of 18/19 Nov and released from there on 8 Dec 1921.

Brett, John (Sean)

Priors Knock, Waterford City.
Age: 24.
Occupation: Carpenter.
Brigade arrest No. 16 I.B. 431.
Following his arrest by Crown Forces, he was taken to Waterford Military Barracks. He was later moved to Kilworth Army Camp and to Cork Male Gaol.
He was transferred from Cork Male Gaol to Spike Island internment compound on 30 June 1921, to 'B' Block, Hut 20. He was later moved to 'A' Block, Hut 1.
He was transferred to Maryborough (Portlaoise) Prison on the night of 18/19 Nov and released from there in Dec 1921.

Brett, Richard

Richard Brett, Kilmachthomas, Co. Waterford.

Carrigcastle, Kilmacthomas, Co. Waterford.
Age: 24.
6th Division arrest No. 251.
Brigade arrest No. 16 I.B. 131.
He was transferred from Kilworth Army Camp to Spike Island internment compound on 5 Mar 1921. He was transferred from Spike to Bere Island internment camp on 11 July 1921 on HMS *Vidette*.

He was transferred back to Spike Island and transferred to Maryborough (Portlaoise) Prison on the night of 18/19 Nov and released from there in Dec 1921.

Buckley, David

Passage West, Co. Cork.
Brigade arrest No. 17 I.B. 243.
He was transferred from Cork Male Gaol to Spike Island internment compound on 24 Feb 1921.

Buckley, Jeremiah

Innishannon, Co. Cork.
Brigade arrest No. 17 I.B. 239.
He was captured by Crown Forces in Jan 1921.
He was transferred from the Brigade Cage in Victoria Barracks, Cork, to Spike Island internment compound on 19 Feb 1921.

Buckley, John

16 Dyke Parade, Cork City.
Occupation: Telegraphist in the General Post Office, Cork.
6th Division arrest No. 609.
Brigade arrest No. 17 I.B. 579.
He was transferred from Cork Male Gaol to Spike Island internment compound on 30 Apr 1921.
He was transferred from Spike to Bere Island internment camp on 11 July 1921 on HMS *Vidette*.

Buckley, John Leo

48 Sheares Street, Cork City.
Brigade arrest No. 17 I.B. 544.
He was the Intelligence Officer of 1 Cork Brigade, alias Jim Buckley. He was arrested in 1920 and lodged in the Brigade Cage in Victoria Barracks, Cork. He was taken to Cork Male Gaol and survived 94 days on hunger strike there from 11 Aug to 12 Nov 1920. After he recovered from the effects of his hunger strike, he was transferred from Cork Male Gaol to Spike Island internment compound on 25 Apr 1921. He was transferred from Spike to Bere Island internment camp and he escaped from there, date not found.[4]

Buckley, John

John Buckley, Millstreet, Co. Cork.

Ballinatona, Millstreet, Co. Cork.
Age: 31
6th Division arrest No. 772.
Brigade arrest No. K.B. 256.
He was transferred from Cork Male

---

4   See his WS, No. 1714.

Gaol to Spike Island internment compound on 22 June 1921.
He was transferred from Spike to Cork Military Hospital on 1 Sept 1921.
He was transferred to Maryborough (Portlaoise) Prison on the night of 18/19 Nov and released from there in Dec 1921.

Buckley, Patrick Francis (Frank)

2 Sharman Crawford Street, Cork City.
Age: 23.
Brigade arrest No. 17 I.B. 990.
He was transferred from the Brigade Cage in Victoria Barracks, Cork, to Spike Island internment compound on 30 June 1921, to 'A' Block, Hut 18.
He was transferred to Maryborough (Portlaoise) Prison on the night of 18/19 Nov and released from there in Dec 1921.

Buckley, Pat

Patrick Buckley, Araglin, Co. Cork.

Coolmohan, Araglin, Kilworth, Co. Cork.
Age: 26.
Brigade arrest No. 16 I.B. 412.

He was arrested on 30 Jan 1920 and taken to Fermoy Military Barracks and later to Cork Male Gaol. He was transferred to Wormwood Scrubs prison in London, where he went on hunger strike for 19 days. He was moved to St Mary's Infirmary, London, and released from there on 8 May 1920.
He was rearrested on 29 Apr 1921 and taken to Moore Park Army Camp, then to Fermoy Military Barracks, Kilworth Army Camp and later to Cork Male Gaol.
He was transferred from Cork Male Gaol to Spike Island internment compound on 30 June 1921, to 'B' Block, Hut 20. He was later moved to 'A' Block, Hut 1, during the Spike hunger strike.
He escaped from Spike on the night of 10/11 Nov 1921 with six other internees. See detailed account of their escape in this book.

Buckley, Stephen

Clonakilty, Co. Cork. Age: 23
Brigade arrest No. 17 I.B. 490.
He was arrested by Crown Forces, on 29 July 1921.
He was transferred from Cork Male Gaol to Spike Island internment compound on 22 Aug 1921, to 'A' Block, Hut 16.
He was transferred to Maryborough (Portlaoise) Prison on the night of 18/19 Nov and released from there in Dec 1921.

Burke, Martin

Main Street, Buttevant, Co. Cork.

Age: 25.

Occupation: Coachbuilder.

6th Division arrest No. 212.

Brigade arrest No. L.242.

He was transferred from Spike to Bere Island internment camp on 11 July 1921 on HMS *Vidette*.

He was transferred from Bere Island back to Spike on 20 Sept on HMS *Stormcloud*, D 89.

He was transferred from Spike to Maryborough (Portlaoise) Prison on the night of 18/19 Nov and released from there in Dec 1921.

Burke, Maurice

Horsemount, Kilcorney, Millstreet, Co. Cork.

Age: 23.

Brigade arrest No. K.B. 300.

He was transferred from Cork Male Gaol to Spike Island internment compound on 22 Aug 1921.

He was transferred to Maryborough (Portlaoise) Prison on the night of 18/19 Nov and released from there in Dec 1921.

Burke, Patrick

Durrow, Stradbally, Co. Waterford.

Age: 30.

Brigade arrest No. 16 I.B. 261.

He was arrested by British soldiers, near Durrow, Co. Waterford in Feb 1921. He was taken to Dungarvan Barracks, to Fermoy Military Barracks and to Kilworth Army Camp.[5]

He was transferred from Kilworth Army Camp to Spike Island internment compound. He was transferred from Spike to Bere Island internment camp, date not found. He was released from Bere Island in Dec 1921.

Butler, Daniel

Shanballymore, Mallow, Co. Cork.

Age: 27.

Brigade arrest No. 16 I.B. 379.

He was transferred from Cork to Spike Island internment compound on 6 July 1921, to 'B' Block, Hut 20. He was later moved to 'A' Block, Hut 10. He was moved again during the Spike hunger strike, to 'A' Block, Hut 2. He was transferred from Spike to Maryborough (Portlaoise) Prison on the night of 18/19 Nov and released from there in Dec 1921.

Butler, James

Ballyragget, Co. Kilkenny.

Age: 32.

Brigade arrest No. 16 I.B. 439.

He was transferred from Cork Male Gaol to Spike Island internment compound on 30 June 1921, to 'B' Block, Hut 20. He was moved to 'A' Block,

---

5 See Patrick Burke, WS No. 1131.

James Butler, Ballyragget, Co. Kilkenny.

Hut 2, during the Spike hunger strike. He was transferred to Maryborough (Portlaoise) Prison on the night of 18/19 Nov and released from there on 8 Dec 1921.

Butler, Matthew
Turtulla, Thurles, Co. Tipperary.
Age: 25.
6th Division arrest No. 133.
Brigade arrest No. 18 I.B. 145.
He was transferred from Cork Male Gaol to Spike Island internment compound on 12 Apr 1921, to 'A' Block, Hut 10.
He was transferred from Spike to Bere Island internment camp on 11 July 1921 on HMS *Vidette*.
He was transferred back to Spike Island and transferred to Maryborough (Portlaoise) Prison on the night of 18/19 Nov and released from there in Dec 1921.

Butler, Pat
Badgers Hill, Glenville, Watergrasshill, Co. Cork.

Age: 40.
Brigade arrest No. 16 I.B. 226.
He was transferred from Kilworth Army Camp to Spike Island internment compound on 17 May 1921, to 'A' Block, Hut 16.
He was transferred to Maryborough (Portlaoise) Prison on the night of 18/19 Nov and released from there in Dec 1921.

Byrne, James
Newtown, Camolin, Bridgetown, Co. Waterford.
Age: 23.
Brigade arrest No. 16 I.B. 483.
He was transferred from Waterford by RN destroyer to Spike Island internment compound on 18 Aug 1921, to 'A' Block, Hut 11.
He was transferred to Maryborough (Portlaoise) Prison on the night of 18/19 Nov and released from there in Dec 1921.

Byrne, Patrick
Castletown, Inch, Gorey, Co. Wexford.
Age: 25.
Brigade arrest No. 16 I.B. 498.
He was transferred from Waterford Gaol by RN destroyer to Spike Island internment compound on 18 Aug 1921.
He was transferred to Maryborough (Portlaoise) Prison on the night of 18/19 Nov and released from there in Dec 1921.

Byrne, Pierce
Charlotte Street, Wexford Town.
Age: 24. Occupation: Carpenter.
Brigade arrest No. 16 I.B. 306.
He was transferred from Kilworth
Army Camp to Spike Island internment
compound on 30 May 1921.
He was transferred to Maryborough
(Portlaoise) Prison on the night of
18/19 Nov and released from there in
Dec 1921.

Cahill, James
No address found.
Brigade arrest No. L.680.
He was transferred from Cork Military
Detention Barracks to Spike Island
internment compound on 9 June 1921.

Cahill, John
375 Blarney Street, Cork City.
Age: 18.
Brigade arrest No. 17 I.B. 1048.
He was transferred from the Brigade
Cage in Victoria Barracks, Cork, to
Spike Island internment compound on
6 July 1921.
He was transferred to Maryborough
(Portlaoise) Prison on the night of
18/19 Nov and released from there on
8 Dec 1921.

Cahill, Richard
Glengall, Ballingarry, Co. Tipperary.
6th Division arrest No. 741.

Brigade arrest No. 16 I.B. 356.
He was transferred from Kilworth
Army Camp to Spike Island
internment compound on 9 June 1921.
He was moved to 'A' Block, Hut 22,
during the Spike hunger strike.
He was transferred from Spike to
Maryborough (Portlaoise) Prison on
the night of 18/19 Nov and released
from there in Dec 1921.

Cahill, Richard (Dick)
Templemichael, Grangemockler,
Carrick-on-Suir, Co. Tipperary.
Age: 24.
Brigade arrest No. 16 I.B. 511.
He was transferred from Waterford
Gaol by RN destroyer to Spike Island
internment compound on 18 Aug
1921. He was moved to 'A' Block, Hut
22, during the Spike hunger strike.
He was transferred from Spike to
Maryborough (Portlaoise) Prison on
the night of 18/19 Nov and released
from there in Dec 1921.

Cahill, Thomas B. (Bob)
Cappahenry, Callan, Co. Kilkenny.
Brigade arrest No. 16 I.B. 386.
He was transferred from Fermoy
Military Barracks to Cork Military
Detention Barracks, on 24 June 1921.[6]
He was transferred from Cork Military
Detention Barracks to Spike Island
internment compound on 25 June 1921.

---

6   See Dan J. Stapleton, WS No. 1208.

Bob Cahill, Cappahenry, Co. Kilkenny.

He was moved to 'A' Block, Hut 22, during the Spike hunger strike.
He was transferred from Spike to Maryborough (Portlaoise) Prison on the night of 18/19 Nov and released from there in Dec 1921.

Cahill, William
Ballyderown, Kilworth, Co. Cork.
Age: 38.
He was arrested on 4 July 1921 and taken to Moore Park Army Camp and from there to Kilworth Army Camp.
Brigade arrest No. 16 I.B. 508.
He was transferred from Kilworth Army Camp to Spike Island internment compound on 15 Sept 1921, to 'B' Block, Hut 9 and later moved to Hut 19.
He was transferred to Maryborough (Portlaoise) Prison on the night of 18/19 Nov and released from there in Dec 1921.

Callaghan, Cornelius (Con)
Lombardstown, Banteer, Co. Cork.

Brigade arrest No. K.B. 190.
He was transferred from Cork Male Gaol to Spike Island internment compound on 16 May 1921.
He was transferred to Maryborough (Portlaoise) Prison on the night of 18/19 Nov and released from there in Dec 1921.

Callaghan, Jeremiah
Knockrour, Co. Cork.
6th Division arrest No. 542.
Brigade arrest No. 17 I.B. 174.
He was transferred from Cork Male Gaol to Spike Island internment compound on 25 Apr 1921.
He was transferred from Spike to Bere Island internment camp on 11 July 1921 on HMS *Vidette*.

Callaghan, John, alias John Lehane
Rathcool, Banteer, Co. Cork.
Brigade arrest No. K.B. 227.
He was transferred from Cork Male Gaol to Spike Island internment compound on 1 June 1921, to Hut 17.
He was moved to 'A' Block, Hut 2, during the Spike hunger strike.
He was transferred from Spike to Maryborough (Portlaoise) Prison on the night of 18/19 Nov and released from there in Dec 1921.

Callaghan, John
Kilmurray, Kenmare, Co. Kerry.
Brigade arrest No. 17 I.B. 877.

He was transferred from the Brigade Cage in Victoria Barracks, Cork, to Spike Island internment compound on 30 June 1921.

He was transferred to Maryborough (Portlaoise) Prison on the night of 18/19 Nov and released from there in Dec 1921.

Callaghan, Michael

Farranhavane, Bandon, Co. Cork.
6th Division arrest No. 571.
Brigade arrest No. 17 I.B. 426.
He was transferred to Spike, to be moved to Bere Island.
He was transferred from Spike to Bere Island internment camp on 11 July 1921 on HMS *Vidette*.

Callanan, John (Jack)

18 St Patrick's Terrace, Magazine Road, Cork City.
Age: 33.
Brigade arrest No. 17 I.B. 914.
He was transferred from Cork Male Gaol to Spike Island internment compound on 25 July 1921, to Hut 21, the internee hospital ward. He was transferred back to Spike and he was transferred to Maryborough (Portlaoise) Prison on the night of 18/19 Nov and released from there in Dec 1921.

Calnan, John

Pedlar's Cross, Ballinascarthy, Clonakilty, Co. Cork.

Brigade arrest No. 17 I.B. 233.
He was transferred from Cork Male Gaol to Spike Island internment compound on 19 Feb 1921.

Calnan, Laurence

Pedlar's Cross, Ballinascarthy, Clonakilty, Co. Cork.
Brigade arrest No. 17 I.B. 231.
He was transferred from Cork Male Gaol to Spike Island internment compound on 19 Feb 1921.

Caniffe, Patrick

Gaggin, Bandon, Co. Cork.
Brigade arrest No. 17 I.B. 209.
He was transferred from the Brigade Cage in Victoria Barracks, Cork, to Spike Island internment compound on 19 Feb 1921.

Carey, Patrick

27 Washington Street, Cork City.
6th Division arrest No. 586.
Brigade arrest No. 17 I.B. 546.
He was transferred from Cork Male Gaol to Spike Island internment compound on 30 Apr 1921.
He was transferred from Spike to Bere Island internment camp on 11 July 1921 on HMS *Vidette*.

Carmody, Maurice

Lisselton, Ballybunion, Co. Kerry.
Age: 32.
6th Division arrest No. 867.
Brigade arrest No. K.B. 304.

He was transferred from Cork Male
Gaol to Spike Island internment
compound on 15 July 1921.
He was transferred to Maryborough
(Portlaoise) Prison on the night of
18/19 Nov and released from there in
Dec 1921.

Carmody, Patrick
Tubridmore, Ardfert, Co. Kerry.
6th Division arrest No. 558.
Brigade arrest No. K.B. 138.
He was transferred from Cork Male
Gaol to Spike Island internment
compound on 25 Apr 1921.
He was transferred from Spike to Bere
Island internment camp on 11 July
1921 on HMS *Vidette*.

Carroll, Dan
Castleinch, Ovens, Co. Cork.
Age: 38. Occupation: Farmer.
Brigade arrest No. 17 I.B. 1161.
He was captured by soldiers from
the Manchester Regiment near
Ballincollig, Co. Cork, in June
1921 and taken to Ballincollig Army
Barracks. In mid-July, he was taken
to the Brigade Cage in Victoria
Barracks and later to Cork
Male Gaol.[7]
He was transferred from Cork Male
Gaol to Spike Island internment
compound on 25 July 1921, to 'A'
Block, Hut 9.

Dan Carroll, Ovens, Co. Cork.

He was transferred from Spike to
Maryborough (Portlaoise) Prison on
the night of 18/19 Nov and released
from there on 8 Dec 1921.

Carroll, Daniel (David)
25 Fitzgerald Place, Cork City.
6th Division arrest No. 597.
Brigade arrest No. 17 I.B. 526.
He was transferred from Cork Male
Gaol to Spike Island internment
compound on 30 Apr 1921.
He was transferred from Spike to Bere
Island internment camp on 11 July
1921 on HMS *Vidette*.

Carroll, Denis
Cloughduv, Crookstown, Co. Cork.
Age: 26.
Brigade arrest No. 17 I.B. 1131.
He was transferred from Cork Male
Gaol to Spike Island internment
compound on 25 July 1921, to 'A'
Block, Hut 9.

---

7   See Timothy O'Keeffe, WS No. 810.

Carroll, Jeremiah F.

Shannon Street, Bandon, Co. Cork.
Age: 21.
Brigade arrest No. 17 I.B. 1122.
He was transferred from Cork Male
Gaol to Spike Island internment
compound on 25 July 1921, to 'A'
Block, Hut 19.

Carroll, Thomas

Clonagoose, Mullinahone, Co.
Tipperary.
He was transferred from Spike to
Maryborough (Portlaoise) Prison on
the night of 18/19 Nov and released
from there in Dec 1921. No other
details found.

Casey, Cornelius

Balynoe, Co. Cork.
Age: 20.
Brigade arrest No. 16 I.B 486.
He was arrested by Crown Forces
on 17 Jan 1921 and held in Fermoy
Military Barracks for five weeks.

Cornelius Patrick Casey, Ballynoe,
Co. Waterford.

He was tried by Summary Court, for
not giving information to the Crown
Forces, and sentenced to six months
imprisonment in Cork Male Gaol. At
the end of his sentence, instead of being
released, he was sentenced to internment.
He was transferred from Cork Male
Gaol to Spike Island internment
compound on 25 July 1921. He was
moved to 'A' Block, Hut 2, during the
hunger strike.
He was transferred from Spike to
Maryborough (Portlaoise) Prison on
the night of 18/19 Nov and released
from there in Dec 1921.

Casey, Eugene

Kinsale, Co. Cork.
6th Division arrest No. 579.
Brigade arrest No. 17 I.B. 359.
He was transferred from Cork Male
Gaol to Spike Island internment
compound on 28 May 1921.
He was transferred from Spike to
Cork Military Hospital in Victoria
Barracks on 21 July 1921.

Casey, Finbarr Patrick

Kileens, Commons Road, Cork City.
6th Division arrest No. 716.
Brigade arrest No. 17 I.B. 515.
He was transferred from Cork Male
Gaol to Spike Island internment
compound on 28 May 1921. He was
moved to 'A' Block, Hut 20, during the
Spike hunger strike.
He was transferred from Spike to

Maryborough (Portlaoise) Prison on the night of 18/19 Nov and released from there in Dec 1921.

Casey, John Bernard

Kileens, Commons Road, Cork City.
Occupation: Gas fitter.
6th Division arrest No. 717.
Brigade arrest No. 17 I.B. 513.
He was transferred from Cork Male Gaol to Spike Island internment compound on 28 May 1921, to 'A' Block, Hut 20.
He was transferred to Maryborough (Portlaoise) Prison on the night of 18/19 Nov and released from there in Dec 1921.

Casey, Michael Joseph

2 Clancy Street, Fermoy, Co. Cork.
Age: 21.
On the night of 4/5 June 1920, a British Army mobile patrol, under the command of Lt G.T. Milnes, drove into The Square in Fermoy. The lead vehicle was an armoured car. Lt Milnes spotted two men on top of a telegraph pole outside the Munster and Leinster Bank. He ordered the two men to climb down and they were taken to the local RIC barracks. They gave their names as Michael Casey and James Barry, both of Fermoy. Casey was searched and a pair of pliers was found in his pocket. When questioned

Michael Casey, Fermoy, Co. Cork.

they stated that they were putting a flag on the pole. The soldiers and police believed that they were about to cut the telephone lines to the local barracks. They were duly arrested.[8]
Brigade arrest No. 16 I.B. 157.
He was transferred from Kilworth Army Camp to Spike Island internment compound on 17 May 1921.
He was released from Spike on 5 Nov, authority received from CA 1068 on 4 Nov 1921.
See also: Barry, James, Fermoy.

Casey, Peter

Blarney Street, Cork City.
Brigade arrest No. 17 I.B. 467.
He was transferred from Cork Male Gaol to Spike Island internment compound on 12 Apr 1921.
He was transferred from Spike to Bere Island internment camp on 14/15 Apr 1921 by RN destroyer.

---

8   UKNA, Kew, London, CO 904/196/48.

Casey, Thomas

35 Stephens Street, Waterford City.
Occupation: Tailor.
Brigade arrest No. 16 I.B. 309.
He was transferred from Cork Military
Detention Barracks to Spike Island
internment compound on 25 June 1921.
He was transferred to Maryborough
(Portlaoise) Prison on the night of
18/19 Nov and released from there in
Dec 1921.

Casey, Thomas A.

Lixnaw, Co. Kerry.
Age: 20.
Brigade arrest No. K.B. 295.
He was transferred from Cork
Military Detention Barracks to Spike
Island internment compound on
6 July 1921, to 'A' Block, Hut 5.
He was transferred to Maryborough
(Portlaoise) Prison on the night of
18/19 Nov and released from there in
Dec 1921.

Casey, Tom

11 Skeffington St, Wexford Town.
He was arrested by Crown Forces
on 7 Jan 1921 and taken to Wexford
Military Barracks. On 4 Feb, he was
moved to Waterford Gaol. On 10 Apr,
he was moved to Kilworth Army
Camp and later to Fermoy Military
Barracks. He was transferred from
Fermoy Military Barracks to Cork
Military Detention Barracks on
24 June 1921.

He was transferred from Cork
Military Detention Barracks to Spike
Island internment compound on
25 June 1921, to 'A' Block, Hut 18.

Cashman, James

Guileen, Whitegate, Co. Cork.
Age: 26.
Brigade arrest No. 17 I.B. 1020.
He was sentenced to 14 days in
gaol. On completion of his sentence
he was served with an Internment
Order and thus remained in custody.
He was transferred from Cork Male
Gaol to Spike Island internment
compound on 25 July 1921, to 'A'
Block, Hut 9.
He was transferred to Maryborough
(Portlaoise) Prison on the night of
18/19 Nov and released from there in
Dec 1921.

Cassidy, John

Callan, Co. Kilkenny.
6th Division arrest No. 259.
He was transferred from Kilworth
Army Camp to Spike Island internment
compound on 13 Apr 1921.
He was transferred from Spike to Bere
Island internment camp on 14/15 Apr
1921 by RN destroyer.

Clair, Michael

C/O Mrs Roche, Church St,
Ennistymon, Co. Clare.
Age: 37.
Brigade arrest No. 18 I.B. 206.

He was arrested by Crown Forces on 18 July 1921.

He was transferred from Cork Male Gaol to Spike Island internment compound on 25 July 1921, to 'A' Block, Hut 19.

He was transferred to Maryborough (Portlaoise) Prison on the night of 18/19 Nov and released from there in Dec 1921.

Clancy, Dan

Farrengeel```, Kanturk, Co. Cork.

Brigade arrest No. K.B. 238.

He was transferred from Cork Male Gaol to Spike Island internment compound on 1 June 1921.

In the aftermath of a disturbance on Spike, he was shot in the foot by a British soldier, resulting in the loss of his big toe. He was transferred to Cork Military Hospital in Victoria Barracks on 20 Sept. He died there of sepsis, on 11 Nov 1921.[9]

Clifford, Jerry

Ballyarthur, Mitchelstown, Co. Cork.

6th Division arrest No. 259.

Brigade arrest No. 16 I.B. 139.

He was transferred from Spike to Bere Island internment camp on 11 July 1921 on HMS *Vidette*.

Jerry Clifford, Mitchelstown, Co. Cork.

Cloke, John

Merristown, Rosslare, Co. Wexford.

No other details.

He was transferred from Spike to Maryborough (Portlaoise) Prison on the night of 18/19 Nov and released from there in Dec 1921.

Coakley, Patrick

Upton, Bandon, Co. Cork.

Brigade arrest No. 17 I.B. 345.

He was transferred from Cork Male Gaol to Spike Island internment compound on 25 Apr 1921.

Cody, William (Bill)

Clonagoose, Mullinahone, Co. Tipperary.

6th Division arrest No. 211.

He is listed as being in 'A' Block, Hut 22, during the Spike hunger strike.

He was transferred to Maryborough (Portlaoise) Prison on the night of 18/19 Nov and released from there in Dec 1921.

---

9   Barry Keane, *Cork's Revolutionary Dead, 1916–1923*, p.280, see also Timothy O'Keeffe, WS No. 810, pp.19–21.

Cogan, Robert

Mardyke, Cork City.

Age: 18.

Brigade arrest No. 17 I.B. 770.

He was transferred from Cork Male Gaol to Spike Island internment compound on 22 Aug 1921, to 'B' Block, Hut 20.

Cogan, Stephen

Crosshaven, Co. Cork.

Brigade arrest No. 17 I.B. 500.

He was transferred from Cork Male Gaol to Spike Island internment compound on 12 Apr 1921.

He was transferred from Spike to Bere Island internment camp on 14/15 Apr 1921 by RN destroyer.

Cohalan (Coughlan), Thomas

Charles Fort, Ballinspittle, Kinsale, Co. Cork.

Age: 36. Occupation: Carpenter.

6th Division arrest No. 65.

While he was in the Spike prison compound, he was served with an Internment Order before his release date. Instead of being released, he was further detained as an internee. He was transferred to Spike internment compound. He was moved to 'A' Block, Hut 3, during the Spike hunger strike.

He was transferred from Spike to Maryborough (Portlaoise) Prison on the night of 18/19 Nov and released from there on 8 Dec 1921.

See Cohalan, Thomas, in the list of Spike prisoners.

Coleman, Charles

Ballymurphy, Upton, Co. Cork.

Age: 28.

6th Division arrest No. 565.

Brigade arrest No. 17 I.B. 499.

He was transferred from Cork Male Gaol to Spike Island internment compound on 30 Apr 1921.

He was transferred from Spike to Bere Island internment camp on 11 July 1921 on HMS *Vidette*.

He was transferred from Bere Island back to Spike on 20 Sept on HMS *Stormcloud*, D 89.

He was transferred from Spike to Maryborough (Portlaoise) Prison on the night of 18/19 Nov and released from there in Dec 1921.

Coleman, Jerome

3 Church Avenue, Blackrock, Cork City.

6th Division arrest No. 300.

Brigade arrest No. 16 I.B. 164.

He was transferred from Kilworth Army Camp to Spike Island internment compound on 4 Mar 1921.

He was transferred from Spike to Bere Island internment camp on 11 July 1921 on HMS *Vidette*.

Coleman, Nicholas

Cork Hill, Youghal, Co. Cork.

6th Division arrest No. 443.

Brigade arrest No. 17 I.B. 375.
He was transferred from Spike to Bere
Island internment camp on 11 July
1921 on HMS *Vidette*.

Colleton, Patrick
Also listed as Collerton.
Greystone St, Carrick-on-Suir,
Co. Tipperary.
Age: 20.
Brigade arrest No. 16 I.B. 527.
He was transferred from Waterford
Gaol by RN destroyer to Spike Island
internment compound on 18 Aug
1921, to 'A' Block, Hut 11.

Collins, Cornelius
Cork City.
Brigade arrest No. 17 I.B. 179.
He was transferred from Cork Male
Gaol to Spike Island internment
compound on 19 Feb 1921.

Collins, Denis
Oldcourt, Kinsale, Co. Cork.
In Jan 1921 he was arrested at home by
British soldiers of the Essex Regiment.
He was taken to Kinsale Barracks, on to
Charles Fort and moved to the Brigade
Cage in Victoria Barracks, Cork.[10]
He was transferred from the Brigade
Cage to Spike Island internment
compound during Mar 1921.
He was transferred from Spike to Bere

Island internment camp on 28 May
and released from there in Dec 1921.

Collins, John M. (Sean)
Woodfield, Clonakilty, Co. Cork.
Age: 43.
Brigade arrest No. 17 I.B. 616.
He was transferred from the Brigade
Cage in Victoria Barracks to Spike
Island internment compound on
16 May 1921, to 'A' Block, Hut 16.
He was transferred from Spike to Cork
Military Hospital in Victoria Barracks
on 12 Oct 1921 to receive treatment
for rheumatic arthritis in his hand.[11]
Brother of *the* Michael Collins.

Collins, John (Sean)
Lislevane, Co. Cork.
6th Division arrest No. 181.
He was transferred from Cork Male
Gaol to Spike Island internment
compound on 25 Apr 1921.
He was transferred from Spike to Bere
Island internment camp on 11 July
1921 on HMS *Vidette*.

Collins, Michael
Inchingerif, Drimoleague, Co. Cork.
6th Division arrest No. 502.
Brigade arrest No. 17 I.B. 424.
He was transferred from Spike Island
to Bere Island internment camp on
11 July 1921 on HMS *Vidette*.

10 See his WS, No. 827.
11 See Richard O'Connell, WS No. 656, p.28.

Collins, Michael

Kilbrittain, Bandon, Co. Cork.
He was transferred from Cork Male
Gaol to Spike Island internment
compound on 19 Feb 1921.

Collins, Patrick

15 Clancy Street, Fermoy, Co. Cork.
6th Division arrest No. 201.
He was transferred from Kilworth
Army Camp to Spike Island
internment compound on
13 Apr 1921.
He was transferred from Spike to Bere
Island internment camp on 14/15 Apr
1921 by RN destroyer.

Collins, Peter

Rockchaple, Meelin, Co. Cork.
Brigade arrest No. K.B. 237.
He was transferred from Kilworth
Army Camp to Spike Island
internment compound on 1 June 1921,
to 'A' Block, Hut 6.
He was transferred to Maryborough
(Portlaoise) Prison on the night of
18/19 Nov and released from there in
Dec 1921.

Collins, Richard

Barryroe, Skibbereen, Co. Cork.
He was transferred from Cork Male
Gaol to Spike Island internment
compound on 19 Feb 1921.

Colivet, Michael Patrick TD

Michael P. Colivet TD, Limerick City.

Castleview Avenue, Limerick City.
Brigade arrest No. 18 I.B. 165.
He was transferred from Cork Male
Gaol to Spike Island internment
compound on 11 May 1921.
As an elected TD, he received early
released from Spike internment
compound on 8 Aug 1921 to
enable him to participate in the
Dáil debates on the proposed Treaty
negotiations. The authority for his
release came from the General Officer
Commanding (GOC) 6th Division,
Gen. Strickland.[12]

Condon, Daniel

Monkstown, Co. Cork.
6th Division arrest No. 240.
Brigade arrest No. 17 I.B. 177.
He was transferred from Cork Male
Gaol to Spike Island internment
compound on 24 Feb 1921.
He was released from Spike on 5 Nov,
authority received from CA 1068.

---

12 UKNA, Kew, London, WO 35/144, Register of the Spike Island Internees.

Condon, Martin

Martin Condon, Rathcormac,
Co. Cork.

Guthroe, Clykeel, Rathcormac,
Co. Cork.
Brigade arrest No. 16 I.B. 89.
He was transferred from Cork
Military Hospital, in Victoria
Barracks, to Spike Island internment
compound on 9 June 1921, to 'A'
Block, Hut 15.
He was transferred to Maryborough
(Portlaoise) Prison on the night of
18/19 Nov and released from there in
Dec 1921.

Condon, Richard

Monkstown, Co. Cork.
6th Division arrest No. 241.
Brigade arrest No. 17 I.B. 176.
He was transferred from Cork Male
Gaol to Spike Island internment
compound on 24 Feb 1921.

Condon, Thomas

Rathcormac, Co. Cork.
Age: 20.
Brigade arrest No. 16 I.B. 484.

He was arrested by Crown Forces on
15 July 1921.
He was transferred from Cork Male
Gaol to Spike Island internment
compound on 25 July 1921. He was
moved to 'A' Block, Hut 2, during the
Spike hunger strike.
He was transferred from Spike to
Maryborough (Portlaoise) Prison on
the night of 18/19 Nov and released
from there in Dec 1921.

Connaire, Pat

2 John's St, Wexford Town.
Age: 21.
Brigade arrest No. 16 I.B. 471.
He was transferred from Waterford
Gaol by RN destroyer to Spike Island
internment compound on 18 Aug
1921, to 'A' Block, Hut 11.

Connell, Michael

Eyeries, Castletownbere, Co. Cork.
Age: 22.
6th Division arrest No. 845.
Brigade arrest No. 17 I.B. 985.
He was transferred from Cork Male
Gaol to Spike Island internment
compound on 15 July 1921.

Connell, William

Ballinacurra, Midleton, Co. Cork.
Brigade arrest No. 17 I.B. 292.
He was transferred from the Brigade
Cage in Victoria Barracks, Cork, to
Spike Island internment compound on
24 Feb 1921.

Connolly, Felix

Fernhill, Clonakilty, Co. Cork.

6th Division arrest No. 374.

Brigade arrest No. 17 I.B. 308.

He was transferred from Cork Male Gaol to Spike Island internment compound on 24 Feb 1921.

He was transferred from Spike to Bere Island internment camp on 11 July 1921 on HMS *Vidette*.

Connolly, John

Fernhill, Clonakilty, Co. Cork.

6th Division arrest No. 373.

Brigade arrest No. 17 I.B. 307.

He was transferred from Cork Male Gaol to Spike Island internment compound on 24 Feb 1921.

He was transferred from Spike to Bere Island internment camp on 11 July 1921 on HMS *Vidette*.

Connolly, Michael

Rossduff, Kilcop, Glenmore, Co. Kilkenny.

6th Division arrest No. 319.

Brigade arrest No. 16 I.B. 195.

He was transferred from Cork Male Gaol to Spike Island internment compound on 28 May 1921, to 'B' Block, Hut 23. He was moved to 'A' Block, Hut 22, during the Spike hunger strike.

He was transferred from Spike to Maryborough (Portlaoise) Prison on the night of 18/19 Nov and released from there in Dec 1921.

Connor, Edward

Ballydonegan, Castletownbere, Co. Cork.

Age: 18.

Brigade arrest No. 17 I.B. 1177.

He was arrested by Crown Forces for membership of the IRA and he was recommended for internment.

He was transferred from Cork Male Gaol to Spike Island internment compound on 25 July 1921, to 'A' Block, Hut 4.

He was transferred to Maryborough (Portlaoise) Prison on the night of 18/19 Nov and released from there in Dec 1921.

Connor, James Patrick

Allihies Mines, Castletownbere, Co. Cork.

Age: 17.

Brigade arrest No. 17 I.B. 1172.

He was arrested by Crown Forces for membership of IRA and recommended for internment.

He was transferred from Cork Male Gaol to Spike Island internment compound on 25 July 1921, to 'A' Block, Hut 4.

He was transferred to Maryborough (Portlaoise) Prison on the night of 18/19 Nov and released from there in Dec 1921.

Connors, James

Address not found.

Brigade arrest No. 18 I.B. 186.

He was transferred from Cork Male

Gaol to Spike Island internment compound on 11 May 1921.

Conry, Thomas
Esker, Jenkinstown, Co. Kilkenny.
Age: 26.
He was arrested on 12 Apr 1921 and taken to Castlecomer. From there to Kilkenny Army Barracks, to Kilkenny Gaol, and after nine weeks he was taken to Kilworth Army Camp.
Brigade arrest No. 16 I.B. 442.
He was transferred from Kilworth Army Camp to Spike Island internment compound on 15 Sept 1921, to 'B' Block, Hut 19.
He was transferred from Spike to Maryborough (Portlaoise) Prison on the night of 18/19 Nov and released from there in Dec 1921.

Considine, Martin
Main Street, Ennistymon, Co. Clare.
Age: 28.
Brigade arrest No. 18 I.B. 208.
He was arrested by Crown Forces on 18 July 1921.
He was transferred from Cork Male Gaol to Spike Island internment compound on 25 July 1921.
He was transferred to Maryborough (Portlaoise) Prison on the night of 18/19 Nov and released from there in Dec 1921.

Conway, James
Abbey Street, Cahir, Co. Tipperary.

Age: 22.
He was arrested in Waterford on 29 May 1921 and transferred to Kilworth on 20 Aug.
Brigade arrest No. 16 I.B. 470.
He was transferred from Kilworth Army Camp to Spike Island internment compound on 15 Sept 1921.
He was transferred from Spike to Maryborough (Portlaoise) Prison on the night of 18/19 Nov and released from there in Dec 1921.

Conway, Patrick
Christendon, Ferrybank, Waterford City.
Age: 20.
Brigade arrest No. 16 I.B. 512.
He was transferred from Waterford Gaol by RN destroyer to Spike Island internment compound on 18 Aug 1921.
He was transferred to Maryborough (Portlaoise) Prison on the night of 18/19 Nov and released from there in Dec 1921.

Cooney, Jimmy
Lombardstown, Mallow, Co. Cork.
He was transferred to Spike Island internment compound, date not found, to 'A' Block, Hut 17.

Corcoran, Eugene
Brown Mills, Kinsale, Co. Cork.
6th Division arrest No. 490.
Brigade arrest No. 17 I.B. 413.
He was transferred from Cork Male

Gaol to Spike Island internment compound on 30 Apr 1921.
He was transferred from Spike to Bere Island internment camp on 11 July 1921 on HMS *Vidette*.

Corcoran, Michael

Glasshouse, Curraglass, Co. Cork.
Age: 46.
He was arrested by Crown Forces on 9 July 1921 and on 22 July he was taken to Kilworth Army Camp.
He was transferred from Kilworth Army Camp to Spike Island internment compound on 16 Sept.
He was transferred from Spike to Maryborough (Portlaoise) Prison on the night of 18/19 Nov and released from there in Dec 1921.

Corkery, Charlie

Lower New Street, Killarney, Co. Kerry.
Brigade arrest No. K.B. 146.
He was arrested by Crown Forces on 23 Mar 1921.
He was transferred from Cork Male Gaol to Spike Island internment compound on 16 May 1921.

Corkery, Pat

10 Friar Street, Cork City.
Brigade arrest No. 17 I.B. 927.
He was arrested by Crown Forces on 22 June 1921.
He was transferred from Cork Male Gaol to Spike Island internment compound on 30 June 1921, to 'B'

Block, Hut 17.
He was transferred to Maryborough (Portlaoise) Prison on the night of 18/19 Nov and released from there in Dec 1921.

Corkery, Thomas

Ballinadee, Co. Cork.
6th Division arrest No. 348.
Brigade arrest No. 17 I.B. 192.
He was transferred from Spike to Bere Island internment camp on 11 July 1921 on HMS *Vidette*.

Cosgrove, Joseph

Ballynookera, Whitegate, Co. Cork.

Joseph Cosgrove, Whitegate, Co. Cork.

Occupation: Estate labourer.
6th Division arrest No. 577.
Brigade arrest No. 17 I.B. 438.
He was transferred from Spike to Bere Island internment camp on 11 July 1921 on HMS *Vidette*.

Cotter, Lawrence F.

30 Abbey Street, Cork City.
Brigade arrest No. 17 I.B. 977.
He was transferred from the Brigade

Cage in Victoria Barracks to Spike Island internment compound on 30 June 1921, to 'A' Block, Hut 17. He was transferred to Maryborough (Portlaoise) Prison on the night of 18/19 Nov and released from there in Dec 1921.

Cotter, Michael
Curraglass, Co. Cork.
Age: 23.
He was arrested on 9 July and taken to Fermoy Military Barracks and from there to Kilworth Army Camp.
Brigade arrest No. 16 I.B. 521.
He was transferred from Kilworth Army Camp to Spike Island internment compound on 16 Sept 1921.
He was transferred from Spike to Maryborough (Portlaoise) Prison on the night of 18/19 Nov and released from there in Dec 1921.

Cottrell, William
Dobbins Hill, Inistioge, Co. Kilkenny.
He was in the Spike internment compound on 25 Oct 1921. During the Spike hunger strike he was in 'A' Block, Hut 22.
He was transferred from Spike to Maryborough (Portlaoise) Prison on the night of 18/19 Nov and released from there in Dec 1921.

Coughlan, Charles
Cork City.
Brigade arrest No. 17 I.B. 182.

He was transferred from Cork Male Gaol to Spike Island internment compound on 19 Feb 1921.

Coughlan, Cornelius
Ballinspittle, Co. Cork.
6th Division arrest No. 306.
Brigade arrest No. 17 I.B. 103.
He was transferred from Cork Male Gaol to Spike Island internment compound on 24 Feb 1921.
He was transferred from Spike to Bere Island internment camp on 11 July 1921 on HMS *Vidette*.

Coughlan, John
Lislevane, Co. Cork.
He was transferred from Cork Male Gaol to Spike Island internment compound on 19 Feb 1921.

Coughlan, James Joseph
74 Evergreen Road, Cork City.
6th Division arrest No. 715.
Brigade arrest No. 17 I.B. 746.
He was transferred from Cork Male Gaol to Spike Island internment compound on 28 May 1921. He was moved to 'A' Block, Hut 15, during the Spike hunger strike.
He was transferred from Spike to Maryborough (Portlaoise) Prison on the night of 18/19 Nov and released from there in Dec 1921.

Coughlan, Pat
Mount Long, Belgooly, Co. Cork.

6th Division arrest No. 501.
Brigade arrest No. 17 I.B. 422.
He was transferred to Spike, to be
moved to Bere Island, date not found.
He was transferred from Spike to Bere
Island internment camp on 11 July
1921 on HMS *Vidette*.

Coughlan, Patrick

Lislevane, Co. Cork.
He was transferred from Cork Male
Gaol to Spike Island internment
compound on 19 Feb 1921.

Coughlan, Patrick

Mondaniel, Rathcormac, Co. Cork.
Age: 22.
He was arrested on 14 June and taken
to Fermoy Military Barracks and from
there to Kilworth on 29 June.
Brigade arrest No. 16 I.B. 479.
He was transferred from Kilworth
Army Camp to Spike Island internment
compound on 15 Sept 1921.
He was transferred from Spike to
Maryborough (Portlaoise) Prison on
the night of 18/19 Nov and released
from there in Dec 1921.

Courtney, Christopher

Killarney, Co. Kerry.
He was transferred from Cork Male
Gaol to Spike Island internment
compound on 19 Feb 1921.

Courtney, Patrick

Home Farm, Killarney, Co. Kerry.

Brigade arrest No. K.B. 178.
He was transferred from Cork Male
Gaol to Spike Island internment
compound on 11 May 1921.

Cowhey, James

Churchtown, Buttevant, Co. Cork.
Brigade arrest No. K.B. 82.
He was transferred from Cork Male
Gaol to Spike Island internment
compound on 24 Feb 1921.

Cox, William John

Jerpoint Church, Thomastown,
Co. Kilkenny.
Brigade arrest No. 16 I.B. 182.
He was transferred from Kilworth
Army Camp to Spike Island
internment compound on 4 Mar 1921.

Coyne, William Joseph

15 Liberty Street, Cork City.
Brigade arrest No. 17 I.B. 691.
He was transferred from Cork Male
Gaol to Spike Island internment
compound on 28 May 1921, to 'A'
Block, Hut 16.
He was transferred to Maryborough
(Portlaoise) Prison on the night of
18/19 Nov and released from there in
Dec 1921.

Crimmins, John D.

Kilbolane, Milford, Charleville,
Co. Cork.
Age: 20.
Brigade arrest No. K.B. 154.

He was arrested by British soldiers at Kilbolane on 1 Apr 1921. He was taken to Buttevant Military Barracks and from there to Cork Male Gaol.[13] He was transferred from Cork Male Gaol to Spike Island internment compound on 16 May.

He was transferred from Spike to Bere Island internment camp, and released from Bere Island on 10 Dec 1921.

Crimmins, Timothy
Kilbolane, Milford, Charleville, Co. Cork.
Brigade arrest No. K.B 153.
He was arrested by British soldiers at Kilbolane on 1 Apr 1921. He was taken to Buttevant Military Barracks and from there to Cork Male Gaol.[14] He was transferred from Cork Male Gaol to Spike Island internment compound on 16 May.
He was transferred from Spike to Bere Island internment camp. He was released from Bere Island on 10 Dec 1921.

Crofts, Tom
alias Tom Flavin
College Road, Cork City.
He was arrested and interned under the alias Tom Flavin.
Age: 29
6th Division arrest No. 424 & 592.

Tom Crofts, College Road, Cork City.

Brigade arrest No. 17 I.B. 532.
He was tried by Court Martial in Victoria Barracks Cork on 4 Mar 1921 for illegal possession of a revolver. He was found not guilty. He was served with an Internment Order, thus remained in custody.
He was transferred from Cork Male Gaol to Spike Island internment compound on 30 Apr 1921, to 'A' Block, Hut 16.
He was transferred from Spike to Bere Island internment camp on 11 July 1921 on HMS *Vidette*.
He was transferred back to Spike and on the night of 10/11 Nov 1921 he escaped with six other internees.
See detailed account of their escape in this book.

Croke, Ned
Ballinure, Co. Tipperary.
Age: 28.
Brigade arrest No. 16 I.B. 143.
He was transferred to Spike Island

---

13 See his WS, No. 1039.
14 See his WS, No. 1051.

internment compound, date not found.
He was transferred from Spike to Bere
Island internment camp on 14/15 Apr
1921 by RN destroyer.
He was transferred from Bere Island
back to Spike on 20 Sept on HMS
Stormcloud, D 89.
He was transferred from Spike to
Maryborough (Portlaoise) Prison on
the night of 18/19 Nov and released
from there in Dec 1921.

Croke, Patrick

Dungarvan, Co. Waterford.
6th Division arrest No. 179.
He was transferred from Kilworth
Army Camp to Spike Island internment
compound on 13 Apr 1921.
He was transferred from Spike to
Bere Island internment camp by RN
destroyer on 14/15 Apr 1921.

Cronin, Arthur

Belgooley, Kinsale, Co. Cork.
6th Division arrest No. 666.
Brigade arrest No. 17 I.B. 696.
He was transferred from Cork Male
Gaol to Spike Island internment
compound on 28 May 1921.
He was transferred to Maryborough
(Portlaoise) Prison on the night of
18/19 Nov and released from there in
Dec 1921.

Cronin, Conor

The Lough, Cork City.
He received treatment in the Spike

Prison hospital ward, on 4 Sept 1921.
No other details found.

Cronin, David

David Cronin, Lombardstown, Co. Cork.

Mohereen, Lombardstown, Co. Cork.
Occupation: Railway Porter.
He was one of the founding
members of the Lombardstown
Company, Irish Volunteers.
As a railway porter he was of
immense value to the brigade and
battalion for smuggling weapons and
for sending and receiving dispatches.
He was a vital cog in General Liam
Lynch's administration as the Second
Brigade HQ was frequently in the
Lombardstown area.
6th Division arrest No. 694.
Brigade arrest No. K.B. 215.
He was transferred from Cork Male
Gaol to Spike Island internment
compound on 28 May 1921, to 'A'
Block, Hut 17.
He was transferred to Maryborough
(Portlaoise) Prison on the night of
18/19 Nov and released from there in
Dec 1921.

Cronin, Denis

Brittas, Lombardstown, Co. Cork.
Age: 22.
Brigade arrest No. K.B. 327.
While he was a prisoner in Cork
Male Gaol, he was served with an
Internment Order before his release
date. Instead of being released, he was
further detained as an internee.
He was transferred from Cork Male
Gaol to Spike Island internment
compound on 14 Nov 1921.
He was transferred from Spike to
Maryborough (Portlaoise) Prison
on the night of 18/19 Nov. He was
released from there in Dec 1921.

Cronin, Edward J.

Aghern, Castlelyons, Co. Cork.
Brigade arrest No. 16 I.B. 445.
He was transferred from Cork Male
Gaol to Spike Island internment
compound on 22 Aug 1921, to 'A'
Block, Hut 2.
He was transferred to Maryborough
(Portlaoise) Prison on the night of
18/19 Nov and released from there in
Dec 1921.

Cronin, Fred

18 Sunday's Well Rd, Cork City.
6th Division arrest No. 562.
Brigade arrest No. 17.I.B.488.
He was transferred from Cork Male
Gaol to Spike Island internment
compound on 25 Apr 1921, to 'A'
Block, Hut 15.

He was transferred from Spike to Bere
Island internment camp on 11 July
1921 on HMS *Vidette*.
He was transferred from Bere Island,
back to Spike and released on parole
on 1 Oct. His parole was extended
and he was released while on parole.

Cronin, John

Ballingeary, Co. Cork.
Brigade arrest No. 17 I.B. 464.
He was transferred from Cork Male
Gaol to Spike Island internment
compound on 12 Apr 1921.
He was transferred from Spike to
Bere Island internment camp by RN
destroyer on 14/15 Apr 1921.

Cronin, Matthew

Nunstown, Aghadoe, Killarney, Co. Kerry.
6th Division arrest No. 696.
Brigade arrest No. K.B. 217.
He was transferred from Cork Male
Gaol to Spike Island internment
compound on 28 May 1921, to 'A'
Block, Hut 14.
He was transferred to Maryborough
(Portlaoise) Prison on the night of
18/19 Nov and released from there in
Dec 1921.

Cronin, Maurice

Transtown, Watergrasshill, Co. Cork.
Age: 26.
Brigade arrest No. 16 I.B. 526.
He was arrested by Crown Forces on
15 July 1921.

He was transferred from Cork Male Gaol to Spike Island internment compound on 25 July 1921. He was moved to 'A' Block, Hut 2, during the Spike hunger strike.

He was transferred from Spike to Maryborough (Portlaoise) Prison on the night of 18/19 Nov and released from there in Dec 1921.

Cronin, Michael

Lixnaw, Co. Kerry.

Brigade arrest No. K.B. 290.

Age: 35.

He was transferred from Cork Military Detention Barracks to Spike Island internment compound on 6 July 1921. He was transferred to Maryborough (Portlaoise) Prison on the night of 18/19 Nov and released from there in Dec 1921.

Cronin, Patrick

Lixnaw, Co. Kerry.

Age: 25.

Brigade arrest No. K.B. 293.

He was transferred from Cork Military Detention Barracks to Spike Island internment compound on 6 July 1921.

Crowe, Michael

Larkfield, Granard, Co. Longford. Also listed as Ballanvalley, Killena, Wexford.

Age: 19.

Brigade arrest No. 16 I.B. 528.

He was transferred from Waterford

Gaol by RN destroyer to Spike Island internment compound on 18 Aug 1921. He was transferred to Maryborough (Portlaoise) Prison on the night of 18/19 Nov and released from there in Dec 1921.

Crowe, Thomas,

alias D. Murphy

Villierstown, Cappoquin, Co. Waterford.

6th Division arrest No. 118.

Brigade arrest No. 16 I.B. 12.

He was transferred from Spike to Bere Island internment camp on 11 July 1921 on HMS *Vidette*.

Crowley, Cornelius

Kilbrittain, Bandon, Co. Cork.

He was transferred from Cork Male Gaol to Spike Island internment compound on 19 Feb 1921.

Crowley, Daniel

Ballea, Carrigaline, Co. Cork.

Age: 23.

6th Division arrest No. 710.

Brigade arrest No. 17 I.B. 729.

He was transferred from Cork Male Gaol to Spike Island internment compound on 6 July 1921. He was moved to 'A' Block, Hut 5, during the Spike hunger strike.

He was transferred from Spike to Maryborough (Portlaoise) Prison on the night of 18/19 Nov and released from there in Dec 1921.

Crowley, Denis
Inchimay, Nadd, Lyre, Banteer, Co. Cork.
Age: 31. Brigade arrest No. K.B. 281.
He was arrested by Crown Forces on
30 June 1921.
He was transferred from Cork Male
Gaol to Spike Island internment
compound on 6 July 1921. He
was transferred to Maryborough
(Portlaoise) Prison on the night of
18/19 Nov and released from there in
Dec 1921.
Brother of internees Patrick and James.

Crowley, James
Inchimay, Nadd, Lyre, Banteer, Co. Cork.
Age: 25.
Brigade arrest No. K.B. 282.
He was arrested by Crown Forces on
30 June 1921.
He was transferred from Cork Male
Gaol to Spike Island internment
compound on 6 July 1921, to 'A'
Block, Hut 3.
He was transferred to Maryborough
(Portlaoise) Prison on the night of
18/19 Nov and released from there in
Dec 1921.
Brother of internees Denis and Patrick.

Crowley, Jeremiah
Bandon, Co. Cork.
Brigade arrest No. 17 I.B. 218.
He was transferred from the Brigade
Cage in Victoria Barracks, Cork, to
Spike Island internment compound on
19 Feb 1921.

Crowley, John
31 Commons Road, Blackpool,
Cork City.
Age: 18.
6th Division arrest No. 710.
Brigade arrest No. 17 I.B. 757.
He was transferred from Cork Male
Gaol to Spike Island internment
compound on 28 May 1921 and
moved to Bere Island internment camp.
He was transferred from Bere Island
back to Spike on 20 Sept on HMS
Stormcloud, D 89.
He was transferred from Spike to
Maryborough (Portlaoise) Prison on
the night of 18/19 Nov and released
from there in Dec 1921.

Crowley, Patrick
Inchimay, Nadd, Lyre, Banteer, Co. Cork.
Age: 18.
Brigade arrest No. K.B. 280.
He was arrested by Crown Forces on
30 June 1921.
He was transferred from Cork Male
Gaol to Spike Island internment
compound on 6 July 1921.
He was transferred to Maryborough
(Portlaoise) Prison on the night of
18/19 Nov and released from there in
Dec 1921.
Brother of internees Denis and James.

Crowley, William
Gurteen North, Bandon, Co. Cork.
Age: 27.
Brigade arrest No. 17 I.B. 1120.

He was transferred from the Brigade Cage in Victoria Barracks via Cork Male Gaol to Spike Island internment compound on 15 July 1921, to 'A' Block, Hut 5.

He was transferred to Maryborough (Portlaoise) Prison on the night of 18/19 Nov and released from there in Dec 1921.

Crowse, Thomas

Occupation: Draper's assistant.

Brigade arrest No. 16 I.B. 12.

He was transferred from Kilworth Army Camp to Spike Island internment compound on 4 Mar 1921.

Culhane, John (Sean)

Glin, Co. Limerick and 19 Parnell Place, Cork City.

Age: 21.

Brigade arrest No. 17 I.B. 502.[15]

He was part of the squad that shot and killed Divisional Commissioner Smyth, RIC, in Cork and District Inspector Swanzy, RIC in Lisburn. He was arrested by British soldiers in Evergreen Rd, Cork City, in May 1921 and taken to Victoria Barracks, Cork.

He was transferred from Cork Male Gaol to Spike Island internment compound on 11 May 1921.

He was transferred from Spike to Bere Island internment camp and escaped from there on 3 Nov 1921.

Cullen, James

Belfield, Enniscorthy, Co. Wexford.

6th Division arrest No. 425.

Brigade arrest No. 16 I.B. 324.

He was transferred from Cork Male Gaol to Spike Island internment compound on 28 May 1921, to 'B' Block, Hut 1.

He was transferred to Maryborough (Portlaoise) Prison on the night of 18/19 Nov and released from there in Dec 1921.

Cullen, Peter

89 North Main Street, Wexford Town & Upper Patrick Street, Kilkenny.

Brigade arrest No. 16 I.B. 359.

He was transferred from Kilworth Army Camp to Spike Island internment compound on 17 May 1921. He was moved to 'A' Block, Hut 21, during the Spike hunger strike.

He was transferred from Spike to Maryborough (Portlaoise) Prison on the night of 18/19 Nov and released from there in Dec 1921.

Cullinane, Charles

Knocknahilan, Aherla, Co. Cork.

6th Division arrest No. 403.

Brigade arrest No. 17 I.B. 282.

He was transferred to Spike for transfer to Bere Island, date not found.

He was transferred from Spike to Bere

---

15 See Sean Culhane, WS No. 746.

Island internment camp on 11 July 1921 on HMS *Vidette*.

Cullinane, John
Dessert, Ballineen, Co. Cork.
Brigade arrest No. 17 I.B 267.
He was transferred from Cork Male Gaol to Spike Island internment compound on 19 Feb 1921.

Cummings, Willy John
Garnish, Castletownbere, Co. Cork.
Age: 19.
Brigade arrest No. 17 I.B. 1174.
He was arrested by Crown Forces for membership of the IRA and recommended for internment.
He was transferred from Cork Male Gaol to Spike Island internment compound on 25 July 1921, to 'A' Block, Hut 4.
He was transferred to Maryborough (Portlaoise) Prison on the night of 18/19 Nov and released from there in Dec 1921.

Cunningham, Cornelius
Dromina, Clonbanin Cross, Co. Cork.
Brigade arrest No. K.B. 150.
He was arrested by Crown Forces on 21 Apr 1921.
He was transferred from Cork Male Gaol to Spike Island internment compound on 30 June 1921, to 'A' Block, Hut 17.
He was transferred to Maryborough (Portlaoise) Prison on the night of

18/19 Nov and released from there in Dec 1921.

Cunningham, Lawrence
Bayle St, Clonakilty, Co. Cork.
Age: 18.
Brigade arrest No. 17 I.B. 460.
He was arrested by Crown Forces on 29 July 1921.
He was transferred from Cork Male Gaol to Spike Island internment compound on 22 Aug 1921, to 'A' Block, Hut 9.
He was transferred from Spike to Maryborough (Portlaoise) Prison on the night of 18/19 Nov and was released from there in Dec 1921.

Dalton, Edward
No address stated.
Brigade arrest No. 17 I.B 310.
He was transferred from Cork Male Gaol to Spike Island internment compound on 11 May 1921.

Daly, James
Shanballymore, Co. Cork
6th Division arrest No. 193.
He was transferred from Kilworth Army Camp to Spike Island internment compound on 13 Apr 1921.
He was transferred from Spike to Bere Island internment camp on 14/15 Apr 1921 by RN destroyer.

Daly, Simon
Cork City.

Brigade arrest No. 17 I.B. 183.
He was transferred from Cork Male
Gaol to Spike Island internment
compound on 19 Feb 1921.

Daly, Thomas
Cork City.
Brigade arrest No. 17 I.B. 178.
He was transferred from Cork Male
Gaol to Spike Island internment
compound on 19 Feb 1921.

Davis, John
10 John Street, Enniscorthy, Co. Wexford.
Age: 34.
Brigade arrest No. 16 I.B. 320.
He was transferred from Kilworth
Army Camp via Cork Male Gaol to
Spike Island internment compound on
9 June 1921.

Deasy, Jeremiah John (Miah)
Kilmacsimon Quay, Bandon, Co. Cork.
Age: 24.
6th Division arrest No. 221.
Brigade arrest No. 17 I.B. 100.
He was arrested after leaving Mass in
Ballinadee Church, Co. Cork, on 6 Jan
1921. He was taken to Kinsale and to
Cork Military Detention Barracks.[16]
He was transferred from Cork
Military Detention Barracks to Spike
Island internment compound on
24 Feb 1921.
He was a brother of Pat Deasy, killed

in action during the Kilmichael
ambush on 28 Nov 1920, and of Liam
Deasy, Brigade Commandant, Third
(West) Cork Brigade, IRA.

Deasy, Patrick
16 Spangle Hill, Commons Road,
Cork City.
Age: 21.
6th Division arrest No. 714.
Brigade arrest No. 17 I.B. 783.
He was transferred from Cork Male
Gaol to Spike Island internment
compound on 28 May 1921, to 'A'
Block, Hut 5.

Delaney, Pat
Kilnaglory, Ballincollig, Co. Cork.
Age: 23.
Brigade arrest No. 17 I.B. 824.
He was transferred from Cork to
Spike Island internment compound on
25 June 1921, to 'A' Block, Hut 9.

Delea, Patrick
Post Office Lane, Blackrock, Cork City.
Age: 21.
Brigade arrest No. 17 I.B. 1117.
He was transferred from Cork Male
Gaol to Spike Island internment
compound on 25 July 1921. He was
moved to 'A' Block, Hut 4, during the
Spike hunger strike.
He was transferred from Spike to
Maryborough (Portlaoise) Prison on

---

16 See his WS, No. 1738.

the night of 18/19 Nov and released from there in Dec 1921.

Deloughrey, Laurence
Parliament Street, Kilkenny City.
6th Division arrest No. 257.
He was transferred from Kilworth Army Camp to Spike Island internment compound on 13 Apr 1921.
He was transferred from Spike to Bere Island internment camp by RN destroyer on 14/15 Apr 1921.

Dennehy, Donal (Daniel)

Daniel Dennehy, Ballyhooley, Co. Cork.

Castleblagh, Ballyhooly, Fermoy, Co. Cork.
6th Division arrest No. 706.
Brigade arrest No. 17 I.B. 774.
He was transferred from Cork Male Gaol to Spike Island internment compound on 28 May 1921.

Dennehy, Daniel
Ballyhooly, Fermoy, Co. Cork.
Age: 25.
Brigade arrest No. 16 I.B. 523.

He was arrested by Crown Forces on 18 July 1921.
He was transferred from Cork Male Gaol to Spike Island internment compound on 25 July 1921.

Dennehy, Timothy
Clash House, Kilbrin, Kanturk, Co. Cork. Age: 23.
Brigade arrest No. K.B. 188.
He was arrested by Crown Forces on 27 Apr 1921.
He was transferred from Cork Male Gaol to Spike Island internment compound on 30 June 1921.

Desmond, Denis
Castlerelact, Bandon, Co. Cork.
Brigade arrest No. 17 I.B. 573.
He was transferred from Cork Male Gaol to Spike Island internment compound on 25 Apr 1921.

Desmond, Denis
Lisasan, Kinsale, Co. Cork.
Age: 31.
Brigade arrest No. 17 I.B. 1118.
He was transferred from the Brigade Cage in Victoria Barracks via Cork Male Gaol to Spike Island internment compound on 15 July 1921.

Desmond, Thomas
Lacka, Lyre, Nadd, Banteer, Co. Cork.
Age: 18.
Brigade arrest No. K.B. 195.
He was transferred from Cork Male

Gaol to Spike Island internment compound on 16 May 1921. He was moved to 'A' Block, Hut 17, during the Spike hunger strike.

He was transferred from Spike to Maryborough (Portlaoise) Prison on the night of 18/19 Nov and released from there in Dec 1921.

Desmond, William

Crowhill, Bandon, Co. Cork.

Age: 24.

Occupation: Farmer.

6th Division arrest No. 563.

Brigade arrest No. 17 I.B. 495.

He was arrested by British soldiers at Crossbarry, Co. Cork, on 19 Mar 1921, the morning of the battle at Crossbarry. He was taken to Bandon Military Barracks, later to the Brigade Cage in Victoria Barracks and from there to Cork Male Gaol.[17]

He was transferred from Cork Male Gaol to Spike Island internment compound on 30 Apr 1921, to 'A' Block, Hut 16.

He was transferred from Spike to Maryborough (Portlaoise) Prison on the night of 18/19 Nov and released from there on 8 Dec 1921.

Devane, Michael

Killarney, Co. Kerry.

Age: 26.

Brigade arrest No. K.B. 322.

While he was in Cork Male Gaol, he was served with an Internment Order before his release date. Instead of being released, he was further detained as an internee.

He was transferred from Cork Male Gaol back to Spike Island internment compound on 14 Nov 1921.

He was transferred from Spike to Maryborough (Portlaoise) Prison on the night of 18/19 Nov and released from there in Dec 1921.

Devereaux, Thomas

Ballinruddery, Listowel, Co. Kerry.

Age: 22.

6th Division arrest No. 726.

Brigade arrest No. L. 539.

He was tried by General Court Martial in Victoria Barracks, Cork. On 30 May 1921, he was found not guilty of the murder of DI Tobias O'Sullivan, RIC, in Listowel, on 21 Jan 1921. He was detained as an internee and sent to Cork Male Gaol.

He was transferred from Cork Male Gaol to Spike Island internment compound on 22 June 1921, to 'B' Block, Hut 1.

DI O'Sullivan, RIC, is generally reported as being killed by the IRA to prevent him identifying prisoners on Spike Island. This is incorrect, as Spike was opened as a prison and internment camp on 19 Feb 1921,

---

17 See his WS, No. 832.

almost one month after he was killed.
The specific prisoner that the British
Army and RIC wanted DI O'Sullivan
to identify was Tom Malone, alias
Sean Forde.
See internee, O'Carroll, Daniel.
See also: Malone/Forde in the list of
Spike prisoners.

Devereaux, Thomas
Danes Castle, Bannow, Co. Wexford.
Age: 40.
Brigade arrest No. 16 I.B. 309.
He was transferred from Cork to
Spike Island internment compound on
6 July 1921.

Devereaux, William
White Rock, Co. Wexford.
Age: 23.
6th Division arrest No. 423.
Brigade arrest No. 16 I.B. 313.
He was transferred from Cork Male
Gaol to Spike Island internment
compound on 28 May 1921, to 'A'
Block, Hut 17. He was later moved to
Hut 18.

Dillon, John
Gurtnapisha, Fethard, Clonmel,
Co. Tipperary.
Age: 22.
6th Division arrest No. 295.
Brigade arrest No. 16 I.B. 169.
He was transferred from Kilworth
Army Camp to Spike Island
internment compound on 4 Mar 1921.

He was transferred from Spike to Bere
Island internment camp on 11 July
1921 on HMS *Vidette*.
He was transferred from Bere Island
back to Spike. During the Spike hunger
strike, he was in 'A' Block, Hut 22.
He was transferred from Spike to
Maryborough (Portlaoise) Prison
on the night of 18/19 Nov. He was
released from there on 8 Dec 1921.

Dillon, Patrick
Kenmare Place, Killarney, Co. Kerry.
6th Division arrest No. 617.
Brigade arrest No. K.B. 169.
He was transferred from Cork Male
Gaol to Spike Island internment
compound on 30 Apr 1921.
He was transferred from Spike to Bere
Island internment camp on 11 July
1921 on HMS *Vidette*.

Dineen, Charles
Mounteen, Ballinascarthy, Co. Cork.
Brigade arrest No. 17 I.B. 212.
He was transferred from the Brigade
Cage in Victoria Barracks, Cork, to
Spike Island internment compound on
19 Feb 1921.

Donoghue, James
Also listed as O'Donoghue.
241 Blarney Street, Cork City.
Age: 23.
Brigade arrest No. 17 I.B. 1050.
He was transferred from the Brigade
Cage in Victoria Barracks, Cork, to

Spike Island internment compound on 6 July 1921, to 'A' Block, Hut 20. On 2 Sept 1921 he was one of the hunger strike orderlies.

He was transferred from Spike to Maryborough (Portlaoise) Prison on the night of 18/19 Nov and released from there on 8 Dec 1921.

Donohue, James

Ross Road, Killuran, Enniscorthy, Co. Wexford.

Age: 25.

Brigade arrest No. 18 I.B. 477.

He was transferred from Waterford Gaol by RN destroyer to Spike Island internment compound on 18 Aug 1921. During the Spike hunger strike he was moved to 'A' Block, Hut 20. He was transferred from Spike to Maryborough (Portlaoise) Prison on the night of 18/19 Nov and released from there on 8 Dec 1921.

Donoghue, Patrick

Ballinvaird, Rossmore, Ballineen, Clonakilty, Co. Cork.

Age: 19.

Brigade arrest No. 17 I.B. 619.

He was transferred from the Brigade Cage in Victoria Barracks, Cork, to Spike Island internment compound on 16 May 1921.

Donovan, Cornelius

Cashelbeg, Bandon, Co. Cork.

Brigade arrest No. 17 I.B. 210.

He was transferred from the Brigade Cage in Victoria Barracks, Cork, to Spike Island internment compound on 19 Feb 1921.

Donovan, Dan

Burrane, Timoleague, Co. Cork.

Age: 21.

Occupation: Farmer.

Brigade arrest No. 17 I.B. 739.

He fought in the major battle at Crossbarry on 19 Mar 1921. He was arrested by troops from the Essex Regiment on 10 May 1921 and taken to Bandon Military Barracks. From there he was moved to Kinsale, to Victoria Barracks and to Cork Male Gaol.[18] He was transferred from Cork Male Gaol to Spike Island internment compound on 28 May 1921.

He was transferred from Spike to Bere Island internment camp on 11 July 1921 on HMS *Vidette* and released from there in Dec 1921.

Donovan, Daniel

6 Mary Street, Cork City.

6th Division arrest No. 672.

Brigade arrest No. 17 I.B. 715.

He was transferred from Cork Male Gaol to Spike Island internment compound on 28 May 1921.

18 See his WS, No. 1608.

Donovan, Denis

Farranlough, Newcestown, Co. Cork.
Brigade arrest No. 17 I.B. 222.
He was transferred from the Brigade
Cage in Victoria Barracks, Cork, to
Spike Island internment compound on
19 Feb 1921.

Donovan, Pat

Lislevane, Co. Cork.
He was transferred from Cork Male
Gaol to Spike Island internment
compound on 25 Apr 1921.

Donovan, Thomas

26 Evergreen Road, Cork City.
Age: 28.
6th Division arrest No. 752.
Brigade arrest No. 17 I.B. 683.
He was transferred from Cork Male
Gaol to Spike Island internment
compound on 22 June 1921, to 'A'
Block, Hut 4. He was later moved to
'B' Block, Hut 21.

Donovan, Thomas

Glanworth, Co. Cork.
Age: 25.
Brigade arrest No. 16 I.B. 447.
He was transferred from Kilworth
Army Camp to Spike Island internment
compound on 15 Sept 1921.
He was transferred from Spike to
Maryborough (Portlaoise) Prison on
the night of 18/19 Nov and released
from there on 8 Dec 1921.

Donovan, Thomas

Also listed as O'Donovan.
Emly, Knocklong, Co. Tipperary.
Age: 30.
Brigade arrest No. L. 464.
He survived 94 days on hunger strike
in Cork Male Gaol from 11 Aug to
12 Nov 1920.
He was transferred from Cork
Military Detention Barracks to Spike
Island internment compound on
11 May 1921, to 'A' Block, Hut 14.
He was transferred from Spike to
Maryborough (Portlaoise) Prison on
18/19 Nov 1921 and released from
there in Dec 1921.

Dooley, Maurice

Brigade arrest No. 16 I.B. 88.
He was transferred from Kilworth
Army Camp to Spike Island
internment compound on 4 Mar 1921.

Dowling, John (Sean)

Davis Lane, Moyderwell, Tralee,
Co. Kerry.
Brigade arrest No. K.B. 130.

John Dowling, Tralee, Co. Kerry.

He was transferred from Cork Male Gaol to Spike Island internment compound on 25 Apr 1921.
He was transferred from Spike to Bere Island internment camp on 11 July 1921 on HMS *Vidette*.

Dowling, William
Castletownbere, Co. Cork.
Age: 23.
6th Division arrest No. 723.
Brigade arrest No. 17 I.B. 617.
He was transferred from Cork Male Gaol to Spike Island internment compound on 22 June 1921, to 'A' Block, Hut 4.

Downey, William
Lehanemore, Castletownbere, Co. Cork.
Age: 22
Brigade arrest No. 17 I.B. 1171.
He was arrested by Crown Forces for membership of the IRA and he was recommended for internment.
He was transferred from Cork Male Gaol to Spike Island internment compound on 25 July 1921, to 'A' Block, Hut 4.

Doyle, William
Tomhadguard, Bridgetown, Co. Wexford.
Age: 30.
6th Division arrest No. 421.
Brigade arrest No. 16 I.B. 312.
He was transferred from Cork Male

Gaol to Spike Island internment compound on 28 May 1921, to 'A' Block, Hut 18.

Drew, Denis
Crowhill, Upton, Co. Cork.
Brigade arrest No. 17 I.B. 211.
He was captured in Jan 1921.
He was transferred from the Brigade Cage in Victoria Barracks, Cork, to Spike Island internment compound on 19 Feb 1921.

Drinan, Patrick
Ballinaboy, Ballinhassig, Co. Cork.
Brigade arrest No. 17 I.B. 469.
He was transferred from Cork Male Gaol to Spike Island internment compound on 12 Apr 1921.
He was transferred from Spike to Bere Island internment camp by RN destroyer on 14/15 Apr 1921.

Duggan, James
Castleliney, Templemore, Co. Tipperary.
Age: 20.
Brigade arrest No. 18 I.B. 172.
He was arrested at home by Crown Forces in mid Jan 1921. He was taken to Templemore Military Barracks and from there to Limerick Barracks. Later he was taken to Newcastlewest, back to Limerick Barracks and later to Cork Male Gaol.[19]
He was transferred from Cork Male

19 See James Duggan, WS No. 1510.

Gaol to Spike Island internment compound on 11 May 1921, to 'A' Block, Hut 10.
He was transferred from Spike to Maryborough (Portlaoise) Prison on the night of 18/19 Nov and released from there on 8 Dec 1921.

Duggan, Jeremiah John
Bilbao, Cappamore, Co. Limerick.
Age: 22.
Brigade arrest No. 18 I.B. 220.
He was transferred from Limerick Gaol to Spike Island internment compound on 22 Aug 1921, to 'A' Block, Hut 19.

Duggan, Patrick
49 Thomas Davis Street, Cork City.
Age: 30.
6th Division arrest No. 750.
Brigade arrest No. 17 I.B. 782.
He was transferred from Cork Male Gaol to Spike Island internment compound on 22 June 1921.[20]
He was transferred from Spike to Maryborough (Portlaoise) Prison on the night of 18/19 Nov and released from there in Dec 1921.

Dunbar, Martin
Castle Place, Ferns, Co. Wexford.
Age: 26.
6th Division arrest No. 430.
Brigade arrest No. 16 I.B. 337.

He was transferred from Cork Male Gaol to Spike Island internment compound on 28 May 1921.

Dunne, Eugene
The Pier, Adrigole, Bantry, Co. Cork.
Age: 33.
Brigade arrest No. 17 I.B. 1183.
He was arrested near Glengarriff, Co. Cork on 3 July 1921. He was taken to Bantry, to Furious Pier, and at the end of Aug to Bere Island Military Prison in the Field.
He was transferred from Bere Island on 20 Sept on HMS *Stormcloud*, D 89, to Spike Island internment compound to 'B' Block, Hut 15.
He was transferred from Spike to Maryborough (Portlaoise) Prison on the night of 18/19 Nov and released from there in Dec 1921.

Dunne, John J.
Callan, Co. Kilkenny.
Age: 49.
Occupation: Auctioneer.
Brigade arrest No. 16 I.B. 171.
He was transferred from Kilworth Army Camp to Spike Island internment compound on 4 Mar 1921.
He was appointed a Staff Officer for the internees. He was moved to 'A' Block, Hut 22, during the Spike hunger strike.
He was transferred to Cork Military

---

20 See Peg Duggan, WS No. 1576.

Hospital on 19 Sept and expected
back within one week.
He was transferred from Spike to
Maryborough (Portlaoise) Prison on
the night of 18/19 Nov and released
from there in Dec 1921.

Dunne, Peter

Catherine Street, Limerick.
6th Division arrest No. 90.
Brigade arrest No. 18 I.B. 127.
He was transferred from Cork Male
Gaol to Spike Island internment
compound on 12 Apr 1921.
He was transferred from Spike to Bere
Island internment camp on 11 July
1921 on HMS *Vidette*.

Durney, Peter Patrick

Buckstown, Mullinavat, Co. Kilkenny.
Age: 30.
Brigade arrest No. 16 I.B. 411.
He was transferred from Fermoy
Military Barracks, to Cork Military
Detention Barracks on 24 June 1921.
He was transferred from Cork
Military Detention Barracks to Spike
Island internment compound on
25 June 1921.

Dwyer, John

Tomalossitt, Enniscorthy, Co. Wexford.
Age: 25.
6th Division arrest No. 436.
Brigade arrest No. 16 I.B. 360.

John Dwyer, Enniscorthy, Co. Wexford.

He was arrested by Crown Forces
near Enniscorthy on 2 Feb 1921 and
transferred to Cork Male Gaol.[21]
He was transferred from Cork Male
Gaol to Spike Island internment
compound on 28 May 1921, to 'A'
Block, Hut 20.
He was transferred from Spike to
Maryborough (Portlaoise) Prison on the
night of 18/19 Nov and released from
there on 8 Dec 1921.

Dwyer, John

Castletownbere, Co. Cork.
Age: 23. Occupation: Farmer.
Brigade arrest No. 17 I.B. 476.
While he was in the Spike prison
compound he was served with an
Internment Order before his release
date. Instead of being released, he
was further detained as an internee.
He was transferred to Spike Island
internment compound on 8 Aug 1921.
He was transferred from Spike to
Maryborough (Portlaoise) Prison on

21 See his WS, No. 1293.

the night of 18/19 Nov and released from there on 8 Dec 1921.

See Dwyer, John, in the list of Spike prisoners.

Dwyer, Patrick

Clerihan, Clonmel, Co. Tipperary.
6th Division arrest No. 184.
Brigade arrest No. 16 I.B. 50.
He was transferred to Spike to be moved to Bere Island.
He was transferred from Spike to Bere Island internment camp on 11 July 1921 on HMS *Vidette*.

Dwyer, Patrick

Killeen, Gould's Cross, Co. Tipperary.
Age: 20. Occupation: Farmer.
6th Division Arrest No. 515.
Brigade arrest No. 16 I.B. 487.
He was originally on Spike as a prisoner and transferred back to Cork Male Gaol.
While he was in Cork Male Gaol, he was served with an Internment Order before his release date and instead of being released, he was further detained as an internee.
He was transferred from Cork Male Gaol back to Spike Island internment compound on 14 Nov 1921.
He was transferred from Spike to Maryborough (Portlaoise) Prison on the night of 18/19 Nov and released from there on 8 Dec 1921.
See also: Dwyer, Pat, in the list of Spike prisoners.

Dwyer, William

Corbally, Waterfall, Co. Cork.
Age: 28.
He was arrested on 27 June 1921.
Brigade arrest No. 17 I.B. 1060.
He was arrested by Crown Forces on 25 June 1921.
He was transferred from Cork to Spike Island internment compound on 25 July 1921, to 'A' Block, Hut 3.

Eddy, Jack

Jack Eddy, Ardmore, Co. Waterford.

Ardmore, Dungarvan, Co. Waterford.
Age: 19.
Brigade arrest No. 16 I.B. 250.
He was transferred from Kilworth Army Camp to Spike Island internment compound on 17 May 1921.
He escaped from Spike with six other internees on the night of 10/11 Nov 1921.
See detailed account of their escape in this book.

Eddy, Pat

Ardmore, Dungarvan, Co. Waterford.
6th Division arrest No. 406.

Brigade arrest No. 16 I.B. 249.
He was transferred from Kilworth
Army Camp to Spike Island internment
compound on 17 May 1921.
He was transferred from Spike to Bere
Island internment camp on 11 July
1921 on HMS *Vidette*.

Egan, Charles

Charles Egan, Mullinahone, Co. Tipperary.

Poulacapple, Mullinahone, Co. Tipperary.
Age: 17.
One of three Egan brothers from
Poulacapple that were arrested
by Auxiliaries from 'H' Company,
Woodstock House at 2 a.m. in early
January 1921.[22]
Brigade arrest No. 16 I.B. 286.
He was transferred from Kilkenny
Gaol to Spike Island internment
compound on 2 May 1921, to 'B'
Block, Hut 22.
Brother of James and Patrick.

Egan, James (Jim)

James Egan, Mullinahone, Co. Tipperary.

Poulacapple, Mullinahone,
Co. Tipperary
Age: 25.
He played centre-half back on the
Tipperary football team against Dublin
in Croke Park, Dublin, on Bloody
Sunday, 21 Nov 1921. His was with
his teammate Michael Hogan (Hogan
Stand, Croke Park) when the latter was
mortally wounded by indiscriminate
gunfire from Crown Forces.[23]
One of three Egan brothers from
Poulacapple that were arrested by
members of 'H' Company, Auxiliary
Police, from Woodstock House, at
2 a.m. in early Jan 1921.[24]
Brigade arrest No. 16 I.B. 284.
He was transferred from Waterford
Gaol to Spike Island internment
compound on 2 May 1921, to 'A'
Block, Hut 22.
In 1922 Jim Egan joined the

---

22 Jim Maher, *The Flying Column West Kilkenny 1916–1921*, 2015 edition, p.133.
23 Ibid.
24 Ibid., pp.133–134. Also Ernest McCall, *The First Anti Terrorist Unit, The Auxiliary Division RIC*, p.312.

pro-Treaty National Army. At the beginning of the Civil War, he joined the anti-Treaty forces. He was killed in action on 19 Apr 1923 while attempting to avoid being captured by National Army troops near his home in Poulacapple in the last week of the Civil War.[25]

Brother of Patrick and Charles.

Egan, John

Church Street, Milltown, Co. Kerry.

6th Division arrest No. 416.

Brigade arrest No. K.B. 90.

He was transferred from Spike to Bere Island internment camp on 11 July 1921 on HMS *Vidette*.

Egan, Patrick

Pat Egan, Mullinahone, Co. Tipperary.

Poulacapple, Mullinahone,
Co. Tipperary

Age: 33.

One of three Egan brothers from Poulacapple that were arrested

by Auxiliaries from 'H' Company, Woodstock House, at 2 a.m. in early January 1921.[26]

Brigade arrest No. 16 I.B. 287.

He was transferred from Waterford Gaol to Spike Island internment compound on 2 May 1921, to 'A' Block, Hut 22.

Brother of Charles and James.

Egan, Patrick

Kenmare, Co. Kerry.

Age: 22.

Brigade arrest No. K.B. 252.

He was transferred from Cork Male Gaol to Spike Island internment compound on 22 Aug 1921, to 'A' Block, Hut 14.

Egan, Thomas

No address found.

6th Division arrest No. 261.

Brigade arrest No. 16 I.B. 141.

He was transferred from Cork Male Gaol to Spike Island internment compound on 28 May 1921.

Ennis, Thomas

6 Paradise Row, McCurtain Street, Wexford Town.

Age: 19.

Brigade arrest No. 16 I.B. 298.

He was transferred from Kilworth Army Camp to Spike Island

---

25 Jim Maher, *The Flying Column West Kilkenny 1916–1921*, p.282.
26 Ibid., p.133.

internment compound on 17 May
1921, to 'A' Block, Hut 18.
He was released from Spike on 5 Nov,
authority received from CA 1068, on
4 Nov 1921.

Eustace, Michael

Main Street, Thurles, Co. Tipperary.
Age: 30.
6th Division arrest No. 136.
Brigade arrest No. 18 I.B. 163.
He was transferred from Cork Male
Gaol to Spike Island internment
compound on 11 May 1921.
He was transferred from Spike to Bere
Island internment camp on 11 July
1921 on HMS *Vidette*.
He was transferred from Bere Island
back to Spike on 20 Sept on HMS
Stormcloud, D 89.
He was transferred from Spike to
Maryborough (Portlaoise) Prison on
the night of 18/19 Nov and released
from there in Dec 1921.

Fahey, Thomas

Abbeyside, Dungarvan, Co. Waterford.
Age: 45.
Brigade arrest No. 16 I.B. 362.
He was transferred from Kilworth
Army Camp to Spike Island internment
compound on 30 May 1921.

Falvey, Michael

Glenbeigh, Co. Kerry.
Age: 22.
6th Division arrest No. 695.

Brigade arrest No. K.B. 218.
He was transferred from Cork Male
Gaol to Spike Island internment
compound on 28 May 1921, to 'A'
Block, Hut 14.

Fanning, Martin

41 John Street, Waterford City.
Age: 20.
He was arrested on 3 May 1921 and
taken to Kilworth Army Camp on
19 May.
Brigade arrest No. 16 I.B. 433.
He was transferred from Kilworth
Army Camp to Spike Island
internment compound on
16 Sept 1921.

Fehen, John

Castlemagner, Co. Cork.
Age: 25.
Brigade arrest No. K.B. 311.
He was transferred from Cork Male
Gaol to Spike Island internment
compound on 22 Aug 1921.

Fehilly, Jeremiah

Rosscarbery, Co. Cork.
6th Division arrest No. 465.
Brigade arrest No. 17 I.B. 403.
He was transferred from Cork Male
Gaol to Spike Island internment
compound on 25 Apr 1921.
He was transferred from Spike to Bere
Island internment camp on 11 July
1921 on HMS *Vidette*.

Finn, John

Dooneen, Old Head, Kinsale, Co. Cork.
Age: 23. Occupation: Labourer.
6th Division arrest no: 518
Brigade arrest No. 17 I.B 344.
He was originally on Spike as a
prisoner and transferred back to Cork
Male Gaol.
While he was in Cork Male Gaol,
he was served with an Internment
Order before his release date. Instead
of being released, he was further
detained as an internee.
He was transferred from Cork Male
Gaol back to Spike Island internment
compound on 14 Nov 1921.
He was transferred from Spike to
Maryborough (Portlaoise) Prison on the
night of 18/19 Nov and released from
there on 8 Dec 1921.
See also: Finn, John, in the list of
Spike prisoners.

Finn, Lawrence

Killowen, Newmarket, Co. Cork.
Brigade arrest No. 17 I.B. 252.
He was transferred from Cork Male
Gaol to Spike Island internment
compound on 24 Feb 1921.

Finn, Patrick

Tullyglass, Bandon, Co. Cork.
Brigade arrest No. 17 I.B. 217.
He was transferred from the Brigade
Cage in Victoria Barracks, Cork, to
Spike Island internment compound on
19 Feb 1921.

Fitzgerald, Jeremiah

Kilbrittain, Bandon, Co. Cork.
He was transferred from Cork
Military Detention Barracks to Spike
Island internment compound on
19 Feb 1921.

Fitzgerald, John Dixon

20 Boherbuee, Tralee, Co. Kerry.
Brigade arrest No. K.B. 129.
He was transferred from Cork Male
Gaol to Spike Island internment
compound on 25 Apr 1921.

Fitzgerald, John

Kilmagner, Fermoy, Co. Cork. Age: 34.
Brigade arrest No. 16 I.B. 112.
He was transferred from Kilworth
Army Camp to Spike Island
internment compound on 5 Mar 1921,
to 'A' Block, Hut 2.

Fitzgerald, Robert

Ballinspittle, Bandon, Co. Cork.
6th Division arrest No. 98.
Brigade arrest No. 17 I.B. 97.
He was transferred from Cork Male
Gaol to Spike Island internment
compound on 24 Feb 1921.

Fitzgibbon, John

Liscarrol, Co. Cork.
6th Division arrest No. 423.
Brigade arrest No. K.B. 109.
He was transferred from Spike to Bere
Island internment camp on 11 July
1921 on HMS *Vidette*.

Fitzmaurice, Patrick
Abbeydorney, Co. Kerry.
Age: 36.
Brigade arrest No. K.B. 174.
He was transferred from Cork Male
Gaol to Spike Island internment
compound on 11 May 1921.

Flavin, Thomas
His real name was Thomas Crofts,
College Road, Cork City.
Age: 29
He was arrested and interned under
the alias Tom Flavin.
6th Division arrest No. 424 & 592.
Brigade arrest No. 17 I.B. 532.
He was tried by Court Martial in
Victoria Barracks Cork on 4 Mar
1921 for the illegal possession of a
revolver. He was found not guilty and
interned, thus remaining in custody.
He was transferred from Cork Male
Gaol to Spike Island internment
compound on 30 Apr 1921, to 'A'
Block, Hut 16.
He was transferred from Spike to Bere
Island internment camp on 11 July
1921 on HMS *Vidette*.
He was transferred back to Spike and
escaped with six other internees on the
night of 10/11 Nov 1921. See detailed
account of their escape in this book.

Flood, John
Brigade arrest No. 16 I.B. 216.

He was transferred from Kilworth
Army Camp to Spike Island
internment compound on 4 Mar 1921.

Flood, Matthew
West Barrack Street, Oliver Plunkett
Hill, Fermoy, Co. Cork.
6th Division arrest No. 354.
Brigade arrest No. 16 I.B. 216.
He was arrested by the RIC for acting
as Irish Republican Police officer in
Fermoy at the funeral of the IRA
officer and hunger striker Comdt
Michael Fitzgerald.
He was transferred from Spike to Bere
Island internment camp on 11 July
1921 on HMS *Vidette*.

Flynn, Daniel
Tullamorthy, Bandon, Co. Cork.
Brigade arrest No. 17 I.B. 235.
He was transferred from Cork Male
Gaol to Spike Island internment
compound on 19 Feb 1921.

Flynn, Daniel
Meentaflugh, Kiskeam, Co. Cork.
Age: 25.
Occupation: Farmer.
Brigade arrest No. K.B. 231.
He was arrested with his flying
column commander Sean Moylan
on 15 May 1921, taken to Kanturk
military post and moved from there to
Victoria Barracks, Cork.[27]

---

27 See his WS, No. 240.

Daniel Flynn, Kiskeam, Co. Cork.

He was transferred from Cork Male
Gaol to Spike Island internment
compound on 1 June 1921.
He was transferred from Spike to Bere
Island internment camp and released
from there in Dec 1921.

Flynn, Eugene
Inchinleary East, Ballyduff,
Co. Waterford. Age: 20.
Brigade arrest No. 16 I.B. 234.
He was transferred from Kilworth
Army Camp to Spike Island internment
compound on 13 Apr 1921.
He was transferred from Spike to Bere
Island internment camp on 14/15 Apr
1921 by RN destroyer.
He was transferred back from Bere
Island to Spike on 20 Sept on HMS
Stormcloud, D 89.
He was transferred from Spike to
Maryborough (Portlaoise) Prison on
the night of 18/19 Nov and released
from there in Dec 1921.

Flynn, John
Cashelmore, Bandon, Co. Cork.

Brigade arrest No. 17 I.B. 219.
He was transferred from Cork Male
Gaol to Spike Island internment
compound on 24 Feb 1921.

Flynn, John
Ballysheehan, Clogheen, Co. Tipperary.
6th Division arrest No. 236.
Brigade arrest No. 16 I.B. 118.
He was transferred from Spike to Bere
Island internment camp on 11 July
1921 on HMS *Vidette*.

Flynn, Michael
Kildarra, Ballinadee, Co. Cork.
Brigade arrest No. 17 I.B. 512.
He was transferred from Cork Male
Gaol to Spike Island internment
compound on 12 Apr 1921.
He was transferred from Spike to
Bere Island internment camp by RN
destroyer on 14/15 Apr 1921.

Flynn, Michael
Tullinmurrihy, Ballinascarthy, Co. Cork.
Brigade arrest No. 17 I.B. 232.
He was transferred from the Brigade
Cage in Victoria Barracks, Cork, to
Spike Island internment compound on
19 Feb 1921.

Flynn, Thomas
Cashelmore, Bandon, Co. Cork.
Brigade arrest No. 17 I.B. 223.
He was transferred from Cork Male
Gaol to Spike Island internment
compound on 24 Feb 1921.

Flynn, Thomas

Stradbally, Co. Waterford.
Brigade arrest No. 16 I.B. 83.
He was transferred from Spike to
Bere Island internment camp by RN
destroyer on 14/15 Apr 1921.

Fogarty, Charles

Charles Fogarty, Gorey, Co. Wexford.

Clonough, Inch, Gorey, Co. Wexford.
Age: 25.
Brigade arrest No. 16 I.B. 496.
He was transferred from Waterford
Gaol by RN destroyer to Spike Island
internment compound on 18 Aug
1921, to 'A' Block, Hut 11.

Fogarty, Jack

Killeen, Templemore, Co. Tipperary.
6th Division arrest No. 144.
Brigade arrest No. 18 I.B. 154.
He was transferred from Spike to Bere
Island internment camp on 11 July
1921 on HMS *Vidette*.

Foley, Cornelius

Clonbanin, Co. Cork.
6th Division arrest No. 361.

Brigade arrest No. K.B. 96.
He was transferred from Spike to Bere
Island internment camp on 11 July
1921 on HMS *Vidette*.

Foley, John R.

11 Springmount Place, Dillon's Cross,
Old Youghal Rd, Cork City.
Age: 23.
Brigade arrest No. 17 I.B. 1097.
He was transferred from Cork Male
Gaol to Spike Island internment
compound on 25 July 1921.

Foley, Michael

Ballyetra, Dungarvan, Co. Waterford.
Brigade arrest No. 16 I.B. 80.
He was arrested at home on Sunday,
23 Jan 1921. He was taken to
Dungarvan, to Fermoy Military
Barracks and to Kilworth Army Camp.
He was transferred from Kilworth
Army Camp to Spike Island
internment compound on 5 Mar 1921.
He was transferred from Spike to
Bere Island internment camp by RN

Michael Foley, Dungarvan,
Co. Waterford.

destroyer on 14/15 Apr 1921. He was released from there on 10 Dec 1921.

Foran, Jeremiah

Killarney, Co. Kerry.
Age: 27.
Brigade arrest No. K.B. 243.
He was transferred from Cork Male Gaol to Spike Island internment compound on 19 Sept 1921.

Forristal, William

William Forristal, Thomastown, Co. Kilkenny.

Jerpoint Church, Thomastown, Co. Kilkenny.
Age: 24.
Brigade arrest No. 16 I.B. 266.
He was transferred from Kilworth Army Camp to Spike Island internment compound on 17 May 1921, to 'A' Block, Hut 21.
On 2 Sept 1921, he was one of the orderlies in his hut during the Spike hunger strike.
He was transferred from Spike to Maryborough (Portlaoise) Prison on

the night of 18/19 Nov and released from there on 8 Dec 1921.

Foskin, John

Ballydow, Kilmacow, Mullinavat, Co. Kilkenny.
Age: 27.
Brigade arrest No. 16 I.B. 381.
He was transferred from Kilworth Army Camp, via Cork, to Spike Island internment compound on 9 June 1921. He was moved to 'A' Block, Hut 21, during the Spike hunger strike.
He was transferred from Spike to Maryborough (Portlaoise) Prison on the night of 18/19 Nov and released from there on 8 Dec 1921.

Foskin, Richard

Richard Foskin, Mullinavat, Co. Kilkenny.

Deer Park, Mullinavat, Co. Kilkenny.
Age: 16.
Brigade arrest No. 16 I.B. 406.
He was transferred from Fermoy Military Barracks to Cork Military Detention Barracks on 24 June 1921 .

He was transferred from Cork Military Detention Barracks to Spike Island internment compound on 25 June 1921.

Fouhy, Martin
Killeagh, Glanworth, Co. Cork.
Age: 21.
He was arrested on 4 May 1921.
Brigade arrest No. 16 I.B. 427.
He was transferred from Kilworth Army Camp to Spike Island internment compound on 15 Sept 1921.
He was transferred from Spike to Maryborough (Portlaoise) Prison on the night of 18/19 Nov and released from there on 8 Dec 1921.

Frizelle, Nicholas J.
1 Farnogue Terrace, Wexford Town.
Age: 55.
Brigade arrest No. 16 I.B. 502.
He was transferred from Waterford Gaol by RN destroyer to Spike Island internment compound on 18 Aug 1921.

Funchion, Patrick
Lower Bridge Street, Callan, Co. Kilkenny.
Age: 43.
Brigade arrest No. 16 I.B. 423.
He was arrested at home by the RIC and taken to Kilworth Army Camp.[28]
He was transferred from Kilworth Army Camp to Spike Island

Paddy Funcheon, Callan, Co. Kilkenny.

internment compound on 16 Sept 1921, to 'B' Block, Hut 17.

Furlong, Philip
Butlerstown, Broadway, Co. Wexford.
Age: 36.
6th Division arrest No. 429.
Brigade arrest No. 16 I.B. 372.
He was transferred from Kilworth Camp via Cork Male Gaol to Spike Island internment compound on 9 June 1921, to 'A' Block, Hut 18.

Furlong, Walter
88 South Main Street, Cork City.
Brigade arrest No. 17 I.B. 472.
He was transferred from Cork Male Gaol to Spike Island internment compound on 12 Apr 1921.
He was transferred from Spike to Bere Island internment camp by RN destroyer on 14/15 Apr 1921.

Gallagher, John J.
9 Bridge Street, Waterford City.

---

28 See Thomas Meagher, WS No. 1672.

John Gallagher, Waterford City.

Age: 49.
He was arrested on 24 May 1921, his birthday, and taken to Waterford Military Barracks. He was transferred to Ballybricken Gaol on 26 May and transferred to Kilworth on 1 June. Brigade arrest No. 16 I.B. 454.
He was transferred from Kilworth Army Camp to Spike Island internment compound on 16 Sept 1921.
He was transferred from Spike to Cork Military Hospital in Victoria Barracks on 31 Oct. Authority received from CA 907 on 29 Oct 1921.

Gallagher, Richard
Curraglass, Co. Cork.
Age: 33.
Brigade arrest No. 16 I.B. 240.
He was transferred from Kilworth Army Camp to Spike Island internment compound on 4 Mar 1921 to be moved to Bere Island internment camp.
He was transferred from Bere Island, back to Spike on 20 Sept on HMS *Stormcloud*, D 89.

Richard Gallagher, Curraglass, Co. Cork.

He was transferred from Spike to Maryborough (Portlaoise) Prison on the night of 18/19 Nov and released from there in Dec 1921.

Geraghty, Francis
16 Auburn Street, Dublin.
Age: 26.
Brigade arrest No. 16 I.B. 358.
He was transferred from Fermoy Military Barracks to Cork Military Detention Barracks on 24 June 1921.
He was transferred from Cork Military Detention Barracks to Spike Island internment compound on 25 June 1921, to 'A' Block, Hut 20.
He was involved in the Spike hunger strike.
He was transferred from Spike to Maryborough (Portlaoise) Prison on the night of 18/19 Nov and released from there in Dec 1921.

Glanville, John
Carrignafoy, Cove (Cobh), Co. Cork.
Age: 20.
Brigade arrest No. 17 I.B. 1155.

He was arrested by Crown Forces on 15 July 1921.

He was transferred from Cork Male Gaol to Spike Island internment compound on 25 July 1921, to 'A' Block, Hut 9.

Glennon, James

Redwood, Lorrha, Co. Tipperary.

Age: 29.

Brigade arrest No. 18 I.B. 217.

He was arrested by Crown Forces on 18 July 1921.

He was transferred from Cork Male Gaol to Spike Island internment compound on 25 July 1921, to 'A' Block, Hut 19.

Godley, Michael

Ballyheigue, Tralee, Co. Kerry.

Brigade arrest No. K.B. 73.

He was arrested by Auxiliary Police near Ballyheigue, Co. Kerry.[29]

He was transferred from Cork Male Gaol to Spike Island internment compound on 24 Feb 1921.

Goggin, James

Muckross, Clonakilty, Co. Cork.

Age: 32.

Brigade arrest No. 17 I.B. 873.

He was transferred from Cork to Spike Island internment compound on 25 June 1921, to 'A' Block, Hut 17.

Golfer, James

Geneva Barracks, Passage East, Co. Waterford.

Age: 25.

Brigade arrest No. 16 I.B. 505.

He was transferred from Waterford Gaol by RN destroyer to Spike Island internment compound on 18 Aug 1921, to 'A' Block, Hut 11.

He was transferred to Maryborough (Portlaoise) Prison on the night of 18/19 Nov and released from there in Dec 1921.

Golfer, Michael (Mick)

Geneva Barracks, Passage East, Co. Waterford,

He was transferred to Spike Island internment compound, date not found, to 'A' Block, Hut 11.

Golfer, Nicholas

Geneva Barracks, Passage East, Co. Waterford.

Age: 23.

Brigade arrest No. 16 I.B. 504.

He was transferred from Waterford Gaol by RN destroyer to Spike Island internment compound on 18 Aug 1921.

He was transferred to Maryborough (Portlaoise) Prison on the night of 18/19 Nov and released from there in Dec 1921.

---

29 See Michael Pierce, WS No. 1190.

Good, John (TC)

62 Grand Parade, Cork City.
Brigade arrest No. 17 I.B. 575.
He was transferred from Cork
Military Detention Barracks to Spike
Island internment compound on
30 Apr 1921.

Grace, Pat

Dromineer, Nenagh, Co. Tipperary.
Age: 22.
6th Division arrest No. 164.
Brigade arrest No. 18 I.B. 176.
He was transferred from Cork Male
Gaol to Spike Island internment
compound on 9 June 1921 to be
moved to Bere Island internment camp.
He was transferred from Bere Island
back to Spike on 20 Sept on HMS
Stormcloud, D 89.
He was transferred from Spike to
Maryborough (Portlaoise) Prison on
the night of 18/19 Nov and released
from there in Dec 1921.

Griffin, Daniel

Aughraught, Ballinadee, Co. Cork.
Brigade arrest No. 17 I.B. 202.
He was transferred from the Brigade
Cage in Victoria Barracks, Cork, to
Spike Island internment compound on
19 Feb 1921.
He was released from Spike on
31 May 1921.

Griffin, Patrick

Ballinspittle, Kinsale, Co. Cork.

Age: 25.
Occupation: Labourer.
6th Division arrest No. 68.
Brigade arrest No. 17 I.B. 1034.
He was transferred to Spike prison
compound on 15 Apr 1921 from
Bere Island. While he was a prisoner
on Spike, he was served with an
Internment Order before his release
date. Instead of being released, he
was further detained as an internee.
He was transferred to Spike Island
internment compound on 20 June. He
was moved to 'A' Block, Hut 3, during
the Spike hunger strike.
He was transferred from Spike to
Maryborough (Portlaoise) Prison on
the night of 18/19 Nov and released
from there in Dec 1921.
See Griffin, Patrick, in the list of
Spike prisoners.

Griffin, Thomas

Thomas Griffin, Ballynoe, Co. Cork.

Tallow Road, Ballynoe, Co. Cork.
Age: 29.
At the time of his arrest he was Officer
Commanding, the Ballynoe Company,

IRA. He was arrested near Ballynoe by British soldiers on 17 Jan 1921. He was marched to Fermoy Military Barracks and on 18 Jan taken to Kilworth Army Camp.
Brigade arrest No. 16 I.B. 102.
He was transferred from Kilworth Army Camp to Spike Island internment compound on 5 Mar 1921. He was appointed the canteen Staff Officer for the internees on Spike.
He initially received one week parole from Spike on 9 Nov 1921. This was extended until Dec and he was released while on parole.
Thomas Griffin's War of Independence medals are on display in the Independence Museum, on Spike.

Griffin, Timothy
Ballinamona, near Kinsale, Co. Cork.
6th Division arrest No. 274.
Brigade arrest No. 16 I.B. 192.
He was transferred from Cork Male Gaol to Spike Island internment compound on 24 Feb 1921.
He was transferred from Spike to Bere Island internment camp on 11 July 1921 on HMS *Vidette*.

Hannon, Jeremiah
Balinspittle, Kinsale, Co. Cork.
Age: 29. Occupation: Labourer.
6th Division arrest No. 66.
Brigade arrest No. 17 I.B. 1035.
He was transferred from Bere Island to Spike Island prison compound on

15 Apr 1921.
While he was a prisoner on Spike, he was served with an Internment Order before his release date. Instead of being released, he was further detained as an internee. He was transferred to Spike Island internment compound on 22 June. He was moved to 'A' Block, Hut 3, during the Spike hunger strike.
He was transferred from Spike to Maryborough (Portlaoise) Prison on the night of 18/19 Nov and released from there in Dec 1921.
See Hannon, Jeremiah, in the list of Spike prisoners.

Harmon, Joseph
3 Courtney's Avenue, Cork City.
Age: 24.
Brigade arrest No. 17 I.B. 752.
He was transferred from Cork Male Gaol to Spike Island internment compound on 25 June 1921, to 'A' Block, Hut 18.

Harper, James
Oylegate, Enniscorthy, Co. Wexford.
Age: 21.
Brigade arrest No. 16 I.B. 367.
He was transferred from Cork Male Gaol to Spike Island internment compound on 6 July 1921, to 'B' Block, Hut 20. He was moved to 'A' Block, Hut 3, during the Spike hunger strike.
He was transferred from Spike to Maryborough (Portlaoise) Prison on

the night of 18/19 Nov and released from there in Dec 1921.

Harper, Thomas
Oylgate, Enniscorthy, Co. Wexford.
Age: 22.
Brigade arrest No. 16 I.B. 368.
He was transferred from Cork Male Gaol to Spike Island internment compound on 6 July 1921 to 'A' Block, Hut 3. He was later moved to 'B' Block, Hut 20.

Harrington, James
Kinsale, Co. Cork.
Age: 25.
Brigade arrest No. 17 I.B. 419.
He was transferred from Bere Island internment camp to Spike Island internment compound on 20 Sept on HMS *Stormcloud*, D 89.
He was transferred from Spike to Maryborough (Portlaoise) Prison on the night of 18/19 Nov and released from there in Dec 1921.

Harrington, Jerome
Inches, Castletownbere, Co. Cork.
Age: 23
6th Division arrest No. 842.
Brigade arrest No. 17 I.B. 982.
He was transferred from Cork Male Gaol to Spike Island internment compound on 15 July 1921.

Harrington, John
Coolvalinane, Kinsale, Co. Cork.

6th Division arrest No. 499.
Brigade arrest No. 17 I.B. 418.
He was transferred to Spike Island internment compound to be moved to Bere Island.
He was transferred from Spike to Bere Island internment camp on 11 July 1921 on HMS *Vidette*.

Harrington, John
Inches, Castletownbere, Co. Cork.
Age: 27.
6th Division arrest No. 844.
Brigade arrest No. 17 I.B. 984.
He was transferred from Cork Male Gaol to Spike Island internment compound on 15 July 1921.

Harrington, John P.
Dromard, Ardgroom, Castletownbere, Co. Cork.
Age: 17.
Brigade arrest No. 17 I.B. 1189.
He was transferred from Bere Island internment camp to Spike Island internment compound on 20 Sept on HMS *Stormcloud*, D 89.
He was transferred from Spike to Maryborough (Portlaoise) Prison on the night of 18/19 Nov and released from there in Dec 1921.

Harrington, Thomas
Clonmeen, Banteer, Co. Cork.
Age: 28.
Brigade arrest No. K.B. 234.
He was transferred from Cork Male

Gaol to Spike Island internment compound on 1 June 1921.

Harte, Bartholomew
Knockavoher, Leap, Co. Cork.
Age: 18.
Brigade arrest No. 17 I.B. 875.
He was transferred from Cork to Spike Island internment compound on 25 June 1921.

Harte, Daniel
Farranlough, Newcestown, Co. Cork.
Brigade arrest No. 17 I.B. 298.
He was transferred from the Brigade Cage in Victoria Barracks, Cork, to Spike Island internment compound on 24 Feb 1921.

Harte, Daniel
Ahalisky, Ballinascarthy, Co. Cork.
Brigade arrest No. 17 I.B. 216.
He was transferred from the Brigade Cage in Victoria Barracks, Cork, to Spike Island internment compound on 19 Feb 1921.

Harte, James
Ballydonaugh, Lisselton, Co. Kerry.
Age: 27.
Brigade arrest No. K.B. 328.
He was transferred from Cork Male Gaol to Spike Island internment compound on 19 Sept 1921.

Harte, Jeremiah
Gaggin, Bandon, Co. Cork.

Brigade arrest No. 17 I.B. 214.
He was transferred from the Brigade Cage in Victoria Barracks, Cork, to Spike Island internment compound on 19 Feb 1921.

Harte, Patrick
Ahalisky, Ballinascarthy, Co. Cork.
Brigade arrest No. 17 I.B. 297.
He was transferred from the Brigade Cage in Victoria Barracks, Cork, to Spike Island internment compound on 24 Feb 1921.

Harte, William
Farranlough, Newcestown, Co. Cork.
Brigade arrest No. 17 I.B. 228.
He was transferred from the Brigade Cage in Victoria Barracks, Cork, to Spike Island internment compound on 19 Feb 1921.

Hartigan, Michael
Droumleigh, Mitchelstown, Co. Cork.
Age: 26.
6th Division arrest No. 431.
Brigade arrest No. 16 I.B. 342.
He was transferred from Cork Male Gaol to Spike Island internment compound on 28 May 1921. He was moved to 'A' Block, Hut 1, during the Spike hunger strike.
He was transferred from Spike to Maryborough (Portlaoise) Prison on the night of 18/19 Nov and released from there in Dec 1921.

Hartnett, Jeremiah

16 Prosperity Square,
off Barrack Street, Cork City.
6th Division arrest No. 497.
Brigade arrest No. 17 I.B. 331.
He was transferred from Spike to Bere
Island internment camp on 11 July
1921 on HMS *Vidette*.

Hartnett, William

Killeens, Upton, Co. Cork.
6th Division arrest No. 564.
Brigade arrest No. 17 I.B. 496.
He was transferred from Cork Male
Gaol to Spike Island internment
compound on 30 Apr 1921.
He was transferred from Spike to Bere
Island internment camp on 11 July
1921 on HMS *Vidette* and escaped
from there.

Hartney, Michael

14 Prospect Villas, Rosbrien,
Co. Limerick.
Brigade arrest No. 18 I.B. 126.
He was a member of 'E' Company,
2 Battalion, Mid Limerick Brigade,
IRA. On 13 Oct 1920, he was arrested
by two RIC constables in Limerick
City and taken to Limerick Gaol. He
was later moved to Limerick Barracks
and from there to Cork Male Gaol.[30]
He was transferred from Cork Male
Gaol to Spike Island internment
compound on 11 May 1921.

He was transferred from Spike to Bere
Island internment camp and released
from there on 10 Dec 1921.

Hassett, Daniel

Mallow, Co. Cork. Age: 22.
Brigade arrest No. K.B. 222.
He was transferred from Cork Male
Gaol to Spike Island internment
compound on 22 June 1921.

Hayes, James

James Hayes, Milford, Co. Cork.

Cromogue, Milford, Co. Cork.
Age: 18.
Brigade arrest No. K.B. 185.
He was transferred from Cork Male
Gaol to Spike Island internment
compound on 11 May 1921, to 'A'
Block, Hut 15.

Hayes, Jeremiah

Passage West, Co. Cork.
Brigade arrest No. 17 I.B. 242.
He was transferred from the Brigade
Cage in Victoria Barracks, Cork, to

---

30 See Michael Hartney, WS No. 1415.

Spike Island internment compound on
19 Feb 1921.

Hayes, Patrick

Mossgrove, Newcestown, Co. Cork.
Brigade arrest No. 17 I.B. 221.
He was transferred from the Brigade
Cage in Victoria Barracks, Cork, to
Spike Island internment compound on
19 Feb 1921.

Hayes, Paul

16 Moore Street, Cork City. Age: 34.
6th Division arrest No. 720.
Brigade arrest No. 17 I.B. 810.
He was transferred from Cork Male
Gaol to Spike Island internment
compound on 22 June 1921.

Healy, Michael

Mocollop, Ballyduff, Co. Waterford.
Age: 21.
Brigade arrest No. 16 I.B. 186.
He was transferred from Kilworth
Army Camp to Spike Island
internment compound on 17 May
1921 to be moved to Bere Island
internment camp.
He was transferred from Bere Island
back to Spike on 20 Sept on HMS
Stormcloud, D 89.
He was transferred from Spike to
Maryborough (Portlaoise) Prison on
the night of 18/19 Nov and released
from there in Dec 1921.

Healy, Pat

Mallow, Co. Cork. Age: 30.
Brigade arrest No. K.B. 262.
He was arrested by Crown Forces on
27 June 1921.
He was transferred from Cork Male
Gaol to Spike Island internment
compound on 6 July 1921.
He was released from Spike on
12 Aug, authority received from CA
693, on 11 Aug 1921.

Healy, Timothy

Tim Healy, Ovens, Co. Cork.

Castleinch, Ovens, Co. Cork.
Age: 29.
Occupation: Farm labourer.
Brigade arrest No. 17 I.B. 1163.
He was captured by British soldiers
from the Manchester Regiment near
Ballincollig on 8 July 1921. He was
taken to Ballincollig Army Barracks,
in mid-July he was moved to the
Brigade Cage in Victoria Barracks and
from there to Cork Male Gaol.[31]
He was transferred from Cork Male

---

31 See Tim O'Keeffe, WS No. 810.

Gaol to Spike Island internment compound on 25 July 1921, to 'A' Block, Hut 9.

He was transferred to Maryborough (Portlaoise) Prison on the night of 18/19 Nov and released from there on 8 Dec 1921.

Heaphy, Thomas

Cahercorney, Holycross, Kilmallock, Co. Limerick.

Age: 26.

Brigade arrest No. 18 I.B. 187.

He was transferred from Cork Male Gaol to Spike Island internment compound on 11 May 1921.

Hegarty, Michael

Ballyvourney, Co. Cork.

6th Division arrest No. 194.

He was transferred from Cork Male Gaol to Spike Island internment compound on 25 Apr 1921.

He was transferred from Spike to Bere Island internment camp on 11 July 1921 on HMS *Vidette*.

Hegarty, Patrick

Ardarow, Glenville, Co. Cork.

Age: 28.

6th Division arrest No. 432.

Brigade arrest No. 16 I.B. 346.

He was transferred from Cork Male Gaol to Spike Island internment compound on 28 May 1921, to 'A' Block, Hut 20.

Hegarty, Peter

Peter Hegarty, Garryvoe, Co. Cork.

Garryvoe, Castlemartyr, Co. Cork.

Arrested on the 23 Mar 1921.

Brigade arrest No. 17 I.B. 528.

He was transferred from Cork Male Gaol to Spike Island internment compound on 30 Apr 1921.

He was transferred from Spike to Bere Island internment camp and escaped from there.

His brother Dick Hegarty was killed in action against Crown Forces during the battle of Clonmult in Co. Cork on 20 Feb 1921.

Hennessy, James

Lower Road, Ringaskiddy, Co. Cork.

Age: 22.

6th Division arrest No. 853.

Brigade arrest No. 17 I.B. 1086.

He was transferred from Kilkenny, via Clonmel, Kilworth Army Camp and Cork Male Goal to Spike Island internment compound on 15 July 1921, to 'A' Block, Hut 10.

He was transferred from Spike to

Maryborough (Portlaoise) Prison on the night of 18/19 Nov and was released from there in Dec 1921.

John Hennessy, Ballynoe, Co. Waterford.

Hennessy, John (Sean)

Ballynoe, Co. Waterford.
6th Division arrest No. 231.
Brigade arrest No. 16 I.B. 110.
He was arrested at home by British soldiers on 17 Jan 1921. He was marched to Fermoy Military Barracks and on 18 Jan taken to Kilworth Army Camp.
He was transferred from Kilworth Army Camp to Spike Island internment compound on 5 Mar 1921, to 'B' Block, Hut 13.
He was transferred from Spike to Bere Island internment camp on 11 July 1921 on HMS *Vidette* and released from there in Dec 1921.
The diary that Hennessy wrote while on Spike Island is now on display in the Independence Museum on Spike.

Hennessy, Timothy (Tadhg)

Danesfort, Threecastles, Co. Kilkenny.
Age: 30.
Occupation: Farmer.
Brigade arrest No. 16 I.B. 300.
He was arrested by Crown Forces on 24 Feb 1921 at his brother Tom's funeral near Threecastles. His brother was killed while ambushing British soldiers in Kilkenny City.
Following his arrest he was taken to Kilkenny, to Clonmel, to Kilworth Army Camp and to Cork Male Gaol.[32]
He was transferred from Cork Male Gaol to Spike Island internment compound on 17 May 1921, to 'B' Block, Hut 23.
He took part in the hunger strike on Spike, which began at 6 p.m. on 30 Aug 1921. He was moved to 'A' Block, Hut 21 during the strike.
He was transferred from Spike to Maryborough (Portlaoise) Prison on the night of 18/19 Nov and released from there in Dec 1921.

Herlihy, Jeremiah

Clashanure, Walshestown, Ovens, Co. Cork.
Age: 29. Occupation: Farmer.
Brigade arrest No. 17 I.B. 1160.
He was captured in June 1921 by soldiers from the Manchester Regiment, near Ballincollig. He was taken to Ballincollig Army Barracks,

---

32 See his WS, No. 1614.

Jeremiah Herlihy, Ovens, Co. Cork.

in mid-July to the Brigade Cage in
Victoria Barracks and from there to
Cork Male Gaol.

He was transferred from Cork Male
Gaol to Spike Island internment
compound on 25 July 1921, to 'A'
Block, Hut 9.

He was transferred from Spike to
Maryborough (Portlaoise) Prison on
the night of 18/19 Nov and released
from there on 8 Dec 1921.

Herlihy, John

Chapel Hill, Fermoy, Co. Cork. Age: 23.
Brigade arrest No. 16 I.B. 407.

He was transferred from Cork to
Spike Island internment compound on
6 July 1921, to 'B' Block, Hut 20.
He participated in the Spike hunger
strike. He was moved to 'A' Block, Hut
1, during the strike.

He was transferred from Spike to
Maryborough (Portlaoise) Prison on
the night of 18/19 Nov and released
from there in Dec 1921.

Herlihy, Timothy

Tim Herlihy, Ovens, Co. Cork.

Clashanure, Walshestown, Ovens,
Co. Cork.

Age: 25. Occupation: Farm labourer.
Brigade arrest No. 17 I.B. 1162

He was captured in June 1921 by
soldiers from the Manchester
Regiment near Ballincollig. He was
taken to Ballincollig Army Barracks.
In mid-July he was moved to the
Brigade Cage in Victoria Barracks and
from there to Cork Male Gaol.[33]

He was transferred from Cork Male
Gaol to Spike Island internment
compound on 25 July 1921, to 'A'
Block, Hut 9.

He was transferred from Spike to
Maryborough (Portlaoise) Prison
on the night of 18/19 Nov. He was
released from there on 8 Dec 1921.

Heskin, Ted

Glandulane, Fermoy, Co. Cork.
6th Division arrest No. 260.
Brigade arrest No. 16 I.B. 140.

---

33 See Timothy O'Keeffe, WS No. 810.

He was transferred from Spike to Bere Island internment camp on 11 July 1921 on HMS *Vidette*.

Hickey, Denis

Denis Hickey, Glenville, Co. Cork.

Glenville, Co. Cork.
Age: 38. Occupation: Farmer.
6th Division arrest No. 585.
Brigade arrest No. 16 I.B. 457
& S.C. /206.
While he was in the Spike prison compound he was served with an Internment Order before his release date. Instead of being released, he was further detained as an internee.
On 12 Sept, he was transferred to Spike Island internment compound, to 'B' Block, Hut 20.
He was transferred from Spike to Maryborough (Portlaoise) Prison on the night of 18/19 Nov and released from there on 8 Dec 1921.
See Hickey, Denis, in the list of Spike prisoners.

Hickey, James
Monkstown, Co. Cork. Age: 23.

6th Division arrest No. 370.
Brigade arrest No. 17 I.B. 288.
He was transferred from the Brigade Cage in Victoria Barracks, Cork, to Spike Island internment compound on 24 Feb 1921.
He was transferred from Spike to Bere Island internment camp on 11 July 1921 on HMS *Vidette*.

Hickie, John A.

John Hickie, Millstreet, Co. Cork.

Main Street, Millstreet, Co. Cork.
Age: 35.
6th Division arrest No. 771.
Brigade arrest No. K.B. 255.
He was transferred from Cork Male Gaol to Spike Island internment compound on 22 June 1921.

Hill, Michael
Cork City.
Brigade arrest No. 17 I.B. 263.
He was transferred from the Brigade Cage in Victoria Barracks, Cork, to Spike Island internment compound on 19 Feb 1921.
He was transferred from Spike to

Bere Island internment camp by RN destroyer on 14/15 Apr 1921.

Hogan, Martin
Ballywilliam, Gortmore, Nenagh, Co. Tipperary. Age: 22.
Brigade arrest No. 18 I.B. 194.
He was transferred from Cork to Spike Island internment compound on 25 June 1921, to 'A' Block, Hut 10.

Hogan, Patrick
Address details not found.
He was transferred from Cork Military Detention Barracks to Spike Island internment compound on 19 Feb 1921.

Hogan, William
Grenane, Co. Tipperary.
Brigade arrest No. 16 I.B. 17.
He was transferred from Kilworth Army Camp to Spike Island internment compound on 4 Mar 1921.
He was released from Spike on 31 May 1921.

Holland, Dan
Timoleague, Courtmacsherry, Co. Cork.
Age: 37. Occupation: Farmer.
6th Division arrest number. 550.
Brigade arrest No. 17 I.B. 993.
He was originally on Spike as a prisoner and he was transferred back to Cork Male Gaol.
While in Cork Male Gaol, he was served with an Internment Order

before his release date. Instead of being released, he was further detained as an internee.
He was transferred from Cork Male Gaol back to Spike Island internment compound on 14 Nov 1921.
He was transferred from Spike to Maryborough (Portlaoise) Prison on the night of 18/19 Nov and released from there on 8 Dec 1921.
See also: Holland, Dan, in the list of Spike prisoners.

Holland, James
Strand Road, Clonakilty, Co. Cork.
Age: 26.
Brigade arrest No. 17 I.B. 459.
He was arrested by Crown Forces on 29 July 1921.
He was transferred from Cork Male Gaol to Spike Island internment compound on 22 Aug 1921, to 'A' Block, Hut 16.

Holland, James
Butlerstown, Co. Cork.
6th Division arrest No. 346.
Brigade arrest No. 17 I.B. 277.
He was transferred from Cork Male Gaol to Spike Island internment compound on 19 Feb 1921.

Holland, Patrick
34 Douglas Street, Cork City.
6th Division arrest No. 497.
Brigade arrest No. 17 I.B. 330.
He was transferred to Spike Island

internment compound, date not found. He was transferred from Spike to Bere Island internment camp on 11 July 1921 on HMS *Vidette*.

Holley, Michael
Convent Street, Listowel, Co. Kerry. Age: 24.
Brigade arrest No. K.B. 161.
He was transferred from Cork Male Gaol to Spike Island internment compound on 19 Sept 1921, to Hut 18.

Holmes, John, Dr.
Scariff, Co. Clare. Age: 37.
6th Division arrest No. 188.
Brigade arrest No. 18 I.B. 204.
He was transferred from Cork Male Gaol to Spike Island internment compound on 15 July 1921, to 'A' Block, Hut 8.
As a doctor, he was the medical officer for the internees. He was released from Spike on medical grounds on 13 Oct 1921, authority received from CA 693, on 15 Oct.

Horan, William
Hollyford, Co. Tipperary.
Age: 24. Occupation: Farmer.
6th Division arrest No. 468
Brigade arrest No. 16 I.B. 488.
He was originally on Spike as a prisoner and transferred back to Cork Male Gaol.
While he was in Cork Male Gaol, he was served with an Internment Order before his release date. Instead of being released, he was further detained as an internee.
He was transferred from Cork Male Gaol back to Spike Island internment compound on 14 Nov 1921.
He was transferred from Spike to Maryborough (Portlaoise) Prison on the night of 18/19 Nov and released from there on 8 Dec 1921.
See also: Horan, William, in the list of Spike prisoners.

Horgan, Daniel
Kilgobbin, Ballinadee, Co. Cork.
6th Division arrest No. 281.
Brigade arrest No. 17 I.B. 208.
He was transferred from Cork Male Gaol to Spike Island internment compound on 24 Feb 1921.
He was transferred from Spike to Bere Island internment camp on 11 July 1921 on HMS *Vidette*.

Horgan, Daniel (Denis)
Ballinora, Carrigrohane, Cork City. Age: 22.
Brigade arrest No. 17 I.B. 648.
He was transferred from the Brigade Cage in Victoria Barracks, Cork, to Spike Island internment compound on 16 May 1921.

Horgan, Denis
Nursetown, Dromahane, Mallow, Co. Cork.
Age: 28.

Denis Horgan, Lombardstown, Co. Cork.

Brigade arrest No. K.B. 212.
He was transferred from Cork Male
Gaol to Spike Island internment
compound on 16 May 1921 for
transfer to Bere Island.
He was transferred from Bere Island
back to Spike on 20 Sept on HMS
Stormcloud, D 89.

Horgan, Patrick
Inchimay, Nadd, Lyre, Banteer,
Co. Cork.
Age: 21.
Brigade arrest No. K.B. 283.
He was arrested by Crown Forces on
30 June 1921.
He was transferred from Cork Male
Gaol to Spike Island internment
compound on 6 July 1921.

Horgan, Timothy
Kilcorney, Co. Cork.
Age: 26.
Brigade arrest No. K.B. 288.
He was arrested by Crown Forces on
30 June 1921.
He was transferred from Cork Male

Gaol to Spike Island internment
compound on 6 July 1921.

Hunt, Frank
Ballinspittle, Ballinadee, Kinsale,
Co. Cork.
6th Division arrest No. 247.
Brigade arrest No. 17 I.B. 98.
He was transferred from Cork Male
Gaol to Spike Island internment
compound on 24 Feb 1921.
He was transferred from Spike to Bere
Island internment camp on 11 July
1921 on HMS *Vidette*.

Hunt, Frank
Parade Field, Bantry, Co. Cork.
Age: 22.
6th Division arrest No. 793.
Brigade arrest No. 17 I.B. 966.
He was transferred from Cork Male
Gaol to Spike Island internment
compound on 15 July 1921.

Hunt, Hubert J. (Bertie), PC
Richmond House, Corofin,
Co. Clare.
Age: 38.
Brigade arrest No. 18 I.B. 215.
He was arrested by Crown Forces on
18 July 1921.
He was transferred from Cork Male
Gaol to Spike Island internment
compound on 25 July 1921, to 'A'
Block, Hut 19.
He was the commander of the
Clare Volunteers.

Hubert J. 'Bertie' Hunt, Corofin, Co. Clare.

Commanding Officer, 5th Battalion, Clare Brigade, Irish Volunteers. Commanding Officer, 3rd Battalion, Mid Clare Brigade, IRA. He was a Peace Commissioner and also a member of Clare County Council.

Hunt, John H.

Parade Field, Bantry, Co. Cork. Age: 24. 6th Division arrest No. 794. Brigade arrest No. 17 I.B. 967. He was transferred from Cork Male Gaol to Spike Island internment compound on 15 July 1921.

Hunt, William

Chapel Street, Bantry, Co. Cork. Age: 19. 6th Division arrest No. 830. Brigade arrest No. 17 I.B. 968. He was transferred from Cork Male Gaol to Spike Island internment compound on 15 July 1921, to 'A' Block, Hut 6.

Hurley, Frank

Clonakilty, Co. Cork. Age: 23. Brigade arrest No. 17 I.B. 1181. He was transferred from Cork Male Gaol to Spike Island internment compound on 22 Aug 1921, to 'A' Block, Hut 16.

Hurley, John

Clonakilty, Co. Cork. Age: 17. Brigade arrest No. 16 I.B. 867. He was transferred from Cork, to Spike Island internment compound on 14 Nov 1921.

Hurley, Richard

Coolaghmore, Callan, Co. Kilkenny. Age: 37. Brigade arrest No. 16 I.B. 277. He was transferred from Waterford Gaol to Spike Island internment compound on 2 May 1921, to 'B' Block. He was moved to 'A' Block, Hut 22, during the Spike hunger strike. He was transferred from Spike to Maryborough (Portlaoise) Prison on 18/19 Nov and released from there in Dec 1921.

Hurley, Thomas

Carrigmore, Conna, Co. Cork. 6th Division arrest No. 229. Brigade arrest No. 16 I.B. 108. He was transferred from Spike to Bere Island internment camp on 11 July 1921 on HMS *Vidette*.

Thomas Hurley, Conna, Co. Cork.

Jackson, Eugene
Cork City.
He was transferred from Cork Male
Gaol to Spike Island internment
compound on 19 Feb 1921.

Jackson, Robert
Cork City.
He was transferred from Cork Male
Gaol to Spike Island internment
compound on 19 Feb 1921.

Jennings, John
College Road, Cork City.
6th Division arrest No. 548.
Brigade arrest No. 17 I.B. 152.
He was transferred from Cork Male
Gaol to Spike Island internment
compound on 30 Apr 1921.
He was transferred from Spike to Bere
Island internment camp on 11 July
1921 on HMS *Vidette*.

Jones, William
Mourneabbey, Mallow, Co. Cork.
Age: 31.
Brigade arrest No. 17 I.B. 148.

He was transferred from Cork
Military Detention Barracks to Spike
Island internment compound on
24 Feb 1921, to 'A' Block, Hut 7.
He was transferred from Spike to Bere
Island internment camp on 11 July
1921 on HMS *Vidette*.

Joyce, James
Killeagh, Co. Cork.
Brigade arrest No. 17 I.B. 455.
He was transferred from Cork Male
Gaol to Spike Island internment
compound on 12 Apr 1921.
He was transferred from Spike to Bere
Island internment camp on 14/15 Apr
1921 by RN destroyer.

Joyce, Michael
Roughdean, Lorrha, Co. Tipperary.
Age: 22.
Brigade arrest No. 18 I.B. 218.
He was arrested by Crown Forces on
18 July 1921.
He was transferred from Cork Male
Gaol to Spike Island internment
compound on 25 July 1921.

Joyce, Thomas Carey
Cronohill, Upper Kilworth, Co. Cork.
Age: 31
Occupation: Farmer's son.
He was arrested on 29 June 1921.
Brigade arrest No. 16 I.B. 507.
He was transferred from Kilworth
Army Camp to Spike Island internment
compound on 15 Sept 1921.

Thomas Carey Joyce, Kilworth, Co. Cork.

He was transferred from Spike to
Maryborough (Portlaoise) Prison on
18/19 Nov and released from there in
Dec 1921.
His brother-in-law, John Joe Joyce, was
killed in action on 20 Feb 1921 during
the battle of Clonmult, Co. Cork.

Kavanagh, Denis

Cronecribbon, Inch, Gorey, Co. Wexford.
Age: 21.
Brigade arrest No. 16 I.B. 497.
He was transferred from Waterford
Gaol by RN destroyer to Spike Island
internment compound on 18 Aug
1921, to 'A' Block, Hut 11.

Kavanagh, James

Churchtown, Buttevant, Co. Cork.
6th Division arrest No. 315.
Brigade arrest No. K.B. 81.
He was transferred from Cork Male
Gaol to Spike Island internment
compound on 24 Feb 1921.

Keane, David

Ballinaruck, Bandon, Co. Cork.

Brigade arrest No. 17 I.B. 220.
He was transferred from the Brigade
Cage in Victoria Barracks, Cork, to
Spike Island internment compound on
19 Feb 1921.

Keane, John (Sean)

King's Street, (Mc Dermott St),
Mitchelstown, Co. Cork.
Age: 22.
Brigade arrest No. 16 I.B. 414.
He was transferred from Fermoy
Military Barracks to Cork Military
Detention Barracks on 24 June.
He was transferred from Cork
Military Detention Barracks to Spike
Island internment compound on
25 June 1921, to 'B' Block, Huts 16.
He was later moved to Hut 20. He
was moved to 'A' Block, Hut 1, during
the Spike hunger strike.
He was transferred from Spike to
Cork Military Hospital, in Victoria
Barracks, for a new glass eye
and returned to Spike on 25 July
1921 from Cork Male Gaol.
He was transferred from Spike to
Maryborough (Portlaoise) Prison on
18/19 Nov and released from there in
Dec 1921.

Keating, Thomas

Castle Street, Cahir, Co. Tipperary.
He was transferred to Spike Island
internment compound, date not found,
to 'A' Block, Hut 20.

Keating, Thomas
8 Parnell Street, Waterford City.
Age: 23.
Brigade arrest No. 16 I.B. 323.
He was transferred from Cork to
Spike Island internment compound on
9 June 1921.

Kehoe, Owen
21 Belstear Street, Wexford Town.
Age: 49.
Brigade arrest No. 16 I.B. 269.
He was transferred from Fermoy
Military Barracks to Cork Military
Detention Barracks on 24 June.
He was transferred from Cork
Military Detention Barracks to Spike
Island internment compound on
25 June 1921, to 'A' Block, Huts 18.

Kelleher, Daniel
Minor Row, Millstreet, Co. Cork.
Age: 27.
Brigade arrest No. K.B. 320.
He was transferred from Cork Male
Gaol to Spike Island internment
compound on 22 Aug 1921.

Kelleher, Daniel J.
Lachabane, Millstreet, Co. Cork.
Age: 27.
Brigade arrest No. K.B. 319.
He was transferred from Cork Male
Gaol to Spike Island internment
compound on 22 Aug 1921, to 'A'
Block, Hut 14.

Kelleher, James
Farrane,.
6th Division arrest No. 464.
Brigade arrest No. 17 I.B.408.
He was transferred from Cork Male
Gaol to Spike Island internment
compound on 25 Apr 1921.
He was transferred from Spike to Bere
Island internment camp on 11 July
1921 on HMS *Vidette*.

Kelleher, John
Farnivane, Bandon, Co. Cork.
Brigade arrest No. 17 I.B. 213.
He was transferred from Cork Male
Gaol to Spike Island internment
compound on 24 Feb 1921.

Kelleher, John
The Glebe, Inchigeela, Co. Cork.
Age: 56.
Brigade arrest No. 17 I.B. 1132.
He was transferred from the Brigade
Cage in Victoria Barracks via Cork
Male Gaol to Spike Island internment
compound on 15 July 1921.
He was released from Spike on 9 Nov,
authority received from CA 693 on
3 Nov 1921.

Kelleher, John (Sean)
Geragh, Ballinacurra, Midleton,
Co. Cork.
Age: 21.
Occupation: Fitter.
6th Division arrest No. 722.
Brigade arrest No. 17 I.B. 807.

Sean Kelleher, Geragh, Midleton, Co. Cork.

He was arrested by Auxiliary Police near Midleton on 16 May 1921 and taken to Midleton RIC Barracks. He was later moved to Belmont huts in Cobh and from there to Cork Male Gaol.[34] He was transferred from Cork Male Gaol to Spike Island internment compound on 22 June 1921. He was released from Spike in early Nov 1921.

Kelleher, Michael
2 Henry Street, Cork City.
6th Division arrest No. 596.
Brigade arrest No. 17 I.B. 504.
He was transferred from Cork Male Gaol to Spike Island internment compound on 30 Apr 1921.
He was transferred from Spike to Bere Island internment camp on 11 July 1921 on HMS *Vidette*.

Kelleher, Michael
Clondrohid, Co. Cork. Age: 41.

6th Division arrest No. 576.
Brigade arrest No. 17 I.B. 458.
He was transferred from Cork Male Gaol to Spike Island internment compound on 22 June 1921, to 'A' Block, Hut 5.

Kelly, Con
Allihies Mines, Lehanemore, Castletownbere, Co. Cork.
Age: 19.
Brigade arrest No. 17 I.B. 1175.
He was transferred from Cork Male Gaol to Spike Island internment compound on 25 July 1921, to 'A' Block, Hut 4.

Kelly, John
35 Mardyke Street, Skibbereen, Co. Cork.
Age: 21.
Brigade arrest No. 17 I.B. 808.
He was arrested by Crown Forces on 22 June 1921.
He was transferred from Cork Male Gaol to Spike Island internment compound on 30 June 1921, to 'B' Block, Hut 17.

Kelly, Martin
Kilgobinet, Dungarvan, Co. Waterford.
Age: 26.
Brigade arrest No. 16 I.B. 133.
He was transferred from Kilworth Army Camp to Spike Island internment compound on 17 May 1921.

---

34 See his WS, No. 1456.

Kelly, Michael

Kilgobnet, Dungarvan, Co. Waterford.

Age: 21

Brigade arrest No. 16 I.B. 126.

He was transferred to Spike to be moved to Bere Island.

He was transferred from Spike to Bere Island internment camp by RN destroyer on 14/15 Apr 1921.

He was transferred from Bere Island back to Spike on 20 Sept on HMS *Stormcloud*, D 89.

He was transferred from Spike to Maryborough (Portlaoise) Prison on 18/19 Nov and released from there in Dec 1921.

Kelly, Richard

Passage West, Co. Cork.

Brigade arrest No. 17 I.B. 65.

He was transferred from the Brigade Cage in Victoria Barracks, Cork, to Spike Island internment compound on 19 Feb 1921.

Kelly, William

35 Mardyke Street, Skibbereen, Co. Cork.

Age: 19.

Brigade arrest No. 17 I.B. 809.

He was arrested by Crown Forces on 22 June 1921.

He was transferred from Cork Male Gaol to Spike Island internment compound on 30 June 1921, to 'B' Block, Hut 17.

Kennedy, Patrick

Patrick Kennedy, Ballyhooly, Co. Cork.

Ballyhooly, Fermoy, Co. Cork.

6th Division arrest No. 223.

He was transferred to Spike to be moved to Bere Island.

He was transferred from Spike to Bere Island internment camp on 14/15 Apr 1921 by RN destroyer.

Kennelly, Michael

Aglish, Co. Waterford.

6th Division arrest No. 281.

Brigade arrest No. 16 I.B. 183.

He was transferred from Kilworth Army Camp to Spike Island internment compound on 4 Mar 1921.

He was transferred from Spike to Bere Island internment camp on 11 July 1921 on HMS *Vidette*.

Kenny, Joseph

Grenagh, Co. Cork.

Brigade arrest No. L. 471

He was arrested at home in Grenagh, Co. Cork, at 3 a.m. on 15/16 July 1920. Ammunition was found in his house that his wife saw being planted

Joseph Kenny, Grenagh, Co. Cork.

by the RIC during the search. He was
taken first to Cork Military Detention
Barracks and that evening to Cork
Male Gaol.

He survived 90 days on hunger strike
in Cork Male Gaol from 15 Aug to
12 Nov 1920.

Around the end of Mar 1921, he
was transferred to Cork Military
Detention Barracks.

He was transferred from Cork
Military Detention Barracks to Spike
Island internment compound on
12 Apr 1921.

He was transferred from Spike to Bere
Island internment camp on 14/15 Apr
1921 by RN destroyer.

He received parole from Bere Island
during Nov. He returned from parole
and he was released from Bere Island
in Dec 1921.

Kenny, Michael

Barnclay Cottage, Mourne Abbey,
Co. Cork.

Age: 25.

Arrested on 28 June 1921.

Brigade arrest No. 16 I.B. 492.

He was transferred from Kilworth
Army Camp to Spike Island internment
compound on 16 Sept 1921.

Keohane, Donald (Daniel)

Kinsale, Co. Cork.

Brigade arrest No. 17 I.B. 246.

He was transferred from Cork Male
Gaol to Spike Island internment
compound on 24 Feb 1921.

He was transferred from Spike to
Bere Island internment camp by RN
destroyer on 14/15 Apr 1921.

Keohane, Tim

Ballinroher, Timoleague, Co. Cork.

Age: 22. Occupation: Labourer.

6th Division arrest No. 542.

Brigade arrest No. 17 I.B. 991.

He was arrested by British soldiers near
Timoleague in June 1921 and taken
to Clonakilty Barracks. He was later
moved to Cork Military Detention
Barracks and to Cork Male Gaol.

He was originally on Spike as a
prisoner and transferred back to Cork
Male Gaol.

While he was in Cork Male Gaol,
he was served with an Internment
Order before his release date. Instead
of being released, he was further
detained as an internee.

He was transferred from Cork Male
Gaol back to Spike Island internment
compound on 14 Nov 1921.

He was transferred from Spike to

Maryborough (Portlaoise) Prison on the night of 18/19 Nov and released from there on 8 Dec 1921.

See also: Keohane, Tim, in the list of Spike prisoners.

Kett, William

Stradbally, Co. Waterford.

Brigade arrest No. 16 I.B. 86.

He was transferred from Spike to Bere Island internment camp by RN destroyer on 14/15 Apr 1921.

Kiely, Roger

Roger Kiely, Millstreet, Co. Cork.

Cullen, Millstreet, Co. Cork.

Age: 25.

Occupation: National Teacher.

6th Division arrest No. 776.

Brigade arrest No. K.B. 260.

He was captured by British soldiers near Kanturk on 11 June 1921.

He was transferred from Cork Male Gaol to Spike Island internment compound on 22 June 1921, to 'A' Block, Hut 12.

He was moved to 'A' Block, Hut 14, during the Spike hunger strike.

He was transferred from Spike to Maryborough (Portlaoise) Prison on 18/19 Nov and released from there in Dec 1921.

He is depicted in the famous Keating painting 'The Men of the South'.

Kierse, Patrick

Killeen, Corofin, Co. Clare.

Age: 24.

Brigade arrest No. 18 I.B. 223.

He was transferred from Limerick via Cork Male Gaol to Spike Island internment compound on 22 Aug 1921, to 'A' Block, Hut 19.

Kingston, Daniel

Lislevane, Co. Cork.

He was transferred from Cork Male Gaol to Spike Island internment compound on 19 Feb 1921.

Kingston, William

Tureen, Skibbereen, Co. Cork.

6th Division arrest No. 390.

Brigade arrest No. 17 I.B. 352.

He was arrested in Jan 1921 and taken to Bandon Military Barracks. From there he was moved to Cork Male Gaol.[35]

He was transferred from Cork Male Gaol to Spike Island internment.

He was transferred from Spike to Bere Island internment camp on 11 July

---

35 See Samuel Kingston, WS No. 620, p.6.

1921 on HMS *Vidette* and released from there in Dec 1921.

Kirby, James

Castlelyons, Co. Cork.
Brigade arrest No. 18 I.B. 325.
He was transferred from Kilworth Army Camp to Spike Island internment compound on 13 Apr 1921.
He was transferred from Spike to Bere Island internment camp on 14/15 Apr 1921 by RN destroyer.

Lacey, James Joseph

Ballycarney, Ferns, Co. Wexford.
Age: 24.
Brigade arrest No. 16 I.B. 361.
He was transferred from Kilworth Army Camp to Spike Island internment compound on 30 May 1921.

Lacy, John

Firoda, Castlecomer, Co. Kilkenny.
Age: 37.
He was arrested on 12 Apr 1921.
Brigade arrest No. 16 I.B. 440.
He was transferred from Kilworth Army Camp to Spike Island internment compound on 16 Sept 1921.

Lane, John

Whitechurch, Cappagh, Co. Waterford.
Brigade arrest No. R.W. 45.
He was transferred from Kilworth Army Camp to Spike Island internment compound on 13 Apr 1921.
He was transferred from Spike to

Bere Island internment camp by RN destroyer on 14/15 Apr 1921.

Lane, Michael

Also listed as Lean.
Killarney, Co. Kerry.
Age: 24.
6th Division arrest No. 770.
Brigade arrest No. K.B. 254.
He was transferred from Cork Male Gaol to Spike Island internment compound on 22 June 1921, to 'A' Block, Hut 14.

Langford, Robert

St Luke's, Cork City.
6th Division arrest No. 707,
Brigade arrest No. 17 I.B. 779.
He was transferred from Cork Male Gaol to Spike Island internment compound on 28 May 1921.

Larkin, Thomas

Seskin, Kilsheelan, Clonmel, Co. Tipperary.
6th Division arrest No. 274.
Brigade arrest No. 16 I.B. 190.
He was transferred from Kilworth Army Camp to Spike Island internment compound on 4 Mar 1921.
He was transferred from Spike to Bere Island internment camp on 11 July 1921 on HMS *Vidette*.

Lavillin, Denis

3 Wise's Cottage, Cork City.
Age: 24.

6th Division arrest No. 751.
Brigade arrest No. 17 I.B. 734.
He was transferred from Cork Male
Gaol to Spike Island internment
compound on 22 June 1921.

Lawless, Michael
Ballinclare, Camolin, Co. Wexford.
Age: 27.
Brigade arrest No. 16 I.B. 495.
He was transferred from Waterford
Gaol by RN destroyer to Spike Island
internment compound on 18 Aug
1921, to 'A' Block, Hut 11.

Patrick J. Lawlor, The Fayth, Co. Wexford.

Lawlor, Patrick
126 Blythe, The Faythe,
Wexford Town.
Age: 19.
Brigade arrest No. 16 I.B. 388.
He was transferred from Fermoy
Military Barracks to Cork Military
Detention Barracks on 24 June.
He was transferred from Cork
Military Detention Barracks to Spike
Island internment compound on
25 June 1921, to 'A' Block, Hut 18.

Lawton, John
Chapel Street, Carrigtwohill, Co. Cork.
Age: 20.
Brigade arrest No. 17 I.B. 1014.
He was transferred from Cork Male
Gaol to Spike Island internment
compound on 25 July 1921.

Leary, Cornelius
5 Brown Street, Cork City.
Age: 20.
6th Division arrest No. 441.
Brigade arrest No. 17 I.B. 372.
He was transferred from Spike to Bere
Island internment camp on 11 July
1921 on HMS *Vidette*.
He was transferred from Bere Island
back to Spike on 20 Sept on HMS
Stormcloud, D 89.
He was released from Spike on 5 Nov,
authority received from CA 1068 on
4 Nov 1921.

Leary, Cornelius
Also listed as O'Leary.
Macroom, Co. Cork.
Age: 21.
Brigade arrest No. 17 I.B. 1130.
He was transferred from the Brigade
Cage in Victoria Barracks, Cork, to
Spike Island internment compound on
15 July 1921, to 'A' Block, Hut 20.

Leary, James
Ballynoe, Co. Cork.
6th Division arrest No. 226.
Brigade arrest No. 16 I.B. 105.

He was transferred to Spike to be
moved to Bere Island.
He was transferred from Spike to Bere
Island internment camp on 11 July
1921 on HMS *Vidette*.
He was transferred from Spike to
Maryborough (Portlaoise) Prison on
18/19 Nov and was released from
there in Dec 1921.

Leary, Patrick
Lisanlea, Upton, Co. Cork.
Age: 28. Occupation: Farmer.
6th Division arrest No. 587.
Brigade arrest No. 17 I.B. 1030.
He was originally on Spike as a
prisoner and transferred back to Cork
Male Gaol.
While he was in Cork Male Gaol,
he was served with an Internment
Order before his release date. Instead
of being released, he was further
detained as an internee.
He was transferred from Cork Male
Gaol back to Spike Island internment
compound on 14 Nov 1921.
He was transferred from Spike to
Maryborough (Portlaoise) Prison on the
night of 18/19 Nov and released from
there on 8 Dec 1921.
See also: Leary, Pat, in the list of
Spike prisoners.

Lee, William
Inistioge, Co. Kilkenny.
Age: 22.
Brigade arrest No. 16 I.B. 278.

He was transferred from Kilkenny
Gaol to Spike Island internment
compound on 2 May 1921.

Lehane, Daniel
Scart, Bantry, Co. Cork.
Age: 19. Occupation: Farmer.
6th Division arrest No. 537.
Brigade arrest No. 17 I.B. 999.
While he was in the Spike prison
compound, he was served with an
Internment Order before his release
date. Instead of being released, he was
further detained as an internee. He was
transferred to Spike Island internment
compound on 7 Sept 1921.
He was transferred from Spike to
Maryborough (Portlaoise) Prison on
the night of 18/19 Nov and released
from there on 8 Dec 1921.
See Lehane, Daniel, in the list of
Spike prisoners.

Lehane, Daniel
21 Dominick Street, Cork City.
Age: 26.
6th Division arrest No. 366.
Brigade arrest No. 17 I.B. 284.
He was transferred from the Brigade
Cage in Victoria Barracks, Cork, to
Spike Island internment compound on
24 Feb 1921.
He was transferred from Spike to Bere
Island internment camp on 11 July
1921 on HMS *Vidette*.
Brother of Frank, Pat and Timothy.

Lehane, Frank
21 Dominick Street, Cork City.
6th Division arrest No. 367.
Brigade arrest No. 17 I.B. 285.
He was transferred from the Brigade
Cage in Victoria Barracks, Cork, to
Spike Island internment compound on
24 Feb 1921.
Brother of Daniel, Pat and Timothy.

Lehane, John
Lehane was his alias, his proper name
was Callaghan, See Callaghan, John.
Rathcoole, Banteer, Co. Cork.
Brigade arrest No. K.B. 227.
He was transferred from Cork Male
Gaol to Spike Island internment
compound on 1 June 1921.
He was moved to 'A' Block, Hut 2,
during the Spike hunger strike.
He was transferred from Spike to
Maryborough (Portlaoise) Prison on
the night of 18/19 Nov and released
from there in Dec 1921.

Lehane, Patrick

Patrick Lehane, Dominick Street,
Cork City.

21 Dominick Street, Cork City.
Age: 34.
6th Division arrest No. 365.
Brigade arrest No. 17 I.B. 283.
He was transferred from the Brigade
Cage in Victoria Barracks, Cork, to
Spike Island internment compound on
24 Feb 1921.
He was transferred from Spike to Bere
Island internment camp on 11 July
1921 on HMS *Vidette*.
Brother of Daniel, Frank and Timothy.

Lehane, Timothy
21 Dominick Street, Cork City.
Age: 30
6th Division arrest No. 368.
Brigade arrest No. 17 I.B. 286.
He was transferred from the Brigade
Cage in Victoria Barracks, Cork, to
Spike Island internment compound on
24 Feb 1921.
He was appointed a Staff Officer for
the internees.
He was transferred from Spike to Bere
Island internment camp on 11 July
1921 on HMS *Vidette*.
Brother of Daniel, Frank and Pat.

Lenane, John
Ballydonough, Liselton, Co. Kerry.
Age: 29
Brigade arrest No. K.B. 329.
He was transferred from Cork Male
Gaol to Spike Island internment
compound on 19 Sept 1921.

Leonard, Martin

Waterford.
6th Division arrest No. 215.
Brigade arrest No. 16 I.B. 95.
He was transferred from Spike to Bere
Island internment camp on 11 July
1921 on HMS *Vidette*.

Linehan, Simon

Kylebeg, Kilworth, Co. Cork.
Age: 41.
Brigade arrest No. 16 I.B. 506.
He was transferred from Kilworth
Army Camp to Spike Island internment
compound on 15 Sept 1921.

Lombard, Patrick

Jack's Bridge, Clonakilty, Co. Cork.
Age: 24.
Brigade arrest No. 17 I.B. 670.
He was transferred from the Brigade
Cage in Victoria Barracks, Cork, to
Spike Island internment compound on
16 May 1921, to 'A' Block, Hut 3. He
was later moved to 'B' Block, Hut 16.

Long, Denis

Curragraigue, near Banteer, Co. Cork.
Age: 19.
Brigade arrest No. K.B. 302.
He was transferred from Cork Male
Gaol to Spike Island internment
compound on 22 Aug 1921.

Long, Richard

Ballytrasna, Macroom, Co. Cork.
Age: 30.

6th Division arrest No. 391.
Brigade arrest No. 17 I.B. 238.
He was transferred from Cork Male
Gaol to Spike Island internment
compound on 24 Feb 1921.

Looney, Tim (Tadhg)

Timothy Looney, Lombardstown,
Co. Cork.

Gortmore, Lombardstown,
Co. Cork.
Age: 27.
He was a member of the
Lombardstown Company IRA
and was drafted on to the Mallow
Battalion flying column. He
participated in the raid on Mallow
Barracks. He participated in guard
duties during Battalion and Second
Brigade meetings.
Brigade arrest No. K.B. 312.
He was transferred from Cork Male
Gaol to Spike Island internment
compound on 22 Aug 1921. He was
moved to 'A' Block, Hut 17, during the
Spike hunger strike.
He was transferred from Spike to
Maryborough (Portlaoise) Prison on

the night of 18/19 Nov and released from there in Dec 1921.

Lordan, Daniel
Kilpatrick, Bandon, Co. Cork.
6th Division arrest No. 569.
Brigade arrest No. 17 I.B. 428.
He was transferred to Spike to be moved to Bere Island.
He was transferred from Spike to Bere Island internment camp on 11 July 1921 on HMS *Vidette*.

Lordan, Denis
Dunkereen, Upton, Co. Cork.
6th Division arrest No. 570.
Brigade arrest No. 17 I.B. 427.
He was transferred from Spike to Bere Island internment camp on 11 July 1921 on HMS *Vidette*.

Lordan, Jeremiah
Gurranes, Timoleague, Co. Cork.
6th Division arrest No. 361.
Brigade arrest No. 17 I.B. 301.
He was transferred from the Brigade Cage in Victoria Barracks, Cork, to Spike Island internment compound on 24 Feb 1921.
He was transferred from Spike to Bere Island internment camp on 11 July 1921 on HMS *Vidette*.

Lordan, Michael
Castlelack, Bandon, Co. Cork.
6th Division arrest No. 277.
Brigade arrest No. 17 I.B. 195.

He was transferred from Cork Male Gaol to Spike Island internment compound on 24 Feb 1921.

Lordan, Patrick
Berehaven, Co. Cork.
Brigade arrest No. 17 I.B. 196.
He was transferred from Cork Male Gaol to Spike Island internment compound on 24 Feb 1921.

Lordan, Timothy
Kilpatrick, Bandon, Co. Cork.
6th Division arrest No. 393.
Brigade arrest No. 17 I.B. 355.
He was transferred from Spike to Bere Island internment camp on 11 July 1921 on HMS *Vidette*.

Lordan, Timothy
Dessert, Ballineen, Co. Cork.
6th Division arrest No. 330.
Brigade arrest No. 17 I.B 268.
He was transferred from Cork Male Gaol to Spike Island internment compound on 19 Feb 1921.
He was transferred from Spike to Bere Island internment camp on 11 July 1921 on HMS *Vidette*.

Lordan, Timothy
Laravoulta, Enniskeane, Co. Cork.
Age: 24. Brigade arrest No. 17 I.B. 505.
He was transferred from Cork Male Gaol to Spike Island internment compound on 28 May 1921, to 'A' Block, Hut 8.

Lovett, Maurice

Lixnaw, Co. Kerry. Age: 21.
Brigade arrest No. K.B. 180.
He was arrested by Crown Forces on
22 June 1921.
He was transferred from Cork Male
Gaol to Spike Island internment
compound on 30 June 1921, to 'A'
Block, Hut 14. He was later moved to
'B' Block, Hut 17.

Lowney, Denis

Lehanemore, Castletownbere, Co. Cork.
Age: 16.
Brigade arrest No. 17 I.B. 1173.
He was arrested by Crown Forces
for membership of the IRA, he was
recommended for internment.
He was transferred from Cork Male
Gaol to Spike Island internment
compound on 25 July 1921, to 'A'
Block, Hut 4.

Lowney, Michael

Fifine Mill, Waterford. Age: 19.
Brigade arrest No. 17 I.B. 1185.
He was transferred from Bere Island
internment camp to Spike Island
internment compound on 20 Sept on
HMS *Stormcloud*, D 89.
He was transferred from Spike to
Maryborough (Portlaoise) Prison on
18/19 Nov and released from there in
Dec 1921.

Lowney, Patrick William

Lehanemore, Castletownbere, Co. Cork.

Age: 22.
6th Division arrest No. 515.
Brigade arrest No. 17 I.B. 1176.
He was arrested by Crown Forces for
membership of the IRA and he was
recommended for internment.
He was transferred from Cork Male
Gaol to Spike Island internment
compound on 25 July 1921, to 'A'
Block, Hut 4.

Luby, William

Lady's Well, Cashel, Co. Tipperary.
Age: 26.
Brigade arrest No. 16 I.B. 218.
He was transferred from Kilworth
Army Camp to Spike Island
internment compound on 17 May
1921, to 'B' Block, Hut 1.

Luddy, Timothy

Coolregan, Mitchelstown, Co. Cork.
Age: 23.
6th Division arrest No. 427.
Brigade arrest No. 16 I.B. 327.
He was transferred from Cork Male
Gaol to Spike Island internment
compound on 28 May 1921, to 'A'
Block, Hut 1.

Lynch, Cornelius

Killarney, Co. Kerry.
Age: 20.
Brigade arrest No. K.B. 244.
He was transferred from Cork Male
Gaol to Spike Island internment
compound on 19 Sept 1921.

Lynch, Daniel
Ballinphelic, Ballinhassig, Co. Cork.
Brigade arrest No. 17 I.B. 240.
He was transferred from the Brigade
Cage in Victoria Barracks, Cork, to
Spike Island internment compound on
19 Feb 1921.

Lynch, James
Lixnaw, Co. Kerry.
Age: 27.
Brigade arrest No. K.B. 294.
He was transferred from Cork Military
Detention Barracks to Spike Island
internment compound on 6 July 1921.

Lynch, John
Curraheen, Carrigrohane, Ballincollig,
Co. Cork.
Age: 26.
6th Division arrest No. 692.
Brigade arrest No. 17 I.B. 712.
He was arrested by British soldiers on
4 May 1921 and taken to Ballincollig
Army Barracks. From there he was
taken to the Brigade Cage in Victoria
Barracks and later to Cork Male Gaol.
He was transferred from Cork Male
Gaol to Spike Island internment
compound on 28 May 1921, to 'A'
Block, Hut 4.

Lynch, John
Kilgobbin, Ballinadee, Co. Cork.
6th Division arrest No. 280.
Brigade arrest No. 17 I.B. 191.
He was transferred from Cork Male

Gaol to Spike Island internment
compound on 24 Feb 1921.
He was transferred from Spike to Bere
Island internment camp on 11 July
1921 on HMS *Vidette*.

Lynch, Patrick
Aherlow, Co. Tipperary.
Age: 35.
Occupation: National school teacher
in Aherlow School.
Brigade arrest No. 16 I.B. 463.
He was transferred from Kilworth
Army Camp to Spike Island internment
compound on 15 Sept 1921.

Lyons, John
Tullyglass, Enniskeane, Co. Cork.
6th Division arrest No. 362.
Brigade arrest No. 17 I.B. 302.
He was transferred from the Brigade
Cage in Victoria Barracks, Cork, to
Spike Island internment compound on
24 Feb 1921, to 'A' Block, Hut 8.
He was transferred from Spike to Bere
Island internment camp on 11 July
1921 on HMS *Vidette*.

Lyons, Patrick Leo
Boyle Street, Bandon, Co. Cork.
6th Division arrest No. 452.
Brigade arrest No. 17 I.B. 388.
He was transferred to Spike, details
not found.
He was transferred from Spike to Bere
Island internment camp on 11 July
1921 on HMS *Vidette*.

Lyons, Patrick

Tullyglass, Enniskeane, Co. Cork. Age: 27.
Brigade arrest No. 17 I.B. 697.
He was transferred from the Brigade
Cage in Victoria Barracks, Cork, to
Spike Island internment compound on
16 May 1921, to 'A' Block, Hut 8.

Lyons, Patrick

Pat Lyons, Lombardstown, Co. Cork.

Creggane, Gortmore, Lombardstown,
Co. Cork. Age: 18.
Brigade arrest No. K.B. 317.
He was transferred from Cork Male
Gaol to Spike Island internment
compound on 22 Aug 1921, to 'A'
Block, Hut 8.

Madden, Daniel

49 Sheares Street, Cork City.
6th Division arrest No. 585.
Brigade arrest No. 17 I.B. 545.
He was transferred from Cork Male
Gaol to Spike Island internment
compound on 30 Apr 1921.
He was transferred from Spike to Bere
Island internment camp on 11 July
1921 on HMS *Vidette*.

Madden, John

12 Curragh Road, Cork City.
Brigade arrest No. 17 I.B. 880.
He was transferred to Spike Island
internment compound, to 'A' Block,
Hut 4.

Magee, John

Also listed as McGee
13 Georges Quay, Cork City.
Age: 28.
6th Division arrest No. 526.
Brigade arrest No. 17 I.B. 435.
He was transferred from Cork to
Spike Island internment compound on
19 Mar 1921.
He was transferred from Spike to Bere
Island internment camp on 11 July
1921 on HMS *Vidette*.

Magner, James

Buttevant, Co. Cork.
Age: 36.
Brigade arrest No. K.B. 233.
He was transferred from Cork Male
Gaol to Spike Island internment
compound on 1 June 1921, to 'A'
Block, Hut 7.

Magner, Michael

Shanballymore, Carrigaline, Co. Cork.
Age: 21.
Brigade arrest No. 17 I.B. 192.
He was transferred from Cork Male
Gaol to Spike Island internment
compound on 11 May 1921.

Maher, John

Innismore, Tralee, Co. Kerry.
6th Division arrest No. 349.
He was transferred from Cork Male
Gaol to Spike Island internment
compound on 24 Feb 1921.
He was transferred from Spike to Bere
Island internment camp on 11 July
1921 on HMS *Vidette*.

Mahoney, Cornelius

Dessert, Ballineen, Co. Cork.
Brigade arrest No. 17 I.B. 269.
He was transferred from Cork Male
Gaol to Spike Island internment
compound on 19 Feb 1921.

Mahoney, Daniel

Ballinora, Waterfall, Co. Cork. Age: 21.
Brigade arrest No. 17 I.B. 135.
He was arrested by British soldiers on
1 Jan 1921 and taken to Ballincollig
Barracks. He was moved from there to
the Brigade Cage in Victoria Barracks
and later moved to Cork Male Gaol.
After five months, he was transferred
from Cork Male Gaol to Spike Island
internment compound on 16 May 1921.

Mahoney, John

3 Grattan Street, Cork City.
Brigade arrest No. 17 I.B. 474.
He was transferred from Cork Male
Gaol to Spike Island internment
compound on 12 Apr 1921.

He was transferred from Spike to
Bere Island internment camp by RN
destroyer on 14/15 Apr 1921.

Mahoney, Michael

Ballyheigue, Tralee, Co. Kerry.
6th Division arrest No. 309.
Brigade arrest No. K.B. 75.
He was arrested by Auxiliary Police,
near Ballyheigue, Co. Kerry.[36]
He was transferred from Cork Male
Gaol to Spike Island internment
compound on 24 Feb 1921.
He was transferred from Spike to Bere
Island internment camp on 11 July
1921 on HMS *Vidette*.

Mahoney, Pat

Mullinarouge, Enniskeane, Co. Cork.
6th Division arrest No. 452.
Brigade arrest No. 17 I.B. 389.
He was transferred from Spike to Bere
Island internment camp on 11 July
1921 on HMS *Vidette*.

Mahoney, Pat Dennis

Castledonovan, Drimoleague,
Co. Cork.
Age: 24.
Brigade arrest No. 17 I.B. 620.
He was transferred from the Brigade
Cage in Victoria Barracks, Cork, to
Spike Island internment compound on
16 May 1921.

---

36 See Michael Pierce, WS No. 1190.

Mahoney, Patrick

Mossgrove, Bandon, Co. Cork.
6th Division arrest No. 276.
Brigade arrest No. 17 I.B. 194.
He was transferred from Cork Male
Gaol to Spike Island internment
compound on 24 Feb 1921.
He was transferred from Spike to Bere
Island internment camp on 11 July
1921 on HMS *Vidette*.

Maloney, Cornelius

Lislevane, Co. Cork.
6th Division arrest No. 398.
Brigade arrest No. 17 I.B. 108.
He was transferred from Spike to Bere
Island internment camp on 11 July
1921 on HMS *Vidette*.

Maloney, John

Lixnaw, Co. Kerry.
Brigade arrest No. K.B. 292.
He was transferred from Cork Military
Detention Barracks to Spike Island
internment compound on 6 July 1921.

Malvey, James

Ardgroom, Castletownbere, Co. Cork.
Age: 19.
Brigade arrest No. 17 I.B. 1186.
He was transferred from Bere Island
internment camp to Spike on 20 Sept
on HMS *Stormcloud*, D 89.
He was transferred from Spike to
Maryborough (Portlaoise) Prison on

18/19 Nov and released from there in
Dec 1921.

Manning, David

Ballinspittle, Co. Cork.
6th Division arrest No. 412.
Brigade arrest No. 17 I.B. 343.
He was transferred from Spike to Bere
Island internment camp on 11 July
1921 on HMS *Vidette*.

Mansfield, Phillip

Mullinahone, Co. Tipperary. Age: 35.
Brigade arrest No. 16 I.B. 47.
He was transferred from Spike to Bere
Island internment camp on 14/15 Apr
1921 by RN destroyer.
He was transferred from Bere Island
back to Spike on 20 Sept on HMS
Stormcloud, D 89.
He was transferred from Spike to
Maryborough (Portlaoise) Prison on
18/19 Nov and released from there in
Dec 1921.

Matthews, John (Sean)

16 The Mall, Waterford City. Age: 34.
Occupation: Shop assistant.
Brigade arrest No. 16 I.B. 248.
He was arrested by Crown Forces at
his place of work in Waterford City
in Nov 1920 and taken to Kilworth
Army Camp.[37]
He was transferred from Kilworth
Army Camp to Spike Island internment

---

37 See his WS, No. 1022.

compound on 17 May 1921.
He was transferred from Spike to
Maryborough Prison on the night of
18/19 Nov and released from there in
Dec 1921.

McAuliffe, Michael

45 Kearney's Lane, Cork City.
Brigade arrest No. 17 I.B. 524.
He was transferred from Cork Male
Gaol to Spike Island internment
compound on 12 Apr 1921.
He was transferred from Spike to
Bere Island internment camp by RN
destroyer on 14/15 Apr by 1921.

McAuliffe, Patrick

Greybrook, Waterfall, Co. Cork.
He was arrested on 27 June and brought
to Cork Military Detention Barracks. He
was tried by Military Court on 1 July
and acquitted. He was further detained
as an internee. He was transferred from
Cork Military Detention Barracks to
Spike Island internment compound on
25 July, to 'A' Block, Hut 3 and later to
Hut 16.

McAuliffe, Thomas

Mallow, Co. Cork.
Age: 30.
6th Division arrest No. 317.
Brigade arrest No. K.B. 83.
He was transferred from Cork Male
Gaol to Spike Island internment
compound on 24 Feb 1921.
He was transferred from Spike to Bere

Tom McAuliffe, Mallow, Co. Cork.

Island internment camp on 11 July
1921 on HMS *Vidette*.

McCarthy, Callaghan (Cal)

Macroom, Co. Cork.
Age: 25. Occupation: Farmer.
While he was in the Spike prison
compound he was served with an
Internment Order before his release
date. Instead of being released, he
was further detained as an internee.
He was transferred to Spike Island
internment compound on 26 June, to
'A' Block, Hut 20.
He was transferred from Spike to
Maryborough (Portlaoise) Prison on the
night of 18/19 Nov and released from
there on 8 Dec 1921.
See McCarthy, Callaghan, in the list of
Spike prisoners.

McCarthy, Charles

Murrintown, Co. Wexford.
Age: 24.
Brigade arrest No. 16 I.B. 308.
He was transferred from Kilworth
Army Camp to Spike Island internment

compound on 17 May 1921, to 'A' Block, Hut 18.

McCarthy, Daniel

Ballyvolane, Co. Cork.
Brigade arrest No. 17 I.B. 203.
He was transferred from the Brigade Cage in Victoria Barracks, Cork, to Spike Island internment compound on 19 Feb 1921.

McCarthy, Edward

8 Rice's Street, Dungarvan, Co. Waterford.
6th Division arrest No. 199.
Brigade arrest No. 16 I.B. 79.
He was transferred from Spike to Bere Island internment camp on 11 July 1921 on HMS *Vidette*.

McCarthy, Hugh

Tullybeg, Camolin, Co. Wexford.
He was transferred to Spike Island internment compound, to 'A' Block, Hut 11.

McCarthy, Frank

Quaker Road, Cork City. Age: 26.
Brigade arrest No. 17 I.B. 816.
He was transferred from Cork to Spike Island internment compound on 14 Nov 1921.

McCarthy, James[38]

Boffikil, Eyeries, Castletownbere, Co. Cork.

Age: 20. Occupation: Farmer.
While he was in the Spike prison compound he was served with an Internment Order before his release date. Instead of being released, he was further detained as an internee.
He was transferred to Spike Island internment compound on 8 Aug 1921, to 'B' Block, Hut 17.
He was transferred from Spike to Maryborough (Portlaoise) Prison on the night of 18/19 Nov and released from there on 8 Dec 1921.
See McCarthy, James, in the list of Spike prisoners.

McCarthy, James

4 Little Hanover Street, Cork City.
Age: 24.
6th Division arrest No. 495.
Brigade arrest No. 17 I.B. 415.
He was transferred from Cork to Spike Island internment compound on 19 Mar 1921, to Hut 12.
He was transferred from Spike to Bere Island internment camp on 11 July 1921 on HMS *Vidette*.

McCarthy, Jeremiah

Main Street, Schull, Co. Cork.
Age: 30.
6th Division arrest No. 602.
Brigade arrest No. 17 I.B. 486.
He was transferred from Cork to Spike Island internment compound on

---

38 See his WS, No. 1567.

30 Apr 1921, to 'A' Block, Hut 16.
He was transferred from Spike to Bere
Island internment camp on 11 July
1921 on HMS *Vidette*.

McCarthy, Joe

Co. Cork.
He was transferred to Spike Island
internment compound, to 'A' Block,
Hut 18.

McCarthy, John

Farrin, Mourne Abbey, Mallow,
Co. Cork.
Age: 30.
6th Division arrest No. 727.
He was transferred from Cork Male
Gaol to Spike Island internment
compound on 9 June 1921, to 'A'
Block, Hut 7.

McCarthy, John George

Grenagh, Blarney, Co. Cork.
Age: 34.
Brigade arrest No. 17 I.B. 329.
He was transferred from Spike to
Bere Island internment camp by RN
destroyer on 14/15 Apr 1921.
He was transferred from Bere Island
back to Spike on 20 Sept on HMS
Stormcloud, D 89.
He was transferred from Spike to
Maryborough (Portlaoise) Prison on
18/19 Nov and released from there in
Dec 1921.

McCarthy, Michael

9 East View Terrace, Quaker Road,
Cork City.
6th Division arrest No. 758.
Brigade arrest No. 17 I.B. 817.
He was transferred from Cork Male
Gaol to Spike Island internment
compound on 22 June 1921.

Michael McCarthy, Lombardstown,
Co. Cork.

McCarthy, Michael

Creggane, Lombardstown, Co. Cork.
Age: 23.
Occupation: Farmer.
He was one of the founding members
of the Lombardstown Company of the
Irish Volunteers. After Gen. Lucas was
captured by the IRA near Fermoy, he
was moved to McCarthy's house. The
soldiers in Fermoy threatened to burn
Fermoy as a reprisal. Gen. Lucas wrote
a letter ordering the soldiers not to do
so. Michael McCarthy was given the
task of cycling the 40km to Fermoy
to deliver the letter. He was later
appointed the Brigade dispatch rider.
Brigade arrest No. K.B. 313.

He was arrested by Crown Forces on 29 June 1921 and taken to Kanturk, later to Buttevant Army Barracks and to Cork Male Gaol.[39]
He was transferred from Cork Male Gaol to Spike Island internment compound on 22 Aug 1921, to 'A' Block, Hut 7.
He was transferred from Spike to Maryborough (Portlaoise) Prison on the night of 18/19 Nov. He was released from there on 8 Dec 1921. Brother of prisoner Daniel McCarthy.

McCarthy, Mortimer

Castletownbere, Co. Cork.
Age: 25. Occupation: Farmer.
While he was in the Spike prison compound, he was served with an Internment Order before his release date. Instead of being released, he was further detained as an internee and transferred to Spike Island internment compound.
He was transferred from Spike to Maryborough (Portlaoise) Prison on the night of 18/19 Nov and released from there on 8 Dec 1921.
See McCarthy, Mortimer, in the list of Spike prisoners.

McCarthy, Patrick

Rathrought, Ballinadee, Co. Cork.
6th Division arrest No. 282.

Brigade arrest No. 17 I.B. 207.
He was transferred from Cork Male Gaol to Spike Island internment compound on 24 Feb 1921.
He was transferred from Spike to Bere Island internment camp on 11 July 1921 on HMS *Vidette*.

McCarthy, Pat

Lahakineen, Mourne Abbey, Mallow, Co. Cork.
Age: 34. Occupation: Farmer.
Brigade arrest No. Div. L. 227.
He was arrested at home by British soldiers on 28 Oct 1920 and taken to Mallow Barracks, later to Cork Military Detention Barracks and in June 1921 to Cork Male Gaol.[40]
He was transferred from Cork Male Gaol to Spike Island internment compound on 9 June 1921, to 'A' Block, Hut 17.
He was transferred from Spike to Maryborough (Portlaoise) Prison on the night of 18/19 Nov and released from there on 8 Dec 1921.

McCarthy, Thomas

Rathrough, Ballinadee, Co. Cork.
Brigade arrest No. 17 I.B. 205.
He was transferred from the Brigade Cage in Victoria Barracks, Cork, to Spike Island internment compound on 19 Feb 1921.

---

39 See his WS, No. 1238.
40 See his WS, No. 1163.

McCarthy, Thomas J.

9 East View Terrace, Quaker Road,
Cork City. Age: 25.
6th Division arrest No. 756.
Brigade arrest No. 17 I.B. 815.
He was transferred from Cork Male
Gaol to Spike Island internment
compound on 22 June 1921.

McCarthy, Timothy

Tullymurrihy, Bandon, Co. Cork.
Brigade arrest No. 17 I.B. 300.
He was transferred from the Brigade
Cage in Victoria Barracks, Cork, to
Spike Island internment compound on
24 Feb 1921.

McCarthy, Timothy

Ballyvolane, Ballinadee, Co. Cork.
Brigade arrest No. 17 I.B. 909.
He was transferred to Spike Island
internment compound, to 'A' Block,
Hut 8.

McCormack, John

Main Street, Thurles, Co. Tipperary.
Age: 27.
Brigade arrest No. 18 I.B. 164.
He was transferred from Cork Male
Gaol to Spike Island internment
compound on 11 May 1921, to 'A'
Block, Hut 15.

McDermott, Michael

Goatstown, Co. Kildare.
He was transferred from Waterford
Gaol by RN destroyer to Spike Island
internment compound on
18 Aug 1921.

McDonald, Denis

Denis McDonald, Crossabeg, Co. Wexford.

Lonsdale, Kyle, Crossabeg, Co.
Wexford. Age: 35.
Brigade arrest No. 16 I.B. 450.
He was transferred from Kilworth
Army Camp to Spike Island internment
compound on 16 Sept 1921.
He was transferred from Spike to
Maryborough Prison on the night of
18/19 Nov and released from there in
Dec 1921.

McDonald, Pat

Ballintlea, Mullinavat, Co. Kilkenny.
He was arrested by Auxiliary
Police on 10 Feb 1921 and taken
to Woodstock House and released
on 18 Feb. Rearrested on 19 Apr
and taken to Kilkenny Military
Barracks and moved to Kilworth on
25 June. He was transferred from
Kilworth Army Camp to Spike Island
internment compound, to 'B' Block,
Hut 23.

McEgan, Michael

Ballyheigue, Tralee, Co. Kerry.
6th Division arrest No. 310.
Brigade arrest No. K.B. 76.
He was arrested by Auxiliary Police
near Ballyheigue, Co. Kerry.[41]
He was transferred from Cork Male
Gaol to Spike Island internment
compound on 24 Feb 1921.
He was transferred from Spike to Bere
Island internment camp on 11 July
1921 on HMS *Vidette*.

McGowan, James

Passage.
He was transferred to Spike Island
internment compound, to 'A' Block,
Hut 12.

McGrath, Laurence

Newtown, Kilmacthomas,
Co. Waterford.
Age: 40.
Brigade arrest No. 16 I.B. 365.
He was transferred from Kilworth
Army Camp to Spike Island internment
compound on 30 May 1921.

McGrath, Martin

Gorey, Co. Wexford.
Age: 24.
Brigade arrest No. K.B. 179.
He was transferred from Cork Male
Gaol to Spike Island internment
compound on 16 May 1921, to 'A'
Block, Hut 17.

McGrath, Martin

Listerlin, Co. Kilkenny. Age: 26.
Brigade arrest No. 16 I.B. 329.
Comdt 6th Battalion, South Kilkenny
Brigade, IRA.
He was arrested by Auxiliary Police
on 11 Mar 1921 and taken to their
Company HQ, at Woodstock House,
Inistioge. He was moved from there to
Kilkenny Military Barracks on 29 Mar.
He was moved to Clonmel and on
9 Apr to Kilworth 'rest camp'.[42]
He was transferred from Kilworth
Army Camp to Spike Island
internment compound on 30 May.
He was moved to 'A' Block, Hut 21,
during the Spike hunger strike.
He was transferred from Spike to
Maryborough (Portlaoise) Prison on
the night of 18/19 Nov and released
from there in Dec 1921.

Martin McGrath, Listerlin, Co. Kilkenny.

---

41 See Michael Pierce, WS No. 1190, p.20.
42 See his own diary notes in Spike Island Independence Museum.

McInerney, Patrick

Kilmihill, Co. Clare.
He was transferred to Spike Island
internment compound, date not found,
to 'A' Block, Hut 8.

McInerney, Thomas

Mountshannon, Co. Clare.
Brigade arrest No. 18 I.B. 209.
He was arrested by Crown Forces on
18 July 1921.
He was transferred from Cork Male
Gaol to Spike Island internment
compound on 25 July 1921, to 'A'
Block, Hut 19.

McInerney, Tommy

9 & 10 Lock Quay and Catherine
Street, Limerick City.
Age: 29.
6th Division arrest No. 171.
Brigade arrest No. 18 I.B. 182.
He was the driver of the car that
plunged off Ballykissane Pier on
Good Friday night 1916, resulting
in the deaths of three fellow Irish
Volunteers.[43] These were the first
fatalities of the 1916 Rising. All
four were on their way to attempt
to steal radios from the Atlantic
Wireless College in Cahersiveen, Co.
Kerry. The radios were required to
attempt to make contact with the gun
running ship *Aud* bringing weapons
and ammunition for the Rising.

Tommy McInerney, Lock Quay,
Limerick City.

Going through Killorglin in the dark,
he missed a turn in the road and
accidentally drove off Ballykissane
Pier. It was discovered later that the
Aud was not equipped with a radio. As
the sole survivor, he was arrested later
that night by the RIC.
He was arrested again in 1921
and interned for suspected
Republican activities.
He was transferred from Cork to
Spike Island internment compound on
9 June 1921, to 'A' Block, Hut 15.
In May 1922, he was fatally injured
as a result of an accidental shooting in
New Barracks, Limerick. McInerney
died of his wound in Barrington's
Hospital, Limerick, on 26 May 1922.

McKernan, Thomas

St Luke's, Cork City.
6th Division arrest No. 601.
Brigade arrest No. 17 I.B. 550.
He was transferred from Cork Male

---

43 Tom Doyle, *The Ballykissane Tragedy, Good Friday 1916, the First Casualties of the Easter
Rising.*

Gaol to Spike Island internment compound on 30 Apr 1921.
He was transferred from Spike to Bere Island internment camp on 11 July 1921 on HMS *Vidette*.

McLoughlin, Patrick
Templederry, Nenagh, Co. Tipperary.
He was transferred to Spike Island internment compound, date not found, to 'A' Block, Hut 19.

McNamara, Cornelius
1 Kelly's Range, Black Boy Pike, Limerick City.
Age: 24.
6th Division arrest No. 173.
Brigade arrest No. 18 I.B.181.
He was transferred from Cork to Spike Island internment compound on 9 June 1921, to 'B' Block, Hut 23.
He was moved to 'A' Block, Hut 21, during the Spike hunger strike.
He was transferred from Spike to Maryborough (Portlaoise) Prison on the night of 18/19 Nov and released from there on 8 Dec 1921.

McNamara, James
Graiguenamanagh, Co. Kilkenny.
He was transferred to Spike Island internment compound, date not found, to 'B' Block, Hut 20. He was moved to 'A' Block, Hut 1, during the Spike hunger strike.
He was transferred from Spike to Maryborough (Portlaoise) Prison on

the night of 18/19 Nov and released from there on 8 Dec 1921.

McSweeney, Michael
166 Blarney Street, Cork City.
Brigade arrest No. 17 I.B. 518.
He was transferred from Cork Male Gaol to Spike Island internment compound on 12 Apr 1921.
He was transferred from Spike to Bere Island internment camp by RN destroyer on 14/15 Apr 1921.

Meade, Jeremiah
Knockleary, Buttevant, Co. Cork.
Age: 22.
Brigade arrest No. K.B. 232.
He was transferred from Cork Male Gaol to Spike Island internment compound on 1 June 1921, to 'A' Block, Hut 7.

Meade, John
Main Street, Kinsale, Co. Cork,
6th Division arrest No. 493.
Brigade arrest No. 17 I.B. 411.
He was transferred from Spike to Bere Island internment camp on 11 July 1921 on HMS *Vidette*.

Meagher, Thomas
Kiely's Cross, near Ardmore, Co. Waterford.
Brigade arrest No. 16 I.B. 177.
He was transferred from Kilworth Army Camp to Spike Island internment compound on 13 Apr 1921.

He was transferred from Spike to Bere Island internment camp on 14/15 Apr 1921.

Mockler, Robert
Laffans Bridge, Co. Tipperary.
Age: 23.
Brigade arrest No. 16 I.B. 199.
He was transferred from Kilworth Army Camp to Spike Island internment compound on 17 May 1921.

Moloney, Jeremiah
Abbeymahon, Lislevane, Timoleague, Co. Cork.
Brigade arrest No. 17 I.B. 265.
He was transferred from Cork Male Gaol to Spike Island internment compound on 19 Feb 1921.

Moloney, John
Castlegrace, Co. Kilkenny.
6th Division arrest No. 119.
He was transferred from Kilworth Army Camp to Spike Island internment compound on 13 Apr 1921.
He was transferred from Spike to Bere Island internment camp by RN destroyer on 14/15 Apr 1921.

Moloney, Paddy
Grange, Lislevane, Co. Cork.
6th Division arrest No. 332.
Brigade arrest No. 17 I.B. 266.
He was transferred from Cork Male

Gaol to Spike Island internment compound on 19 Feb 1921.
He was transferred from Spike to Bere Island internment camp on 11 July 1921 on HMS *Vidette*.

Moloney, Thomas
Abbeymahon, Timoleague, Co. Cork.
6th Division arrest No. 334.
Brigade arrest No. 17 I.B. 264.
He was transferred from Cork Male Gaol to Spike Island internment compound on 19 Feb 1921.

Molyneaux, Thomas J.
3 Árd na Gréine, Evergreen Road, Cork City.
Brigade arrest No. 17 I.B. 503.
He was transferred from Cork Male Gaol to Spike Island internment compound on 11 May 1921.

Moore, Stephen
Beechmount, Upton, Co. Cork.
Brigade arrest No. 17 I.B. 225.
He was captured by Crown Forces in Jan 1921.[44]
He was transferred from the Brigade Cage in Victoria Barracks, Cork, to Spike Island internment compound on 19 Feb 1921.

Morris, James
Ballyneenan, Co. Tipperary.
Age: 22.

---

44 See Frank Neville, WS No. 443, p.12.

Brigade arrest No. 16 I.B. 429.
He was transferred from Cork to
Spike Island internment compound on
14 Nov 1921.

Morris, Tom

10 Dempsey's Terrace, Wexford Town.
He was transferred from Waterford
Gaol by RN destroyer to Spike Island
internment compound on 18 Aug
1921, to 'A' Block, Hut 11.

Morrison, James

Castlelyons, Fermoy, Co. Cork.
6th Division arrest No. 331.
He was transferred from Kilworth
Army Camp to Spike Island internment
compound on 13 Apr 1921.
He was transferred from Spike to
Bere Island internment camp by RN
destroyer on 14/15 Apr 1921.

Morrissey, Geoffrey

Knockavannia, Ballymacarbery, Co.
Waterford.
Brigade arrest No. 16 I.B. 173.

Geoffrey Morrissey, Ballymacarbery,
Co. Waterford.

He was arrested by Crown Forces in
Dungarvan in early January 1921 and
taken to Kilworth Army Camp.
He was transferred from Kilworth
Army Camp to Spike Island
internment compound on 4 Mar 1921.
He was later transferred to Bere Island
internment camp.

Morrogh, William

19 Merville Terrace, Evergreen Road,
Cork City.
Age: 21.
6th Division arrest No. 705.
Brigade arrest No. 17 I.B. 799.
He was transferred from Cork Male
Gaol to Spike Island internment
compound on 28 May 1921.

Moynihan, Jeremiah

Banteer, Co. Cork Age: 28.
Brigade arrest No. K.B. 215
He was transferred from Cork Male
Gaol to Spike Island internment
compound on 16 May 1921.

Moynihan, William

Banteer West, Co. Cork.
Age: 21.
Brigade arrest No. K.B. 192.
He was transferred from Cork Male
Gaol to Spike Island internment
compound on 16 May 1921, to 'A'
Block, Hut 17.
He was transferred from Spike, to
Cork by launch, on Tuesday, 16 Aug
1921. He arrived at Custom House
Quay, Cork, at 10 a.m.

Mulcahy, James
Clogheen, Cahir, Co. Tipperary.
He was transferred to Spike Island
internment compound, date not found,
to 'A' Block, Hut 10.

Mulcahy, Patrick James
Mallow, Co. Cork.
He was transferred from Cork Male
Gaol to Spike Island internment
compound on 19 Feb 1921.

Mulhall, Patrick
Castlecomer, Co. Kilkenny.
Age: 50.
Brigade arrest No. 16 I.B. 441.
He was transferred from Kilworth
Army Camp to Spike Island internment
compound on 16 Sept 1921.
He was shot in the foot by British
soldiers during a disturbance in the
moat on 19 Oct. He was transferred
from the Spike hospital to Cork
Military Hospital in Victoria Barracks,
later that day.

Mullally, Martin
Priestown, Drangan, Co. Tipperary.
Brigade arrest No. 16 I.B. 531.
He was arrested by Crown Forces on
21 July 1921.
He was transferred from Cork Male
Gaol to Spike Island internment
compound on 22 Aug 1921, to 'B'
Block, Hut 20.
He was moved to 'A' Block, Hut 22,
during the Spike hunger strike.

He was transferred from Spike to
Maryborough (Portlaoise) Prison on the
night of 18/19 Nov and released from
there on 8 Dec 1921.

Mullane, Cornelius
Also listed as O'Mullane.
Banteer, Co. Cork. Age: 18.
Brigade arrest No. K.B. 191.
He was transferred from Cork Male
Gaol to Spike Island internment
compound on 16 May 1921, to 'A'
Block, Hut 17.

Mullane, Jeremiah
Also listed as O'Mullane.
Banteer, Co. Cork. Age: 22.
Brigade arrest No. K.B. 193.
He was transferred from Cork Male
Gaol to Spike Island internment
compound on 16 May 1921, to 'A'
Block, Hut 17.

Mullane, Timothy
Ballinaraha, Ballyhooly, Killavullen,
Co. Cork. Age: 35.
Brigade arrest No. 16 I.B. 364.
He was transferred from Kilworth
Army Camp to Spike Island internment
compound on 30 May 1921.

Mullins, Thomas
Kinsale, Co. Cork.
He was transferred from Cork Male
Gaol to Spike Island internment
compound on 19 Feb 1921.

Murnane, John

Passage West, Co. Cork.

Brigade arrest No. 17 I.B. 244.

He was transferred from the Brigade
Cage in Victoria Barracks, Cork, to
Spike Island internment compound on
19 Feb 1921.

Murphy, Charles

81 Douglas Street, Cork City.

Age: 38.

6th Division arrest No. 460.

Brigade arrest No. 17. I.B.397.

He was transferred from Cork Male
Gaol to Spike Island internment
compound on 25 Apr 1921, to 'A'
Block, Hut 15.

He was transferred from Spike to Bere
Island internment camp on 11 July
1921 on HMS *Vidette*. He was later
transferred back to Spike.

He was transferred from Spike to Cork
Military Hospital on 6 Sept 1921.

Murphy, Daniel F.

3 Hanover Street, Cork City.

Brigade arrest No. 17 I.B.487.

He was transferred from Cork Male
Gaol to Spike Island internment
compound on 12 Apr 1921.

He was transferred from Spike to
Bere Island internment camp by RN
destroyer on 14/15 Apr 1921.

Murphy, Edward

Kellystown, Co. Wexford. Age: 29.

Brigade arrest No. 16 I.B. 311.

He was transferred from Kilworth
Army Camp to Spike Island internment
compound on 30 May 1921, to 'A'
Block, Hut 18.

Murphy, James

Stanton's Lane, Bandon, Co. Cork.

Age: 25.

Occupation: Insurance Agent.

6th Division arrest No. 548.

Brigade arrest No. 17 I.B. 998.

He was originally on Spike as a
prisoner and he was transferred back
to Cork Male Gaol. While he was
in Cork Male Gaol, he was served
with an Internment Order before his
release date. Instead of being released,
he was further detained as an internee.

He was transferred from Cork Male
Gaol back to Spike Island internment
compound on 14 Nov 1921.

He was transferred from Spike to
Maryborough (Portlaoise) Prison on the
night of 18/19 Nov and released from
there on 8 Dec 1921.

See also: Murphy, James, in the list of
Spike prisoners.

Murphy, Joe

Castletownbere, Co. Cork.

He was transferred to Spike Island
internment compound, date not found,
to 'A' Block, Hut 6.

Murphy, John

Templemartin, Bandon, Co. Cork.

6th Division arrest No. 389.

Brigade arrest No. 17 I.B. 983 or 303.
He was transferred from Cork Male
Gaol to Spike Island internment
compound on 15 July 1921.
He was transferred from Spike to Bere
Island internment camp on 11 July
1921 on HMS *Vidette*.

Murphy, John
Coolnabrone, Graiguenamanagh,
Co. Kilkenny.
Age: 23.
Brigade arrest No. 16 I.B. 276.
He was transferred from Kilworth
Army Camp to Spike Island
internment compound on 30 May
1921, to 'B' Block, Hut 1. He was
later moved to Hut 23. He was
moved to 'A' Block, Hut 22, during
the Spike hunger strike.
He was transferred from Spike to
Maryborough (Portlaoise) Prison on the
night of 18/19 Nov and released from
there on 8 Dec 1921.

Murphy, John
Ballydaheen, Mallow, Co. Cork.
Age: 20.
6th Division arrest No. 728.
He was transferred from Cork Male
Gaol to Spike Island internment
compound on 9 June 1921, to 'A'
Block, Hut 7.

Murphy, John
Clonroe (Clonea Upper), Dungarvan,
Co. Waterford.

Brigade arrest No. 16 I.B. 398.
He fought in the Dungarvan ambush on
19 Mar 1921 and was arrested that day.
He was transferred to Spike Island
internment compound, date not found.

Murphy, John (Jack)
Old Hall, Bridgetown, Co. Wexford.
Brigade arrest No. 16 I.B. 409
He was transferred to Spike Island
internment compound, date not
found, to 'B' Block, Hut 16. He was
moved to 'A' Block, Hut 1, during
the Spike hunger strike.
He was transferred from Spike to
Maryborough (Portlaoise) Prison on
the night of 18/19 Nov and released
from there in Dec 1921.

Murphy, Larry
Carrigduff, near Millstreet, Co. Cork.
Brigade arrest No. K.B. 301.
He was transferred from Cork Male
Gaol to Spike Island internment
compound on 22 Aug 1921.

Murphy, Matthew
34 Ballintemple, Blackrock,
Ballintemple, Cork City.
Age: 26.
6th Division arrest No. 700.
Brigade arrest No. 17 I.B. 714.
He was transferred from Cork Male
Gaol to Spike Island internment
compound on 28 May 1921, to 'A'
Block, Hut 15, and later moved to
Hut 21.

Murphy, Matthew

Ferns, Co. Wexford. Age: 33.
Brigade arrest No. 16 I.B. 336.
He was transferred from Kilworth
Army Camp to Spike Island internment
compound on 30 May 1921.

Murphy, Michael

Killowen, Co. Cork.
Brigade arrest No. K.B. 318.
He was transferred from Cork Male
Gaol to Spike Island internment
compound on 22 Aug 1921.

Murphy, Michael

Inchigeela, Macroom, Co. Cork.
Brigade arrest No. 17 I.B. 907.
He was arrested by Crown Forces on
22 June 1921.
He was transferred from Cork Male
Gaol to Spike Island internment
compound on 30 June 1921. He was
moved to 'A' Block, Hut 1, during the
Spike hunger strike.
He was transferred from Spike to
Maryborough (Portlaoise) Prison on the
night of 18/19 Nov and released from
there on 8 Dec 1921.

Murphy, Michael

Cahir, Ardgroom, Castletownbere,
Co. Cork. Age: 19.
Brigade arrest No. 17 I.B. 1190.
He was transferred from Bere
Island, to Spike on 20 Sept on HMS
Stormcloud, D 89.
He was transferred from Spike to

Maryborough (Portlaoise) Prison on
18/19 Nov and released from there in
Dec 1921.

Murphy, Patrick

Tulla, Co. Clare.
Brigade arrest No. 18 I.B. 210.
He was arrested by Crown Forces on
18 July 1921.
He was transferred from Cork Male
Gaol to Spike Island internment
compound on 25 July 1921, to 'A'
Block, Hut 19.

Murphy, Thomas

Shehane, Ballinhassig, Co. Cork.
6th Division arrest No. 408.
Brigade arrest No. 17 I.B. 338.
He was transferred to Spike Island
internment compound, date not found.
He was transferred from Spike to Bere
Island internment camp on 11 July
1921 on HMS *Vidette*.

Murphy, Thomas

4 Keohane's Lane, Blarney Street,
Cork City.
Age: 22.
6th Division arrest No. 712.
Brigade arrest No. 17 I.B. 685.
He was transferred from Cork Male
Gaol to Spike Island internment
compound on 22 June 1921, to 'A'
Block, Hut 4.

Murphy, Timothy

Clashflugh, near Timoleague, Co. Cork.

Brigade arrest No. 17 I.B. 1182.
He was transferred from Cork Male
Gaol to Spike Island internment
compound on 22 Aug 1921.

Murphy, Timothy
Bank, Waterfall, Castletownbere,
Co. Cork.
Brigade arrest No. 17 I.B. 844.
He was arrested by Crown Forces
on 24 May 1921. On 26 May he was
taken to Bere Island, 5 June to Bantry,
7 June to the Brigade Cage in Victoria
Barracks Cork and on 17 June to
Cork Male Gaol.
He was transferred from Cork Male
Gaol to Spike Island internment
compound on 25 June 1921, to 'A'
Block, Hut 20.

Murphy, William
Crowhill, Upton, Co. Cork. Age: 32.
Brigade arrest No. 17 I.B. 607.
He was transferred from the Brigade
Cage in Victoria Barracks, Cork, to
Spike Island internment compound on
16 May 1921.

Murphy, William
Cork City.
Brigade arrest No. 17 I.B. 241.
He was transferred from Cork Male
Gaol to Spike Island internment
compound on 19 Feb 1921.

Murray, John
Kinsale, Co. Cork. Age: 25.

Occupation: Farmer.
6th Division arrest No. 70.
While he was in the Spike prison
compound he was served with an
Internment Order, before his release
date. Instead of being released, he was
further detained as an internee. He was
transferred to Spike Island internment
compound on 8 Aug 1921.
He was transferred from Spike to
Maryborough (Portlaoise) Prison on the
night of 18/19 Nov and released from
there on 8 Dec 1921.
See Murray, John, in the list of
Spike prisoners.

Murray, Pat
Clonakilty, Co. Cork.
6th Division arrest No. 498.
Brigade arrest No. 17 I.B. 412.
He was transferred from Spike to Bere
Island internment camp on 11 July
1921 on HMS *Vidette*.

Nagle, Maurice
Creggane, Lombardstown, Mallow,
Co. Cork. Age: 16.
Brigade arrest No. K.B. 316.
He was transferred from Cork Male
Gaol to Spike Island internment
compound on 22 Aug 1921.

Nelligan, Patrick
Ballymacphilip, Ballyhooly, Fermoy,
Co. Cork.
Age: 25.
Brigade arrest No. 16 I.B. 446.

He was transferred from Cork, to Spike Island internment compound on 14 Nov 1921.

Neville, Michael, aka 'Bubbles'

Monkstown, Co. Cork. Age: 26.
6th Division arrest No. 376.
Brigade arrest No. 17 I.B. 315.
He was transferred from the Brigade Cage in Victoria Barracks, Cork, to Spike Island internment compound on 24 Feb 1921.
He was transferred from Spike to Bere Island internment camp on 11 July 1921 on HMS *Vidette*.

Neville, Patrick

'Arcadia', Ballinlough Road, Cork City.
Age: 21.
Brigade arrest No. 17 I.B. 690.
He was transferred from Cork to Spike Island internment compound on 14 Nov 1921.
He was transferred from Spike to Maryborough Prison on the night of 18/19 Nov and released from there in Dec 1921.

Neville, Timothy

3 De Vesci Place, Monkstown, Co. Cork.
Age: 21.
6th Division arrest No. 239.
Brigade arrest No. 17 I.B. 175.
He was transferred from Cork Male Gaol to Spike Island internment compound on 24 Feb 1921. He was transferred from Spike to Bere Island internment camp, date not found.
He was transferred from Bere Island back to Spike on 20 Sept on HMS *Stormcloud*, D 89.
He was transferred from Spike to Maryborough (Portlaoise) Prison on 18/19 Nov and released from there in Dec 1921.

Noonan, Maurice

Milford, Charleville, Co. Cork.
Age: 26.
Brigade arrest No. K.B. 152.
He was arrested by British soldiers at Kilbolane on 1 Apr 1921. He was taken to Buttevant Military Barracks and later to Cork Male Gaol.[45]
He was transferred from Cork Male Gaol to Spike Island internment compound on 16 May 1921, to 'A' Block, Hut 7.
He was transferred from Spike to Maryborough (Portlaoise) Prison on

Maurice Noonan, Charleville, Co. Cork.

---

45 See his WS, No. 1098.

the night of 18/19 Nov and released from there in Dec 1921.

Nunan, Michael
Toorard, Newmarket, Co. Cork.
6th Division arrest No. 422.
Brigade arrest No. K.B. 108.
He was transferred from Spike to Bere Island internment camp on 11 July 1921 on HMS *Vidette*.

Nyhan, John
Ballinspittle, Co. Cork.
Brigade arrest No. 17 I.B. 276.
He was transferred from Cork Male Gaol to Spike Island internment compound on 19 Feb 1921.

O'Brien, Daniel
Innishannon, Bandon, Co. Cork.
6th Division arrest No. 669.
Brigade arrest No. 17 I.B. 527.
He was transferred from Cork Male Gaol to Spike Island internment compound on 28 May 1921, to 'A' Block, Hut 16.

O'Brien, Daniel
Glengarriff Road, Bantry, Co. Cork.
Age: 21.
Brigade arrest No. 17 I.B. 1013.
He was transferred from Cork Male Gaol to Spike Island internment compound on 15 July 1921, to 'A' Block, Hut 5.

O'Brien, Denis
Co. Waterford.
He was transferred to Spike Island internment compound, date not found, to 'A' Block, Hut 3.

O'Brien, Denis
Carraheen, Lislevane, Co. Cork.
6th Division arrest No. 430.
Brigade arrest No. 17 I.B. 296.
He was transferred from Spike to Bere Island internment camp on 11 July 1921 on HMS *Vidette*.

O'Brien, Denis
Butlerstown, Timoleague, Co. Cork.
Age: 25.
Brigade arrest No. 17 I.B. 693.
He fought in the battle at Crossbarry on 19 Mar 1921. He was arrested on 30 Apr 1921, he was taken to Bandon Military Barracks and later to Cork Male Gaol.[46]
He was transferred from Cork Male Gaol to Spike Island internment compound on 25 July 1921, to 'A' Block, Hut 3.

O'Brien, Denis
Kilally, Kilworth, Co. Cork.
Age: 25.
He was arrested on 9 Feb 1921 and taken to Moore Park Camp near Fermoy. He was released on 10 Mar. He was rearrested on 1 June and held

---

46 See his WS, No. 1306.

in Moore Park for one day before being moved to Kilworth Army Camp. Brigade arrest No. 16 I.B. 458. He was transferred from Kilworth Army Camp to Spike Island internment compound on 15 Sept 1921, to 'B' Block, Hut 19.

O'Brien, George

Greenfield, Ballincollig, Co. Cork.
Age: 27.
Brigade arrest No. 17 I.B. 918.
He was transferred from the Brigade Cage in Victoria Barracks, Cork, to Spike Island internment compound on 30 June 1921, to 'A' Block, Hut 9.

O'Brien, James

St. John's Siding, Enniscorthy,
Co. Wexford.
Age: 19.
Brigade arrest No. 16 I.B. 375.
He was transferred from Cork, to Spike Island internment compound on 6 July 1921.

O'Brien, James

48 Irish Street, Enniscorthy, Co. Wexford.
Age: 32.
Brigade arrest No. 16 I.B. 267.
He was transferred from Kilworth Army Camp to Spike Island internment compound on 16 Sept 1921.

O'Brien, John

Ballincollig, Co. Cork.
Brigade arrest No. 17 I.B.

He was transferred from Cork Military Detention Barracks to Spike Island internment compound on 24 Feb 1921.

O'Brien, John J.

Minane Bridge, Carrigaline, Co. Cork.
6th Division arrest No. 410.
Brigade arrest No. 17 I.B. 241.
He was transferred from Spike to Bere Island internment camp on 11 July 1921 on HMS *Vidette*.

O'Brien, John P.

Ballyheady, Ballinhassig, Co. Cork.
Age: 22.
Brigade arrest No. 17 I.B. 362.
He was transferred from Cork, to Spike Island internment compound on 3 Mar 1921.
He was released from Spike on 8 Nov, authority received from CA 1068 on 4 Nov 1921.

O'Brien, Michael

Duneen Mines, Clonakilty, Co. Cork.
Age: 26.
Brigade arrest No. 17 I.B. 874.
He was transferred from Cork Male Gaol to Spike Island internment compound on 25 June 1921, to 'A' Block, Hut 17.
He was transferred from Spike to Maryborough (Portlaoise) Prison on the night of 18/19 Nov and released from there on 8 Dec 1921.

O'Brien, Mogue
Kilbegnet, Castletown Inch, Gorey,
Co. Wexford.
Age: 32.
Brigade arrest No. 16 I.B. 500.
He was transferred from Waterford
Gaol by RN destroyer to Spike Island
internment compound on 18 Aug 1921.
He was transferred to Maryborough
(Portlaoise) Prison on the night of
18/19 Nov and released from there in
Dec 1921.

O'Brien, Thomas J.
Ballinvoher, Kilally, Kilworth, Co. Cork.
Age: 20.
Brigade arrest No. 16 I.B. 459.
Arrested on 9 July 1921 and taken to
Moore Park Camp near Fermoy and
moved to Kilworth Camp on 2 Aug.
He was transferred from Kilworth
Army Camp to Spike Island internment
compound on 15 Sept 1921.

O'Byrne, John
Gorey, Co. Wexford.
6th Division arrest No. 163.
He was transferred from Kilworth
Army Camp to Spike Island internment
compound on 13 Apr 1921.
He was transferred from Spike to
Bere Island internment camp on
14/15 Apr 1921.

O'Byrne, Pierce
Charlotte St, Wexford Town.
He was transferred to Spike Island
internment compound, date not
found, to 'B' Block, Hut 19.

O'Callaghan, Cornelius
Lombardstown, Co. Cork.
He was transferred to Spike Island
internment compound, date not found,
to 'A' Block, Hut 17.

O'Callaghan, Daniel
North Main Street, Bandon, Co. Cork.
Age: 22.
Brigade arrest No. 17 I.B. 1121.
He was transferred from Cork Male
Gaol to Spike Island internment
compound on 25 July 1921.

O'Callaghan, Ignatius
11 Southern Road, Cork City. Age: 22.
Brigade arrest No. 17 I.B. 894.
He was transferred from Cork to
Spike Island internment compound on
25 June 1921, to 'A' Block, Hut 15.

O'Callaghan, James
Ballynoe, Co. Cork.
6th Division arrest No. 228.
Brigade arrest No. 16 I.B. 107.
He was transferred to Spike to be
moved to Bere Island.
He was transferred from Spike to Bere
Island internment camp on 11 July
1921 on HMS *Vidette*.

O'Callaghan, Jeremiah
Coolineagh, Coachford, Co. Cork.
He was captured after the failed

ambush at Dripsey, Co. Cork, on 28 Jan 1921.

Although an active IRA man, he escaped execution because he was able to convince the Military Court officers, with references given to him by a Maj. Woodley, that he was not involved in the ambush.[47]

He was transferred to Spike Island internment compound, date not found, to Hut 14.

O'Callaghan, John

Mossgrove, Bandon, Co. Cork.
6th Division arrest No. 463.
Brigade arrest No. 17 I.B. 407.
He was transferred from Cork Male Gaol to Spike Island internment compound on 22 June 1921, to 'A' Block, Hut 5.

O'Callaghan, Luke

Minane Bridge, Carrigaline, Co. Cork.
6th Division arrest No. 703.
Brigade arrest No. 17 I.B. 731.
He was transferred from Cork Male Gaol to Spike Island internment compound on 28 May 1921, to 'A' Block, Hut 18.

O'Callaghan, Michael Joseph

6 Richmond Hill, Cork City and formerly of Ardglass, Charleville, Co. Cork.
Age: 21.

Michael Joseph O'Callaghan, Charleville, Co. Cork.

Brigade arrest No. 17 I.B. 1055.
He was transferred from Cork Male Gaol to Spike Island internment compound on 25 July 1921, to 'A' Block, Hut 7.

O'Callaghan, Peter

Ballynoe, Co. Cork.
6th Division arrest No. 254.
Brigade arrest No. 16 I.B. 134.
He was transferred to Spike to be moved to Bere Island.
He was transferred from Spike to Bere Island internment camp on 11 July 1921 on HMS *Vidette*.

O'Carroll, Daniel

Dromclough, Lixnaw, Co. Kerry.
Age: 33.
6th Division arrest No. 725.
Brigade arrest No. L. 536.
On 30 May 1921 following a General Court Martial in Victoria Barracks, Cork, he was found not guilty of the

---

47 P.J. Feeney, *Glory O, Glory O, Ye Bold Fenian Men*, p.132.

murder of DI Tobias O'Sullivan, RIC, in Listowel on 21 Jan 1921.

Instead of being released, he was served with an Internment Order and interned. He was transferred from Cork Male Gaol to Spike Island internment compound on 22 June 1921.

DI O'Sullivan is generally reported as being killed by the IRA to prevent him identifying prisoners on Spike Island. This is incorrect as Spike was opened as a prison and internment camp on 19 Feb 1921, four weeks after DI O'Sullivan was killed. The specific prisoner that the British Army and RIC wanted DI O'Sullivan to identify was Tom Malone, alias Sean Forde. See also: Spike internee, Devereaux, Thomas and Malone/Forde in the list of Spike prisoners.

O'Connell, Cornelius

Killumney, Ballincollig, Co. Cork. Age: 27.

Brigade arrest No. 17 I.B. 831.

He was transferred from Cork to Spike Island internment compound on 25 June 1921, to 'A' Block, Hut 9.

O'Connell, John

Cork City.

Brigade arrest No. 17 I.B. 187.

He was transferred from the Brigade Cage in Victoria Barracks, Cork, to

Spike Island internment compound on 19 Feb 1921.

O'Connell, Michael

Michael O'Connell, Thurles, Co. Tipperary.

24 Liberty Square, Main Street, Thurles, Co. Tipperary. Age: 32.

Brigade arrest No. 16 I.B. 205.

He was the acting Brigade Commandant of the Mid Tipperary Brigade, Irish Volunteers. He was heavily involved in the planning at short notice of the successful rescue of Séan Hogan at Knocklong railway station, Co. Tipperary, on 13 May 1919.[48] He was arrested at home on 7 June 1919 by Crown Forces under the command of DI Hunt RIC. DI Hunt was killed in Thurles by the IRA on 23 June 1919.

He was transferred to Cork Male Gaol, from Kilworth Army Camp, on 14 May 1921. He was transferred from Cork Male Gaol to Spike Island internment compound on 16 May, to 'A' Block, Hut 10.

---

48 Neville O'Connell, *History Ireland, March/April 2020*, pp.34–37.

O'Connell, Mortimer

Cahersiveen, Co. Kerry.

Brigade arrest No. 17 I.B. 396.

He was transferred to Spike to be moved to Bere Island.

He was transferred from Spike to Bere Island internment camp on 14/15 Apr 1921 by RN destroyer.

He escaped from Bere Island on 15 Sept 1921 while returning from swimming with other internees escorted by British soldiers. The internees had been swimming near the rifle range. He was smuggled to the mainland by a Bere Island fisherman.[49]

O'Connell, Patrick

Chapel Street, Bantry, Co. Cork.

Age: 28.

6th Division arrest No. 503.

Brigade arrest No. 17 I.B. 160.

He was transferred from Bere Island to Spike Island internment compound on 12 Apr 1921.

He is the only internee in the ledger that was listed as being transferred from Bere Island to Spike on that date.

He was transferred from Spike, back to Bere Island internment camp on 11 July 1921 on HMS *Vidette*.

O'Connell, Richard

Caherconlish, Co. Limerick. Age: 29.

Brigade arrest No. 18 I.B. 178.

He was arrested by the RIC near Pallas and taken to Killaloe Barracks. He was later moved to Limerick and to Cork Male Gaol.[50]

He was transferred from Cork Male Gaol to Spike Island internment compound on 11 May 1921.

He volunteered to be transferred to Bere Island instead of internee John Collins of Woodfield.[51]

He was transferred from Spike to Bere Island internment camp, from where he escaped with six others.

O'Connell, Timothy

Ahakeera, Dunmanway, Co. Cork.

Brigade arrest No. 17 I.B. 189.

He was transferred from Cork Male Gaol to Spike Island internment compound on 24 Feb 1921.

O'Connor, James

Ballyheigue, Tralee, Co. Kerry.

Brigade arrest No. K.B. 80.

He was arrested by Auxiliary Police near Ballyheigue, Co. Kerry.[52]

He was transferred from Cork Male Gaol to Spike Island internment compound on 24 Feb 1921.

O'Connor, Patrick

Newmarket, Co. Cork.

---

49 See Ted O'Sullivan, *Bere Island, a Short History*, pp.27–28.

50 See his WS, No. 656.

51 Ibid., p.28.

52 See Michael Pierce, WS No. 1190, p.20.

Patrick O'Connor, Newmarket, Co. Cork.

6th Division arrest No. 209.
Brigade arrest No. L. 243.
He was transferred to Spike to be
moved to Bere Island, date not found.
He was transferred from Spike to Bere
Island internment camp on 11 July
1921 on HMS *Vidette*.

O'Connor, Patrick

Patrick O'Connor, Freemount, Co. Cork.

Curraheen, Freemount, Co. Cork.
Age: 25.
Brigade arrest No. K.B. 228.
He was transferred from Cork Male
Gaol to Spike Island internment
compound on 1 June 1921.

O'Connor, Robert

Kanturk, Co. Cork.
He was transferred from Cork Male
Gaol to Spike Island internment
compound on 19 Feb 1921.

O'Connor, Thomas

Thomas O'Connor, Ballyheigue,
Co. Kerry.

Ballyheigue, Tralee, Co. Kerry.
6th Division arrest No. 311.
Brigade arrest No. K.B. 77.
He was arrested by Auxiliary Police
near Ballyheigue, Co. Kerry.[53]
He was transferred from Cork Male
Gaol to Spike Island internment
compound on 24 Feb 1921.
He was transferred from Spike to Bere
Island internment camp on 11 July
1921 on HMS *Vidette*.

O'Connor, William

Ballyclough, Mallow, Co. Cork. Age: 36.
Brigade arrest No. K.B. 284.
He was arrested by Crown Forces on
30 June 1921.

---

53 Ibid.

He was transferred from Cork Male Gaol to Spike Island internment compound on 6 July 1921, to 'A' Block, Hut 5.

O'Dea, Patrick
Scropul, Mullagh, Miltown Malbay, Co. Clare.
Age: 30.
6th Division arrest No. 147.
Brigade arrest No. 18 I.B. 160.
He was transferred from Cork Male Gaol to Spike Island internment compound on 9 June 1921, to 'A' Block, Hut 8.

O'Donnell, Frank
Kilrush, Co. Clare.
He was transferred from Cork Male Gaol to Spike Island internment compound on 19 Feb 1921.

O'Donnell, Jim
Castletownbere, Co. Cork.
Age: 22.
Occupation: Clerk.
Brigade arrest No. 17 I.B. 704.
While he was in the Spike prison compound, he was served with an Internment Order, before his release date. Instead of being released, he was further detained as an internee. He was transferred to Spike Island internment compound on 8 Aug 1921. He was transferred from Spike to Maryborough (Portlaoise) Prison on the night of 18/19 Nov and released

from there on 8 Dec 1921.
See O'Donnell, Jim, in the list of Spike prisoners.

O'Donnell, Philip
Kilrush, Dungarvan, Co. Waterford.
Age: 21.
6th Division arrest No. 303.
Brigade arrest No. 16 I.B. 161.
He was transferred from Cork to Spike Island internment compound on 24 Feb 1921.
He was appointed a Staff Officer for the internees.
He was transferred from Spike to Bere Island internment camp on 11 July 1921 on HMS *Vidette*.

O'Donoghue, Humphrey

Humphrey O'Donoghue, Cullen, Co. Cork.

Cullen, Millstreet, Co. Cork and Headford, Co. Kerry.
Age: 26. Occupation: Farmer.
6th Division arrest No. 774.
Brigade arrest No. K.B. 258.
He was arrested by British soldiers from Kanturk during a major round-up on 11 June 1921 and he was

taken to Kanturk Military post.[54]
He was transferred from Cork Male
Gaol to Spike Island internment
compound on 22 June 1921.
He was transferred from Spike to
Maryborough (Portlaoise) Prison on the
night of 18/19 Nov and released from
there on 8 Dec 1921.

O'Donoghue, James

Also listed as Donoghue.
241 Blarney Street, Cork City. Age: 23.
Brigade arrest No. 17 I.B. 1050.
He was transferred from the Brigade
Cage in Victoria Barracks, Cork, to
Spike Island internment compound on
6 July 1921 to, 'A' Block, Hut 20.
He was one of the orderlies in his hut
during the Spike hunger strike.
He was transferred from Spike to
Maryborough (Portlaoise) Prison on the
night of 18/19 Nov and released from
there on 8 Dec 1921.

O'Donoghue, Patrick

Ballinvaird, Rossmore, Ballineen,
Clonakilty,
Co. Cork.
He was transferred to Spike Island
internment compound, date not found,
to 'A' Block, Hut 8.

O'Donoghue, Patrick

3 Highfield West, College Road,
Cork City. Age: 23.
Brigade arrest No. 17 I.B. 1095.

He was arrested by Crown Forces on
10 July 1921.
He was transferred from Cork Male
Gaol to Spike Island internment
compound on 25 July 1921.

O'Donovan, John

Also listed as Donovan.
Balteenbrack, Ardfield, Clonakilty,
Co. Cork. Age: 22.
6th Division arrest No. B.198.
Brigade arrest No. 17 I.B 429.
He was transferred from Cork to
Spike Island internment compound on
19 Mar 1921, to 'A' Block, Hut 5.
He was released from Spike on 5 Nov,
authority received from CA 1068, on
4 Nov 1921.

O'Donovan, Thomas

Front Glen, Kinsale, Co. Cork.
Age: 21.
6th Division arrest No. 489.
Brigade arrest No. 17 I.B. 414.
He was transferred from Cork to
Spike Island internment compound on
19 Mar 1921, to 'A' Block, Hut 15.
He was transferred from Spike to Bere
Island internment camp on 11 July
1921 on HMS Vidette.

O'Donovan, Thomas

Also listed as Donovan.
Emly, Knocklong, Co. Tipperary.
Age: 30. Brigade arrest No. L. 464.

---

54 See his WS, No. 1351.

He was transferred from Cork Military Detention Barracks to Spike Island internment compound on 11 May 1921, to 'A' Block, Hut 14. He was transferred from Spike to Maryborough (Portlaoise) Prison on 18/19 Nov and released from there in Dec 1921.

He survived 94 days on hunger strike in Cork Male Gaol, from 11 Aug to 12 Nov 1920.

O'Driscoll, John

Clonbanin, Banteer, Co. Cork.
Age: 19.
Brigade arrest No. K.B. 186.
He was transferred from Cork Male Gaol to Spike Island internment compound on 16 May 1921, to 'A' Block, Hut 7.

O'Driscoll, John

Mill Street, Timoleague, Co. Cork.
Age: 25. Occupation: Farmer.
6th Division arrest No. 551.
Brigade arrest No. 17 I.B. 992.
While he was in the Spike prison compound, he was served with an Internment Order before his release date. Instead of being released, he was further detained as an internee. He was transferred to Spike Island internment compound on 14 Nov 1921.
He was transferred from Spike to Maryborough (Portlaoise) Prison on the night of 18/19 Nov and released from there on 8 Dec 1921.

See O'Driscoll, John, in the list of Spike prisoners.

O'Driscoll, Timothy

Fort Hill, Kinsale, Co. Cork.
6th Division arrest No. 436.
Brigade arrest No. 17 I.B. 361.
He was transferred to Spike to be moved to Bere Island.
He was transferred from Spike to Bere Island internment camp on 11 July 1921 on HMS *Vidette*.

O'Dwyer, James K.

Ballydavid, Littleton, Thurles, Co. Tipperary.
Age: 30.
Brigade arrest No. 18 I.B. 150.
He was transferred from Cork Male Gaol to Spike Island internment compound on 12 Apr 1921.
He was transferred from Spike to Bere Island internment camp by RN destroyer on 14/15 Apr 1921.
He was transferred from Bere Island back to Spike on 20 Sept on HMS *Stormcloud*, D 89.
He was transferred from Spike to Maryborough (Portlaoise) Prison on 18/19 Nov and released from there in Dec 1921.

O'Grady, Michael

Castletownroche, Co. Cork. Age: 33.
Brigade arrest No. K.B. 205.
He was transferred from the Brigade Cage in Victoria Barracks, Cork, to

Spike Island internment compound on 6 July 1921, to 'A' Block, Hut 7.

O'Grady, Michael
Kanturk, Co. Cork.
He was transferred to Spike Island internment compound, date not found, to 'A' Block, Hut 17.

O'Halloran, Timothy
1 Corcoran's Quay, Blackpool, Cork City.
6th Division arrest No. 693.
Brigade arrest No. 17 I.B. 718.
He was transferred from Cork Male Gaol to Spike Island internment compound on 28 May 1921, to 'A' Block, Hut 5.

O'Hea, Jeremiah, (Jerome)
Lissercremin, Co. Cork.
6th Division arrest No. 342.
Brigade arrest No. 17 I.B. 273.
He was transferred from Cork Male Gaol to Spike Island internment compound on 19 Feb 1921.
He was transferred from Spike to Bere Island internment camp on 11 July 1921 on HMS *Vidette*.

O'Hehir, Michael
Mount Prospect, North Circular Road, Limerick City.
Brigade arrest No. 16 I.B. 307.
He was transferred from Kilworth Army Camp to Spike Island internment compound on 17 May 1921.

O'Hourihane, Peter
Skibbereen, Co. Cork.
Brigade arrest No. 17 I.B. 475.
He was transferred from Cork Male Gaol to Spike Island internment compound on 12 Apr 1921.
He was transferred from Spike to Bere Island internment camp by RN destroyer on 14/15 Apr 1921.

O'Keeffe, Daniel
Dengham, Mitchelstown, Co. Cork.
Age: 28.
Brigade arrest No. 16 I.B. 256.
He was transferred from Kilworth Army Camp via Cork Male Gaol to Spike Island internment compound on 9 June 1921, to 'B' Block, Hut 1.

O'Keeffe, Denis
Kingsland, Ballinhassig, Co. Cork.
6th Division arrest No. 409.
Brigade arrest No. 17 I.B. 339.
He was transferred to Spike to be moved to Bere Island.
He was transferred from Spike to Bere Island internment camp on 11 July 1921 on HMS *Vidette*.

O'Keeffe, Edward
Ballingarry, Co. Limerick.
Age: 27.
Brigade arrest No. 18 I.B. 221.
He was transferred from Cork Male Gaol to Spike Island internment compound on 22 Aug 1921.
He was released from Spike on

10 Nov, authority received from CA 1068, on 9 Nov 1921.

O'Keeffe, John
Churchtown, Buttevant, Co. Cork.
Age: 16.
Brigade arrest No. K.B. 235.
He was transferred from Cork Male Gaol to Spike Island internment compound on 1 June 1921.
He was released from Spike on 8 Nov, authority received from CA 1068, on 4 Nov 1921.

O'Keeffe, John
Clogheen Cottage, Clonakilty, Co. Cork.
Age: 66.
Brigade arrest No. 17 I.B. 839.
He was transferred from Cork Male Gaol to Spike Island internment compound on 14 Nov 1921.
He was transferred from Spike to Maryborough (Portlaoise) Prison on the night of 18/19 Nov and he was released from there on 28 Nov by order of the RIC.

O'Keeffe, Martin
Ballynoe, Co. Cork.
Brigade arrest No. 16 I.B. 111.
He was transferred to Spike to be moved to Bere Island.
He was transferred from Spike to Bere Island internment camp by RN destroyer on 14/15 Apr 1921 and escaped from there.

Martin O'Keeffe, Ballynoe, Co. Cork.

O'Keeffe, Patrick
Ardra, Rostellan, Co. Cork.
6th Division arrest No. 406.
Brigade arrest No. 17 I.B. 336.
He was transferred to Spike to be moved to Bere Island.
He was transferred to Bere Island internment camp on 11 July 1921 on HMS *Vidette*.

O'Keeffe, Patrick
Kanturk, Co. Cork.
Age: 38.
Brigade arrest No. K.B. 326.
He was transferred from Cork Male Gaol to Spike Island internment compound on 22 Aug 1921.

O'Keeffe, Richard
Ballynoe, Co. Cork. Age: 29.
Brigade arrest No. 16 I.B. 485.
He was arrested by Crown Forces on 15 July 1921.
He was transferred from Cork Male Gaol to Spike Island internment compound on 25 July 1921, to 'A' Block, Hut 2.

Richard O'Keeffe, Ballynoe, Co. Cork.

O'Keeffe, Thomas

Ballinavourty, Glenrose, Kilfinnane,
Co. Tipperary.
6th Division arrest No. 129.
Brigade arrest No. 18 I.B. 141.
He was transferred from Cork Male
Gaol to Spike Island internment
compound on 12 Apr 1921.
He was transferred from Spike to Bere
Island internment camp on 11 July
1921 on HMS *Vidette*.

O'Keeffe, William

Shade Place, Cork City.
6th Division arrest No. 583.
Brigade arrest No. 17 I.B. 537.
He was transferred from Spike to Bere
Island internment camp on 11 July
1921 on HMS *Vidette*.

O'Leary, Cornelius

Killarney, Co. Kerry.
He was transferred from Cork Male
Gaol to Spike Island internment
compound on 19 Feb 1921.

O'Leary, Con

Market Street, Bandon, Co. Cork.
Age: 28. Occupation: Saddler.
6th Division arrest No. 549.
Brigade arrest No. 17 I.B. 997.
While he was in the Spike prison
compound he was served with an
Internment Order before his release
date. Instead of being released, he was
further detained as an internee. He was
transferred to Spike Island internment
compound on 14 Nov 1921.
He was transferred from Spike to
Maryborough (Portlaoise) Prison on
the night of 18/19 Nov.
He was transferred from
Maryborough (Portlaoise) Prison to
the Curragh Military Hospital on
30 Nov. He was released in Dec 1921.
See O'Leary, Cornelius, in the list of
Spike prisoners.

O'Leary, Cornelius

Also listed as Leary.
Macroom, Co. Cork. Age: 21.
Brigade arrest No. 17 I.B. 1130.
He was transferred from the Brigade
Cage in Victoria Barracks, Cork, to
Spike Island internment compound on
15 July 1921, to 'A' Block, Hut 20.

O'Leary, Daniel

Timoleague, Co. Cork.
Brigade arrest No. 17 I.B. 193.
He was transferred from Cork Male
Gaol to Spike Island internment
compound on 24 Feb 1921.

O'Leary, Denis

Ballycromane, Durras, Bantry, Co.
Cork. Age: 21.
6th Division arrest No. 801.
Brigade arrest No. 17 I.B. 1012.
He was transferred from Cork Male
Gaol to Spike Island internment
compound on 15 July 1921, to 'A'
Block, Hut 5.

O'Leary, Florence

Florence O'Leary, College Road, Cork City.

22 College Road, Cork City.
Age: 22.
Brigade arrest No. 17 I.B. 928.
He was arrested on the South Mall,
Cork City, on 18 June 1921 and
taken in an armoured car to the
Bridewell. He was taken next to
Victoria Barracks, Cork, and put into
the Brigade Cage. On Wednesday
29 June he was taken from the Brigade
Cage to Cork Male Gaol. He was
transferred from Cork Male Gaol to
Spike Island internment compound
on 30 June 1921, to 'B' Block, Hut 17.
He was moved to 'A' Block, Hut 21,
during the Spike hunger strike.

He was transferred from Spike to
Maryborough (Portlaoise) Prison on
the night of 18/19 Nov and released
from there in Dec 1921.

O'Leary, John

Cork City.
Brigade arrest No. 17 I.B. 180.
He was transferred from Cork Male
Gaol to Spike Island internment
compound on 19 Feb 1921.

O'Leary, John

Telephone Street, Blarney, Co. Cork.
6th Division arrest No. 335.
Brigade arrest No. 17 I.B. 248.
He was transferred from Cork
Military Detention Barracks to Spike
Island internment compound on
19 Feb 1921.
He was transferred from Spike to Bere
Island internment camp on 11 July
1921 on HMS *Vidette*.

O'Leary, John

Cullen, Millstreet, Co. Kerry. Age: 30.
6th Division arrest No. 775.
Brigade arrest No. K.B. 259.
He was captured by British soldiers
near Kanturk on 11 June 1921.
He was transferred from Cork Male
Gaol to Spike Island internment
compound on 22 June 1921.

O'Leary, Lawrence

Timoleague, Co. Cork.
6th Division arrest No. 269.

Brigade arrest No. 17 I.B. 201.
He was transferred from Cork Male
Gaol to Spike Island internment
compound on 24 Feb 1921.
He was transferred from Spike to Bere
Island internment camp on 11 July
1921 on HMS *Vidette*.

O'Leary, Patrick
24 Mangerton Terrace, Blarney,
Co. Cork.
Age: 23. Occupation: Medical Student.
6th Division arrest No. 762.
Brigade arrest No. 17 I.B. 563.
He was taken from Cork Military
Hospital, in Victoria Barracks, to
Cork Male Gaol.
He was transferred from Cork Male
Gaol to Spike Island internment
compound on 25 July 1921.

O'Leary, Timothy
Kilmurry, Berrings, Co. Cork.
Brigade arrest No. 17 I.B. 247.
He was transferred from the Brigade
Cage in Victoria Barracks, Cork, to
Spike Island internment compound on
19 Feb 1921.

O'Loughlin, Patrick
Also listed as Loughlin.
Urlingford, Co. Kilkenny. Age: 23.
Brigade arrest No. 16 I.B. 401.
He was transferred from Cork Male
Gaol to Spike Island internment

compound on 30 June 1921, to 'B'
Block, Hut 20. He was moved to
'A' Block, Hut 1, during the Spike
hunger strike.
He was transferred from Spike to
Maryborough (Portlaoise) Prison on
the night of 18/19 Nov and released
from there in Dec 1921.

O'Mahoney, Daniel
Newcestown, Co. Cork.
6th Division arrest No. 324.
Brigade arrest No. 17 I.B. 104.
He was transferred from Cork Male
Gaol to Spike Island internment
compound on 24 Feb 1921.

O'Mahony, Denis[55]
Belrose, Upton, Co. Cork.
6th Division arrest No. 607.
Brigade arrest No. 17 I.B. 574.
He was arrested by Crown Forces at
the end Apr 1921.
He was transferred from Cork Male
Gaol to Spike Island internment
compound on 25 Apr 1921. He
was transferred from Spike to Bere
Island internment camp on 11 July
1921 on HMS *Vidette*. O'Mahony's
house at Belrose, Upton, was used
regularly by the officers of Third
(West) Cork Brigade for Brigade
council meetings until it was burned
down by Crown Forces.

---

55 See Frank Neville, WS No. 443, p.15

O'Mahony, Denis

Conna, Co. Cork.
6th Division arrest No. 241.
He was transferred from Kilworth
Army Camp to Spike Island internment
compound on 13 Apr 1921.
He was transferred from Spike to
Bere Island internment camp on
14/15 Apr 1921.

O'Mahoney, Edward

Castleisland, Co. Kerry.
6th Division arrest No. 472.
He was transferred to Spike to be
moved to Bere Island.
He was transferred from Spike to Bere
Island internment camp on 11 July
1921 on HMS *Vidette*.

O'Mahony, M.J. Henry

Dock Street, Monkstown, Passage
West, Co. Cork. Age: 25.
6th Division arrest No. 369.
Brigade arrest No. 17 I.B. 287.
He was arrested by Cameron

Henry O'Mahony, Passage West, Co. Cork.

Highlanders in Monkstown on
8 Feb 1921 and taken to their HQ in
Cobh. From there he was taken to
Victoria Barracks and lodged in the
Brigade Cage.[56]
He was transferred from the Brigade
Cage to Spike Island internment
compound on 24 Feb 1921.
He was elected O/C of the
internment compound.
He escaped from Spike on the night of
10/11 Nov 1921 with six other internees.
See detailed account of their escape in
this book.

O'Mahony, James

9 Victoria Cottages, Cork City.
Age: 26.
6th Division arrest No. 235.
Brigade arrest No. 17 I.B. 164.
He was transferred from Cork Male
Gaol to Spike Island internment
compound on 24 Feb 1921.
He was transferred from Spike to Bere
Island internment camp on 11 July
1921 on HMS *Vidette*.

O'Mahony, John

Kilrush, Bandon, Co. Cork.
6th Division arrest No. 611.
Brigade arrest No. 17 I.B. 583.
He was transferred from Cork Male
Gaol to Spike Island internment
compound on 25 Apr 1921.
He was transferred from Spike to Bere

---

56 See his WS, No. 1506.

Island internment camp on 11 July 1921 on HMS *Vidette*.

O'Mahony, Joseph
Newcastle West, Co. Limerick.
Age: 23.
6th Division arrest No. 173.
Brigade arrest No. 18 I.B.192.
He was transferred from Cork Male Gaol to Spike Island internment compound on 9 June 1921 to 'B' Block, Hut 23. He was moved to 'A' Block, Hut 21, during the Spike hunger strike. He was transferred from Spike to Maryborough (Portlaoise) Prison on the night of 18/19 Nov and released from there in Dec 1921.

O'Mahony, Larry
Macroom, Co. Cork.
He was transferred from Cork Male Gaol to Spike Island internment compound on 19 Feb 1921.

O'Mahony, Martin
Garryduff, Clonmult, Dungourney, Co. Cork.

Martin O'Mahony, Clonmult, Co. Cork.

Brother of William below.
Brigade arrest No. 16 I.B. 154.
He was arrested by Crown Forces on 16 July 1921.
He was transferred from Cork Male Gaol to Spike Island internment compound on 25 July 1921, to 'A' Block, Hut 1.
Brother of William below.

O'Mahony, William

William O'Mahony, Clonmult, Co. Cork.

Garryduff, Clonmult, Dungourney, Co. Cork.
Brigade arrest No. 16 I.B. 99.
He was transferred to Spike, to be moved to Bere Island.
He was transferred from Spike to Bere Island internment camp on 14/15 Apr 1921 by RN destroyer.
Brother of Martin above.

O'Mullane, Cornelius
Also listed as Mullane.
Banteer, Co. Cork. Age: 18.
Brigade arrest No. K.B. 191.
He was transferred from Cork Male Gaol to Spike Island internment

compound on 16 May 1921, to 'A' Block, Hut 17.

O'Mullane, Jeremiah

Also listed as Mullane.
Banteer, Co. Cork.
Age: 22.
Brigade arrest No. K.B. 193.
He was transferred from Cork Male Gaol to Spike Island internment compound on 16 May 1921, to 'A' Block, Hut 17.

O'Neill, Daniel David

13 Carrigveen Street, Co. Wexford.
Age: 29.
Brigade arrest No. 16 I.B. 383.
He was transferred from Kilworth Army Camp via Cork Male Gaol to Spike Island internment compound on 9 June 1921, to 'A' Block, Hut 18.

O'Neill, Daniel

Kilbrittain, Co. Cork.
He was transferred to Spike Island internment compound, date not found, to 'A' Block, Hut 16.

O'Neill, Daniel (Donal)

Loughbeg, Ringaskiddy, Co. Cork.
Age: 30.
6th Division arrest No. 854.
Brigade arrest No. 17 I.B. 1087.
He was transferred from Cork Male Gaol to Spike Island internment compound on 15 July 1921, to 'A' Block, Hut 10.

O'Neill, Daniel

Maryborough, Timoleague, Co. Cork.
Age: 28.
Brigade arrest No. 17 I.B. 1193.
He was arrested by Crown Forces on 20 July 1921.
He was transferred from Cork Male Gaol to Spike Island internment compound on 22 Aug 1921.

O'Neill, Michael

Cromfane, Eyeries, Castletownbere, Co. Cork. Age: 20.
6th Division arrest No. 847.
Brigade arrest No. 17 I.B. 986.
He was transferred from Cork Male Gaol to Spike Island internment compound on 15 July 1921, to 'A' Block, Hut 6.
He was transferred from Spike to Maryborough (Portlaoise) Prison on the night of 18/19 Nov and released from there on 8 Dec 1921.

O'Neill, Michael

8 Railway Cottages, Kilbarry, Co. Cork.
Age: 55.
He was arrested at Limerick Junction Railway Station on 23 May 1921 and taken to Tipperary Army Barracks and to Kilworth Army Camp on 27 May.
Brigade arrest No. 16 I.B. 448.
He was transferred from Kilworth Army Camp to Spike Island internment compound on 16 Sept 1921.

He was released from Spike on 5 Nov,
authority received from CA 1068, on
4 Nov 1921.

O'Neill, Peter

Passage West, Co. Cork.
Brigade arrest No. 17 I.B.
He was transferred from Cork Male
Gaol to Spike Island internment
compound on 24 Feb 1921.

O'Rahilly, Alfred, Prof.

Alfred O'Rahilly, Listowel, Co. Kerry.

Listowel, Co. Kerry and University
College Cork.
Brigade arrest No. 17 I.B. 634
He was transferred from Cork Male
Gaol to Spike Island internment
compound on 11 May 1921 and he
was later transferred to Bere Island
internment camp.

O'Regan, Tom

The Cottage, Rathkeale, Co. Limerick.
Brigade arrest No. 18 I.B. 149.
He was transferred from Cork Male
Gaol to Spike Island internment
compound on 12 Apr 1921.

O'Riordan, Stephen

Cork City.
Brigade arrest No. 17 I.B 184.
He was transferred from Cork Male
Gaol to Spike Island internment
compound on 19 Feb 1921.

O'Shea, Florence

Curragh, Skibbereen, Co. Cork.
Age: 24. Occupation: Trade union
secretary.
6th Division arrest No. 588.
Brigade arrest No. 17 I.B. 1090.
While he was in the Spike prison
compound he was served with an
Internment Order before his release
date. Instead of being released, he
was further detained as an internee.
He was transferred to Spike Island
internment compound on
14 Nov 1921.
He was transferred from Spike to
Maryborough (Portlaoise) Prison on the
night of 18/19 Nov and released from
there on 8 Dec 1921.
See O'Shea, Florence, in the list of
Spike prisoners.

O'Shea, John

Gurteen, Bandon, Co. Cork.
6th Division arrest No. 359 & 709.
Brigade arrest No. 17 I.B. 299.
He was transferred from Cork
Military Detention Barracks to Spike
Island internment compound on
24 Feb 1921.
He was transferred from Spike to Bere

Island internment camp on 11 July 1921 on HMS *Vidette*.

O'Shea, John

Tralee, Co. Kerry.

Age: 45.

Brigade arrest No. L 625.

He was transferred from Cork Military Detention Barracks to Spike Island internment compound on 6 July 1921.

He was released from Spike on 15 Aug, authority received from CA 693.

O'Shea, John (Jack)

John O'Shea, Great William O'Brien Street, Cork City.

76 Great William O'Brien Street, Cork City.

Age: 30.

Occupation: Flax worker.

Brigade arrest No. 17 I.B.780.

He was first arrested by Crown Forces on 5 Nov 1920.

He was rearrested at home with his brother Joe by British soldiers on 21 May 1921 and taken to Cork Military Detention Barracks. He was later moved to Cork Male Gaol.[57]

He was transferred from Cork Male Gaol to Spike Island internment compound on 28 May 1921, to 'A' Block, Hut 5.

He was transferred from Spike to Maryborough (Portlaoise) Prison on 18/19 Nov and released from there in Dec 1921.

Brother of Joseph below.

O'Shea, Joseph

Joe O'Shea, Great William O'Brien Street, Cork City.

76 Great William O'Brien Street, Cork City.

Age: 23.

Occupation: Dock worker.

6th Division arrest No. 708.

Brigade arrest No. 17 I.B. 781.

He was arrested at home with his brother John by British soldiers on 21 May 1921. He was taken to Cork

---

57 See Joseph O'Shea, WS No. 1675.

Military Detention Barracks and later moved to Cork Male Gaol.[58] He was transferred from Cork Male Gaol to Spike Island internment compound on 28 May 1921, to 'B' Block, Hut 21. He was moved to 'A' Block, Hut 5, during the Spike hunger strike. He was transferred from Spike to Maryborough (Portlaoise) Prison on the night of 18/19 Nov and released from there on 8 Dec 1921. Brother of John above.

O'Shea, Padraig

Castlegregory, Co. Kerry. He was transferred to Spike Island internment compound, date not found, to 'A' Block, Hut 6.

O'Shea, Patrick

Farrantaun, Castlegregory, Co. Kerry. Age: 32. 6th Division arrest No. 382. Brigade arrest No. K.B. 88. He was transferred from Cork to Spike Island internment compound on 3 Mar 1921. He was transferred from Spike to Bere Island internment camp on 11 July 1921 on HMS *Vidette*.

O'Shea, Timothy

Dunmanway, Co. Cork. 6th Division arrest No. 455. Brigade arrest No. 17 I.B. 391. He was transferred to Spike, to be moved to Bere Island. He was transferred from Spike to Bere Island internment camp on 11 July 1921 on HMS *Vidette*.

O'Shea, Timothy

Lower New Street, Killarney, Co. Kerry. Age: 35. Brigade arrest No. K.B. 271. He was arrested by Crown Forces on 30 June 1921. He was transferred from Cork Male Gaol to Spike Island internment compound on 15 July 1921, to 'A' Block, Hut 14. He was transferred from Spike to Maryborough (Portlaoise) Prison on the night of 18/19 Nov. He was released on parole from there on 5 Dec 1921. He was released while on parole.

O'Sullivan, Christopher

Boherbue, Co. Cork. Occupation: Blacksmith. 6th Division arrest No. 378. Brigade arrest No. K.B. 84. He was arrested on 6 Feb 1921. He was tried by military court and acquitted of illegal possession of a revolver. Instead of being released, he was classified as an internee. He was transferred from Cork Male Gaol to Spike Island internment compound on 30 Apr 1921. He was transferred from Spike to Bere

Island internment camp on 11 July 1921 on HMS *Vidette*.

O'Sullivan, Cornelius

Also listed as Sullivan. Drumkeen, Ballymountain, Innishannon, Co. Cork. Age: 24. Brigade arrest No. 17 I.B. 393. He was arrested by British soldiers in Innishannon, Co. Cork, on 27 Feb 1921. He was taken to Bandon Military Barracks and later taken to Cork Military Detention Barracks.[59] He was transferred from Cork Military Detention Barracks to Spike Island internment compound on 19 Mar 1921, to 'A' Block, Hut 16. He was transferred from Spike to Maryborough (Portlaoise) Prison on the night of 18/19 Nov and released from there on 8 Dec 1921.

O'Sullivan, Cornelius

Inchigeela, Co. Cork. Brigade arrest No. 17 I.B. 465. He was transferred from Cork Male Gaol to Spike Island internment compound on 12 Apr 1921. He was transferred from Spike to Bere Island internment camp on 14/15 Apr 1921 by RN destroyer.

O'Sullivan, Daniel

Cromfane, Eyeries, Castletownbere, Co. Cork. Age: 18.

6th Division arrest No. 699 & 848. Brigade arrest No. 17 I.B. 989. He was transferred from Cork Male Gaol to Spike Island internment compound on 15 July 1921.

O'Sullivan, Daniel C.

Glenduff, Kilbrittain, Bandon, Co. Cork. Age: 20. Brigade arrest No. 17 I.B. 275. He was transferred from Cork Male Gaol to Spike Island internment compound on 19 Feb 1921, to Hut 8. He was transferred from Spike to Cork Military Hospital, in Victoria Barracks, on 17 Oct, authority received from CA 907, dated 14 Oct 1921.

O'Sullivan, Daniel

Daniel O'Sullivan, Lombardstown, Co. Cork.

Gortmore, Lombardstown, Co. Cork. Age: 20. Brigade arrest No. K.B. 315. He was transferred from Cork Male

Gaol to Spike Island internment
compound on 22 Aug 1921.
He was released from Spike on 8 Nov,
with the authority of CA 1068, dated
4 Nov 1921.

O'Sullivan, Daniel R.
Barracalla, Ardgroom,
Castletownbere, Co. Cork.
Age: 26
Brigade arrest No. 17 I.B. 720.
He was transferred from Cork Male
Gaol to Spike Island internment
compound on 28 May 1921, to 'B'
Block, Hut 1.

O'Sullivan, Denis
Also listed as Sullivan.
Kilbritain, Co. Cork. Age: 21.
Brigade arrest No. 17 I.B. 281.
He was transferred from Cork, to
Spike Island internment compound on
3 Mar 1921, to 'A' Block, Hut 3.
He was released from Spike on 8 Nov,
authority received from CA 1068,
dated 4 Nov 1921.

O'Sullivan, Edward (Ned)
Ballyhooley, Fermoy, Co. Cork.
6th Division arrest No. 223.
He was transferred from Kilworth
Army Camp to Spike Island internment
compound on 13 Apr 1921.
He was transferred from Spike to Bere
Island internment camp on 14/15 Apr
1921 by RN destroyer.

O'Sullivan, Eugene
Gurteen Bridge, Ardgroom,
Castletownbere, Co. Cork. Age: 20.
6th Division arrest No. 698.
Brigade arrest No. 17 I.B. 721.
He was transferred from Cork Male
Gaol to Spike Island internment
compound on 28 May 1921, to 'A'
Block, Hut 20.
Brother of internee O'Sullivan,
Michael J.

O'Sullivan, Frank
Also listed as Sullivan.
Douglas Road, Cork City.
Age: 24.
Brigade arrest No. 17 I.B. 700.
He was transferred from Cork
Military Detention Barracks to Spike
Island internment compound on
16 May 1921, to 'A' Block, Hut 4.

O'Sullivan, Jeremiah
262 Blarney Street, Cork City. Age: 22.
Brigade arrest No. 17 I.B. 879.
He was transferred from Cork to
Spike Island internment compound on
25 June 1921.

O'Sullivan, Jeremiah M.
Killarney, Co. Kerry.
Age: 24.
Brigade arrest No. K.B. 87.
He was transferred from Cork Male
Gaol to Spike Island internment
compound on 24 Feb 1921.

O'Sullivan, John

16 Abbey Street, Cork City.
6th Division arrest No. 627.
Brigade arrest No. 17 I.B. 603.
He was transferred from Cork Military
Detention Barracks to Spike Island
internment compound on 30 Apr 1921.
He was transferred from Spike to Bere
Island internment camp on 11 July
1921 on HMS *Vidette*.

O'Sullivan, John (Sean)

Lixnaw, Co. Kerry. Age: 25.
Brigade arrest No. K.B. 291.
He was transferred from Cork Military
Detention Barracks to Spike Island
internment compound on 6 July 1921.

O'Sullivan, John Joseph

Brandonwell, Ardfert, Co. Kerry.
Age: 22. Brigade arrest No. K.B. 157.
He was transferred from Cork Male
Gaol to Spike Island internment
compound on 16 May 1921, to 'A'
Block, Hut 14.

O'Sullivan, John L.

Carrigroe, Clonakilty, Co. Cork.
Age: 19. Brigade arrest No. 17 I.B. 309.
He was transferred from the Brigade
Cage in Victoria Barracks, Cork, to
Spike Island internment compound on
19 Mar 1921, to 'A' Block, Hut 8.
He was transferred from Spike to
Maryborough (Portlaoise) Prison on
the night of 18/19 Nov and released
from there on 6 Dec 1921.

O'Sullivan, Lawrence

Mill Street, Timoleague, Co. Cork.
Age: 34.
Brigade arrest No. 17 I.B. 380.
He was transferred from Cork Male
Gaol to Spike Island internment
compound on 19 Mar 1921.

O'Sullivan, Michael J.

Gurteen Bridge, Ardgroom,
Castletownbere, Co. Cork.

Michael O'Sullivan, Castletownbere,
Co. Cork.

Age: 26.
6th Division arrest No. 697.
Brigade arrest No. 17 I.B. 719.
He was transferred from Cork Male
Gaol to Spike Island internment
compound on 28 May 1921, to 'B'
Block, Hut 1.
Brother of internee, O'Sullivan, Eugene.

O'Sullivan, Morris (Maurice)

Also listed as Sullivan.
Castleisland, Co. Kerry.
Age: 24.
Brigade arrest No. K.B. 472.
He was transferred from Cork to

Spike Island internment compound on 19 Mar 1921, to 'A' Block, Hut 6.

O'Sullivan, Mortimer
Bantry, Co. Cork.
He was transferred to Spike Island internment compound, date not found, to 'A' Block, Hut 9.

O'Sullivan, Mortimer
32 Horgan's Buildings, Cork City.
Age: 32.
Brigade arrest No. 17 I.B. 869.
He was arrested by Crown Forces on 10 July 1921.
He was transferred from Cork Male Gaol to Spike Island internment compound on 25 July 1921.

O'Sullivan, Patrick
Carrigroe, Rosscarbery, Co. Cork.
He was transferred from Cork Male Gaol to Spike Island internment compound on 19 Feb 1921.

O'Sullivan, Peter
Bantry, Co. Cork.
He was transferred to Spike Island internment compound, date not found, to 'A' Block, Hut 9.

O'Sullivan, Peter
53 Hibernian Buildings, Cork City.
Age: 25.
Brigade arrest No. 17 I.B. 872.
He was arrested by Crown Forces on 10 July 1921.

He was transferred from Cork Male Gaol to Spike Island internment compound on 25 July 1921.

O'Sullivan, Peter
Allihies Mines, Castletownbere, Co. Cork.
Age: 25.
Brigade arrest No. 17 I.B. 1169.
He was arrested by Crown Forces for membership of the IRA and recommended for internment.
He was transferred from Cork Male Gaol to Spike Island internment compound on 25 July 1921, to 'A' Block, Hut 4.

O'Sullivan, T.M.
New Street, Killarney, Co. Kerry.
He was transferred to Spike Island internment compound, date not found, to 'A' Block, Hut 6. He was later moved to Hut 14.

Parker, John
Conna, Co. Cork.
6th Division arrest No. 224.

John Parker, Conna, Co. Cork.

Brigade arrest No. 16 I.B. 103.
He was transferred to Spike Island
internment camp, date not found, to
'B' Block, Hut 2.

Pearce, Patrick
Also listed as Pierce.
Upper Shannon, Enniscorthy, Co.
Wexford.
Age: 23.
Brigade arrest No. 16 I.B. 351
He was transferred from Cork Male
Gaol to Spike Island internment
compound on 9 June 1921, to 'A'
Block, Hut 20.
Beginning on 2 Sept 1921, he spent
63 hours on hunger strike on Spike
Island.
He was transferred from Spike to
Maryborough (Portlaoise) Prison on
the night of 18/19 Nov and released
from there in Dec 1921.

Pearse, Patrick A.
Cork Street, Kinsale, Co. Cork.

Patrick Pearse, Kinsale, Co. Cork.

Age: 23.
6th Division arrest No. 580.
Brigade arrest No. 17 I.B. 360.
He was transferred from Cork Male
Gaol to Spike Island internment
compound on 28 May 1921, to 'A'
Block, Hut 2.
He was killed in action during the
Civil War fighting against National
Army troops near Upton in Co. Cork
on 4 Oct 1922.[60] He was buried in the
Abbey graveyard in Kinsale, Co. Cork.

Pendergast, Joseph
Stonehall, Kilcornan, Co. Limerick.
Age: 30.
Brigade arrest No. 18 I.B. 222.
He was transferred from Limerick
via Cork Male Gaol to Spike Island
internment compound on 22 Aug
1921.
He was released from Spike on
10 Nov, authority received from CA
1068 on 9 Nov 1921.

Phillips, Michael
69 Poleberry, Waterford City, also
Talbot Street, Tramore, Co. Waterford.
Age: 24.
Brigade arrest No. 16 I.B. 270.
He was transferred from Kilworth
Army Camp to Spike Island
internment compound on 17 May,
1921.

---

60 *The Last Post, 1985 edition,* p.152.

Michael Philips, Poleberry, Waterford City.

Pierce, John

Ballyheigue, Tralee, Co. Kerry.
Brigade arrest No. K.B. 79.
He was arrested by Auxiliary Police
near Ballyheigue, Co. Kerry.[61] He was
transferred from Cork Male Gaol to
Spike Island internment compound on
24 Feb 1921.

Pollard, Patrick

Killenaule, Co. Tipperary.
6th Division arrest No. 262.
Brigade arrest No. 16 I.B. 142.
He was transferred to Spike to be
moved to Bere Island.
He was transferred from Spike to Bere
Island internment camp on 11 July
1921 on HMS *Vidette*.

Power, Edmond (Edward)[62]

52 Slievekeale Rd, Kilmacthomas,
Co. Waterford. Age: 25.
Brigade arrest No. 16 I.B. 481.
During Apr 1921, he was arrested

by British soldiers in Kilmacthomas.
He was taken to Dungarvan and
to Fermoy Military Barracks. He
was convicted of IRA membership
and sentenced to two months
imprisonment with Hard Labour. He
was imprisoned in Cork Male Gaol.
On completion of his sentence he was
served with an Internment Order.
He was transferred from Cork Male
Gaol to Spike Island internment
compound on 30 June 1921, to 'A'
Block, Hut 2. He was later moved to
'B' Block, Hut 16.
He was transferred from Spike to
Maryborough (Portlaoise) Prison on the
night of 18/19 Nov and released from
there on 6 Dec 1921.

Power, Edward

Brenor, Piltown, Co. Kilkenny.
Age: 25.
He was arrested on 25 May and taken
to Kilkenny Military Barracks and
moved to Kilworth Army Camp on
25 June 1921.
Brigade arrest No. 16 I.B. 482.
He was transferred from Kilworth
Army Camp to Spike Island internment
compound on 15 Sept 1921.

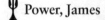

Power, James

Lixnaw, Co. Kerry.
Age: 30.

---

61 See Michael Pierce, WS No. 1190, p.20.
62 See his WS, No. 1130.

Brigade arrest No. K.B. 289.
He was transferred from Cork Military
Detention Barracks to Spike Island
internment compound on 6 July 1921.

Power, John

John Power, Cashel, Co. Tipperary.

Rosegreen, Cashel, Co. Tipperary.
Age: 20. Brigade arrest No. L 463.
He was transferred from Cork Male
Gaol to Spike Island internment
compound on 12 Apr 1921.
He was transferred from Spike to Bere
Island internment camp on 14/15 Apr
1921 by RN destroyer.
He was transferred from Bere Island
back to Spike on 20 Sept on HMS
Stormcloud, D 89.
He was transferred from Spike to
Maryborough (Portlaoise) Prison on
18/19 Nov and was released from
there in Dec 1921.
He survived 94 days on hunger strike
in Cork Male Gaol from 11 Aug to
12 Nov 1920.

Power, John

33 or 53 Commons Road, Cork City.

John Power, Commons Road, Cork City.

Age: 21. 6th Division arrest No. 719.
Brigade arrest No. 17 I.B. 756.
He was transferred from Cork Male
Gaol to Spike Island internment
compound on 22 June 1921, to 'A'
Block, Hut 5.

Prenderville, John (Jack)

Clonacurrig, Castleisland, Co. Kerry.
6th Division arrest No. 553.
Brigade arrest No. K.B. 106.
He was transferred from Cork Male
Gaol to Spike Island internment
compound on 25 Apr 1921.
He was transferred from Spike to Bere
Island internment camp on 11 July
1921 on HMS *Vidette*.

Purcell, Patrick

Castletown, Inch, Gorey, Co. Wexford.
Age: 37.
Brigade arrest No. 16 I.B. 499.
He was transferred from Waterford
Gaol by RN destroyer to Spike
Island internment compound on
18 Aug 1921.

Purcell, Pierce

65 O'Connell St, Waterford City.
Age: 28.
Brigade arrest No. 16 I.B. 514
He was transferred from Waterford
Gaol by RN destroyer to Spike Island
internment compound on 18 Aug
1921, to 'A' Block, Hut 11.
He was transferred from Spike to
Maryborough (Portlaoise) Prison on the
night of 18/19 Nov and released from
there on 6 Dec 1921.

Purcell, Pierce

Bawnmore, Johnstown, Co. Kilkenny.
He is listed in 'A' Block, Hut 11 during
the Spike hunger strike.
No other details found. Possibly the
previously listed individual using a
different address.

Quinlan, Gerard

C/o R. Denphy, Stradbally, Co. Laois.
6th Division arrest No. 290.
Brigade arrest No. 16 I.B. 174.
He was transferred from Kilworth
Army Camp to Spike Island
internment compound on 4 Mar 1921.
He was transferred from Spike to Bere
Island internment camp on 11 July
1921 on HMS *Vidette*.

Quinlan, William

Annacarty, Co. Tipperary.
Age: 22 .
Occupation: Book keeper.
6th Division arrest No. 607.

Brigade arrest No. 16 I.B. 489 & S.C/62.
While he was in the Spike prison
compound he was served with an
Internment Order before his release
date. Instead of being released, he was
further detained as an internee. He was
transferred to Spike Island internment
compound on 14 Nov 1921.
He was transferred from Spike to
Maryborough (Portlaoise) Prison on the
night of 18/19 Nov and released from
there on 8 Dec 1921.
See Quinlan, William, in the list of
Spike prisoners.

Quinn, James

Kildorney, Kilsheelan, Co. Tipperary.
6th Division arrest No. 191.
He was transferred from Kilworth
Army Camp to Spike Island internment
compound on 13 Apr 1921.
He was transferred from Spike to Bere
Island internment camp on 14/15 Apr
1921 by RN destroyer.

Quinn, John (Jack)

Villierstown, Cappoquin, Co. Waterford.
Age: 20. Brigade arrest No. 16 I.B. 254.
He was transferred from Kilworth
Army Camp to Spike Island internment
compound on 17 May 1921.

Quinn, Maurice

Ballinspittle, Co. Cork
He was transferred from Cork Male
Gaol to Spike Island internment
compound on 19 Feb 1921.

Quirke, James

Ballyduff, Co. Waterford.

Age: 28. Occupation: Farmer.

6th Division arrest No. 560.

Brigade arrest No. 16 I.B. 490 & S.C/ 215.

While he was in the Spike prison compound he was served with an Internment Order before his release date. Instead of being released, he was further detained as an internee. He was transferred to Spike Island internment compound on 14 Nov 1921.

He was transferred from Spike to Maryborough (Portlaoise) Prison on the night of 18/19 Nov and released from there on 8 Dec 1921.

See Quirke, James, in the list of Spike prisoners.

Quirke, John

Carragorne, Ballyduff Upper, Co. Waterford. Age: 26.

6th Division arrest No. 404.

Brigade arrest No. 16 I.B. 160.

He was transferred from Kilworth Army Camp to Cork Male Gaol on 4 Mar 1921.

He was transferred from Cork Male Gaol to Spike Island internment compound on 9 June 1921, to 'B' Block, Hut 20.

Quirke, William[63]

Burke Street, Fethard, Co. Tipperary.

Bill Quirke, Fethard, Co. Tipperary.

Age: 26. Brigade arrest No. 16 I.B. 168.

He was arrested by Crown Forces in Jan 1921.

He was transferred from Kilworth Army Camp to Spike Island internment compound on 9 June 1921, to 'B' Block.

He was elected commander of 'B' Block. He was moved to 'A' Block, Hut 22, during the Spike hunger strike. He escaped from Spike with six other internees on the night of 10/11 Nov 1921.

See detailed account of their escape in this book.

Radford, Lawrence

Oldpound, Co. Waterford.

Age: 29.

Brigade arrest No. 16 I.B. 305.

He was transferred from Kilworth Army Camp to Spike Island internment compound on 17 May 1921, to 'A' Block, Hut 18.

---

63 See James Keating, WS No. 1220, p.10.

Raftis, Liam
Ferrybank, Co. Waterford.
6th Division arrest No. 194.
He was transferred from Kilworth
Army Camp to Spike Island internment
compound on 13 Apr 1921.
He was transferred from Spike to Bere
Island internment camp on 14/15 Apr
1921 by RN destroyer.

Raftis, Pat
Ballylusky, Mullinavat, Co. Kilkenny.
Age: 31.
Brigade arrest No. 16 I.B. 405.
He was transferred from Fermoy
Military Barracks to Cork Military
Detention Barracks on 24 June 1921.
He was transferred from Cork
Military Detention Barracks to Spike
Island internment compound on
25 June. He was moved to 'A' Block,
Hut 21, during the Spike hunger strike.
He was transferred from Spike to
Maryborough (Portlaoise) Prison on the
night of 18/19 Nov and released from
there on 8 Dec 1921.

Rahilly, Michael
Abbeydorney, Killarney, Co. Kerry.
Age: 50.
Brigade arrest No. K.B. 172.
He was transferred from Cork Male
Gaol to Spike Island internment
compound on 16 May 1921. He was
moved to 'A' Block, Hut 22, during the
Spike hunger strike.
He was transferred from Spike to

Maryborough (Portlaoise) Prison on the
night of 18/19 Nov and released from
there on 8 Dec 1921.

Raleigh, James
Mitchel Street (Feather St),
Mullinahone, Co. Tipperary.
Age: 29.
Brigade arrest No. 16 I.B. 295.
He was transferred from Kilkenny
Gaol to Spike Island internment
compound on 2 May 1921. He was
moved to 'A' Block, Hut 22, during
the Spike hunger strike.
He was transferred from Spike to
Maryborough (Portlaoise) Prison on the
night of 18/19 Nov and released from
there on 8 Dec 1921.

Raleigh, Michael
Mullinahone, Co. Tipperary.
Age: 24.
Brigade arrest No. 16 I.B. 208.
He was transferred from Kilworth
Army Camp to Spike Island
internment compound on 17 May
1921. He was moved to 'A' Block, Hut
22, during the Spike hunger strike.
He was transferred from Spike to
Maryborough (Portlaoise) Prison on the
night of 18/19 Nov and released from
there on 8 Dec 1921.

Reddy, John
Raheen, Camolin, Co. Wexford.
Age: 23.
He was transferred from Waterford

Gaol to Spike Island internment compound by RN destroyer on 18 Aug 1921, to 'A' Block, Hut 11.

Reidy, John

Main Street, Rathkeale, Co. Limerick.
Age: 21.
Brigade arrest No. 18 I.B. 148.
He was transferred from Cork Male Gaol to Spike Island internment compound on 12 Apr 1921, to 'A' Block, Hut 6.

Reilly, Daniel

Inchigeela, Macroom, Co. Cork.
Age: 28.
Brigade arrest No. 17 I.B. 908.
He was arrested by Crown Forces on 22 June 1921.
He was transferred from Cork Male Gaol to Spike Island internment compound on 30 June 1921, to 'B' Block, Hut 20. He was moved to 'A' Block, Hut 1, during the Spike hunger strike.
He was transferred from Spike to Maryborough (Portlaoise) Prison on the night of 18/19 Nov and released from there on 8 Dec 1921.

Ringrose, Thomas

Meelick, Co. Clare.
Age: 25.
He was arrested and transferred to Cork Male Gaol and to Spike Island with his friend Patrick White, who was shot on Spike.
Brigade arrest No. 18 I.B. 143.

Thomas J. Ringrose, Meelick, Co. Clare.

He was transferred from Cork Male Gaol to Spike Island internment compound on 12 Apr 1921, to 'A' Block, Hut 6.
He was released from Spike on 8 Nov, authority received from CA 1068 on 4 Nov 1921.

Riordan, Daniel J.

Cullen, Millstreet, Co. Cork.
Age: 24.
6th Division arrest No. 773.
Brigade arrest No. K.B. 257.
He was captured by British soldiers near Kanturk on 11 June 1921.
He was transferred from Cork Male Gaol to Spike Island internment compound on 22 June 1921.

Riordan, Jeremiah

Rossmore, Kilbarry, Co. Cork.
Age: 39.
Brigade arrest No. 17 I.B. 1129.
He was transferred from the Brigade Cage in Victoria Barracks via Cork Male Gaol to Spike Island internment compound on 15 July 1921.

Riordan, John

Knockavorheen, Kiskeam, Co. Cork.
Age: 24.
Brigade arrest No. K.B. 229.
He was transferred from Cork Male
Gaol to Spike Island internment
compound on 1 June 1921, to 'A'
Block, Hut 6.

Riordan, Michael

Lisvernane, Glen of Aherlow, Co.
Tipperary.
6th Division arrest No. 236.
He was transferred from Kilworth
Army Camp to Spike Island internment
compound on 13 Apr 1921.
He was transferred from Spike to Bere
Island internment camp on 14/15 Apr
1921 by RN destroyer.

Riordan, Michael

Bandon, Co. Cork.
Age: 25.
Brigade arrest No. 17 I.B. 1119.
He was transferred from the Brigade
Cage in Victoria Barracks, Cork, via
Cork Male Gaol to Spike Island
internment compound on 15 July 1921.

Riordan, Patrick

Firies, Longfield, Co. Kerry.
Age: 30.
Brigade arrest No. K.B. 87.
He was transferred to Spike to be

moved to Bere Island.
He was transferred from Spike to Bere
Island internment camp on 14/15 Apr
1921 by RN destroyer.
He was transferred from Bere Island
back to Spike on 20 Sept on HMS
Stormcloud, D 89.
He was transferred from Spike to
Maryborough (Portlaoise) Prison on
18/19 Nov and was released from
there in Dec 1921.

Roberts, Patrick

He was transferred from Cork
Military Detention Barracks to Spike
Island internment compound on
19 Feb 1921.

Roche, James

Templeglantine, Co. Limerick.
Age: 26. Brigade arrest No. 18 I.B. 185.
He was arrested on Sunday
10 Apr 1921 by British soldiers
near Newcastlewest and taken to
Newcastlewest. From there he was
moved to Limerick Gaol and later to
Cork Male Gaol.[64]
He was transferred from Cork Male
Gaol to Spike Island internment
compound on 11 May 1921, to 'A'
Block, Hut 8.

Roche, James

Rathencare, Glenmore, Co. Kilkenny.
Age: 27. Brigade arrest No. 16 I.B. 529.

---

64 See his WS, No. 1286.

He was transferred from Waterford Gaol to Spike Island internment compound by RN destroyer on 18 Aug 1921, to 'A' Block, Hut 11.

Roche, Jeremiah (Jerry)

Gortmore, Lombardstown, Co. Cork.
Age: 25.
He was a very active member of the Lombardstown Company, Irish Volunteers, and participated in the attack on Mallow Barracks with his brother William. His family home was a selected safe house and Second Brigade IRA headquarters was often located there.
Brigade arrest No. K.B. 314.
He was transferred from Cork Male Gaol to Spike Island internment compound on 22 Aug 1921, to 'A' Block, Hut 7.
He was transferred from Spike to Maryborough (Portlaoise) Prison on 18/19 Nov and was released from there in Dec 1921.
Brother of William, below.

Jeremiah Roche, Lombardstown, Co. Cork.

Roche, John

Ballyhooley, Fermoy, Co. Cork.
Age: 21.
Brigade arrest No. 16 I.B. 217.
He was transferred from Kilworth Army Camp to Spike Island internment compound on 4 Mar 1921, to 'A' Block, Hut 8.

Roche, Michael

Doonaha, Carrigaholt, Co. Clare.
Age: 21.
Brigade arrest No. 18 I.B. 189.
He was transferred from Cork Male Gaol to Spike Island internment compound on 11 May 1921.

Roche, William

William Roche, Lombardstown, Co. Cork.

Gortmore, Lombardstown, Co. Cork.
Age: 20.
He was a very active member of the Lombardstown Company, Irish Volunteers, and participated in the attack on Mallow Barracks with his brother Jerry. His family home was a selected safe house and Second

Brigade IRA headquarters was often located there.

Brigade arrest No. K.B. 214.
He was transferred from Cork Male Gaol to Spike Island internment compound on 16 May 1921 to be transferred to Bere Island.
He was transferred from Bere Island back to Spike on 20 Sept on HMS *Stormcloud*, D 89.
He was transferred from Spike to Maryborough (Portlaoise) Prison on 18/19 Nov and was released from there in Dec 1921.
Brother of Jerry, above.

Ronan, Patrick (RDC)

Ballyandrew, Ferns, Co. Wexford.
Age: 26. Brigade arrest No. 16 I.B. 371.
He was arrested by the RIC on 21 Nov 1920 and taken to Enniscorthy RIC Barrack. Later he was moved to the Courthouse Barracks, to Waterford Gaol and to Kilworth Army Camp.[65]
He was transferred from Kilworth Army Camp to Spike Island internment compound on 15 Sept 1921.
He was transferred from Spike to Maryborough (Portlaoise) Prison on the night of 18/19 Nov and released from there in Dec 1921.

Ronan, Ted (Ned)

Fermoy, Co. Cork. Age: 27.

Brigade arrest No. 16 I.B. 213.
He was transferred from Kilworth Army Camp to Spike Island internment compound on 17 May 1921.
He was released from Spike on 5 Nov 1921, authority received from CA 1068 on 4 Nov 1921.

Rumley, John (Jack)

John Rumley, Ballynoe, Co. Cork.

Ballynattin, Ballynoe, Co. Cork.
Age: 28. Brigade arrest No. 16 I.B. 109.
He was arrested near Ballynoe by British soldiers on 17 Jan 1921. He was marched to Fermoy Military Barracks and on 18 Jan he was taken to Kilworth Army Camp.
He was transferred from Kilworth Army Camp to Spike Island internment compound on 5 Mar 1921, to 'A' Block, Hut 2.

Russell, Bart (Finbarr)

Farnivane, Mount Pleasant, Bandon, Co. Cork.
Brigade arrest No. 17 I.B. 215.

---

65 See his WS, No. 1157.

He was transferred from the Brigade Cage in Victoria Barracks, Cork, to Spike Island internment compound on 19 Feb 1921.

Russell, John

Mount Pleasant, Bandon, Co. Cork.
Age: 18.
Brigade arrest No. 17 I.B. 392.
He was transferred from Cork Male Gaol to Spike Island internment compound on 19 Mar 1921, to 'A' Block, Hut 5.

Russell, Maurice

Shronell, Tipperary Town.
Age: 28.
Arrested in June 1921 and detained in Tipperary Army Barracks for seven weeks. Moved to Kilworth during the Truce.
Brigade arrest No. 16 I.B. 467.
He was transferred from Kilworth Army Camp to Spike Island internment compound on 15 Sept 1921, to 'B' Block, Hut 19.

Ryan, Cornelius

Curraglass, Borrisoleigh, Co. Tipperary.
Age: 25.
Brigade arrest No. 18 I.B. 153.
He was transferred from Cork Male Gaol to Spike Island internment compound on 12 Apr 1921, to 'A' Block, Hut 10.
He was released from Spike on 8 Nov, authority received from CA 1068 on 4 Nov.

Ryan, Daniel

Ballinakilla, Bartlemy, Co. Cork.
Age: 41.
Brigade arrest No. 16 I.B. 98.
He was transferred from Kilworth Army Camp to Spike Island internment compound on 5 Mar 1921. He was in 'A' Block, Hut 2, during the Spike hunger strike.
He was transferred from Spike to Maryborough (Portlaoise) Prison on the night of 18/19 Nov and released from there on 8 Dec 1921.

Ryan, Denis

52 Grattan Street, Cork City.
Age: 18.
Brigade arrest No. 17 I.B. 569.
He was transferred from Cork Male Gaol to Spike Island internment compound on 30 Apr 1921, to 'A' Block, Hut 16.

Ryan, Denis

Lombardstown, Mallow, Co. Cork.
Age: 21.
6th Division arrest No. 856.

Denis Ryan, Lombardstown, Co. Cork.

Brigade arrest No. K.B. 269.

He was arrested by Crown Forces on 30 June 1921.

He was transferred from Cork Male Gaol to Spike Island internment compound on 15 July 1921, to 'A' Block, Hut 17.

Ryan, Jim, Dr, TD

James Ryan, Taghmon, Co. Wexford.

Wexford Town.

Brigade arrest No. 16 I.B. 81.

He was transferred to Spike to be moved to Bere Island.

He was transferred from Spike to Bere Island internment camp on 14/15 Apr 1921 by RN destroyer.

Ryan, James

Knockeen, Graiguenamanagh, Co. Kilkenny.

Age: 30.

Brigade arrest No. 16 I.B. 397.

He was transferred from Kilworth Army Camp via Cork Male Gaol to Spike Island internment compound on 9 June 1921, to 'A' Block, Hut 21.

He was transferred from Spike to

James Ryan, Graiguenamanagh, Co. Kilkenny.

Maryborough (Portlaoise) Prison on the night of 18/19 Nov and released from there in early Dec 1921.

Ryan, James

Bridge Street, Castletownroche, Co. Cork. Age: 26.

Brigade arrest No. 16 I.B. 452.

He was arrested on 28 May 1921 and taken to Fermoy Military Barracks and to Kilworth on 5 June. He was transferred from Kilworth Army Camp to Spike Island internment compound on 16 Sept 1921, to 'B' Block, Hut 19.

Ryan, John

Cashel, Co. Tipperary.

He was transferred from Cork Male Gaol to Spike Island internment compound on 19 Feb 1921.

Ryan, John

Cormackstown, Thurles, Co. Tipperary.

Age: 28.

Brigade arrest No. 18 I.B. 146.

He was transferred from Cork Male Gaol to Spike Island internment compound on 12 Apr 1921, to 'B' Block, Hut 20.

Ryan, John

John Ryan, Drombane Cross, Co. Tipperary.

Drombane Cross, Holy Cross, Thurles, Co. Tipperary. Age: 22.
Brigade arrest No. 18 I.B. 228.
He was arrested by Crown Forces at Upperchurch, Thurles, Co. Tipperary, on 7 Sept 1921.
He was transferred from Cork Male Gaol to Spike Island internment compound on 20 Sept 1921, to 'A' Block, Hut 10.
Brother of prisoner, Peter Ryan.

Ryan, Martin

Loisheen Moyne, Templemore, Thurles, Co. Tipperary.
Also listed as Kildowney, Moyne, Thurles. Age: 25.
Brigade arrest No. 18 I.B. 151.
He was transferred from Cork Male Gaol to Spike Island internment compound on 12 Apr 1921, to 'A' Block, Hut 10.

Ryan, Michael

Droumlough, Ballinspittle, Co. Cork.
Age: 21.
Brigade arrest No. 17 I.B. 382.
He was transferred from Cork to Spike Island internment compound on 19 Mar 1921.
He was released from Spike on 23 Aug, authority received from CA 693 on 22 Aug 1921.

Ryan, Michael

Mardyke Walk, Cork City.
Brigade arrest No. 17 I.B. 243
He was transferred from Cork Male Gaol to Spike Island internment compound on 24 Feb 1921.

Ryan, Patrick

Kerry St, Fethard, Co. Tipperary.
Age: 26
Brigade arrest No. 16 I.B. 517
He was transferred from Kilworth Army Camp to Spike Island internment compound on 15 Sept 1921.
He was transferred from Spike to Maryborough (Portlaoise) Prison on the night of 18/19 Nov. He was released from Maryborough Prison on 8 Dec 1921.

Ryan, Patrick Joseph

Kenyon St, Nenagh, Co. Tipperary.
Age: 30. Brigade arrest No. 18 I.B. 207.

He was arrested by Crown Forces on
18 July 1921.
He was transferred from Cork Male
Gaol to Spike Island internment
compound on 25 July 1921, to 'A'
Block, Hut 19.

Ryan, Thomas

Tom Ryan, Bonnybrook, Co. Kilkenny.

Bonnybrook, Thomastown,
Co. Kilkenny. Age: 31.
Brigade arrest No. 16 I.B. 283.
He was transferred from Kilworth
Army Camp to Spike Island
internment compound on 17 May
1921, to 'B' Block, Hut 23.
He took part in the hunger strike on
Spike, beginning at 6 p.m. on 30 Aug
1921. He was moved to 'A' Block, Hut
21, during the hunger strike.
He was transferred from Spike to
Maryborough (Portlaoise) Prison on
the night of 18/19 Nov and released
from there on 8 Dec 1921.

Ryan, Thomas

6 Harbour Hill, Queenstown (Cobh),
Co. Cork.

Brigade arrest No. 17 I.B. 462.
He was transferred from Cork Male
Gaol to Spike Island internment
compound on 25 Apr 1921.

Ryan, Thomas

Sixmilebridge, Co. Clare.
His name and address have appeared
in a number of Spike Island autograph
books. No further details found.

Ryan, Thomas J.

Labasheeda, Co. Clare. Age: 25.
Brigade arrest No. 18 I.B. 202.
He was arrested by Crown Forces on
18 July 1921.
He was transferred from Cork Male
Gaol to Spike Island internment
compound on 25 July 1921, to 'A'
Block, Hut 4.

Ryan, Thomas Joseph

Cronovone, Borrisoleigh, Co. Tipperary.
Age: 23. Brigade arrest No. 18 I.B. 179.
He was transferred from Cork Male
Gaol to Spike Island internment
compound on 25 June 1921, to 'A'
Block, Hut 20.

Ryan, William

Kilcloonagh, Templetouhy,
Templemore, Co. Tipperary. Age: 29.
Brigade arrest No. 18 I.B. 214.
He was transferred from Limerick
via Cork Male Gaol to Spike Island
internment compound on 22 Aug
1921, to 'A' Block, Hut 19.

Ryan, William

Hollypark, Cappamore, Co. Limerick.
Age: 24.
Brigade arrest No. 18 I.B. 219.
He was transferred from Limerick
via Cork Male Gaol to Spike Island
internment compound on 22 Aug
1921, to 'B' Block, Hut 14. He was
moved to 'A' Block, Hut 22, during the
Spike hunger strike.
He was transferred from Spike to
Maryborough (Portlaoise) Prison on the
night of 18/19 Nov and released from
there on 8 Dec 1921.

Ryan, William J.

Lower Cork Street (Connolly St),
Mitchelstown, Co. Cork. Age: 42.
Brigade arrest No. 16 I.B. 413.
He was transferred from Cork, to
Spike Island internment compound on
6 July 1921.
He was paroled from Spike from
22 Nov to 3 Dec 1921. He was
released while on parole.

Samson, John P.

Ballinamuck, Churchtown, Buttevant,
Co. Cork. Age: 36.
Brigade arrest No. K.B. 213
He was transferred from Cork Male
Gaol to Spike Island internment
compound on 16 May 1921.
He was paroled from Spike from 5 to
19 Dec 1921. He was released while
on parole.

Santry, John

Lislevane, Co. Cork. Age: 30.
Brigade arrest No. 17 I.B. 119.
He was transferred from Cork Male
Gaol to Spike Island internment
compound on 24 Feb 1921.

Santry, Pat

Ballydurane, Clonakilty, Co. Cork.
Age: 22.
Brigade arrest No. 17 I.B. 586.
He was transferred from the Brigade
Cage in Victoria Barracks, Cork, to
Spike Island internment compound on
16 May 1921, to 'A' Block, Hut 3.

Santry, Timothy

Lislevane, Co. Cork. Age: 18.
Brigade arrest No. 17 I.B. 621.
He was transferred from the Brigade
Cage in Victoria Barracks, Cork, to
Spike Island internment compound on
16 May 1921.

Santry, William

52 Patrick St, Clonakilty, Co. Cork.
Age: 26.
Brigade arrest No. 17 I.B. 489.
He was transferred from Cork Male
Gaol to Spike Island internment
compound on 22 Aug 1921.

Saunders, Joseph

75 Upper Carey's Road, Limerick City.
Age: 22.
Brigade arrest No. 18 I.B. 199.
He was transferred from Cork Male

Gaol to Spike Island internment compound on 25 June 1921.

Savage, Patrick

Broadford, Co. Clare. Age: 25.
Brigade arrest No. 18 I.B. 205.
He was arrested by Crown Forces on 18 July 1921.
He was transferred from Cork Male Gaol to Spike Island internment compound on 25 July 1921, to 'A' Block, Hut 19.

Scanlan, Martin

Bridge House and West Street, Tallow, Co. Waterford. Age: 46.
Brigade arrest No. 16 I.B. 231.
He was arrested in Tallow by Auxiliary Police on 17 Jan 1921.
From Tallow he was taken to Fermoy Military Barracks. On 9 Mar, he was taken to Kilworth Army Camp and to Cork Male Gaol on 27 Mar. He was transferred from Cork Male Gaol to Spike Island internment compound on 30 June 1921, to 'B' Block, Hut 16.

Scanlon, Richard

Castlelyons, Fermoy, Co. Cork.
6th Division arrest No. 258.
He was transferred from Kilworth Army Camp to Spike Island internment compound on 13 Apr 1921.
He was transferred from Spike to Bere Island internment camp on 14/15 Apr 1921 by RN destroyer.

Scully, Christopher

Glencar, Co. Kerry.
Brigade arrest No. K.B. 135.
He was transferred from Cork Male Gaol to Spike Island internment compound on 25 Apr 1921.

Sexton, Cornelius

Ballinadee, Co. Cork. Age: 21.
Brigade arrest No. 17 I.B. 206.
He was transferred from Cork Male Gaol to Spike Island internment compound on 24 Feb 1921.

Sexton, Michael

Lislevane, Timoleague, Co. Cork.
Age: 23.
Brigade arrest No. 17 I.B. 272.
He was transferred from Cork Male Gaol to Spike Island internment compound on 19 Feb 1921, to 'A' Block, Hut 3.

Sexton, Timothy

Skeaf, Timoleague, Co. Cork. Age: 30.
Brigade arrest No. 17 I.B. 381.
He was transferred from Cork Male Gaol to Spike Island internment compound on 19 Mar 1921, to 'A' Block, Hut 20. He was moved to 'A' Block, Hut 5, during the Spike hunger strike.
He was transferred from Spike to Maryborough (Portlaoise) Prison on the night of 18/19 Nov and released from there on 8 Dec 1921.

Sexton, Timothy James

Killavarrig, Timoleague, Co. Cork.
Age: 26.
Brigade arrest No. 17 I.B. 425.
He was transferred from the Brigade
Cage in Victoria Barracks, Cork, to
Spike Island internment compound
on 12 Apr 1921. He was moved to
'A' Block, Hut 20, during the Spike
hunger strike.
He was transferred from Spike to
Maryborough (Portlaoise) Prison on the
night of 18/19 Nov and released from
there on 8 Dec 1921.

Sexton, Timothy

Kinsale, Co. Cork.
Age: 17. Occupation: Labourer.
6th Division arrest No. 67.
While he was in the Spike prison
compound he was served with an
Internment Order before his release
date. Instead of being released, he
was further detained as an internee.
He was transferred to Spike Island
internment compound on 4 July 1921.
See Sexton, Timothy, in the list of
Spike prisoners.

Shalloo, Thomas

Caherclough, Ennistymon, Co. Clare.
Age: 24.
Vice O/C, 5th Battalion, Mid Clare
Brigade, IRA.
Brigade arrest No. 18 I.B. 227.
He was transferred from Limerick
via Cork Male Gaol to Spike Island

Tom Shaloo, Ennistymon, Co. Clare.

internment compound on 22 Aug
1921, to 'A' Block, Hut 19.

Shanahan, Patrick

Aglish, Co. Waterford.
6th Division arrest No. 180.
He was transferred from Kilworth
Army Camp to Spike Island internment
compound on 13 Apr 1921.
He was transferred from Spike to Bere
Island internment camp on 14/15 Apr
1921 by RN destroyer.

Shea, John

Castletownbere, Co. Cork.
Age: 20. Occupation: Farmer.
Brigade arrest No. 17 I.B. 612.
While he was in the Spike prison
compound he was served with an
Internment Order before his
release date. Instead of being
released, he was further detained as
an internee. He was transferred to
Spike Island internment compound
on 8 Aug 1921.
He was transferred from Spike to
Maryborough (Portlaoise) Prison on the

night of 18/19 Nov and released from
there on 8 Dec 1921.
See Shea, John, in the list of
Spike prisoners.

Sheehan, Jack
Thurles, Co. Tipperary.
He was transferred from Cork Male
Gaol to Spike Island internment
compound on 19 Feb 1921.

Sean Sheehan, Templeglantine,
Co. Limerick.

Sheehan, Jeremiah
Donoure, Kilcorney, Co. Cork.
Age: 20.
Brigade arrest No. K.B. 287.
He was arrested by Crown Forces on
30 June 1921.
He was transferred from Cork Male
Gaol to Spike Island internment
compound on 6 July 1921.

Sheehan, John
Cork City.
Brigade arrest No. 17 I.B. 181.
He was transferred from Cork Male
Gaol to Spike Island internment
compound on 19 Feb 1921.

Sheehan, John (Sean)
Templeglantine, Co. Limerick.
Age: 30. His family home was a safe
house during the War of Independence.
Gen. Lucas, the senior British Army
officer captured near Fermoy in June
1920, was briefly held captive there.[66]

6th Division arrest No. 841.
Brigade arrest No. 17 I.B 803.
He was transferred from Cork Male
Gaol to Spike Island internment
compound on 15 July 1921, to 'A'
Block, Hut 8.
While on Spike he taught Irish to his
fellow internees.

Sheehan, Patrick
Donoure, Kilcorney, Co. Cork.
Age: 22. Brigade arrest No. K.B. 286.
He was arrested by Crown Forces on
30 June 1921.
He was transferred from Cork Male
Gaol to Spike Island internment
compound on 6 July 1921.

Sheehy, Pat
Timoleague, Co. Cork. Age: 26.
Brigade arrest No. 17 I.B. 197.
He was transferred from Cork Male
Gaol to Spike Island internment
compound on 24 Feb 1921.

66 *Rebel Cork's Fighting Story*, Anvil edition, pp.73–75.

Shelley, Michael

Michael Shelley, Callan, Co. Kilkenny.

Callan, Co. Kilkenny. Age: 59.
Brigade arrest No. 16 I.B. 172.
He was transferred from Kilworth
Army Camp to Spike Island internment
compound on 17 May 1921.
He was appointed a Staff Officer for
the internees.

Silles, Thomas

Ballinavoher, Lixnaw, Co. Kerry.
Brigade arrest No. K.B. 142.
He was transferred from Cork Male
Gaol to Spike Island internment
compound on 25 Apr 1921.

Sinnott, John (Seán)

7 Grattan Terrace, Wexford Town.
Age: 37.
He attempted to organise a
rising in Wexford during Easter
week 1916 without success. He
was subsequently arrested and
imprisoned in Dublin, Stafford
Prison in England, and Frongoch
in North Wales. He was released
in Oct and rearrested in Nov 1916.

John Sinnott, Grattan Terrace,
Wexford Town.

He was arrested again in 1920 and
held in Waterford Gaol, Cork
Military Detention Barracks and
Cork Male Gaol. He was transferred
to Wormwood Scrubs Prison and
Brixton Prison in London.
He was arrested again on 11 Apr
1921 and taken to Waterford Military
Barracks. He was moved to Kilworth
Army Camp on 19 May and to Cork
Male Gaol on 27 June.
Brigade arrest No. 16 I.B. 399.
He was transferred from Cork Male
Gaol to Spike Island internment
compound on 30 June 1921.
He was transferred from Spike to
Maryborough (Portlaoise) Prison
on the night of 18/19 Nov. He was
released from there on 8 Dec 1921.

Sinnott, Michael

Ballylando, Davidstown, Enniscorthy,
Co. Wexford. Age: 26.
Brigade arrest No. 16 I.B. 15.
He was transferred from Kilworth
Army Camp to Spike Island internment

Michael Sinnott, Enniscorthy,
Co. Wexford.

compound on 17 May 1921, to 'A'
Block, Hut 20.

Slattery, Maurice

Milltown, Co. Kerry. Age: 18.
Brigade arrest No. K.B. 91.
He was transferred from Cork Male
Gaol to Spike Island internment
compound on 25 Apr 1921.

Smyth, John

Cloneen, Co. Tipperary. Age: 21.
Brigade arrest No. 16 I.B. 170.
He was transferred from Kilworth
Army Camp to Spike Island
internment compound on 17 May
1921. He was later transferred from
Spike to Bere Island internment camp.
He was transferred from Bere Island
back to Spike on 20 Sept 1921 on
HMS *Stormcloud*, D 89.
He was transferred from Spike to
Maryborough (Portlaoise) Prison on
18/19 Nov and was released from
there in Dec 1921.

Spillane, Edmund or Edward

Loughatane, Glenflesk, Killarney,
Co. Kerry. Age: 40.
Brigade arrest No. K.B. 1681.
He was transferred from Cork Male
Gaol to Spike Island internment
compound on 30 Apr 1921, to 'A'
Block, Hut 14.
He was paroled from 5 to 19 Dec
1921 and released while on parole.

Spillane, Edward (Ned)

Curraglass, Tallow, Co. Waterford.
Age: 22. Brigade arrest No. 16 I.B. 181.
He was transferred from Kilworth
Army Camp to Spike Island
internment compound on 17 May
1921, to 'A' Block, Hut 2.
Brother of John and Maurice.

Spillane, John (Jack)

Curraglass, Tallow, Co. Waterford.
Age: 25. Brigade arrest No. 16 I.B. 106.
He was transferred from Kilworth
Army Camp to Spike Island
internment compound on 5 Mar 1921,
to 'A' Block, Hut 1.
Brother of Ned and Maurice.
Their brother Maurice was due to
be transferred from Kilworth Army
Camp to Spike Island on the night
of 15 Sept 1921. Before he could
be transferred he escaped from
Kilworth earlier that night through
a tunnel with the remainder of the
internees.

Stack, Maurice (Moss)

Stagmount, Rockchapel, Co. Cork.
Age: 37.
Brigade arrest No. K.B. 279.
He was arrested by Crown Forces on
30 June 1921.
He was transferred from Cork Male
Gaol to Spike Island internment
compound on 6 July 1921, to 'A'
Block, Hut 13.

Sugrue, Patrick

Patrick Sugrue, Foynes, Co. Kerry.

Foynes, Co. Kerry.
He was transferred from Cork Male
Gaol to Spike Island internment
compound on 25 Apr 1921.
Also known as Pádraig Ó Siochfhradha
or under his pen name, An Seabhac,
'The Hawk'. He was a well-known
author of Irish language books.

Sullivan, Daniel

Keilslaugh, Butlerstown, Lislevane,
Co. Cork. Age: 24.
Brigade arrest No. 17 I.B. 271.
He was transferred from Cork Male
Gaol to Spike Island internment
compound on 19 Feb 1921, to 'A'
Block, Hut 3.

Sullivan, Denis

Also listed as O'Sullivan.
Garranassig, Kilbritain, Co. Cork.
Age: 21. Brigade arrest No. 17 I.B. 281.
He was transferred from Cork, to
Spike Island internment compound on
3 Mar 1921, to 'A' Block, Hut 3.
He was released from Spike on 8 Nov
1921, authority received from CA
1068 on 4 Nov 1921.

Sullivan, John

Rathscannel, Abbeydorney, Co. Kerry.
Age: 24. Brigade arrest No. K.B. 136.
He was transferred from Cork Male
Gaol to Spike Island internment
compound on 25 Apr 1921.

Sullivan, John

Urhan, Eyeries, Co. Cork.
Age: 26.
Brigade arrest No. 17 I.B. 1187.
He was transferred from Bere Island
internment camp to Spike Island
internment compound on 20 Sept
1921 on HMS *Stormcloud*, D 89.
He was transferred from Spike to
Maryborough (Portlaoise) Prison on
18/19 Nov and was released from
there in Dec 1921.

Sullivan, Morris (Maurice)

Also listed as O'Sullivan.
Castleisland, Co. Kerry.

Age: 24.

Brigade arrest No. K.B. 472.

He was transferred from Cork to Spike Island internment compound on 19 Mar 1921, to 'A' Block, Hut 6.

Sullivan, Michael

Castletownbere, Co. Cork.
Age: 22. Occupation: Labourer.
Brigade arrest No. 17 I.B. 613.
While he was in the Spike prison compound he was served with an Internment Order before his release date. Instead of being released, he was further detained as an internee. He was transferred to Spike Island internment compound on 8 Aug 1921. He was moved to 'A' Block, Hut 1, during the Spike hunger strike. He was transferred from Spike to Maryborough (Portlaoise) Prison on the night of 18/19 Nov and released from there on 8 Dec 1921.
See Sullivan, Michael, in the list of Spike prisoners.

Sullivan, Michael

Carpa, Bandon, Co. Cork.
Age: 20.
He was arrested by Crown Forces on 26 July 1921.
Brigade arrest No. 17 I.B. 608.
He was transferred from Cork Male Gaol to Spike Island internment compound on 22 Aug 1921, to 'A' Block, Hut 16.

Sullivan, Patrick

Ballinroher, Timoleague, Co. Cork.
He was transferred from Cork Male Gaol to Spike Island internment compound on 19 Feb 1921.

Sullivan, Phillip

Allihies Mines, Castletownbere, Co. Cork. Age: 20.
Brigade arrest No. 17 I.B. 1178.
He was arrested by Crown Forces for membership of the IRA and recommended for internment. He was transferred from Cork Male Gaol to Spike Island internment compound on 25 July 1921.

Sullivan, Timothy

Also listed as O'Sullivan.
Castletownbere, Co. Cork. Age: 21.
6th Division arrest No. 637.
Brigade arrest No. 17 I.B. 642
He was transferred from Cork Male Gaol to Spike Island internment compound on 28 May 1921. He was moved to 'A' Block, Hut 21, during the Spike hunger strike.
He was transferred from Spike to Maryborough (Portlaoise) Prison on 18/19 Nov and was released from there in Dec 1921.

Swanton, William Maurice

Castletownbere, Co. Cork. Age: 35.
Occupation: Pharmaceutical Chemist.
Brigade arrest No. 17 I.B. 457.

William Swanton, Castletownbere,
Co. Cork.

He was transferred from Cork Male
Gaol to Spike Island internment
compound on 12 Apr 1921.
He was transferred from Spike to Bere
Island internment camp on 14/15 Apr
1921 by RN destroyer.
He was transferred from Bere Island
back to Spike on 20 Sept on HMS
Stormcloud, D 89.
He was transferred from Spike to
Maryborough (Portlaoise) Prison on
18/19 Nov and was released from
there in Dec 1921.

Sweeney, Daniel
Gaggin, Bandon, Co. Cork.
6th Division arrest No. 339.
Brigade arrest No. 17 I.B. 270.
He was transferred from Cork Male
Gaol to Spike Island internment
compound on 19 Feb 1921.

Sweeney, Michael
King Street, Fermoy, Co. Cork.
6th Division arrest No. 211.
He was transferred from Kilworth

Army Camp to Spike Island internment
compound on 13 Apr 1921.
He was transferred from Spike to Bere
Island internment camp on 14/15 Apr
1921 by RN destroyer.

Talbot, Patrick
Lesduff, Urlingford, Co. Kilkenny.
Age: 28.
Brigade arrest No. 16 I.B. 232.
He was transferred from Cork Male
Gaol to Spike Island internment
compound on 11 May 1921, to 'A'
Block, Hut 14.

Tobin, John (Jack)
Burncourt, Clogheen, Co. Tipperary.
Age: 22. Brigade arrest No. 16 I.B. 117.
He was transferred from Kilworth
Army Camp to Spike Island
internment compound on 5 Mar 1921,
to 'A' Block, Hut 10.

Tobin, Patrick
West Street, Tallow, Co. Waterford.
Age: 33. Brigade arrest No. 16 I.B. 166.
He was transferred from Kilworth
Army Camp to Spike Island
internment compound on 17 May
1921, to 'B' Block, Hut 1.
He was paroled from 28 Nov to 8 Dec
1921 and released while on parole.

Torpie, Patrick
Rathculbin, Kells, Co. Kilkenny.
Age: 23. Brigade arrest No. 16 I.B. 425.
He was transferred from Waterford

Gaol, to Spike Island internment compound by RN destroyer on 18 Aug 1921.

Treacy, Patrick
Kanturk, Co. Cork.
Age: 30. Brigade arrest No. K.B. 325.
He was transferred from Cork Male Gaol to Spike Island internment compound on 22 Aug 1921.
He was released from Spike on 13 Sept 1921, with the authority of CA 693 dated 9 Sept 1921.

Twomey, Daniel
Killowney, Old Head of Kinsale, Co. Cork.
Age: 28. Occupation: Farmer.
6th Division arrest No. 517.
Brigade arrest No. 17 I.B. 969B.
While he was in the Spike prison compound he was served with an Internment Order before his release date. Instead of being released, he was further detained as an internee. He was transferred to Spike Island internment compound on 14 Nov 1921.
He was transferred from Spike to Maryborough (Portlaoise) Prison on the night of 18/19 Nov and released from there on 8 Dec 1921.
See Twomey, Daniel, in the list of Spike prisoners.

Twomey, Jeremiah
Cahergariffe, Castletownbere, Co. Cork.
Age: 19. Brigade arrest No. 17 I.B. 1184.

He was transferred from Bere Island internment camp to Spike Island internment compound on 20 Sept 1921 on HMS *Stormcloud*, D 89.
He was transferred from Spike to Maryborough (Portlaoise) Prison on 18/19 Nov and was released from there in Dec 1921.

Twomey, Maurice (Moss)

Michael Twomey, Fermoy, Co. Cork.

Listed as Michael, Clondulane, Fermoy, Co. Cork.
Age: 24. Brigade arrest No. 16 I.B. 155.
He was transferred from Cork Male Gaol to Spike Island internment compound on 16 May 1921, to 'A' Block, Hut 2.
He escaped with six other internees from Spike on the night of 10/11 Nov 1921.
See a detailed account of their escape in this book.
He later became Chief of Staff of the IRA.

Upton, Christopher
Ballylanders, Co. Limerick.
Age: 22. 6th Division arrest No. 753.

Christopher Upton, Ballylanders,
Co. Limerick.

Brigade arrest No. L. 467.
He was arrested on 16 July 1920.
A party of police arrived in Ballylanders,
Co. Limerick, at 1.15 a.m. on 16 July
1920 and were fired upon from
Crowley's public house. The police
returned fire and after half an hour
rushed the house. Michael O'Reilly,
John and Peter Crowley were found in
a top room. Revolvers and ammunition
were found in a trap in the ceiling. They
were found not guilty of attacking the
police with firearms. They were found
guilty of being present and abetting
certain persons unknown, in the attack
on the police. Christopher Upton was
found in the same house, hiding under
the stairs. He was also tried, found not
guilty and detained as an internee.[67]
He was eventually taken to Cork
Male Gaol.
He survived 94 days on hunger strike
in Cork Male Gaol from 15 Aug to
12 Nov 1920.

He was transferred from Cork Male
Gaol to Spike Island internment
compound on 22 June 1921, to 'A'
Block, Hut 1.
He was paroled from Spike from
23 Nov to 3 Dec 1921. He was
released while on parole.
See also: the two Crowley brothers
and Michael Reilly on the Spike
prisoners list.

Verling, John (Jack)
9 Newtown, Cobh, Co. Cork.
Age: 28. Brigade arrest No. 17. 1093.
He was transferred from Cork Male
Gaol to Spike Island internment
compound on 15 July 1921, to 'A'
Block, Hut 15.

Walsh, Daniel
3 Ferry Hill, off Popes Quay,
Cork City. Age: 19.
Brigade arrest No. 17 I.B. 1092.
He was transferred from Cork Male
Gaol to Spike Island internment
compound on 25 July 1921, to 'A'
Block, Hut 19.

Walsh, David
Clonakilty, Co. Cork. Age: 39.
Brigade arrest No. 17 I.B. 278.
He was transferred from Cork Male
Gaol to Spike Island internment
compound on 3 Mar 1921.

---

67 UKNA, Kew, London, WO 35/135, p.150.

He was discharged from Spike for release to Clonakilty on 21 July 1921, with the authority of CA 693.

Walsh, Edmund (Ned)

Killally, Kilworth, Co. Cork. Age: 20. He was arrested on 9 Feb 1921 and taken to Moore Park Camp and moved to Kilworth Camp on 19 Feb. Released on 10 Mar. Rearrested on 1 June and taken to Moore Park and moved to Kilworth.
Brigade arrest No. 16 I.B. 460.
He was transferred from Kilworth Army Camp to Spike Island internment compound on 15 Sept 1921.

Walsh, Eugene

Eugene Walsh, Bandon, Co. Cork.

Cloundereen, Kilbrittain, Bandon, Co. Cork.
He was a member of the Clogagh Company, Irish Volunteers.
6th Division arrest No. 392.
Brigade arrest No. 17 I.B. 354.
He was arrested by Crown Forces during 1920 and interned on Spike Island during 1921.

Walsh, James

James Walsh, Blarney Street, Cork City.

22 Sive's Lane, off Blarney St, Cork City. Age: 45.
He was a member of 'D' Company, First Battalion, Cork City, IRA.
He was also a member of the Sinn Féin Executive and chairman of the Dáil Ceantair for Cork City.
Brigade arrest No. 17 I.B. 1049.
He was transferred from the Brigade Cage in Victoria Barracks, Cork, to Spike Island internment compound on 6 July 1921, to 'A' Block, Hut 18.

Walsh, James

Knockea, Clonakilty, Co. Cork. Age: 47. Occupation: Farmer.
6th Division arrest No. L. 624.
Brigade arrest No. 17 I.B. 657.
While he was in the Spike prison compound he was served with an Internment Order before his release date. Instead of being released, he was further detained as an internee. He was transferred to Spike Island internment compound on 25 Aug 1921.
He was transferred from Spike to

Maryborough (Portlaoise) Prison on the night of 18/19 Nov and released from there on 8 Dec 1921. See Walsh, James, in the list of Spike prisoners.

Walsh, Joseph

Mullinahone, Co. Tipperary. Age: 25. Brigade arrest No. 16 I.B. 503. While he was in Cork Male Gaol, he was served with an Internment Order before his release date. Instead of being released, he was further detained as an internee.
He was transferred from Cork Male Gaol back to Spike Island internment compound on 14 Nov 1921.
He was transferred from Spike to Maryborough (Portlaoise) Prison on the night of 18/19 Nov and released from there on 8 Dec 1921.

Walsh, Jeremiah

Cashelmore, Bandon, Co. Cork. Brigade arrest No. 17 I.B. 236. He was transferred from Cork Male Gaol to Spike Island internment compound on 19 Feb 1921.

Walsh, John

Cashelmore, Bandon, Co. Cork. Brigade arrest No. 17 I.B. 226 He was transferred from the Brigade Cage in Victoria Barracks, Cork, to Spike Island internment compound on 19 Feb 1921.

Walsh, Maurice

Maurice Walsh, St Lelia Street, Limerick City.

10 St Lelia Street, Limerick City. Brigade arrest No. 17 I.B 185. He was transferred from Cork Male Gaol to Spike Island internment compound on 19 Feb 1921, to 'B' Block, Hut 23. He was moved to 'A' Block, Hut 20, during the Spike hunger strike.
He was transferred from Spike to Maryborough (Portlaoise) Prison on the night of 18/19 Nov and released from there in Dec 1921.

Walsh, Maurice

9 Princess Street, Cork City. Age: 25. Brigade arrest No. 17 I.B. 590. He was transferred from Cork Male Gaol to Spike Island internment compound on 16 May 1921.

Walsh, Michael

Beaumont Cottages, Ballintemple, Cork City. Age: 25.
6th Division arrest No. 675. Brigade arrest No. 17 I.B. 717.

He was arrested by Black and Tans in Blackrock, Cork City, in May 1921. He was taken to Union Quay RIC Barracks, to the Bridewell and to the Brigade Cage in Victoria Barracks.[68] He was transferred from the Brigade Cage to Spike Island internment compound on 28 May 1921, to 'A' Block, Hut 15.

He was transferred from Spike to Maryborough (Portlaoise) Prison on the night of 18/19 Nov and released from there in Dec 1921.

Walsh, Patrick

Ballyarthur, Mitchelstown, Co. Cork. Age: 30. Brigade arrest No. 16 I.B. 146. He was transferred from Kilworth Army Camp to Spike Island internment compound on 5 Mar 1921, to 'A' Block, Hut 10.

Walsh, Patrick J.

Annelley St (Lower Cork St), Mitchelstown, Co. Cork. Age: 21. Brigade arrest No. 16 I.B. 121. He was transferred from Kilworth Army Camp to Spike Island internment compound on 17 May 1921, to 'A' Block, Hut 10. He was later moved to 'B' Block, Hut 1.

Walsh, Patrick K.

Bilboa, Doon, Co. Limerick. 6th Division arrest No. 176.

Brigade arrest No. 18 I.B. 198. He was transferred from Fermoy Military Barracks, to Cork Military Detention Barracks on 24 June 1921. He was transferred from Cork Military Detention Barracks to Spike Island internment compound on 25 June 1921.

Walsh, Thomas

Garnish, Castletownbere, Co. Cork. Age: 20. Brigade arrest No. 17 I.B. 1170. He was arrested by Crown Forces for membership of the IRA and recommended for internment. He was transferred from Cork Male Gaol to Spike Island internment compound on 25 July 1921, to 'A' Block, Hut 4.

Walsh, William

15 Pound Street and 14 Sally Park, Waterford City. Age: 35. He was arrested on 31 May 1921 and taken to Waterford Military Barracks and moved to Kilworth Army Camp on 10 June. Brigade arrest No. 16 I.B. 474. He was transferred from Kilworth Army Camp to Spike Island internment compound on 16 Sept 1921 to 'B' Block, Hut 16.

---

68 See WS, No. 1521.

Whelton, Batt
Lislevane, Co. Cork.
Age: 27
Brigade arrest No. 17 I.B.
He was transferred from Cork Male
Gaol to Spike Island internment
compound on 25 Apr 1921, to 'A'
Block, Hut 3.

Whelton, William
The Mills, Clonakilty, Co. Cork.
Age: 22.
Brigade arrest No. 17 I.B. 431.
He was transferred from Cork Male
Gaol to Spike Island internment
compound on 19 Mar 1921.

White, Patrick
Kilkieran, Inistioge, Co. Kilkenny.
Age: 31. Brigade arrest No. 16 I.B. 292.
He was transferred from Kilkenny
Gaol to Spike Island internment
compound on 2 May 1921, to 'A'
Block, Hut 22.

White, Patrick
Meelick, Co. Clare.
He was transferred from Cork Male
Gaol to Spike Island internment
compound on 12 Apr 1921.
He was shot and mortally wounded
by a sentry on Spike on 31 May
1921. See an extensive account of the
incident in this book.

Patrick White, Meelick, Co. Clare.

Wickam, Mark
8 Merchants Quay, Cork City. Age: 22.
Brigade arrest No. 17 I.B. 161.
He was arrested by Crown Forces on
25 Jan 1921.[69]
He was transferred from Cork
Military Detention Barracks to Spike
Island internment compound on
19 Mar 1921.

Wills, Henry
Allihies, Bantry, Co. Cork. Age: 21.
Brigade arrest No. 17 I.B. 1168.
He was arrested by Crown Forces on
18 July 1921 for membership of the
IRA and recommended for internment.
He was transferred from Cork Male
Gaol to Spike Island internment
compound on 25 July 1921.

Wills, Thomas
Allihies, Bantry, Co. Cork.
Age: 20.
Brigade arrest No. 17 I.B. 1188.
He was transferred from Bere Island

internment camp to Spike Island internment compound on 20 Sept on HMS *Stormcloud*, D 89.

He was transferred from Spike to Maryborough (Portlaoise) Prison on 18/19 Nov and was released from there in Dec 1921.

Winter, James

Aghaburren, Churchtown, Buttevant, Co. Cork. Age: 30.

Brigade arrest No. K.B. 170.

He was transferred from Cork Male Gaol to Spike Island internment compound on 30 Apr 1921, to 'A' Block, Hut 7.

Withero, John (Sean)

Sean Withero, Spittle Street, Tipperary Town.

Spittle Street, Cashel Road, Tipperary Town. Age: 20.

He was arrested by British soldiers in Tipperary Town on the night of 26 Nov 1920. That night an Army patrol was proceeding down Main Street and the British soldiers saw two men ahead of them, Patrick O'Halloran of Scallagheen and John Withero of Spittle Street, Tipperary Town. The officer called on the two men to halt. Both ran off and were pursued by the British Army officer. One of the men turned around and fired on the officer, who returned fire. In a follow-up search, Withero was found at home with a bullet wound in his leg. O'Halloran was found in a doctor's surgery with a chest wound; he was identified as the man who fired on the officer.[70]

6th Division arrest No. 495.

Brigade arrest No. 16 I.B. 447.

He was transferred from Cork Male Gaol to Spike Island internment compound on Wednesday, 22 June 1921, to 'B' Block, Hut 1.

See also: O'Halloran, Patrick, in the prisoners list.

Woodlock, John

Rathdrum, Lisronagh, Ardfinnan, Co. Tipperary. Age: 23.

He was arrested on 6 July and taken to Tipperary Military Barracks and from there to Kilworth Camp.

Brigade arrest No. 16 I.B. 516.

He was transferred from Kilworth Army Camp to Spike Island internment compound on 15 Sept 1921.

---

70 UKNA, Kew, London, WO 35/136, p.79.

LIST OF APPENDICES

APPENDIX 1: The IRA Brigades in the Martial Law Area[1]

Mid Clare Brigade and West Clare Brigade.
  North Kerry No. 1 Brigade, Mid Kerry No. 2 Brigade, South Kerry No. 3 Brigade.
  East Limerick Brigade, Mid Limerick Brigade and East Limerick Brigade.
  No. 1 (North Tipperary) Brigade, No. 2 (Mid Tipperary) Brigade and No. 3 (South Tipperary) Brigade.
  First (East, Mid, South and City) Cork Brigade, Second (North) Cork Brigade and Third (West) Cork Brigade. In July 1921 the Second Cork Brigade was divided in half. After that the Second Brigade covered the north-east of the county and the new Fourth Cork Brigade covered the north-west of the county.
  West Waterford Brigade and East Waterford Brigade.
  Kilkenny Brigade.
  Wexford Brigade.

APPENDIX 2: IRA Men Executed in the Martial Law Area

All the executions in Cork during 1921 took place in the exercise yard of Cork Military Detention Barracks by firing squad and all the bodies were buried in what were the grounds of Cork Male Gaol and now part of UCC campus.[2]

Captain Cornelius Murphy, Rathmore, Co. Kerry, 1 February 1921
Captain John Allen, Tipperary Town, 28 February 1921
Volunteer Timothy McCarthy, Donoughmore, Co. Cork, 28 February 1921
Volunteer Thomas O'Brien, Dripsey, Co. Cork, 28 February 1921
Volunteer Daniel O'Callaghan, Dripsey, Co. Cork, 28 February 1921
Volunteer John Lyons, Coachford, Co. Cork, 28 February 1921
Volunteer Patrick O'Mahony, Berrings, Co. Cork, 28 February 1921
Volunteer Maurice Moore, Cobh, Co. Cork, 28 April 1921
Lieutenant Patrick O'Sullivan, Cobh, Co. Cork, 28 April 1921
Volunteer Thomas Mulcahy, Mourne Abbey, Co. Cork, 28 April 1921
Volunteer Patrick Ronayne, Mourne Abbey, 28 April 1921
Volunteer Patrick Casey, Grange Co. Limerick, 2 May 1921
Volunteer Daniel O'Brien, Liscarrol, Co. Cork, 16 May 1921

A number of the prisoners on Spike Island were colleagues of some of these men and some were tried by Military Courts with them. Denis Murphy and Jeremiah O'Callaghan were tried and sentenced to death with their colleagues listed above for Dripsey. Likewise Jeremiah O'Leary was captured at Clonmult and sentenced to death with his two Flying Column colleagues from Cobh.

---

1   *With the IRA in the Fight for Freedom, 1919 to the Truce, The Red Path to Glory*, pp.13–25.
2   Harvey and White, *The Barracks, A History of Victoria/Collins Barracks, Cork*, pp.240–242.

Executed in New Barracks, Limerick

Captain Thomas Keane, Limerick, by firing squad on 4 June 1921 and he was buried in the Republican Plot, Mount St Lawrence Cemetery, Limerick.[3]

Spike prisoners Timothy Murphy and Edward Punch from Limerick were both sentenced to death with Thomas Keane and their death sentences were commuted to PS for Life.

APPENDIX 3: The Operational Strength of the British Army's 6th Division[4]

16th Infantry Brigade, headquarters in Fermoy Military Barracks
3,899 military
85 Auxiliary Police

17th Infantry Brigade, headquarters in Victoria Barracks, Cork
4,259 military
146 Auxiliary Police

18th Infantry Brigade, headquarters in Limerick Military Barracks
4,289 military
173 Auxiliary Police

Kerry Infantry Brigade, headquarters in Buttevant Military Barracks
2,036 military
133 Auxiliary Police

Totals: 12,483 military, 537 Auxiliary Police

APPENDIX 4: Prisons and Internment Camps in the Martial Law Area

Cork Male Gaol.
Limerick Civilian Gaol.
Waterford Civilian Gaol.
Kilkenny Civilian Gaol.
Spike Island Military Prison in the Field (MPIF) referred to as the prison compound, in effect the north-east casemates.
Spike Island Internment Camp, referred to as the internment compound and initially the north-east casemates, later the 'A' and 'B' Blocks.
Bere Island Military Prison in the Field and Internment Camp.
Kilworth Army Camp.
Cork Military Detention Barracks.
The Brigade Cage in Victoria Barracks.

---

3 Thomas Toomey, *The War of Independence in Limerick 1912–1921*, pp.616–618, also *The Last Post*, p.140.

4 For an extensive list of the deployment of all British Army troops in the south of Ireland from Mar 1920–July 1921 see *The Irish Sword, The Irish Rebellion in the 6th Division Area, No. 107, Spring 2010, Appendix 11*, pp.152–156. Also UK NA, Kew, London, WO 35/179/1 and Charles Townshend, *The British Campaign in Ireland 1919–1921*, p.220.

APPENDIX 5: The Spike Island Hunger Strikers by Counties

30 August 1921[5]

From Co. Cork	185
Co. Tipperary	28
Co. Dublin	1
Co. Carlow	1
Co. Mayo	1
Co. Wexford	31
Co. Kerry	15
Co. Kilkenny	2
Co. Limerick	8
Co. Clare	12
Co. Waterford	9
Total	293

APPENDIX 6: Spike Island Prisoners Staff[6]

Dr Holmes, Scarriff, Co. Clare

Assisted by medical orderlies
James Barry, Maiville Terrace, Cork City, Hut XV (15)
Paddy O'Leary, medical student, Blarney, Co. Cork, Hut XV (15)
Seán Collins, Woodfield, Clonakilty, Co. Cork, Hut XVI (16)
Tom Donovan, hunger striker, Tipperary, Hut XIV (14)
Chris Upton, hunger striker, Mitchelstown, Co. Cork, I B
Bill Ryan, hunger striker, Mitchelstown, Co. Cork

Hospital Staff
Dr Holmes, Scarriff, Co. Clare
Assisted by staff officers:
Seán Mc Gee, George's Quay, Cork City
Tom Heaphy, Kilmallock, Co. Limerick, listed as Tipperary

Military Medical Staff During the Hunger Strike
Dr Russell, (Capt. RAMC) Spike
Dr Biggs, (Maj. RAMC) Victoria Barracks
Dr McDonnell (Lt Col, ADMS) Victoria Barracks

---

5   See John Sinnott's original autograph book in the Spike Island reference library. Also Timothy Healy's autograph book.

6   Internee Richard Brett's original notebook in the Spike Island reference library.

APPENDIX 7: British Army Officers, Spike Island, 1921

Commandants, Military Prison in the Field
Col Gregory, Royal Garrison Artillery (RGA)
Maj. C.F. Kennedy, King's Own Scottish Borderers, (KOSB)

British Army Censor Officers
Lt G.J. de Mullens, 4th Dragoon Guards
Capt. F.W.F. Card, 1st Dragoon Guards
Lt R.V.D. Cullen, 4th Dragoon Guards
Capt. G.B. Martin, 1st Battalion Manchester Regt
Capt. A.B.H.N. Richardson

British Army Medical Officers, Spike Island
Dr Ronayne, Major, Royal Army Medical Corps (RAMC)
Dr V.J.A. Wilson, Capt., RAMC
Dr Russell, Capt., RAMC
Dr Biggs, Maj., RAMC from Victoria Barracks
Dr McDonnell, Lt Col, from Victoria Barracks
Lt Victor Bickersteth Murray, 2 Battalion the Cameron Highlanders

APPENDIX 8: Daily Ration Scale for Prisoners and Internees

Tea, loose	1oz (28g)
Sugar	2oz (56g)
Bread	1lb (450g)
Meat	8oz (227g)
Potato	1
Milk	¼ pint (122ml)
Margarine	2 oz (56g)

The prisoners and internees were permitted to supplement the above with food parcels from home and were also permitted to purchase foodstuffs and other essential items from the canteen through the canteen officer, Thomas Griffin of Ballynoe.[7]

---

7   *Internee Canteen Account Ledger*, Local Studies and Reference Library, County Library
    Building, County Hall, Cork.

APPENDIX 9: The Ten Spike Escapees

The three prisoners who escaped on Saturday, 30 April 1921

Tom Malone alias Sean Forde, from Tyrrellspass, Co. Westmeath.
Sean MacSwiney, Cork City.
Cornelius Twomey, Cork City.

The seven internees who escaped on 10/11 November 1921

Dick Barrett, Upton, Co. Cork
Paddy Buckley, Araglin, Co. Cork
Tom Crofts, alias Tom Flavin, Cork City
Jack Eddy, Ardmore, Co. Waterford
Henry O'Mahony, Passage West, Co. Cork
Bill Quirke, Fethard, Co. Tipperary
Moss Twomey, Fermoy, Co. Cork

APPENDIX 10: The Former Spike Prisoners Who Escaped from Kilkenny Gaol on Tuesday, 22 November 1921

Michael Burke, Thurles, Co. Tipperary
Cornelius Conroy, Cork City
Thomas Kearns, Limerick City
William McNamara, Ennis, Co. Clare
Timothy Murphy, Rathpeacon, Co. Cork
Timothy Murphy, Limerick City
Edward O'Dwyer, Limerick City
Patrick O'Halloran, Tipperary Town
James Pollock, Cork City
James Power, Kilmachthomas, Co. Waterford
Edward Punch, Limerick City
Frank Pyne, Ballyporeen, Co. Tipperary
Jeremiah Ryan, Thurles, Co. Tipperary

Appendix 11: The Former Spike Men Who Escaped from Bere Island and CMH

Bere Island

Buckley, John, Leo, 48 Sheares Street, Cork City
Culhane, John (Sean), Glin, Co. Limerick and 19 Parnell Place, Cork City
Hartnett, William, Killeens, Upton, Co. Cork
Hegarty, Peter, Garryvoe, Co. Cork
O'Connell, Mortimer, Cahersiveen, Co. Kerry
O'Connell, Richard, Caherconlish, Co. Limerick
O'Keeffe, Martin, Ballynoe, Co. Cork
Hartnett, William, Kileens, Upton, Co. Cork

Cork Military Hospital (CMH), Victoria Barracks

O'Mahony, Francis, 29 South Terrace, Cork City

Appendix 12: The Spike Island Journal *Saoirse*

Irisleabhair Oileain Spice
(1921)
Spike Island Journal *Freedom*

During October 1921 it was decided by some of the internees on Spike Island to publish a camp journal, called *Saoirse (Freedom)*. Above are the details, in Irish, of the title page of the first and only issue. The original handwritten and typed versions are available to view in the National Library of Ireland in Dublin.

The articles in all versions are the same and are as follows, translations added here:

CLÁR (Contents)

Dár Léitheoirí (For the readers)	2*
'Saoirse'	1
Labour in the New Irish State	3
The Shadow Passeth	7
Twenty Years After	9
Open Letter to Lloyd George	14
Roger Casement: a memory	17
The Resurrection of the National Spirit	19
Written on a Child's Album	22
Invocatory : 1 Felicitas atque Calamitas	26
11 Bellum atqua Pax	27
Notes	28

Anecdotes from Saoirse

Internee: You are suffering from acute escapeitis. Sorry you cannot visit Spike to investigate your case. Am sending by registered post a course of treatment.
  Testimonials from Kilworth and the Curragh,
    P.S. Keep out from the wire.

Internee No. 2: A Spike Islander must have the constitution of a 'Scrub' bull, the digestion of an ostrich and the stomach of a camel.

Tunnel: You are right in assuming they grow in the ground like potatoes. They are very plentiful at present and will, we understand, be stocked in the canteen.

Medical: We would not recommend 'Iodine' as a solvent for a wooden leg. Consult your own medical advisor.

Food: The cooking arrangements for our staff at 'A' Block were jettisoned by Noah, salved by one of his grandsons and sold to Spike.

Statistician: The number of internees on Spike is:
'A' Block   -   361, 'B' Block   -   191, Total   -   552

We acknowledge with gratitude a consignment of gifts for indoor and outdoor amusements from the Society of Friends who have been always so interested in the cause of 'suffering humanity'.

A professionally produced, typed version exists in Octavo. It was printed 'Lúnasa, 1954, blain Mhuire', in May 1954, the Marian Year, by Fáiscán na Réaltóige (the Star Press) in Bunclody, Co. Wexford, and was in the collection of War of Independence memorabilia belonging to internee Sean (John) Sinnott of Wexford. His artefacts, including the copy of *Saoirse*, were very kindly donated to the 'Independence' museum on Spike Island by his family. The second copy, with a very slightly different cover and identical contents to the above, came from Co. Tipperary. This copy was also donated to Spike Island.

APPENDIX 13: Medals Awarded to Spike Island Prisoners and Internees[8]

1917–21 Service Medals & the Truce Commemorative Medal 1971

The medals with 'Comhrac' (Action) bar, below left, were awarded to all persons including prisoners and internees who rendered active service in operations against Crown Forces from 1 April 1920 to 11 July 1921, the day the Truce began.[9] The medals without bar, below centre, were awarded to non-combatants, but who were members of the IRA, the Cumann na mBan and na Fíanna Éireann or the Irish Citizen Army for the three months ended on 11 July 1921.[10] Both medals were awarded officially named and numbered to all IRA men and women that were killed during the War of Independence as well as to those that were entitled to the medal but had died prior to its presentation in 1941. All other recipients received their medal unnamed. In 1971 all surviving recipients of both medals received the Truce Commemorative Medal, below right.

---

8   E.H. O'Toole, *Decorations and Medals of the Republic of Ireland,* (Medallic Publishing Company, Connecticut, U.S.A., 1990), pp.25–27.

9   *The Military Service (1916–1923) Pensions Collection, the Medals Series,* Defence Forces Printing Press, 2016, p.9. Also, *Medals of the Irish Defence Forces* (DFPP) 2010, p.94.

10 Ibid

APPENDIX 14: How Many MPs from the Martial Law Area are Interned?

Westminster Parliamentary Question (PQ)
Received 6 Division HQ, 15 June 1921

Reply,
Irish MPs (TDs) interned or undergoing sentences.

J.J. Walsh	Cork City	5 years Penal Servitude
John Hayes	West Cork	6 months imprisonment with Hard Labour
John Nolan	Co. Cork	Interned (Ballykinlar)
Ed Dee	Waterford	Interned (Ballykinlar)
James Doyle	Wexford	Interned (Ballykinlar)
John Moylan	Co. Cork	15 years Penal Servitude
Michael Colivet	Limerick	Interned (Spike)
Dr James Ryan	Wexford	Interned (Bere)
Edward Roche	Limerick	3 years Penal Servitude
James Crowley	Kerry	Arrested in Dublin

Total 10

Answer given on phone to DAG, GHQ

5 Internees, 5 Under sentence, as of 15/6/21

APPENDIX 15: Known Spike Island Autograph Books from 1921

Originals of some of these ABs listed below are on display and copies of all are available to view on Spike Island.

AB 01, Internee Florence O'Leary, College Road, Cork City.
AB 02, Internee Patrick Tobin, Tallow, Co. Waterford.
AB 03, Internee Daniel Dennehy, Ballyhooly, Co. Cork.
AB 04, Prisoner Thomas Conway, Fedamore, Co. Limerick.
AB 05, Internee Michael O'Sullivan, Castletownbere, Co. Cork.
AB 06, Internee Patrick O'Connor, Kanturk, Co. Cork.
AB 07, Prisoner Patrick O'Halloran, Tipperary Town.
AB 08, Prisoner Denis Murphy, Dripsey, Co. Cork.
AB 09, Internee John Brett, Killenaule, Co. Tipperary.
AB 10, Internee Patrick Barry, Blarney Street, Cork City.
AB 11, Prisoner William Dower, Villierstown, Co. Waterford.
AB 12, Internee James Butler, Ballyragget, Co. Kilkenny.
AB 13, Internee Patrick O'Donoghue, College Road, Cork City.

AB 14, Internee John Dowling, Moyderwell, Tralee, Co. Kerry.
AB 15, Internee Maurice Walsh, St Lelia Street, Limerick City.
AB 16, Internee Denis McDonald, Crossabeg, Co. Wexford.
AB 17, Internee John Sinnott, Grattan Terrace, Wexford Town.
AB 18, Internee Timothy Healy, Castleinch, Ovens, Co. Cork.
AB 19, Prisoner Michael Murphy, 97 Barrack Street, Cork City, alias John O'Brien.

The original and a display copy of the diary of internee John Hennessy, Ballynoe, Co. Waterford.
The original and a display copy of the notebook of internee Richard Brett, Kilmacthomas, Co. Waterford.

APPENDIX 16: The Death of Patrick White, Tuesday, 31 May 1921

A shot; a cry; and there a sudden hush,
A priest; a priest a fallen comrade cries,
Attracted by his piercing wail we rush,
He falls in quivering death before our eyes.

Beside him with a crucifix held fast,
One grey with years kneels down upon the sod,
The cross he lays within his dying clasp,
And prayers for mercy he raises to his God.

Reciting in the dying comrades ears
Contrition for the fading ebbing life,
With anxious look the comrades hear,
Repeats the words forgets his country's strife,

And all around drooped heads in prayers are seen
An Coróin Mhuire* breaks the mighty spell sublime,
Hurley and ball are lying in the green
While mocking sentries mock their latest crime.

*The Rosary

Written on Spike Island by internee Peadar Cullen, 89 North Main Street, Wexford Town.

APPENDIX 17: Lament for Patrick White[11]

Brave was the heart that perished
In Spike Islands lonely square.
With a bullet deep in his bosom
and his blood flowing freely there
and his comrades knelt around him
As his moans they rent the air
For his dear and loving parents
Who were far away in Clare.

In memory of P. White shot and mortally wounded on 31 May 1921.

Written on 5 October 1921 on Spike Island by internee Michael O'Sullivan, Ardgroom, Castletownbere, Co. Cork.

APPENDIX 18: The Spike Island Hunger Strike

I'm sitting in the hut Mary,
I'm feeling sick and sore,
For the boys are going on hunger strike,
They won't eat here no more,
They want to be released right now
and homeward we must go.
But we cannot leave this island
Until Lloyd George says so.
I'm sick of being in here Mary,
The Tommie's make bad friends,
and we'd sooner die in hunger strike,
than be herded here like pigs.

Written by Michael J. O'Sullivan, Ardgroom, Castletownbere, Co. Cork, Spike internee, pp.63–64 in his autograph book.

---

11 Spike Island autograph book from 1921.

PRIMARY SOURCE MATERIAL

Bureau of Military History, 1913–21, Individual Witness Statements (W.S.) relating to Spike Island 1921

Barry, Tom	String, Glanworth	W.S. 430	Spike prisoner
Berry, Pat J.	Dublin	W.S. 941	Warder in Maryborough
Brady, J.J.	Ringaskiddy	W.S. 190	Re. the Spike escape
Brennan, Tom	Waterford	W.S. 1104	Spike prisoner
Buckley, Leo	Cork City	W.S. 1714	Spike internee
Burke, Patrick,	Waterford	W.S. 1131	Spike internee
Collins, Denis	Kinsale	W.S. 827	Spike internee
Crimmins, John D.	Milford	W.S. 1039	Spike internee
Crimmins, Tim	Milford	W.S. 1051	Spike internee
Culhane, Sean	Cork City	W.S. 746	Spike internee
Dargan, Thomas	Limerick	W.S. 1404	Spike internee
Deasy, Jeremiah	Bandon	W.S. 1738	Spike internee
Desmond, William	Bandon	W.S. 832	Spike internee
Donovan, Dan	Timoleague	W.S. 1608	Spike internee
Duggan, James	Templemore	W.S. 1510	Spike internee
Duggan, Peg	Cork City	W.S. 1576	Sister of internee
Dunne, Eugene	Adrigole	W.S. 1537	Spike internee
Dwyer, John	Wexford	W.S. 1293	Spike internee
Fitzgerald, Seamus	Cobh	W.S. 1737	Public figure in Cork
Flynn, Daniel	Newmarket	W.S. 240	Spike internee
Fraher, James	Dungarvan	W.S. 1232	Spike prisoner
Hartney, Michael	Limerick	W.S. 1415	Spike internee
Healy, Sean	Cork City	W.S. 1643	
Healy, Sean	Cork City	W.S. 1476	Ref. the Brigade Cage
Hennessy, Sean	Ballynoe	W.S. 1090	Spike internee & diary
Hennessy, Tim	Kilkenny	W.S. 1614	Spike internee

Tim Herlihy & seven others	North Cork	W.S. 810	
Holland, Daniel	Courtmacsherry	W.S. 1341	Spike prisoner & internee
Kealy, Martin	Kilkenny	W.S. 1006	Prisoner in Kilkenny
Keating, James	Tipperary	W.S. 1220	
Kelleher, John	Midleton	W.S. 1456	Spike internee
Kelleher, Matthew	Banteer	W.S. 1319	
Keohane, Tim	Timoleague	W.S. 1295	Spike prisoner & internee
Kingston, Samuel	Drinagh	W.S. 620	Brother of internee
Leahy, James	Tipperary	W.S. 1454	
Lynch, P.J.	Cork	W.S. 1543	
Lyons, Patrick	Kerry	W.S. 1166	Spike internee
Malone, Tom	Limerick	W.S. 845	Spike prisoner
Matthews, Sean	Waterford	W.S. 1022	Spike internee
McCarthy, Dan	Lombardstown	W.S. 1239	Spike prisoner
McCarthy, James	Eyeries	W.S. 1567	Spike prisoner & internee
McCarthy, John	Limerick	W.S. 883	
McCarthy, Michael	Lombardstown	W.S. 1238	Spike internee
McCarthy, Patrick	Mourne Abbey	W.S. 1163	Spike internee
McKenna, James	Monaghan	W.S. 1028	
McNamara, William	Clare	W.S. 1135	Spike prisoner
Meagher, Tom	Callan	W.S. 1672	
Moylan, Sean	Kiskeam	W.S. 505	Spike prisoner & 838
Murphy, Matthew	Millstreet	W.S. 1375	
Murphy, Michael	Cork City	W.S. 1547	Spike prisoner
Neville, Frank	Upton	W.S. 443	
Neville, Laurence	Blackrock, Cork	W.S. 1639	
Neylon, John J.	Clare	W.S. 1042	Spike prisoner
Noonan, Maurice	Milford	W.S. 1098	Spike internee
O'Brien, Denis	Timoleague	W.S. 1306	Spike internee
O'Brien, John J.	Limerick	W.S. 1647	
O'Connell, Michael	Lombardstown	W.S. 1428	
O'Connell, Richard	Caherconlish	W.S. 656	Spike internee
O'Doherty, Felix	Blarney	W.S. 739	
O'Donoghue, H.	Cullen, Millstreet	W.S. 1351	Spike internee
O'Driscoll, Dan	Drimoleague	W.S. 1352	Spike prisoner
O'Hannigan, D.	Limerick	W.S. 600	
O'Leary, Diarmuid	Killeagh	W.S. 1589	Spike prisoner
O'Mahony, Henry	Monkstown	W.S. 1506	C/O of Spike internees
O'Mahony, Seamus	Mitchelstown	W.S. 730	
O'Shea, Joe	Cork City	W.S. 1675	Spike internees
O'Sullivan, Con	Innishannon	W.S. 1740	Spike internee
Pierce, Michael	Kerry	W.S. 1190	
Power, Edmond	Monkstown	W.S. 1130	Spike internee
Roche, James	Templeglantine	W.S. 1286	Spike internee
Ronan, Patrick	Ferns	W.S. 1157	Spike internee
Ryan, Jerry	Tipperary	W.S. 1487	Spike prisoner
Stack, Una	Kerry	W.S. 214	Spike 1916
Stapleton, Dan J.	Kilkenny	W.S. 1208	
Tobin, Edmund	Limerick	W.S. 1451	

Walsh, Michael	Ballintemple, Cork	W.S. 1521	Spike internee
Whelan, Patrick J.	Wexford	W.S. 1449	
Wickham, Mark	Cork City	W.S. 558	Spike internee

Internee canteen officer Thomas Griffins' Spike Island internees Canteen Ledger, in the Local Studies and Reference Library, County Library Building, County Hall, Cork.
Seamus Healy's audio interview of former internee Timothy Herlihy.
Richard Brett's notebook available on Spike Island.

United Kingdom National Archives (UKNA), Kew, London

WO 35/136   UKNA for brief details of specific military trials.
WO 35/138   UKNA ref for Spike 1921 nominal rolls of prisoners and internees.
WO 35/140   UKNA for Spike Island general prison correspondence 1921.
WO 35/ 141   UKNA for Internment Camps and Prisons.
WO 35/144   UK National Archives ref for the 1921 Spike prisoners ledger and the 1921 Spike internees ledger.
WO 35/159B/35   UK National Archives ref. for the Military Court of Inquiry in lieu of Inquest into the death of Patrick White, (internee) Spike Island.

BIBLIOGRAPHY

Published Works

Abbott, Richard, *Police Casualties in Ireland, 1919–1922* (Cork: Mercier Press, 2000) ISBN 1 85635 314 1.

Anvil Press, *Sworn to be Free, The Complete Book of IRA Jailbreaks 1918–1921* (Tralee: Anvil Press, 1971).

Barry, Michael B., *The Fight for Irish Freedom, An Illustrated History of the War of Independence* (Dublin: Andalus Press, 2018) ISBN 978-0-9933554-6-2.

Barry, Tom, *Guerrilla Days in Ireland* (Dublin: Irish Press Ltd, 1949).

Barton, Brian, *From Behind a Closed Door, Secret Court Martial Records of the 1916 Easter Rising* (Belfast: Blackstaff Press, 2002) ISBN 0 85640 697 X.

Bennett, R., *The Black and Tans* (London: E. Hulton & Co. Ltd, 1959).

Breen, Dan, *My Fight for Irish Freedom* (Tralee: Anvil Press, 1975).

Brennan Michael, *The War in Clare, 1911–1921* (Dublin: Four Courts Press/Irish Academic Press, 1980) ISBN 0 906127 26 2.

Carroll, Aideen, *Sean Moylan, Rebel Leader* (Cork: Mercier Press, 2010) ISBN 978 1 85635 669 5.

Cork County Council Heritage Unit, *Heritage Centenary Sites of Rebel County Cork* (Co. Cork: Carrig Print Litho Press, 2016) ISBN 978 0 9935969 1 9, PB, and ISBN 978 0 9935969 2 6, HB.

Crowley, John, Ó Drisceoil, Donal, and Murphy, Mike, editors, *Atlas of the Irish Revolution* (Cork: Cork University Press, 2017) ISBN 9781782051176.

Doyle, Tom, *The Ballykissane Tragedy, Good Friday 1916* (Killorgin: Killorglin Archive Society, 2016).

Durney, James, *Interned, the Curragh Internment Camps in the War of Independence* (Cork: Mercier Press, 2019) ISBN 978 1 78117 588 0.

Feeney, P.J., *Glory O, Glory O, Ye Bold Fenian Men* (Dripsey, Co. Cork: Self-published, 1996).

Foxton, David, *Revolutionary Lawyers, Sinn Féin Courts in Ireland and Britain 1916–1923* (Dublin: Four Courts Press, 2008) ISBN 978-1-84682-068-7.

Gillis, Liz, *The Hales Brothers and the Irish Revolution* (Cork: Mercier Press, 2016) ISBN 978 1 78117 375 6.

Hart, Peter, *The IRA and its Enemies, Violence and Community in Cork, 1916–1923* (Oxford: Oxford University Press, 1998) ISBN 0-19-820537-6.

Hart, Peter, *The IRA at War 1916–1923* (Oxford: Oxford University Press, 2003) ISBN 0 19 925258 0.

Harvey, D. and White, G., *The Barracks, A History of Victoria/Collins Barracks, Cork* (Cork: Mercier Press, 1997) ISBN 1 85635 194 7.

Hogan, David, (pseudo. Frank Gallagher), *The Four Glorious Years* (Dublin: Irish Press Ltd, 1953).

Hogan, Seán, *The Black and Tans in North Tipperary, Policing, Revolution and War, 1913–1922*, (Nenagh, Co. Tipperary: Guardian Print & Design, 2013) ISBN 1 901370 45 4.

Hopkinson, Michael, *The Irish War of Independence* (Dublin: Gill and Macmillan, 2002) ISBN 0 7171 3010 X.

Jeffers, John, *Death on the Pier* (Carrigtohill, Co. Cork: Lettertec Publishing, 2017)

Jordan, Kieran, *Kilworth and Moore Park British Army Camps from 1896–1922* (Fermoy, Co. Cork: Strawhall Press, 2004) ISBN 0-9548417-0-0.

Keane, Barry, *Cork's Revolutionary Dead 1916–1923* (Cork: Mercier Press, 2017) ISBN 978 1 78117 495 1.

Macardle, Dorothy, *The Irish Republic* (Dublin: Irish Press Ltd, 1951).

Mac Eoin, Uinseann, *Survivors* (Dublin: Argenta Publications, 1980).

McCall, Ernest, *Tudor's Toughs, The Auxiliaries, 1920–1922* (Newtownards, Co. Down: Red Coat Publishing, 2010) ISBN 978-0-9538367-3-4.

Malone, Tom, *Alias Sean Forde* (Dublin: Danesfort Publications, 2000) ISBN 1-902232-24-0.

McCall, Ernest, *The Auxies, 1920–1922, a Pictorial History* (Newtownards, Co. Down: Red Coat Publishing, 2013) ISBN 978-0-9538367-5-8.

McCall, Ernest, *The First Anti-Terrorist Unit, The Auxiliary Division, RIC* (Newtownards, Co. Down: Red Coat Publishing, 2018) ISBN 978-0-9538367-6-5.

McCann, John, 'Thirty Pieces of Silver', in *War by the Irish* (Tralee: The Kerryman, 1946).

McCarthy, Cal, *Cumann na mBan and the Irish Revolution*, revised edition (Cork: The Collins Press, 2014) ISBN 9781848892224.

McCarthy, Kieran/Christensen, Maj-Britt, *Cobh's Contribution to the Fight for Irish Freedom, 1913–1990* (Cobh, Co. Cork: Oileann Mór Publications, 1992).

Maher, Jim, *The Flying Column of West Kilkenny, 1916–1921* (Dublin: Geography Publications, first edition 1988)

Maher, Jim, *The Flying Column of West Kilkenny, 1916–1921* (Dublin: Geography Publications, second edition 2015) ISBN 978-0-906602-683.

Murphy, Gerard, *The Year of Disappearances, Political Killings in Cork 1921–1922* (Dublin: Gill and Macmillan, 2010) ISBN 978 07171 4748 9.

Murphy, William, *Political Imprisonment & the Irish, 1912–1921* (Oxford: Oxford University Press, 2014) ISBN 978-0-19-956907-6.

National Graves Association, *The Last Post, Details and Stories of Irish Republican Dead, 1916–1985* (Dublin: Elo Press, 1985).

O'Callaghan, Sean, *Execution* (London: Frederick Muller Limited, 1974).

O Duibhir, Liam, *Prisoners of War, Ballykinlar Internment Camp 1920–1921* (Cork: Mercier Press, 2013) ISBN 978 1 78117 041 0.

O'Farrell, Padraic, *Who's Who in the Irish War of Independence 1916–1921* (Dublin and Cork: Mercier Press, 1980) ISBN 0 85342 604 6.

O'Halpin, Eunan & Ó Corráin Daithí, *The Dead of the Irish Revolution* (Yale: Yale University Press, 2020) ISBN 978-0-300-12382-1.

O'Neill, Tom, *The Battle of Clonmult, The IRA's Worst Defeat*, revised edition (Cheltenham: The History Press, 2019) ISBN 978 0 7509 9221 3.

Ó Ruairc, Pádraig Óg, *Blood on the Banner, the Republican Struggle in Clare* (Cork: Mercier Press, 2009) ISBN 978 1 85635 613 8.

O'Sullivan, John L., *Cork City Gaol* (Ballinhassig, Co. Cork: Ballyheada Press, 1996)

O'Sullivan, Ted, *Bere Island a Short History* (Cork: Inisgragy Books, 1992) ISBN 0 951 9186 0 5.

Kerryman, *With the IRA in the Fight for Freedom 1919 to the Truce, the Red Path of Glory* (Tralee: The Kerryman, 1950).

Kerryman, *Rebel Cork's Fighting Story, from 1916 to the Truce with Britain* (Tralee: The Kerryman).

Kerryman, *Rebel Cork's Fighting Story, from 1916 to the Truce with Britain* (Tralee: The Kerryman, Anvil Edition)

Scott-Daniell, David, *The Regimental History of the Royal Hampshire Regiment, Vol. 3, 1918–1954* (Aldershot: Gale and Polden, 1955).

Toomey, Thomas, *The War of Independence in Limerick, 1912–1921* (Self-published, 2011) ISBN 978 0 9522568 5 4.

Townshend, Charles, *The British Campaign in Ireland 1919–1921, The Development of Political and Military Policies* (Oxford: Oxford University Press, 1975).

White, G., and O'Shea, B., *The Irish Volunteer Soldier 1913–23*, Warrior Series No. 80 (Wellingborough, UK: Osprey Publishing, 2003) ISBN 1 84176 685 2.

White, G., and O'Shea, B., *The Burning of Cork* (Cork: Mercier Press, 2006) ISBN 1 856355225.